Bahrain, Oman,
Qatar, and the UAE

CSIS Middle East Dynamic Net Assessment

Bahrain, Oman, Qatar, and the UAE

Challenges of Security

Anthony H. Cordesman

WestviewPress

A Division of HarperCollins*Publishers*

Published in 1997 in the United States of America by Westview Press, 5500 Central Avenue, Boulder, Colorado 80301-2877, and in the United Kingdom by Westview Press, 12 Hid's Copse Road, Cumnor Hill, Oxford OX2 9JJ

Library of Congress Cataloging-in-Publication Data
Cordesman, Anthony H.
  Bahrain, Oman, Qatar, and the UAE : challenges of security /
  p. cm.
  Includes bibliographical references (p.   ).
  ISBN 0-8133-3239-7 (hc). — ISBN 0-8133-3240-0 (pbk.)
  1. Persian Gulf States—Strategic aspects. 2. National security—
Persian Gulf States. 3. Persian Gulf States—Defenses. I. Title.
DS247.A13C67 1997
953.6—dc21
                                                              96-46288
                                                              CIP

This book was typeset by Letra Libre, 1705 Fourteenth Street, Suite 391, Boulder, Colorado 80302.

The paper used in this publication meets the requirements of the American National Standard for Permanence of Paper for Printed Library Materials Z39.48-1984.

10   9   8   7   6   5   4   3   2   1

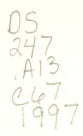

Contents

v

Tables and Illustrations

Charts

Maps

Preface

This volume is part of an ongoing dynamic net assessment of the Gulf. The project was conceived by David Abshire and Richard Fairbanks of the Center for Strategic and International Studies, and focuses on the foreign policy, military forces, politics, economics, energy sector, and internal security of each Gulf state, and US strategy and power projection capabilities in the Gulf. Separate volumes are available on Kuwait, Iran, Iraq, Saudi Arabia, and US forces. Bahrain, Oman, Qatar, and the UAE are combined into a single volume.

Each of these volumes is interlinked to provide comparable data on the current situation and trends in each country, and to portray the overall trends in key areas like economy and the military balance. The volume on Iran provides a detailed graphic overview of the military trends in the region, but each volume shows how the key economic and military developments in each country relate to the developments in other Gulf countries.

At the same time, this series deliberately emphasizes nation-by-nation analysis. Iran and Iraq clearly deserve separate treatment. The Southern Gulf states are largely independent actors and are driven by separate strategic, political, economic, and military interests. In spite of the creation of the Arab Gulf Cooperation Council (GCC), there is little practical progress in strategic, economic, or military cooperation, and there are serious rivalries and differences of strategic interest between Bahrain, Kuwait, Oman, Qatar, Saudi Arabia, and the UAE. The Southern Gulf cannot be understood in terms of the rhetoric of the Arab Gulf Cooperation Council, or by assuming that developments in Bahrain, Kuwait, Oman, Qatar, Saudi Arabia, and the UAE are similar and these states have an identity of interest.

These Gulf studies are also part of a broader dynamic net assessment of the Middle East, and a separate study is available of the trends in the Arab-Israeli military balance and the peace process. See Anthony H. Cordesman, *Perilous Prospects*, Boulder, Westview, 1996.

Anthony H. Cordesman

Acknowledgments

This volume is part of a six-volume series reporting on a dynamic net assessment of the Gulf. The project was conceived by David Abshire and Richard Fairbanks of the Center for Strategic and International Studies, and is part of a broader dynamic net assessment of the entire Middle East.

The author would like to thank Kimberly Goddes and Kiyalan Batmanglidj for their research and editing help in writing this series, and Thomas Seidenstein and David Hayward for helping to edit each volume.

Many US and international analysts and agencies played a role in commenting on drafts of the manuscript. So did experts in each Southern Gulf country. The author cannot acknowledge these contributions by name or agency but he is deeply grateful. The author would also like to thank his colleagues at the CSIS who reviewed various manuscripts and commented on the analysis. These colleagues include Richard Fairbanks and Arnaud de Borchgrave, and his Co-Director of the Middle East Program, Judith Kipper.

A.H.C.

1

The Southern Gulf States

This volume of the CSIS Dynamic Net Assessment of the Middle East provides detailed studies of four Southern Gulf countries: Bahrain, Oman, Qatar, and the UAE. The choice of these countries, however, is a matter of publishing convenience, and not an indication of the fact that the smaller Gulf countries can be treated as if they had common interests or are similar in character.

It may be tempting for many in the West to divide the Gulf into three parts: Iran, Iraq, and the Southern Gulf, and then describe the Southern Gulf in terms of strategic short hand—using the Gulf Cooperation Council (GCC) as a synonym for all the Southern Gulf states. Any net assessment of the Gulf, however, must focus on the fact that the differences between the Southern Gulf states are as important as the similarities.

Table One shows how great the differences are between the Southern Gulf states in terms of size, population, wealth, and military forces. These differences are only part of the story. Each Southern Gulf state has different strategic interests, politics, economics, demographics, ethnic structures, religious practices, internal security situations, and military capabilities.

While the six Southern Gulf states are loosely allied within the Gulf Cooperation Council (GCC), each Southern Gulf state is dependent on the strength of its own individual military capabilities and the power projection capabilities of the US and other Western states. The GCC is not NATO. Its efforts at unity are more rhetoric than reality, and this is particularly true of its military efforts. The Southern Gulf has made only limited progress towards developing effective collective economic and security arrangements, and the Southern Gulf states are deeply divided over how best to strengthen the role of the GCC in creating integrated military forces, defense plans, and procurement efforts.

Problems in Economics, Demographics, and Social Development

The Southern Gulf states are all oil and gas exporters, but they are scarcely an economic bloc. Table Two shows that they differ radically in

TABLE ONE The Size, Economy, and Military Capabilities of the Gulf States in 1996

Country	Size (Sq. Km.)	Population (1,000,000s)	GDP ($B)	Military Spending ($B)	Active Military Manpower	Tanks	Combat Aircraft	Combat Ships
Iran	1,648,000	64,625	59.8	5.0	513,000	1,445	295	56
Iraq	434,920	20,644	18.5	2.7	382,500	2,700	380	17
Sub-total	2,082,920	85,269	78.3	7.7	895,500	4,145	675	73
Bahrain	620	576	4.6	.3	10,700	106	24	11
Kuwait	17,820	1,817	7.6	2.9	16,600	220	76	10
Oman	212,460	2,125	12.0	1.6	43,500	91	46	12
Qatar	11,000	534	7.7	0.3	11,100	24	12	9
Saudi Arabia	2,149,690	18,730	128.1	12.5	161,500	910	295	44
UAE	83,600	2,924	36.7	1.9	70,000	133	97	20
Sub-total	2,475,190	26,706	196.7	19.5	313,700	1,484	550	106
Total Gulf	4,558,110	111,975	275.0	27.2	1,208,900	5,629	1,225	179
Yemen	527,970	14,728	23.4	0.8	39,500	1,125	69	10

Source: Estimated by Anthony H. Cordesman using CIA and World Bank data.

TABLE TWO   Gulf and World Gas Reserves and Production

Comparative Oil Reserves in 1994 in Billions of Barrels

Country	Identified	Undiscovered	Identified and Undiscovered	Proven	% of World Total
Bahrain	—	—	—	.35	
Iran	69.2	19.0	88.2	89.3	8.9
Iraq	90.8	35.0	125.8	100.0	10.0
Kuwait	92.6	3.0	95.6	96.5	9.7
Oman	—	—	—	5.0	NA
Qatar	3.9	0	3.9	3.7	0.4
Saudi Arabia	265.5	51.0	316.5	261.2	26.1
UAE	61.1	4.2	65.3	98.1	9.8
Total	583.0	112.2	695.2	654.1	64.9
Rest of World	—	—	—	345.7	35.1
World	—	—	—	999.8	100.0

Comparative Oil Production in Millions of Barrels per Day

Country	Reserves in 1995 TCF	Reserves in 1995 BCM	Percent of World Supply	Production in 1993 (BCM)
Bahrain	—	—	—	—
Iran	741.6	21,000	14.9	60.0
Iraq	109.5	3,100	2.2	2.75
Kuwait	52.9	1,498	1.1	5.17
Oman	—	600–640	—	—
Qatar	250.0	7,070	5.0	18.4
Saudi Arabia	185.9	5,134	4.2	67.3
UAE	208.7	5,779*	4.2	31.63
Gulf	1,548.6	—	31.1	185.25
Rest of World	3,431.7	104,642	68.9	—
World Total	4,980.3	148,223	100.0	—

Note: *Other sources estimate 6,320–7,280 BCM for Abu Dhabi only.

Source: Adapted by Anthony H. Cordesman from estimates in IEA, *Middle East Oil and Gas,* Paris, OED/IEA, 1995, Annex 2 and DOE/EIA, *International Energy Outlook, 1995,* Washington, DOE/EIA, June 1995, pp. 26–30. Reserve data for Bahrain and Oman estimated by author based on country data.

oil and gas resources—the main measure of economic power in the Gulf. While there is no question that the Gulf states have a common Arab identity, their economic identity is tied largely to trade with developed oil importing states outside the Arab world. All of the Southern Gulf states get well over 85% of their imports from outside the Arab world, and over 90% of their imports from outside the Gulf. Well over 80% of all Gulf foreign investment is in the Western developed world, and there is little chance that this will change significantly in the foreseeable future.

At the same time, each Southern Gulf state must find its own path to increasing the legitimacy of its regime, and to providing for its social and economic development. The Gulf states have already undergone several decades of massive social change, converting from small coastal city states and/or largely tribal societies to heavily urbanized states that are dependent on oil wealth for many of the benefits provided by the economies of developed nations. In most cases, this process has weakened or broken up traditional ties or relationships between groups and individuals. It has often created a serious gap in wealth between ruler and ruled—although Western educated elites and technocrats have usually benefited in the process. In several cases, social and economic change have also exacerbated ethnic and religious tensions.

Each Southern Gulf state faces serious internal challenges. Table Three shows that each state remains dependent on oil and gas revenues. The native population of each Gulf state has more than doubled since the early 1970s, and this has had a major impact on Gulf economies, and Chart One shows that export income has remained or declined since the mid-1980s, when oil wealth had already dropped sharply below its peak.

Oil wealth can decline quickly in relative terms. Table Four and Chart Two show that oil wealth is only about one-third to one-half of the per capita level the Southern Gulf states reached when peak oil prices peaked in the 1970s. Most estimates indicate that the Southern Gulf states will only experience a slow growth in real export revenue during the coming decade. Given the fact that most Southern Gulf states have a current net population increase in excess of three percent, this means that oil wealth per capita may well drop by another 30% to 50% by the year 2010.

Cuts in oil wealth are already creating major problems for each Gulf state in terms of budget deficits and are making their efforts to fund both "guns" and "butter" increasingly difficult. Many states have had to cut back on the subsidies and welfare payments that underpin their internal unity and make up the informal "social contract" they developed in the 1970s and 1980s. Many states have been forced to cut educational benefits, social services, as well as subsidies.

In spite of some recent reductions in population growth rates, Chart Three and Table Five show that the Gulf will suffer a population explo-

TABLE THREE   Economic Dependence of Middle Eastern States on Oil
Production

Oil Exporter	Trade in Fuels as a Percent of GDP*				Share of Total Exports 1993
	1970	1974	1984	1993**	1993
Gulf					
Bahrain***	140	105	72	67	90
Iran	20	47	7	15	90
Iraq	3	2	9	2	35
Kuwait	62	80	47	40	80
Oman	78	70	47	30	95
Saudi Arabia	46	90	37	33	99
Gulf Cooperation Council	50	85	35	35	95
Other Middle East					
Algeria	15	30	22	20	85
Egypt	5	2	6	7	45
Syria	6	8	7	14	42
Total Middle East and North Africa					
Percent	25	60	20	30	90
Total Value of Exports in $ Current Billions	10	90	100	110	80

Notes: *Mineral fuels, including petroleum and products, natural gas, and natural gas liquids.
**Estimate.
***Includes fuel processed from Saudi Arabia.
Source: Adapted by Anthony H. Cordesman from World Bank, *Claiming the Future,* Washington, World Bank, 1995, p. 17.

sion during 1995–2030, and one that will lead to growth that states like Iran, Iraq, Oman, and Saudi Arabia will have great difficulty in dealing with. Furthermore, Chart Four shows that the Southern Gulf countries have exceptionally young populations—roughly 40% of the native population is under 15 years of age. They also have massive disguised unemployment. At least two, and sometimes four, native males are unemployed in each government job for every male that is needed to perform a real job. In most cases, there is also growing direct unemployment of native males.

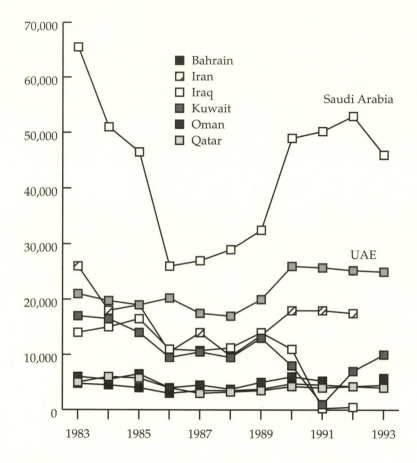

CHART ONE   Real Export Income of the Gulf States ($93 Millions).
Source: Adapted by Anthony H. Cordesman from ACDA, *World Military Expenditures and Arms Transfers, 1993–1994,* Table II.

This combination of economic and demographic forces will have a growing impact. Well over 20% of the Gulf's young population will reach an age where it would normally leave its extended family during the next six years. Yet, no Gulf state has any prospect of creating more than a third of the real jobs required to employ its youth and correcting the level of disguised unemployment that already exists. Every Gulf state will be confronted with new challenges in trying to find careers and jobs for its youth, and there is little chance that most states can give their youth the same level of personal wealth or rapid promotion as their parents or provide all their job seekers with meaningful and rewarding employment.

TABLE FOUR   The Per Capita GDP of the Gulf States: 1985–1994 (GNP in $94 Millions, Per Capita in $94 Dollars)

Country	GNP	World Bank Estimate GNP Per Capita	Average Annual Real Growth in % 1985–1994	US Government Estimate of GNP Per Capita	
				1984	1994
Iran	—	—	-1.0	2,527	1,981
Iraq	—	—	—	3,185	685
Average	—	—	—	(2,856)	(1,333)
Bahrain	4,114	7,500	-0.9	12,740	7,140
Kuwait	31,433	19,040	-1.3	22,480	16,600
Oman	10,779	5,200	0.6	6,892	4,915
Qatar	7,810	14,540	-0.8	31,100	15,070
Saudi Arabia	126,597	7,240	-1.2	11,450	6,725
UAE	—	20,040	0.2	27,620	14,100
Average	—	(12,090)	—	(18,713)	(10,758)
Total Gulf	—	—	—	—	—
Yemen	3,884	280	—	—	—

Source: Estimated by Anthony H. Cordesman using World Bank data in *The World Bank Atlas, 1996*, Washington, World Bank, 1996, and US Arms Control and Disarmament Agency, computer print out dated May 14, 1996.

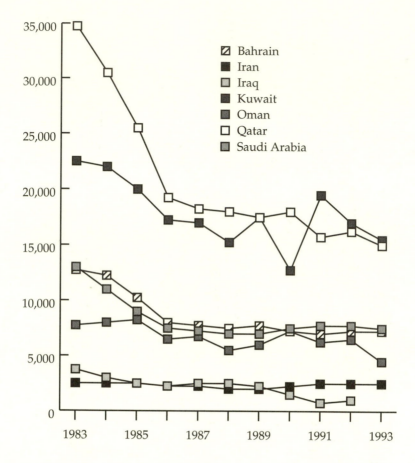

CHART TWO   Real Per Capita Income in the Gulf: 1983–1993 ($93 Millions).
Source: Adapted by Anthony H. Cordesman from ACDA, *World Military Expenditures and Arms Transfers, 1993–1994,* Washington, ACDA, 1995, and material provided by the CIA.

Most Southern Gulf states have institutionalized another economic problem that threatens their social cohesion and cultural identity. All the Southern Gulf states are heavily dependent on foreign labor. All have failed to develop a work ethic and employment patterns that make adequate use of native talent. In several countries, a large percentage of the total population is foreign.

The demographics involved are described in detail in the country studies in this series, and there are many different estimates of the exact numbers involved. Most estimates indicate that foreigners make up 50–60% of

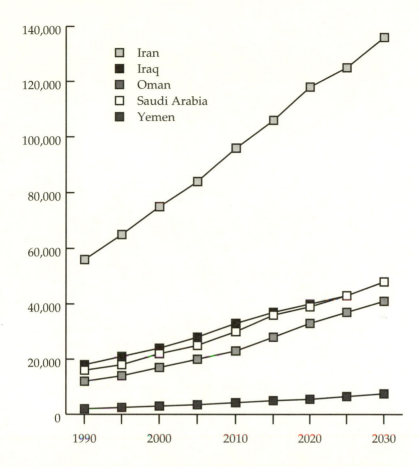

CHART THREE   Estimated Trends in Population of the Gulf High Growth States During 1990–2030 in 1,000s. *Source:* Adapted by Anthony H. Cordesman from World Bank, *World Population Projections, 1994–1995,* Washington, World Bank, 1994, and material provided by the CIA.

the total population in Kuwait, 38% in Bahrain, 41% in Saudi Arabia, 78% in Qatar, and 80% in the UAE. There is a sharp difference in estimates for Oman, ranging from 23% to 60%.

Estimates of the percentage of foreigners in the work force of the Southern Gulf states are much higher. Estimates dating back to 1990 indicate that 51% of the work force is foreign in Bahrain, 86% in Kuwait, 70% in Oman, 92% in Qatar, 60% in Saudi Arabia, and 89% in the UAE. While these percentages are uncertain, they are still likely to be well over 60% in most of the Southern Gulf states. Further, they only reflect part of the

TABLE FIVE   The Population Growth of the Gulf States: 1990–2030 (Growth in Percent and Population in Millions)

Country	Growth Rate in 1994	Fertility Rate in 1994	1990	1995	2000	2005	2010	2015	2020	2025	2030
Iran	3.3	4.9	55.78	64.81	74.63	85.13	96.00	106.67	116.68	125.66	134.42
Iraq	2.9	5.6	18.10	21.00	24.55	28.42	32.54	36.63	40.53	44.19	47.50
Sub-total	—	—	73.88	85.81	99.18	113.55	128.54	143.30	157.21	169.85	181.92
Bahrain	3.1	3.7	0.50	0.57	0.64	0.70	0.77	0.84	0.90	0.96	1.00
Kuwait	—	3.1	2.14	1.59	1.88	2.08	2.28	2.46	2.62	2.77	2.91
Oman	4.4	7.1	1.52	1.88	2.30	2.76	3.29	3.88	4.51	5.16	5.80
Qatar	4.5	4.3	0.49	0.54	0.60	0.65	0.69	0.72	0.77	0.80	0.82
Saudi Arabia	3.6	6.3	15.8	18.6	22.0	25.8	30.0	34.4	38.8	42.9	47.1
UAE	3.3	4.2	1.59	1.79	2.00	2.16	2.34	2.50	2.64	2.74	2.83
Sub-total	—	—	22.04	24.97	29.42	34.15	39.37	44.80	50.24	52.59	60.46
Total Gulf	—	—	95.92	110.78	128.60	147.70	167.91	188.10	207.45	222.44	242.38
Yemen	4.1	7.5	11.28	14.24	17.00	20.09	23.63	27.60	31.90	36.42	40.93

Source: Estimated by Anthony H. Cordesman using World Bank data in *World Population Projections, 1994–1995*, Washington, World Bank, 1996, and *The World Bank Atlas, 1996*, Washington, World Bank, 1996.

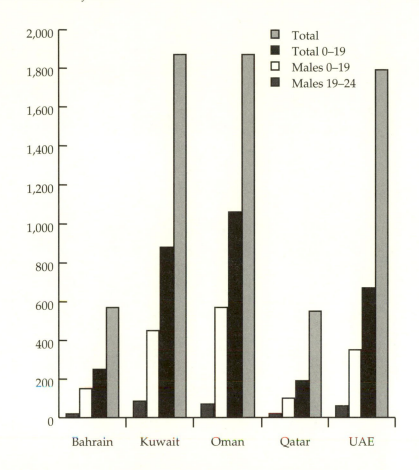

CHART FOUR   Youth in the Smaller Gulf States: 1995 (Thousands).
Source: Adapted by Anthony H. Cordesman from World Bank, *World Population Projections, 1994–1995*, Washington, World Bank, 1994, and material provided

problem that the Southern Gulf states face in creating economies that rely on native labor and reward citizens for a competitive work ethic. The state, petroleum, other state-dominated, and service sectors of most Southern Gulf states are filled with "non jobs" for citizens. While no precise estimates are possible, it seems likely that 50% or more of the jobs currently held by the citizens of the Southern Gulf countries serve no productive purpose and are little more than disguised unemployment. As such, these jobs are little more than concealed welfare and offer little hope or career opportunity to most job holders.

TABLE SIX   Ethnic and Religious Divisions Affecting Gulf Security

Gulf Region	Ethnic	Religious	Labor
Bahrain	68% Bahraini 13% Asian 10% Other Arab 8% Iranian 1% Other (Arabic, English, Farsi, Urdu)	70% Shiite 30% Sunni	58% Foreign 85% Comm & Indust 5% Agriculture 5% Services 3% Government
Iran	51% Persian 25% Azerbaijani 9% Kurd 8% Gilaki/Mazandarani 2% Lur 1% Baloch 1% Arab 3% Other (58% Persian, 26% Turkic, 9% Kurdish, 7% Other)	95% Shiite 4% Sunni 1% Bahai, Jewish, Christian, Zoroastrian	33% Agriculture 21% Manufacturing
Iraq	75–80% Arab 15–20% Kurd 5% Turkoman/Assyrian (Arabic, Kurdish, Assyrian, Armenian)	60–65% Shiite 32–37% Sunni 3% Christian & Other	48% Services 30% Agriculture 22% Industry
Kuwait	39% Kuwaiti 35% Other Arab 9% South Asian 4% Iranian 2% Other (Arabic, English)	45% Sunni 30% Shiite 10% Other Muslim 15% Christian, Hindu, Parsi	70% Foreign 45% Services 20% Construction 12% Trade 8.6% Manufacturing 2.6% Finan/Real Est 1.9% Agriculture

(continues)

TABLE SIX (continued)

Gulf Region	Ethnic	Religious	Labor
Oman	27% Expatriate Arab with Balochi, Zanzibari, and South Asian (Arabic, English, Urdu, Balochi, Indian dialects)	75% Ibadhi Muslim Sunni Shiite Hindu	58% Foreign 40% Agriculture
Qatar	25% Qatari Arab 75% Expatriate 15% Other Arab 18% Pakistani 18% Indian 10% Iranian 14% Other (Arabic, English)	95% Muslim	85% Foreign
Saudi Arabia	69% Saudi Arab 21% Asian 8% Arab 2% African 1% Other (Arabic)	86% Sunni 8% Shiite 6% Other	60% Foreign 34% Government 28% Indust & Oil 22% Services 16% Agriculture
UAE	24% Emirian Arab 12% Other Arab 30% Indian 16% Pakistani 12% Other Asian 1% European (Arab, English, Hindu, Urdu)	80% Sunni 16% Shiite 4% Christian, Hindu, Other	80% Foreign 85% Indust & Comm 5% Agriculture 5% Services 5% Government

Source: Author's estimate, based on CIA and IISS statistics.

Only a few Gulf states face serious ethnic divisions within their native populations. At the same time, Table Six shows that the Southern Gulf states do have significant differences in their ethnic and religious composition. Social change and alienation have created new problems in terms of Islamic fundamentalism and extremism in a number of states, and there is growing tension between the large royal families of most Southern Gulf states and those outside the power elite.

There also are deep and growing divisions between the ruling elites of the Southern Gulf states. These divisions are sometimes concealed by the rhetoric of the Gulf Cooperation Council, and reports of "border settlements," but they are all too real. They are reflected in the tensions between Bahrain and Qatar, and between Qatar, Saudi Arabia and the UAE. They are also reflected in tensions between Kuwait and other Southern Gulf states, between Oman and Saudi Arabia, and between the UAE and Oman. Such tensions are unlikely to shatter the apparent unity of the Southern Gulf in dealing with many issues, but they are another reason that each state must be assessed separately.

These political and socio-economic problems are likely to be as important in shaping the security and stability of each Southern Gulf state as are external threats and military capabilities. While priorities differ significantly by country, there cannot be stability without reform. In broad terms, each of the Southern Gulf states must:

- Limit population growth through education, birth control, and other measures.
- Force radical reductions in the number of foreign workers. Eliminate economic disincentives for employers in hiring native labor, and create disincentives for hiring foreign labor. The UAE's young and increasingly well-educated population needs to replace its foreign workers as quickly as possible, and it will only develop a work ethic and suitable skills once it is thrust into the labor market.
- Reduce those aspects of state subsidies and welfare that distort the economy and discourage the native population from seeking jobs. Reduce dependence on welfare, and replace subsidies with jobs and economic opportunities.
- Price water, electricity, motor gasoline, basic foods, and services at market levels.
- Restructure educational systems to focus on job training and competitiveness. Create strong new incentives for faculty and students to focus on job-related education, sharply down-size other forms of educational funding and activity, and eliminate high overhead educational activities without economic benefits.

- Unify and reform the structure of national budgets to reduce the amount of money going directly to royal accounts, and ensure that most of the nation's revenues and foreign reserves are integrated into the national budget and into the planning process. Clearly separate royal and national income and investment holdings.
- Place limits on the transfer of state funds to princes and members of the royal family outside the actual ruling family, and transfers of unearned income to members of other leading families.
- Ensure that all income from enterprises with state financing is reflected in the national budget and is integrated into the national economic development and planning program.
- Freeze and then reduce the number of civil servants. Restructure and down-size the civil service to focus on productive areas of activity with a much smaller pool of manpower. Cut back sharply on state employees.
- Establish market criteria for major state and state-supported investments. Require detailed and independent risk assessment and projections of comparative return on investment, with a substantial penalty for state versus privately funded projects and ventures. Down-size the scale of programs to reduce investment and cash flow costs and the risk of cost-escalation.
- Carry out more rapid and extensive privatization to increase the efficiency of investments in downstream and upstream operations, create real jobs and career opportunities for native workers, and create investment opportunities for a much wider range of investors. Manage privatization in ways that ensure an opportunity for all native citizens to share in the privatization process.
- Avoid offset requirements that simply create disguised unemployment or non-competitive ventures that act as a further state-sponsored distortion of the economy.
- Create new incentives to invest in local industries and business and disincentives for the expatriation of capital. Encourage outside investment.
- Tax earnings and sales with progressive taxes that reduce or eliminate budget deficits. Use taxes to encourage local investment, and which create strong disincentives for the expatriation of capital, including all foreign holdings of capital and property by members of elite and ruling families.
- Establish a firm rule of law for all property, contract, permitting, and business activity and reduce state bureaucratic and permitting barriers to private investment.
- Place national security spending on the same basis as other state spending. Integrate it fully into the national budget, including in-

vestment and equipment purchases. Replace the present emphasis on judging purchases on the basis of initial procurement costs and technical features with a full assessment of life cycle cost—including training, maintenance, and facilities—and with specific procedures for evaluating the value of standardization and interoperability with existing national equipment and facilities, those of other Gulf states, and those of the US and other power projection forces.

Strategic Needs and Vulnerabilities

Each of the individual Southern Gulf states has different strategic needs and vulnerabilities. Kuwait and northwestern Saudi Arabia (the location of most of the Kingdom's oil facilities) are vulnerable to land attack from Iraq. Kuwait's small forces, limited territory, and proximity to Iraq make it a natural target for Iraqi ambitions. As a result, the strategic priorities and military balance in the upper Gulf will always be determined by different factors from those that affect the central and lower Gulf. Kuwait and Saudi Arabia will always be vulnerable to rapid Iraqi mobilization and attack, and will have to be prepared to rapidly fight a major land-air battle for the defense of Kuwait and the Eastern Province.

Saudi Arabia is the largest Southern Gulf state in terms of both geography and military forces and is the key to any successful effort at regional cooperation in defense. Yet, Saudi Arabia has a low ratio of forces to the space in its critical defensive areas—particularly along its border with Iraq. It cannot create an effective defense without its neighbors.

Kuwait shares a common border with Iraq and is only a short distance from Iran. No foreseeable mix of Kuwaiti, other Southern Gulf, other Arab, and/or US forces can offer Kuwait full security against another round of Iraqi surprise attacks or surprise Iranian air, amphibious, and missile attacks. Kuwait 's small territory and population keep its military vulnerable while it has massive oil and gas resources to protect.

The smaller Southern Gulf states face more serious problems. They spread along the coast of the Southern Gulf. If any of these states fell into hostile hands, it would be a major strategic springboard for intervention by Iran or Iraq, or a constant threat to the internal security of its neighbors. A hostile air force or navy based in the Southern Gulf could also make it far more difficult for other Arab states or the US to project power into the region.

Iran presents different challenges. The waters of the Gulf provide a barrier to Iranian land and amphibious attacks on the main territory of the other Southern Gulf states. At the same time, Iran's coast covers virtually all of the Northern Gulf and extends into the Gulf on Oman. The Gulf does not act as a barrier to strategic attacks, naval attacks, infiltration, or arms smuggling.

Bahrain, Qatar, UAE, and Oman have special problems. They do not share a common border with Iran or Iraq, but they all lack strategic depth and adequate air and coastal defense capabilities and are vulnerable to Iraqi and Iranian attacks. Bahrain is small and relatively poor. Qatar is small, and has too small a native population to develop effective armed forces. The UAE shares the demographic and geographic problems of its littoral neighbors, and is further weakened by tensions between its individual Sheikdoms. Oman must defend the Straits of Hormuz against any challenge by Iran and a long border with Yemen.

All of the Southern Gulf states are vulnerable to attacks on Gulf shipping and oil facilities in the Gulf, or to Iranian control of the Straits of Hormuz. Bahrain is small enough to be vulnerable to amphibious and air attack from Iran, and Oman is potentially vulnerable to an Iranian attack on the Musandam Peninsula or its ports and shipping in the Gulf of Oman. All of the Southern Gulf states are vulnerable to attacks on key water facilities and desalinization plants near their shores, and most have only one major city which defines their national existence—a fact that makes them highly vulnerable to attack by weapons of mass destruction.

The key statistical details of the military forces of the Southern Gulf states are summarized in Table Seven, along with the forces of Iran, Iraq, and Yemen. While the Southern Gulf states may collectively have enough manpower and weapons to provide a regional deterrent and considerable self-defense capability, Table Seven shows that each country has very different military resources and a very different force structure.

Table Seven reveals a number of additional details about the regional balance:

- Iran and Iraq both have armed forces totaling close to half a million men. They have massive land forces by regional standards with large numbers of armored weapons, artillery, and major air forces.
- At the same time, Iran still has fewer land weapons and aircraft than it did at the time of the Shah. Iran has not yet been able to rebuild its land forces to compensate for its catastrophic military defeats in the Iran-Iraq War during the spring and summer of 1988—defeats that cost it at least 40% of its inventory of major land combat equipment. While it has recently built its tank strength up to a many as 1,350 tanks, it does not have anything approaching the massive tank forces of Iraq. Iran has a limited strength of other armored vehicles. It has large numbers of artillery weapons, but many of these weapons are towed. While Iran does have nearly 300 combat aircraft and over 100 armed helicopters in inventory, many

TABLE SEVEN Gulf Military Forces in 1996

	Iran	Iraq	Bahrain	Kuwait	Oman	Qatar	Saudi Arabia*	UAE	Yemen
Manpower									
Total Active	320,000	382,500	10,700	16,600	43,500	11,100	161,500	70,000	39,500
Regular	220,000	382,500	10,700	16,600	37,000	11,100	105,500	70,000	39,500
National Guard & Other	100,000	0	0	0	6,500	0	57,000	0	0
Reserve	350,000	650,000	0	23,700	0	0	0	0	40,000
Paramilitary	135,000	24,800	9,250	5,200	4,400	0	15,500	2,700	30,000
Army and Guard									
Manpower	260,000	350,000	8,500	10,000	31,500	8,500	127,000	65,000	37,000
Regular Army Manpower	180,000	350,000	8,500	10,000	25,000	8,500	70,000	65,000	37,000
Reserve	350,000	450,000	0	0	0	0	20,000	0	40,000
Tanks	1,350	2,700	81	220	85	24	910	133	1,125
AIFV/Recce, Lt. Tanks	515	1,600	46	130	136	50	1,467	515	580
APCs	550	2,200	235	199	7	172	3,670	380	560
Self Propelled Artillery	294	150	13	38	6	28	200	90	30
Towed Artillery	2,000	1,500	36	0	96	12	270	82	483
MRLs	890	120	9	0	0	4	60	48	220
Mortars	3,500	2,000+	18	24	74	39	400	101	800
SSM Launchers	46	12	0	0	0	0	10	6	30
Light SAM Launchers	700	3,000	65	48	62	58	650	36	700
AA Guns	1,700	5,500	0	0	18	12	10	62	372
Air Force Manpower	20,000	15,000	1,500	2,500	4,100	800	18,000	3,500	1,000
Air Defense Manpower	15,000	15,000	0	0	0	0	4,000	0	0

(continues)

TABLE SEVEN (*continued*)

	Iran	Iraq	Bahrain	Kuwait	Oman	Qatar	Saudi Arabia*	UAE	Yemen
Total Combat Aircraft	295	353	24	76	46	12	295	97	69
Bombers	0	6	0	0	0	0	0	0	0
Fighter/Attack	150	130	12	40	19	11	112	41	27
Fighter/Interceptor	115	180	12	8	0	1	122	22	30
Recce/FGA Recce	8	0	0	0	12	0	10	8	0
AEW C4I/BM	0	1	0	0	0	0	5	0	0
MR/MPA**	6	0	0	0	7	0	0	0	0
OCU/COIN	0	18	0	11	13	0	36	15	12
Combat Trainers	92	200	0	11	22	5	66	35	19
Transport Aircraft**	68	34	3	4	14	0	49	20	0
Tanker Aircraft	4	2	0	0	0	0	16	0	0
Armed Helicopters**	100	120	10	16	0	20	12	42	8
Other Helicopters**	509	350	8	36	37	7	138	42	21
Major SAM Launchers	204	340	12	24	0	0	128	18	87
Light SAM Launchers	60	200	0	12	28	9	249	34	0
AA Guns	0	0	0	12	0	0	420	0	0
Navy Manpower	38,000	2,500	1,000	1,500	4,200	1,800	17,000	1,500	1,500
Major Surface Combatants									
Missile	5	0	3	0	0	0	8	0	0
Other	2	1	0	0	0	0	0	0	0
Patrol Craft									
Missile	10	1	4	2	4	3	9	10	7

(*continues*)

TABLE SEVEN (continued)

	Iran	Iraq	Bahrain	Kuwait	Oman	Qatar	Saudi Arabia*	UAE	Yemen
Other	26	7	5	12	8	6	20	18	3
Submarines	2	0	0	0	0	0	0	0	0
Mine Vessels	3	4	0	0	0	0	5	0	3
Amphibious Ships	8	0	0	0	2	0	0	0	2
Landing Craft	17	3	4	6	4	1	7	4	2

Notes: Does not include equipment in storage. Air Force totals include all helicopters, and all heavy surface to air missile launchers.

*60,000 reserves are National Guard Tribal Levies. The total for land forces includes active National Guard equipment. These additions total 262 AIFVs, 1,165 APCs, and 70 towed artillery weapons.

**Includes navy, army, national guard, and royal flights, but not paramilitary.

Source: Adapted by Anthony H. Cordesman from International Institute for Strategic Studies *Military Balance* (IISS, London), in this case, the 1995–1996 edition; *Military Technology, World Defense Almanac, 1994–1995*; and Jaffee Center for Strategic Studies, *The Military Balance in the Middle East, 1993–1994* (JCSS, Tel Aviv, 1994).

of these weapons are not operational and most are systems the US supplied 15–20 years ago. Similarly, much of Iran's fleet suffers severely from age, a lack of Western resupply, and damage done by clashes with the US and British navies during 1987–1988.

- Iraqi forces also have important limitations. In spite of losing nearly half of its land force equipment in the Gulf War, Iraq has the largest land and air forces in the Gulf. It remains a major military power by Gulf standards. At the same time, Iraq has only had minimal resupply since the beginning of the Gulf War, and UN sanctions have put severe limits on its ability to repair combat damage and bring its equipment and aircraft inventories back to full operational readiness. Unlike Iran, Iraq is not a significant sea power by regional standards, and few of Iraq's combat vessels survived the war.

- While any estimate of Yemen's total force numbers is uncertain, because of the difficulty in estimating the totals that survived the Yemeni civil war in 1994, Yemen's forces are still large enough to present a potential threat to dispersed Saudi forces, many of which must be kept near other fronts. Saudi Arabia must be a Red Sea, as well as a Gulf Power.

- The Southern Gulf states have a large potential pool of military resources. However, even if their total resources are analyzed in strictly quantitative terms, their collective land forces still have only about half the tanks of Iraq and half the manpower of Iran. Their greatest strength is in aircraft, where they collectively have nearly twice the combat aircraft of either Iran or Iraq. They also have far more collective naval strength than Iraq, and many more combat ships than Iran.

- The numbers in Table Seven do not include the forces the US might contribute to the balance in the region. It is impossible to show a single set of comparable figures for US and other Western powers because these forces would vary sharply according to a given scenario. Yet, any comparison of the balance which does not include the Western forces that could play a critical role in determining the balance in any real world war fighting situation is inherently misleading.

Relative Military Expenditures and Arms Transfers

Comparisons of military expenditures and arms sales provide another picture of the trends in the Gulf balance and of the differences between the Southern Gulf states. The data shown in Table Eight show the extent to which Iran, Iraq, and Saudi Arabia dominate the regional arms race, and reveal several other trends in the military balance in the Gulf:

TABLE EIGHT Gulf Country Military Expenditures and Arms Sales (in Constant $1994 Millions)

	1984	1985	1986	1987	1988	1989	1990	1991	1992	1993	1994	Total
Total Military Expenditures												
Northern Gulf												
Iran	8,386	9,044	11,490	9,436	8,406	6,886	7,117	6,597	4,133	4,502	3,042	79,039
Iraq	23,306	16,920	19,370	20,770	22,330	15,360	15,820	9,462	2,800	2,400	2,100	150,638
Sub-total	31,692	25,964	30,860	30,206	30,736	22,246	22,937	16,059	6,933	6,902	5,142	229,677
Southern Gulf												
Bahrain	205	201	209	202	227	227	240	254	262	256	256	2,539
Kuwait	1,958	2,015	1,673	1,575	1,529	2,257	14,370	17,190	19,910	3,670	3,086	69,233
Oman	2,621	2,587	2,250	1,913	1,638	1,802	1,899	1,554	1,843	1,726	1,818	21,651
Qatar	174	163	171	168	176	202	480	1,001	372	336	302	3,545
Saudi Arabia	28,230	28,490	22,530	20,430	16,510	17,050	25,780	38,060	36,510	20,900	17,200	271,690
UAE	2,656	2,522	2,041	1,987	1,913	1,831	2,863	5,216	2,172	2,154	1,907	27,262
Sub-total	35,844	35,978	28,874	26,275	21,993	23,369	45,632	63,275	61,069	29,042	24,569	395,920
Total	67,536	61,942	59,734	56,481	52,729	45,615	68,569	79,334	68,002	35,944	29,711	625,597
Arms Sales												
Northern Gulf												
Iran	3,737	2,537	3,381	2,521	3,155	1,742	2,003	2,251	375	1,021	390	23,113
Iraq	12,870	6,544	7,802	7,310	6,796	2,782	3,116	131	90	90	90	47,621
Sub-total	16,607	9,081	11,183	9,831	9,951	4,524	5,119	2,382	465	1,111	480	70,734

(continues)

TABLE EIGHT   (continued)

	1984	1985	1986	1987	1988	1989	1990	1991	1992	1993	1994	Total
Southern Gulf												
Bahrain	55	80	52	366	121	105	323	54	136	61	80	1,433
Kuwait	900	494	234	252	316	546	312	515	1,043	765	250	5,627
Oman	429	187	143	139	36	70	11	54	10	122	50	1,251
Qatar	291	53	7	0	36	209	111	21	42	0	0	770
Saudi Arabia	9,827	9,348	9,493	8,570	7,525	6,851	8,681	8,039	8,864	6,940	5,200	89,338
UAE	263	294	221	189	146	1,016	1,558	397	375	439	200	5,098
Sub-total	11,765	10,456	10,150	9,516	8,180	8,797	10,996	9,080	10,470	8,327	5,780	103,517
Total	28,372	19,537	21,333	19,347	18,131	13,321	16,115	11,462	10,935	9,438	6,260	174,251

Note: Definitions of military expenditures and arms transfers are not always comparable between countries shown.
Source: Adapted by Anthony H. Cordesman from US Arms Control and Disarmament Agency, *World Military Expenditures and Arms Transfers, 1994–1995*, Washington, GPO, 1996. Estimates by the author are included for Iraq and Qatar.

- Gulf military expenditures and arms transfers reached truly massive levels during the Iran-Iraq War of 1980–1988, the "tanker war" of 1987–1988, and the Gulf War of 1990–1991. During the decade between 1982 and 1992, military expenditures totaled over $634 billion in constant 1993 dollars. Arms transfers totaled nearly $155 billion.
- Iraq was able to spend far more than Iran on military expenditures and arms transfers during the Iran-Iraq War—three to four times in some years. Iraqi arms imports average over $7 billion annually during 1984–1988. However, virtually all arms imports to Iraq halted as a result of the Gulf War, while Iran continued to make significant imports.
- Iran's economic and political problems have led to a major cut in Iranian arms imports since the early 1990s. Iran's arms imports have dropped from an average level of over $2 billion a year during 1984–1991, to as little as $400 million in 1994.
- Bahrain has only made a limited military effort by the standards of its neighbors, but has sustained a consistent effort over time. It has also maintained a relatively good balance between total military spending and arms imports.
- Kuwaiti military expenditures and arms imports were relatively limited until the Iraqi invasion. Kuwait was then forced to make massive expenditures during 1990–1992 to build up its military capabilities and assist Coalition countries in liberating Kuwait. It has since cut its military expenditures to about twice its pre-war levels and its arms imports to pre-war levels.
- Oman has made consistent efforts to build up its military forces, but Omani arms imports have fallen far below the ratio necessary to support Omani military expenditures.
- Qatari military expenditures were even lower than those of Bahrain during the period before the Gulf War. They have since risen to levels averaging over $300 million annually. Qatari arms imports rose during the early years of the Iran-Iraq War, then fell to low levels until the Iraqi invasion of Kuwait. They did not peak during the Gulf War, and have remained too low to fund a conversion to modern armored and air forces.
- Saudi Arabia has made massive military efforts, both in terms of total expenditures and arms imports. Saudi expenditures rose to new heights during the liberation of Kuwait, but have since dropped to pre-war levels. Saudi arms imports have been cut sharply since 1992 because of Saudi Arabia's growing budget problems.
- The UAE's military expenditures also rose during the early years of the Iran-Iraq War, dropped after 1986, and then rose again as a result of the Iraqi invasion of Kuwait. The UAE has, however, sustained far

higher levels of arms imports than the other, smaller Gulf states and has funded a substantially higher level of arms imports and modernization.

Tables Nine and Ten provide further data on recent arms transfers, and reveal the lack of standardization and interoperability in Southern Gulf military equipment and suppliers. These data also show:

- International sanctions have virtually cut Iraq off from Russia and Europe—its traditional sources of arms—since 1990.
- Iran not only cut its total arms imports significantly after the Iran-Iraq War, it turned to Russia as a major new supplier of arms. Roughly $1.0 billion worth of the arms Iran imported between 1992 and 1994 came from Russia, versus $40 million from Germany, $525 million from China, $20 from other Middle Eastern countries, $30 million from East European countries, $110 million from East Asian states, and $40 million from other countries.[1] This shift to Russia as a major supplier gave Iran a critical new source of more advanced weapons and military technology.
- Bahrain is dependent on the US for arms imports. Bahrain imported $270 million worth of arms during 1992–1994. A total of $260 million came from the US, and $10 million from the smaller West European countries.
- Kuwait has increased its imports from the US since the Gulf War, but has scarcely standardized on any supplier. Kuwait has often made a deliberate effort to import from a wide variety of countries, emphasizing politics over interoperability and standardization. Kuwait imported $2.04 billion worth of arms during 1992–1994. A total of $1.8 billion came from the US, $100 million from France, $30 million from other Middle Eastern countries, $80 million from other East European countries, and $30 million from other countries. During 1981–1994, however, only about half of Kuwait's arms came from the US.
- Oman remains dependent on the UK—although it has increasingly imported arms from the US. Oman imported $180 million worth of arms during 1992–1994. A total of $20 million came from the US, $150 million from the UK, $5 million from other Middle Eastern countries, and $5 million from other countries.
- Qatar remains dependent on Europe—particularly France—for virtually all of its arms imports. Qatar imported $45 million worth of arms during 1992–1994. A total of $5 million came from the US, $10 million from France, $20 million from other West European countries, and $10 million from other countries.

TABLE NINE   Arms Sales Agreements Affecting the Gulf (Millions of Current US Dollars)

Recipient Country	US	Russia	PRC	Major West European	All Other European	All Others	Total
1987–1990							
Bahrain	600	0	0	0	0	0	600
Iran	0	2,500	3,400	200	2,100	2,000	10,200
Iraq	0	4,100	800	2,700	1,200	1,700	10,500
Kuwait	2,100	200	100	100	200	100	800
Oman	100	0	0	300	0	0	400
Qatar	0	0	0	100	0	0	100
Saudi Arabia	14,300	200	3,300	25,700	2,000	200	45,700
UAE	300	0	0	300	0	400	1,000
1991–1993							
Bahrain	200	0	0	0	0	0	200
Iran	0	1,200	400	100	100	900	2,700
Iraq	0	0	0	0	0	0	0
Kuwait	3,900	600	0	1,200	0	0	5,700
Oman	0	0	0	600	0	0	600
Qatar	0	0	0	2,000	0	0	2,000
Saudi Arabia	20,200	0	0	9,500	500	0	30,200
UAE	800	400	0	3,600	100	100	5,000

(continues)

TABLE NINE (continued)

Recipient Country	US	Russia	PRC	Major West European	All Other European	All Others	Total
1987–1994							
Bahrain	800	0	0	0	0	0	800
Iran	0	3,700	3,800	300	2,200	2,900	12,900
Iraq	0	4,100	800	2,700	1,200	1,700	10,500
Kuwait	6,000	800	0	1,400	500	500	9,200
Oman	100	0	0	900	0	0	1,000
Qatar	0	0	0	2,100	0	0	2,100
Saudi Arabia	34,500	200	3,300	35,200	2,500	200	75,900
UAE	1,100	400	0	3,900	100	500	6,000

Source: Adapted by Anthony H. Cordesman, CSIS, from Richard F. Grimmett, "Conventional Arms Transfers to Developing Nations, 1987–1994," CRS 85-862F, Congressional Research Service, August 4, 1995, pp. 56–57 and 67–69. All data are rounded to nearest $100 million. Major West European states include Britain, France, Germany, and Italy.

TABLE TEN Arms Deliveries Affecting the Gulf (Millions of Current US Dollars)

Recipient Country	US	Russia	PRC	Major West European	All Other European	All Others	Total
1987–1990							
Bahrain	500	0	0	300	0	0	800
Iran	0	1,100	2,500	500	1,900	1,800	7,800
Iraq	0	7,400	1,800	2,900	3,000	1,500	16,600
Kuwait	200	200	0	200	200	500	1,300
Oman	0	0	0	200	0	0	200
Qatar	0	0	0	300	0	0	300
Saudi Arabia	6,500	100	3,000	15,100	900	700	26,300
UAE	300	0	0	2,100	0	100	2,500
1991–1993							
Bahrain	300	0	0	0	0	0	300
Iran	0	2,400	1,100	100	0	300	3,900
Iraq	0	0	0	0	0	0	0
Kuwait	2,100	0	0	200	100	100	2,500
Oman	100	0	0	200	0	0	300
Qatar	0	0	0	0	0	0	0
Saudi Arabia	10,900	100	300	14,700	1,800	100	27,900
UAE	600	300	0	200	0	200	1,300

(*continues*)

TABLE TEN (continued)

Recipient Country	US	Russia	PRC	Major West European	All Other European	All Others	Total
1987–1994							
Bahrain	800	0	0	300	0	0	1,100
Iran	0	3,500	3,600	600	1,900	2,100	11,700
Iraq	0	7,400	1,800	2,900	3,000	1,500	16,600
Kuwait	2,300	200	0	400	300	600	3,800
Oman	100	0	0	400	0	0	500
Qatar	0	0	0	300	0	0	300
Saudi Arabia	17,400	200	3,300	29,800	2,700	800	54,200
UAE	900	300	0	2,300	0	300	3,800

Source: Adapted by Anthony H. Cordesman, CSIS, from Richard F. Grimmett, "Conventional Arms Transfers to Developing Nations, 1987–1994," CRS 85-862F, Congressional Research Service, August 4, 1995, pp. 56–57 and 67–69. All data are rounded to nearest $100 million. Major West European states include Britain, France, Germany, and Italy.

- Saudi Arabia draws its arms imports from a wide range of sources. About 40% of Saudi Arabia's arms have come from the US over the last decade, and about 40% from Western Europe. Saudi Arabia imported $20.47 billion worth of arms during 1992–1994. A total of $8.6 billion came from the US, $9.4 billion from the UK, $30 million from Germany, $525 million from France, $170 million from China, $900 million from Canada, $750 million from other West European countries, $30 million from other Middle Eastern countries, $10 million from East Asian countries, and $80 million from other countries.
- The UAE also gets its arms from a wide range of sources. The UAE imported $995 million worth of arms during 1992–1994. A total of $360 million came from the US, $260 million from Russia,, $110 million from France, $10 million from other West European countries, $5 million from other Middle Eastern countries, $30 million from East European countries, $30 million from East Asian countries, and $190 million from other countries.
- Yemen faced problems in funding significant arms imports well before the Yemeni civil war—largely because of the cut off of Soviet-bloc aid at the end of the Cold War, and the loss of Southern Gulf aid when Yemen supported Iraq in the Gulf War.

The Southern Gulf states have more problems than a lack of standardization and interoperability. While they are gradually improving in individual military capability, many are still "showpiece" forces which cannot operate effectively except in carefully planned exercises. Their forces include manpower and equipment with a wide range of different capabilities. Much of their equipment counted is held by low grade active and reserve units with only limited readiness and limited combat capability.

The Southern Gulf states have relatively small manpower pools to draw on, given the territory they must defend. Southern Gulf military forces also generally suffer from major diseconomies of scale. These problems have been compounded by poorly structured arms purchases. In many cases, the Southern Gulf states have bought weapons for their prestige—or "glitter factor"—rather than their deterrent or combat capabilities. Most of the military forces in the smaller Southern Gulf states have inadequate warning sensors, and weak command and control systems.

Most of the smaller Southern Gulf armies lack modern communications, battle management, and target acquisition systems. There is little heliborne or amphibious capability to rapidly move troops. There are limited airborne early warning (AEW) and air control and warning assets. Most Southern Gulf ships have inadequate air and missile defenses. The smaller navies have no mine warfare capability, and all forces have poor ability to conduct combined arms and joint operations. There are few modern reconnaissance and intelligence assets.

These military problems are as critical in shaping the security and stability of each Southern Gulf state as are external threats and military capabilities. Once again, priorities differ significantly by country, but there cannot be stability without reform. To varying degrees, each Southern Gulf state must work with its neighbors in:

- Creating an effective planning system for collective defense, and truly standardized and/or interoperable forces.
- Integrating its C^{4}I and sensor nets for air and naval combat, including beyond-visual-range and night warfare.
- Focusing on deploying its forces to support the joint land defense of the Kuwaiti/Northwestern Saudi borders and reinforcing other Gulf states like Oman in the event of any Iranian amphibious or air borne action.
- Creating joint air defense and air attack capabilities.
- Creating joint air and naval strike forces.
- Establishing effective cross reinforcement and tactical mobility capabilities.
- Preparing fully for outside or over-the-horizon reinforcement by the US and other Western powers.
- Setting up joint training, support, and infrastructure facilities.
- Creating common advanced training systems that develop a brigade and wing-level capability for combined arms and joint warfare, and which can support realistic field training exercises of the kind practiced by US and Israeli forces.
- Improving its capability to provide urban and urban area security and to fight unconventional warfare and low intensity combat.

At the same time, most Southern Gulf states need to stop making political and "glitter factor" procurements. They need to steadily reduce their number of different suppliers and major weapons types and to focus on procuring interoperable and/or standardized equipment to provide the capability to perform the following missions:

- Heavy armor, artillery, attack helicopters, and mobile air defense equipment for defense of the upper Gulf.
- Interoperability and standardization with US power projection forces.
- Interoperable offensive air capability with stand-off, all-weather precision weapons and anti-armor/anti-ship capability.
- Interoperable air defense equipment, including heavy surface-to-air missiles, beyond-visual-range/all-weather fighters, airborne early

warning & surveillance capability, anti-radiation missile & electronic countermeasure capability.

- Maritime surveillance systems, and equipment for defense against maritime surveillance, and unconventional warfare.
- Mine detection and clearing systems.
- Improved urban, area, and border security equipment for unconventional warfare and low intensity conflict.
- Advanced training aids.
- Support and sustainment equipment.

Differences and Similarities

In summary, the differences between each Southern Gulf state are as important as the similarities—particularly in a world which is critically dependent on energy imports and trade with the Gulf. It may be convenient to think in terms of strategic short hand, but such thinking does not explain the internal dynamics of the Southern Gulf, the economics and trade policies of individual states, or the strategic realities that affect regional and Western interests.

The Southern Gulf states do have many similarities, and far more similarities than they do to Iran and Iran. Nevertheless, Saudi Arabia has a territory seven times that of all of its Southern Gulf neighbors combined, and over twice their population. Saudi Arabia's GDP is 27 times that of Bahrain and almost four times that of the UAE—which has the second largest GDP of any Southern Gulf state. Kuwait's primary threat is a land attack by Iraq. Oman, some 600 miles away by air and 750 miles away by sea, faces a naval and air threat from Iran. Qatar, which is similar to Bahrain in some respects, has nearly 15 times as many oil reserves. The political, cultural, and ethnic differences between the Southern Gulf states described earlier may be less tangible, but they are at least as important.

The following chapters on Bahrain, Oman, Qatar, and the UAE make these points in far more detail, as do the separate volumes on Iran, Iraq, and Saudi Arabia. No one can deny the Muslim character of the Gulf region, that it is largely Arab, and that it is largely dependent on oil and gas exports. A net assessment of the Gulf, however, is ultimately a net assessment of states and not of a region. It is the differences which explain the most, and not the similarities.

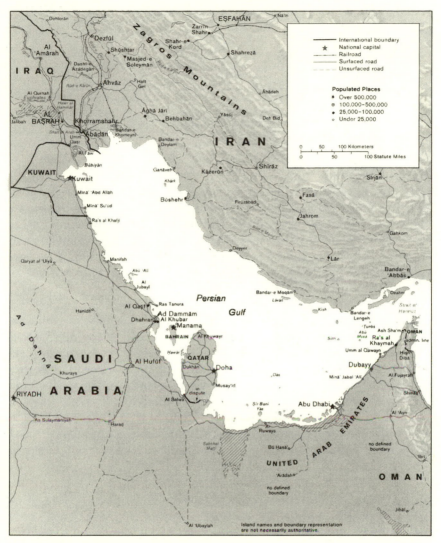

MAP ONE   The Gulf

2

Bahrain

Bahrain is one of the smallest countries in the Middle East, with a total land area of 620 square kilometers. Its territory is largely composed of a single main island—roughly the size of the greater metropolitan area of Washington, DC. This main island has a coastline of 161 kilometers and is connected by a 25 kilometer causeway with Saudi Arabia. There are two smaller inhabited islands, and Bahrain has sovereignty over a total of 33 islands and their surrounding waters.[2]

Despite its small territory, Bahrain has great strategic importance. It is within eight minutes flying time from Iran and 30 minutes flying time from Iraq. Its location near Iran and Iraq, and the main shipping channels to Kuwait and Saudi Arabia make the existence of a friendly Bahrain critical to both collective security efforts in the Gulf and Western power projection efforts. Bahrain is also one of the most strategically exposed Gulf States. It is within a few minutes flying time of Iran and Iraq, and it is vulnerable to air attacks, naval infiltration, attacks on its lines of communications, mining operations, and Iranian amphibious operations.

Bahrain's History

Bahrain's history dates back as far as 2400 B.C., and the time of Dilmun. Its modern history, however, dates back to the early 1500s and a series of Persian, Portuguese, and Turkish struggles to control the main island that helped make Bahrain a major military and trading center. These struggles ended in the Persian conquest of Bahrain in 1602, and its forts and settlements came under the control of the Matareesh. The Matareesh were an Omani Arab family based in Bushehr in Iran, and owed fealty to the Persian Empire. Under their rule, Bahrain continued to be a major trade and pearling center, and was used for raids on other Southern Gulf ports and shipping.[3]

Beginning in the 1760s, however, the Matareesh encountered growing rivalry from the Al Khalifa family. The Al Khalifas were part of the Utub

(Utoob) tribe and had migrated into the region from southern Arabia during the 17th Century. They settled in Kuwait in the early 1700s, and then set up a base at Az Zubarah on Qatar's Western coast in 1763. The Al Khalifas fortified Az Zubarah in 1768, and used it as a base to dominate much of modern Qatar. They also exploited the reefs near Az Zubarah for pearling, created a port free of the duties and taxes charged in Bahrain, and strongly encouraged merchant settlements.

In 1782, Sheik Nasr Al-Mazkoor, the Matareesh governor of Bahrain and Bushehr, responded to Az Zubarah's growing economic power by attacking shipping going in and out of the port. The next year, Sheik Nasr waited until Sheik Khalifa went on the Haj, and laid siege to Az Zubarah. The siege was badly organized, however, and Ahmed Bin Mohammed Al Khalifa, Sheik Khalifa's brother, organized an effective defense that lifted the siege and drove the Persian-Matareesh forces out of Qatar.

Sheik Ahmed became the leader of the Al Khalifa family when his brother died during the Haj, and moved to counterattack. He formed a coalition with other branches of the Bani Utub, including the Al Sabahs of Kuwait. This coalition invaded and conquered Bahrain later in 1783, and forced Sheik Nasr Al-Mazkoor to flee to Bushehr. As a result, the Al Khalifa family gained control of a territory with better water and agricultural resources than Qatar and which was easier to defend. Sheik Ahmed became the first Al Khalifa Amir of Kuwait and ruled from 1783–1796. During his rule, he expanded Bahrain's ports, trade, and pearling industry, and most of the Al Khalifa family migrated from Qatar to Bahrain.

The Al Khalifas maintained their rule over Bahrain from 1783–1861—although they sporadically acknowledged the authority of Iran, Muhammed Ali, the Ottoman Empire, and even the Wahhabi Emirs of the Najd, when the Al Khalifas found this to be politically expedient or useful as a way of avoiding attack. On several occasions, the Al Khalifas paid fealty to several outside states at once—balancing the power of one state against another until the complex power struggles in the Gulf again allowed the Al Khalifas to assert their independence.[4]

This maneuvering reached a crisis in 1859, when the Amir of Bahrain acknowledged both Persian and Turkish sovereignty, and then attempted to exploit this arrangement by attacking shipping and by taxing the British Indian traders on the island. At the same time, the Al Khalifa family became involved in a series of dynastic battles.

Britain responded by forcing the Amir of Bahrain to sign a treaty on May 31, 1861, in which he agreed to a perpetual maritime truce in return for British protection. Britain took this action primarily to secure its shipping interests in the Gulf. Britain also acted, however, to keep Bahrain from Turkish and Iranian control, and to secure the approaches to India.

New administrative arrangements made Bahrain part of the British Trucial States in 1868, and the Al Khalifas signed treaties with Britain in 1880 and 1892 that further strengthened this relationship, and established a British political resident and agent.

Dynastic Stability, Oil, and Independence

British rule did not, however, resolve growing dynastic conflicts between the Al Khalifas. A year after Bahrain became part of the Trucial States, the ruling Amir—Ali ibn Khalifa al Khalifa was killed by his brother and nephew, who seized power. Britain refused to accept the new Amir, however, and made Ali ibn Khalifa al Khalifa's son, Isa bin Ali Al Khalifa the new Amir. The new Amir ruled from 1869 to 1923 and brought a new stability to Bahrain. He also established a rule of primogeniture. Unlike the other Gulf Arab regimes, the succession in Bahrain now goes to the ruler's eldest son.

The next major change in Bahrain's history occurred in the early 1930s. During most of the late 1800s and early 1900s, Bahrain's economy was shaped by the pearling industry and it remained a wealthy state by Gulf standards until the pearling industry was nearly devastated by the development of cultivated pearls in the 1920s. Fortunately for Bahrain, oil was discovered in 1932, and Bahrain was able to begin exporting oil in 1934. Bahrain became the first state in the Southern Gulf to become a significant oil exporter, and oil wealth revitalized Bahrain's economy and made it one of the most sophisticated states in the Gulf. It also gave Bahrain extensive exposure to Western culture and business practices, and helped prepare it for independence.

Bahrain concentrated on the development of its oil economy until Britain announced in January, 1968 that it would end its treaty relations with the Southern Gulf states and withdraw its forces "East of Suez" in 1971. This decision forced Bahrain to both define itself as a state and seek new sources of security.

During the period between 1968 and 1971, Britain attempted make Bahrain part of a federation that included Qatar and the seven sheikdoms that later became the United Arab Emirates (UAE). This effort failed for several reasons. Bahrain and Qatar were feuding over territorial claims. Bahrain was more advanced than the other Emirates and had little reason to join in a federation that promised to create as many political and economic problems as it solved. Finally, the Shah's recognition of Bahrain's independence in 1970 deprived Bahrain of an external threat that might have kept it in the union of emirates. As a result, Bahrain chose full independence on December 16, 1971, when Britain left the Gulf.

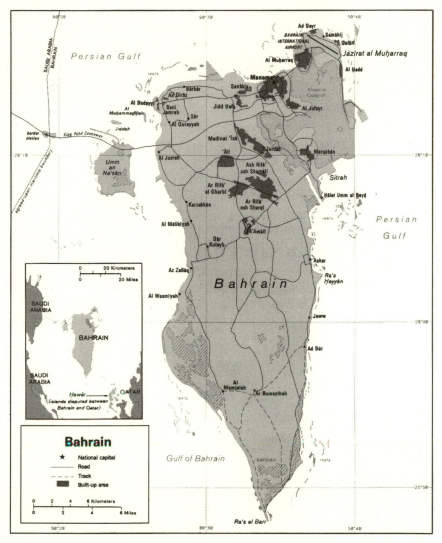

MAP TWO   Bahrain

Bahrain's Changing Strategic Position
and Relations with the US

Once Bahrain achieved independence, however, it faced the potential threats from the Arab radicalism of states like Iraq and had to deal with the Shah of Iran's ambitions to make Iran the dominant power in the Gulf. Although the Shah of Iran had recognized Bahrain's independence before British withdrawal, it was clear that Iran might reassert its claim if

Bahrain appeared to be exposed and vulnerable. As a result, Bahrain turned to the US and Saudi Arabia to help compensate for the loss of British protection, and Bahrain has maintained close ties to Saudi Arabia and the United States ever since.

Bahrain's ties to the US began long before Bahrain's independence. The three ships in the US Navy Middle East Force (MEF) were first head-quartered in Bahrain in 1949, and the US leased office accommodation in the British Naval Compound at Jufair, adjacent to the port of Mina Sulman. The US strengthened this relationship with Bahrain as Britain withdrew from the Gulf, and signed a lease for 10 acres at Jufair to support the MEF on December 31, 1971. The new lease included the use of a transmitter and antenna, priority use of Berth 1 at the port, use of waterfront ship repair facilities, and landing rights and hangar and office space at Muharraq Airfield.

Bahrain had to officially terminate this arrangement on October 20, 1973, as a result of tensions between the US and the Arab world that followed the October War. This termination, however, had only limited practical effect on Bahrain's relations with the US. Bahrain quietly reinstated the lease in July 1975, and expanded its scope on August 12, 1975, and on June 30, 1977.

Bahrain again had to ask the US to make their arrangements informal in July, 1977, because of complaints by other Arab states. As a result, the US ceased to officially headquarter its forces in Bahrain, and changed the title of its headquarters to "temporary duty administrative unit," which as known locally as an ASU (Administrative Support Unit). Once again, this change made little real difference to Bahraini and US cooperation. The US continued to "homeport" its command ship and Gulf naval forces in Manama, use Bahrain's airport, and use the port facility at Mina Sulman—although the admiral of the MEF was now the only US military officer in the fleet allowed to have his family live in Bahrain. The US was supposedly restricted in the number of days it could deploy in Bahrain, but this restriction consisted largely of a log of port usage.

US and Bahraini cooperation became more open during the second half of the 1980s. Bahrain provided extensive support, basing, and repair facilities to the US during "Operation Earnest Will"—the "tanker war" between the US, Britain, and Iran during 1987–1988. The US used 27 warships in this operation and conducted 127 missions in the Gulf from July 1987 to December 1988. These ships were often fueled with bunker fuel from Bahrain's refinery. Bahrain played a critical role in helping the US recover the *USS Stark* after it was mistakenly hit by an Iraqi Exocet, with the loss of 33 lives. Bahrain also supported the US during Operation Praying Mantis—when the US carried out a measured retaliatory strike against Iranian oil platforms in the Gulf in response to the aggressive activities of the Iranian revolutionary guards.

Bahrain and the US cooperated even more closely as allies during the Gulf War, and reached a 10 year bilateral agreement after the war that restored a formal US presence in Bahrain, and establishes an even closer security relationship between the two countries. Bahrain signed a this security agreement with the US in 1991, and Bahrain signed a further agreement on July 1, 1995, making Bahrain the headquarters of the new US 5th Fleet. As a result, the 15 ships in the fleet are now officially "home ported" at the port of Mina Sulman in Bahrain, and approximately 1,500 US personnel are stationed in the country.[5]

Bahrain, Saudi Arabia, and the Gulf Cooperation Council

Bahrain has cooperated closely with Saudi Arabia as well as the US. Bahrain provides an important forward buffer to any Iranian or Iraqi air and naval attacks on Saudi Arabia. At the same time, Saudi Arabia has provided Bahrain with political and military protection, some economic and military aid, and low cost oil. The expansion of the Saudi Air Force and Navy steadily increased Saudi Arabia's ability to assist Bahrain with forward air and naval defense, and the creation of a causeway between Bahrain and Saudi Arabia made it easier for Saudi Arabia to assist Bahrain with land forces.

Bahrain also helped to create the Gulf Cooperation Council (GCC) in 1981, and has strongly supported the strengthening of regional security efforts ever since. In March 1995, Bahrain joined the other members of the GCC in signing a new Gulf Security Agreement. This agreement gave more structure to the cooperation between the GCC's military forces. It establishes the position of Assistant Secretary General of the GCC with an office located in the GCC Secretariat in Riyadh. It called for increased consultation between the GCC states in the development of their future military capabilities, and calls for greater military integration and inter-operability. Bahrain also supported Prince Abdullah of Saudi Arabia at the December, 1995 meeting of the GCC when he stated that, "the only method of confronting (our) challenges is by collecting human, economic, political, and military resources to form in totality a single effective force."[6]

Bahrain is fully aware, however, that the GCC is currently more a symbol than a military reality. It is aware of the fact that the divisions between the GCC states are preventing or delaying many aspects of collective defense, and that it is Bahrain's bilateral relations with Saudi Arabia and the US which largely determine its security. Bahrain is also aware that its security interests are somewhat different from those of its Southern Gulf neighbors. Kuwait and Saudi Arabia must focus on the threat of an Iraqi land attack, although these "upper Gulf" states must also be concerned with the same naval, air, and amphibious threats as Bahrain. In contrast, the "lower Gulf" states like the UAE and Oman are more concerned with Iran than Iraq. These differences in strategic focus present further problems in translating the rhetoric used in the GCC into deterrent and war fighting capabilities that benefit Bahrain.

Bahrain's External Security

Bahrain faces several external challenges to its security. The most important such challenge is Iran which poses a threat to Bahrain's internal security, as well as more direct military threats to its security. At the same time, Bahrain cannot separate its security position from that of Kuwait and Saudi Arabia, and must consider the threat from Iraq. Further, there are long-standing tensions between Bahrain and Qatar which have grown worse with time, although both nations have sought to reach a compromise on the issues involved.

The Problem of Iran and Iraq

Iraq has not directly threatened Bahrain, although it did support radical Arab groups during the 1960s and through the mid-1970s—such as the National Front for the Liberation of Bahrain and PFLOAG. These groups never established a strong political base in Bahrain, and Bahrain was always able to use its internal security forces to control their activity.

Iraq is a still potential threat to Bahrain because of Bahrain's strong support for the UN Coalition and participation in the Gulf War, and because Bahrain has since supported the UN's efforts to make Iraq comply with all UN resolutions. At the same time, there seems to be little current prospect that Iraq will single out Bahrain for retaliation, or will be able to pose a direct military threat to Bahrain. Iraq has almost no influence over Bahrain's secular and Sunni opposition groups, and Iraq's repressive regime faces wide opposition among Bahrain's Shi'ites—the group most likely to oppose Bahrain's government and ties to the West.

Bahrain's relations with Iran are a different story. Iran's claims to Bahrain are tenuous even by the loose standards of the Gulf. Nevertheless, some Iranian leaders have made claims to Bahrain which are based largely upon on the fact that Bahrain was conquered by forces loyal to Shah Abbas I in 1602, and on the fact that the Al Khalifas paid occasional fealty and tribute to the Persian Empire. The former claim ignores the Al

Khalifas' decisive victory in 1783, and the latter claim that ignores the fact the Al Khalifas simultaneously paid tribute to Turkey, never came under direct Persian rule, and had no ties to Persia after 1861.

Iranian nationalists have continued to claim Bahrain since the early 1900s, however, and Iran protested to the League of Nations in 1927, when Britain signed a treaty with Saudi Arabia that recognized Bahrain's sovereignty and Britain's role in protecting it. Reza Shah's son renewed these claims when he came to power in World War II, and Iran protested Britain's transfer of its political agent in the Gulf from Bushehr to Bahrain when this took place in 1946. Iran often showed Bahrain as part of Iran on its maps, and the Iranian Majlis even passed laws applying to Bahrain—although they had no power or effect.

Some of these Iranian actions were little more than political gestures, but the Shah strongly reasserted Iran's claim to Bahrain in a note to the British government in early 1968, shortly after Britain had announced that it would leave the Gulf. This note led to negotiations between Iran and Britain which resulted in an agreement in late 1969 that the issue would be referred to the Secretary General of the United Nations. The Secretary General was then to appoint a mission of inquiry to determine the wishes of the people of Bahrain.

It was clear at the time when Britain and Iran reached this agreement that it would lead to Bahrain's independence under the Al Khalifas, although the agreement served the Shah's interest to the extent that the UN mission made it less likely that Britain could unite Bahrain into a federation of Emirates that united most of the smaller states in the Southern Gulf, and create a political counterweight to Iran.[7]

The resulting Winspeare-Gucciardi mission held a referendum in 1970, which confirmed that the Bahraini people supported a government headed by Sheik Isa Bin Sulman Al Khalifa. The report of the United Nations fact-finding mission also confirmed that the people of Bahrain wished to exist as a sovereign independent state. The Shah did not challenge either the results of the referendum or the UN report, and this effectively ended any Iranian basis for claims to any rights over Bahrain. As a result, Bahrain soon became a member of the United Nations, the Arab League and many other international organizations.

In 1979, however, the Shah's fall and the rise of Khomeini changed Iran's politics. Shortly after Khomeini's rise to power in 1979, he reasserted the Shah's claim that Bahrain was part of Iran. He also sent "messengers" to Bahrain to promote Iran's religious revolution. Khomeini's messengers had some success. The Iranian revolution appealed to some of Bahrain's Shi'ites, and Iran's religious leaders had considerable influence because many of Bahrain's Shi'ite clergy trained in Iran, and Bahrain had many Iranian residents.

Iranian efforts helped lead to riots in Bahrain as early as August, 1979—when some 1,500 Shi'ite demonstrators rallied in support of the Iranian revolution. As a result, Bahrain's security forces arrested many of the demonstrators, exiled some, and expelled at least one pro-Iranian Sheik and several members of the Shi'ite clergy. Further Shi'ite demonstrations occurred at the time of the student seizure of the US embassy in Tehran, including some violent protests against the US presence in Bahrain.[8]

These developments almost inevitably helped make Bahrain a strong supporter of Iraq at the start of the Iran-Iraq War. Bahrain allowed Iraq to disperse some of its aircraft in Bahrain, and the Al Khalifa family made it clear that it supported Iraq's initial victory claims. This led to new protests in April, 1980. The security forces arrested at least 50 Shi'ite leaders and were forced to organize a new structure designed to control and infiltrate Shi'ite opposition. At the same time, Iran actively began to provide funds, training, and arms for its supporters in Bahrain.

The resulting tensions between Bahrain and Iran reached a crisis point in mid-December, 1981. Bahrain's government found that Iran was supporting a coup attempt. It arrested 73 people, including 58 Bahraini nationals, 13 Saudis, 1 Kuwaiti, and 1 Omani, and eventually deported up to 300 others. All were members of a Shi'ite group called the Islamic Front for the Liberation of Bahrain, and had planned a coup for Bahrain's national day on December 16, 1980. Many had trained in Iran, and they had smuggled in arms, men, and some $120,000 in cash from Iran. The group had obtained Bahraini police uniforms and planned to assassinate key members of the Al Khalifa family and government officials. They planned to declare an Islamic republic when their leader arrived from Iran.

The plot was discovered by an immigration official in Dubai—who noted suspicious movements from Iran to Bahrain. Bahraini security officials then discovered that the Iranian charge d'affaires in Manama was bringing in equipment like walkie-talkies in his diplomatic pouch from London, and was funding the group. Another 13 members of the group were found to be operating in Saudi Arabia and others in the UAE.

While the arrests of the group's members did not lead to public protests, the group was found to have received considerable support in the Diraz and A'ali districts of Bahrain, and was found to have some 150–200 guerrillas training in Iran. The group also had ties to Hadi al-Modarasi, a Shi'ite mullah who had lived in Bahrain while the Shah was in power and who subsequently became the head the Gulf Affairs Section of Iran's Revolutionary Guards.

These discoveries led Bahrain to be cautious in dealing with those it arrested for the coup attempt. Any signs of public demonstrations were carefully suppressed when the government held trials in 1982. The government expelled another 200–300 Shi'ites rather than arrest them, and kept new arrests it made in 1983 secret. Bahrain also made a major effort to expand economic opportunities for Shi'ites, while expanding its efforts to penetrate every Shi'ite group and cell. These government efforts largely contained violent protests and pro-Iranian actions, although low level sabotage and occasional incidents continued until the end of the Iran-Iraq War in 1988.[9]

Iran seems to have reduced its support of radical groups in Bahrain after the end of the Iran-Iraq War and the death of Khomeini. Anti-government Shi'ite activity in Bahrain was also limited during the Gulf War. In 1992, however, Bahrain began to experience growing economic problems, which have led to serious internal unrest among some of Bahrain's Shi'ites. Iran encouraged this unrest, using by Iranian-trained, Bahraini Shi'ite clergy and students—many of whom were educated in Qom. Iran also continues to permit the Islamic Front for the Liberation of Bahrain to maintain an office in Tehran, and seems to be providing funds to the group's main office in London—the location of a number of other Bahraini exile organizations.[10]

Bahraini officials believe that Iran has been steadily more active in supporting Shi'ite unrest in Bahrain since that time, and has active ties to a number of the more extreme Shi'ite clerics that have helped trigger demonstrations and riots. Bahrain expelled a Iranian diplomat, Third Secretary Abdul-Rasool Dokoohki, for "activities incompatible with his diplomatic status" in early February, 1996.[11]

Bahraini officials note that the Iranian official media in Tehran have provided "moral support" for many of the acts of sabotage which have taken place during the disturbances during Bahrain. They note that,

> While the official Iranian 'state' circles purport to maintain a stance neutral to the situation in Bahrain, the revolutionary circles close to the office of the 'Guardian of the Revolution' overtly encourage the movement of disorderly elements in Bahrain. There has also been Iranian diplomatic support for such actions as the distribution of pro-disturbance leaflets by the Iranian Embassy in Kuwait. The pro-Iranian Party of the Hezbollah in Lebanon has trained some Bahraini activists who took part in sabotage in Bahrain.

Bahraini officials feel that Iran is providing support to two Shi'ite movements: The hard-line Islamic Front for the Liberation of Bahrain, and Bahrain Freedom Movement. The Bahrain Freedom Movement expresses its views in terms of peaceful change, but the Government of Bahrain believes it is a front for some of the groups behind the disturbances. It believes the Bahrain Freedom Movement has extensive links to the

Hezbollah in Bahrain. Indeed, one of the leaders of the group is the son of Abdul Amir Al Jamri, the spiritual leader of the Bahrain Hezbollah.

Bahraini officials believe that some of the activists have been trained in Lebanon by the Iranian-backed Hezbollah, and that others have been trained in Iran. They note that many of the leaders of recent demonstrations and protests trained at the Bahrain Study Center in Qom. While most explosives to date have been small and "home made," they are concerned that Iran may provide arms and larger explosives, and feel that Iran may be providing money to dissidents inside and outside Bahrain.

Key officials like Prime Minister Sheik Khalifa bin Sulman and Foreign Minister Sheik Mohammed bin Mubarak Al Khalifa see Iran as a primary cause of the problems that have emerged in 1994 and 1995. They see Iran as encouraging protests and violence, as a threat that may seek to precipitate broad social violence or revolution, and as a threat that may take more direct subversive or military action if the situation in Bahrain continues to deteriorate. They are also concerned about the possible threat posed by the many Iranians living in Bahrain.[12]

These concerns took on a far more dramatic character on June 3, 1996, when Bahrain announced that it had uncovered evidence that Iran might be supporting a new coup attempt. Bahrain's Ministry of the Interior stated, "A serious conspiracy has been uncovered which reveals that an organization known as the military wing of the Hezbollah-Bahrain have been plotting since early 1993 to undermine Bahrain's security." Ibrahim al-Mutawe announced that Bahrain was recalling its ambassador to Tehran and would down grade its representation in Iran to the level of a charge d'affaires. The cabinet office also announced that that Hezbollah-Bahrain, "was planning to overthrow the rule of Bahrain's government by force and establish a pro-Iran rule . . . the movement's main aim is to stage an armed revolution to overthrow the Bahrain government and replace it with a pro-Iranian regime."[13]

Bahrain also claimed that the Bahrain-Hezbollah was founded in Qom in 1993 with the financial and political "backing of the Iranian authorities and the Intelligence Department of the at Iranian Revolutionary Guards Corps. It claimed that the military wing of the Bahrain-Hezbollah was linked to the Iranian Intelligence Committee headed by Gasem Hasan Mansour, and that the Financial Committee and Committee of Coordination of Affairs worked under Iranian intelligence and was headed by Ali Ahmad Al-Kazem Abd Ali. It reported that some of the young Bahrainis in the Bahrain-Hezbollah trained at Iranian Revolutionary Guards Corps camps in Iran before moving to Hezbollah camps in Lebanon.[14]

This was the first time that Bahrain's government had openly accused Iran of direct involvement in the unrest in Bahrain, and Sheik Isa immediately sent envoys to the other Southern Gulf states to brief them on the conspiracy. The accusation came only days after the GCC Foreign Ministers had condemned Iran for interfering "in the internal affairs of Bahrain and other member countries," and for seeking to develop an arsenal that "exceeds its ordinary and legitimate defense needs."[15]

Iran responded with denials. A spokesman for the Iranian Foreign Ministry stated on June 4 that, "the Islamic Republic of Iran advises the Bahraini government against being influenced by the "conspiracies of the enemies of the Islamic Ummah," and stated that the accusations were, "a result of the instigations of outsiders." Iran's Interior Minister, Ali Mohammed Basharati stated on June 5 that, "Despite the imaginary claims by Bahrain, there are no bases anywhere in Iran for the military training of foreigners." Bahraini opposition groups charged that the government was fabricating an outside threat to disguise its own failures, and a number of US experts felt that Bahrain was exaggerating Iran's role and/or the seriousness of the conspiracy to win public support.[16]

On June 5, however, the Bahraini government announced that it had made 44 arrests in the conspiracy. It also televised confessions by six of those who had been arrested. One such confession stated that an Iranian official supporting the conspiracy had told the suspect that he reported to Iran's spiritual leader, the Ayatollah Ali Khamenei. Another suspect stated that he had been asked to gather data on the US forces in Bahrain. A third, Hussain Youssef Ibrahim Mohammed, stated that several of the conspirators had been trained by pro-Iranian Hezbollah in Lebanon who, "gave us training on light, medium, and heavy weapons. . . . They trained us on using explosives and techniques of making bombs . . . We had training on booby traps and explosives." Bahrain's Interior Minister, Mohammed bin Khalifa Khalifa, also announced that many of the detained suspects had been recruited 18 months before riots began in December 1994.[17]

Like most Southern Gulf states, Bahrain has reacted to the threats from Iran and Iraq by supporting the build-up of Southern Gulf military capabilities and strengthening its alliance with the US and the West. Bahrain has strongly supported efforts to limit Iranian and Iraqi efforts to rebuild their military capabilities, and to enforce the terms of the UN Security Council resolutions dealing with Iraq. At the same time, Bahrain has opposed efforts for the total political and economic isolation of Iran and Iraq. Like most of the other Gulf states, Bahrain sees the US policy of "dual containment" as more likely to provoke the sort of Iranian and Iraqi extremism of the kind that has already threatened Bahrain, rather than to moderate the leadership of either state.

Bahrain's Tensions with Qatar

Bahrain and Qatar are divided by a long-standing dispute over the control of the Hawar Islands, the offshore waters between Bahrain and Qatar, and Az Zubarah. This dispute has its origins in the struggles for the control of Bahrain and Qatar which began in the 1700s. The Al Khalifa and Al Jalahima branches of the Bani Utub tribe migrated to Qatar in the 1760s, at a time when Qatar was sparsely inhabited, and the Turks had driven the Portuguese from the Gulf. The Al Khalifas and Al Jalahimas feuded over control of Qatar, but the Al Khalifa's became the dominant ruling family because of their familial and trading ties to Kuwait, and because they had established their headquarters at Az Zubarah, on Qatar's northwestern coast, the most important port in the region.

As has been discussed earlier, the growing wealth of this port encouraged an Omani sheik, who then ruled Bahrain from the port of Bushehr in Iran, to attack Az Zubarah. The Al Khalifas and several other families in Qatar responded by invading Bahrain, and seizing control of the island in 1783. This conquest led most members of the Al Khalifa family to migrate to Bahrain because of the island's superior wealth, shipping, agricultural, and water resources and the Al Khalifas only left a limited presence in Az Zubarah. As a result, the Al Thani family—a major family on Qatar's east coast—began to acquire steadily growing power over the Qatari peninsula.

From the 1780s to the mid 1800s, the Al Khalifas engaged in a complex struggle for control of Bahrain and Qatar. This struggle reached a crisis point in 1867, when the Al Khalifa family sent forces from Bahrain to attack the ports of Doha and Al Wakrah on Qatar's western coast. The British political agent in the Gulf intervened to protect shipping in the region, and helped to reach a settlement in 1868 which acknowledged the new role of the Al Thani family in Qatar. The Al Khalifa family only retained a small enclave at Az Zubarah, although the leading families in Qatar agreed to continue to pay them tribute.

This arrangement lasted for only a few years. The Al Thanis allied with the Turks who were expanding their role in the Gulf, and the Al Thanis seized control over most of Qatar in 1871. The Al Thanis then recognized Turkish sovereignty over Qatar in 1872, and stopped paying tribute to the Al Khalifas. Half a decade later, Qasim ibn Muhammed Al Thani charged that pirates loyal to the Al Khalifa family were attacking shipping to Qatar. Qasim then attacked and destroyed Az Zubarah in 1878, although the Al Khalifas retained control over most of the islands and waters between Bahrain and Qatar.[18]

This history has left a heritage of lasting animosity, and Bahrain and Qatar have continued to dispute control of the 16 Hawar Islands and the shoal of Fasht-e-Dibal in the waters between Bahrain's main island and the peninsula of Qatar. The issue took on new importance in 1936, when the dispute over the island threatened to lead to war between Bahrain and Qatar. Britain decided in favor of Bahrain's claims, and its decision was based on both the fact that Bahrain had long had long maintained control of the Hawar Islands and had a small military garrison on the largest island, and on a British analysis of the legal history of each nation's claims. Qatar claimed afterwards, however, that the decision was biased because the British adviser to Bahrain was able to present Bahrain's case in Western legal terms while Qatar could not. As a result, Qatar renewed its claims in 1971.

Qatar and Bahrain also continued to dispute control of Az Zubarah, on Qatar's northwestern coast. Although the Al Khalifa settlement at Az Zubarah was destroyed in 1878, the Naim tribe in the region maintained their ties to the Al Khalifas. This led to a new round of fighting in 1937, when Abdullah bin Qasim Al Thani sent an armed force into the area and defeated the Naim tribe which had asserted its independence after the British award of the Hawar Islands to Bahrain. The British political agent supported Qatar in these actions, and warned Hamad Ibn Isa Al Khalifa—then the Amir of Bahrain—not to take military action. Hamad responded by imposing an embargo on trade and travel to Qatar which made relations between the two countries still worse.

There have since been a number of public and not so public cases in which Bahraini and Qatari troops and ships have entered the disputed islands and waters. One such clash occurred in early 1986, when Qatari forces attacked a Bahraini position on the Fasht e-Dibal. Bahrain had built up a small base on an artificial island on the reef, and was turning the island into a coast guard station. On April 26, 1986, Qatari helicopters fired on construction crews working on the Fasht e-Dibal, and Qatari troops landed by helicopter and arrested the 29 workers on the island. Bahrain indicated in response that its work crews were actually building a GCC facility to monitor tanker traffic, pursuant to an agreement reached in 1992, which was followed up with GCC funds for the project.[19] Both nations then called military alerts, and Bahrain reinforced its positions on Hawar while Qatar reinforced its positions on the Fasht ad Dibal.[20] Qatar continued to occupy the site for over a month, until Bahrain agreed to destroy its facilities on the Fasht ad Dibal.[21] The captured workers were released in May, 1986.[22]

Another clash occurred in June, 1991, when Qatari Navy ships entered the waters off the Hawar Islands and Bahrain responded by sending fighters into Qatari air space. While GCC attempts at mediation succeeded, and a GCC observation team was sent to end the disagreement, this did not prevent further exchanges of accusations and new tension after the Gulf War. Qatar then filed a claim with the International Court of Justice in the Hague in July, 1991. Bahrain refused to accept the court's jurisdiction because it felt that Bahrain had previously entered into an agreement with Qatar whereby both parties together—rather than either one of them unilaterally—might proceed to the Court once a proper form of agreement have been reached between them setting out the terms on which the case might be presented to the court.

In May 1993, Bahrain passed a Territorial Sea Decree pursuant to the United Nations Convention on the Law of the Sea of 1982. This Decree reflected the terms of the United Nations Convention in that it promulgated a territorial sea of 12 miles from the coast and a contiguous zone of 24 miles. Neither the base points nor the baselines referred to in the Decree have been promulgated, but there is no reference in it to islands or reefs. Qatar fielded new documents in February 1994, as part of its earlier proceedings, but did not file a new case.

While the International Court of Justice ruled in February, 1995 that it had jurisdiction over the Hawar Islands dispute, Bahrain called for bilateral negotiations or GCC mediation. It called for Saudi mediation on the basis of principles that had been laid down in 1978, and Saudi Arabia offered to mediate because of its concern that a decision by the International Court of Justice would open up other boundary disputes to non-Arab courts. Qatar agreed to discuss such mediation, although it felt that Saudi Arabia might be biased in favor of Bahrain, and that if any such mediation took place, it should have to come from an Arab state outside the Gulf.

Relations between Bahrain and Qatar became worse in late 1995 and early 1996. Qatar walked out of the Gulf Cooperation Council meeting in December 1995, because it felt that Saudi Arabia had pushed the GCC into appointing a new Saudi Secretary General of the GCC in spite of the fact that there was a tacit agreement to rotate the nationality of the Secretary General in alphabetic order (the previous Secretary Generals had been Kuwaiti and Omani). This walk out occurred after Sheik Zayed of the UAE had attempted to mediate, and Bahrain, Saudi Arabia, and the UAE felt that they had been insulted by the way in which Qatar carried out its walk out.

The resulting tensions went far beyond the past rivalry between Qatar and Bahrain. Bahrain, Saudi Arabia, and the UAE welcomed the deposed ex-Emir of Qatar, Sheik Khalifa bin Hamad al-Thani, as if he were a head of state. They did even though Sheik Khalifa openly claimed that he wanted to regain power from Qatar's new Emir, Sheik Hamad bin Khalifa al-Thani.

Qatar responded by allowing two members of the Bahraini opposition, Mansour al-Jamri and Sheik Ali Salman, to broadcast calls for "democracy" over Qatari state television and by reprinting excerpts of these TV interviews in its newspapers. The media in some Gulf states then printed attacks on Qatar's government, and Saudi and UAE newspapers printed implicit attacks on Emir, Sheik Hamad bin Khalifa al-Thani and his Foreign Affairs Minister, Sheik Hamad bin Jassim Bin Jabr al-Thani.[23]

Qatar's Emir, Sheik Hamad bin Khalifa al-Thani, gave an interview in January 1996 in which he stated that the negotiations on over the Hawar Islands, "are in the courts and the Saudis are meditating . . . Whenever there is a solution between the two countries, we are ready to pull it from the courts." He also stated that the dispute was one in which the former Emir, Sheik Khalifa bin Hamad could not make concessions, "Do you believe that the Qataris will allow him to do that? This cannot be accepted by anyone in Qatar."[24]

These tensions eased in March and April 1996, when Qatar, Bahrain, Saudi Arabia, and the UAE reached the compromise on the selection of a Secretary General. Bahrain also indicated that it might accept the jurisdiction of the International Court of Justice. Nevertheless, relations between the ruling families of Qatar and Bahrain remain poor. Qatar felt Bahrain had become a tool of the Saudis and had helped sponsor a coup attempt by Sheik Khalifa bin Hamad al-Thani. Qatar also felt that Bahrain's ruling family had failed to modernize its political leadership and that its conservatism was responsible for most of the Shi'ite unrest in Bahrain. Bahrain, in contrast, felt that Qatar's rulers had violated the normal courtesies between Gulf ruling elites, were deliberately being provocative, and had exploited Bahrain's internal crisis at a particularly sensitive time.

These disputes between Bahrain and Qatar are not petty to the nations involved. They have strategic and economic importance because they divide two nations that play an important role in the defense of the upper Gulf, and because the Hawar Islands may have off-shore oil resources. They involve nearly one-third of Bahrain's territory and water, and could have a vital impact on Bahrain's future. Further, Bahrain feels that it has historically exercised control over the Hawar Islands since the Al Khalifa family first came to power, and considers that the Hawar Islands are an integral part of its territorial archipelago. It claims that the islands have long been used by Bahraini fishermen, and by senior Bahraini families for hunting and fishing purposes. As a result, they cannot be dismissed simply as an anachronistic feud between rival royal families, and they act as a serious barrier to cooperation between the Southern Gulf states.[25]

Bahrain's Internal Security

Like most Southern Gulf states, Bahrain faces challenges to its internal stability because of rapid social and demographic changes, a decline in its oil economy and the resulting ability to fund social services, and problems in broadening popular political participation and redefining the role of its Ruling Family. Further, these economic problems are combining in Bahrain's case with ethnic problems to create a growing internal security problem that may not be easy to resolve without significant changes to Bahrain's current social and labor policies and outside financial aid.

The Government and the Role of the Ruling Family

Sheik Isa bin Sulman Al Khalifa is the head of the government and the ruling Amir. One of his brothers, Sheik Khalifa bin Sulman Al Khalifa, is the Prime Minister, and many other members of the Al Khalifa family play a leading role in the government and the military. The succession to the Crown Prince, Sheik Hamad bin Isa, is well established. One of the Amir's brothers, Sheik Mohamed bin Sulman Al Khalifa, is more or less ostracized. He has only a small following, however, and plays no role in the government.

Despite growing Shi'ite unrest, Bahrain's Amir, Sheik Isa ibn Salman al Khalifa, still seems to be widely respected and is still popular with much of the population. He continues to hold bi-weekly meetings of an open Majlis for the general public, and has reacted to the current crisis by reorganizing his cabinet, adopting social and economic reforms to reduce Shi'ite grievances, and broadening dialogue with the Shi'ite community. He has also made statements that promise increased public participation in government, although he has never promised or accepted the concept of Western-style democracy.

Nevertheless, Bahrain does face growing political challenges. Its government has been slow to broaden its popular base, and some observers feel that it has failed to coopt a large part of the Shi'ite portion of its population into the process of government, and its political reforms have so far been too limited in character to meet its needs.

The Cabinet

Bahrain's Council of Ministers, or Cabinet, acts as its main instrument of government. It contains a mix of members of the Ruling Family and leading technocrats. About one-third of the Ministers are Shi'ite although they do not hold sensitive positions. It manages most day-to-day functions of government, although the military services and internal security forces are under the direct control of the Ruling Family. It serves as the chief body coordinating Bahrain's economic development and national budget, and reviewing legislation.

In the spring of 1995, the Cabinet was reorganized for the first time since 1971. This reorganization came as a reaction to Bahrain's growing economic problems and sectarian divisions, Five long-standing members were dropped (Development and Industry, Information, Commerce and Agriculture, Education, and Legal Affairs).

The reshuffle did produce a renewed level of public optimism that the government would address its problems with economic growth, and improve education, provide effective vocational training, and reduce unemployment. However, all political power remained vested in the office of the Prime Minister, and the Al Khalifa family continued to control all sensitive positions. Seven of the sixteen ministers in the new cabinet were Al Khalifas, four others were Sunnis not connected to the ruling family, and five were Shi'ites (Labor, Commerce, Works and Agriculture, Health, and Minister of State Without Portfolio).

The Majlis and Political Reform

It is not clear that the current structure of Bahrain's government offers enough opportunities to resolve Bahrain's social problems peacefully and to debate key issues in ways that can coopt Bahrain's Shi'ites and reach a consensus on critical issues—although Bahrain's style of government provides for informal participation in the decision-making process of a kind different from that in the West.

Bahrain has a constitution which was drafted by a Constituent Assembly that included a mix of elected and appointed officials. This constitution was adopted in 1973, and provided for freedom of speech and extensive legal protection of individual rights, and created a National Assembly.

Elections were held for the National Assembly in December, 1973, with the franchise limited to male citizens. A total of 30 representatives were elected. One bloc of eight members openly supported the banned, pro-Marxist National Front for the Liberation of Bahrain, and called for the repeal of many of Bahrain's internal security laws. Another bloc of six representatives emerged, which was pro-Shi'ite, and favored the imposition of Islamic custom and law. The remaining 16 representatives were a mix of independents because political parties had been banned before the election and only established polarized groups had a pre-election political identity.

These blocs of opposition groups made the debates within the National Assembly increasingly extreme. They became an open challenge to the Amir's control of the budget, the Amir's internal security powers, and Bahrain's restrictive national security laws during the winter and spring of 1973. The Amir then issued a new national security law in December, 1974, and both the pro-Marxist and pro-Shi'ite blocs, along with many independents, demanded that the laws be submitted to the National Assembly for ratification.

These demands increasingly became an open test of power between the Assembly and the Amir. As a result, the Amir disbanded the Assembly in August, 1975, at the time of its summer recess. He suspended the

National Assembly indefinitely in August, 1976.[26] The only political activity permitted in Bahrain after that date was informal discussion—largely as part of participation in professional associations. This situation continued through the late 1970s, the fall of the Shah, the Iran-Iraq War, and the Gulf War.

The aftermath of the Gulf War seemed to offer Bahrain a new degree of regional security, however, and some Bahrainis pressed for broader, popular participation in the government. In response, the Amir appointed a 30 member Consultative Council or Majlis. This Council met for the first time in the fall of 1992, had its second session during October, 1993 to May, 1994, and began its third session in May, 1995.

Unlike the Cabinet, the Majlis has no members of the Ruling Family or the government. Its chairman is a Shi'ite who previously served as a minister, and its membership is evenly divided between Sunni and Shi'ite. The Majlis does not have formal legislative power and its earlier meetings were closed with no minutes made public. It can, however, draft legislation and comment on legislation presented by ministries to the cabinet. Many of its recommendations have been accepted by the Cabinet, or to have contributed in some way to the formulation of government policy. Further, its meetings now receive more detailed press and television coverage.

In 1995 the Majlis debated a number of contentious social and economic issues, including unemployment, labor policy, and education, drafting proposals on these and other subjects for government consideration. According to the Speaker of the Majlis, the Government responded positively to about "85 percent" of the Majlis's recommendations by incorporating them into legislation or by taking other appropriate actions. Although the Government intends to keep the Majlis an advisory body, it promised in September 1995 to give it more powers and scope, and repeated this promise in an announcement in June 1996—which also referred to expanding its numerical representation.

The creation of the Majlis has not, however, reduced the desire of some Bahrainis for an elected National Assembly, nor has it offered an outlet for those Bahrainis seeking an independent path to political power or who are critics of the government. During 1994, some 14 prominent secular and religious officials began to circulate a petition calling for the return of the National Assembly and elections. This petition was not formally submitted to the government, but continued to be circulated. It has since been a source of considerable contention. Those in opposition have claimed that it had gained some 20,000 signatures by the end of 1994, and nearly 25,000 by mid-1995. If true, this would be a significant number of signatures in a nation with Bahrain's small native population, but Bahraini officials claim it has only a fraction of these signatures and it's being used as opposition propaganda rather than as a real petition.[27]

The US State Department reports that there is no evidence that the government has arrested anyone for signing or circulating the petition. However, one of the original 14 signers, Sa'id Abdulla Asbool, lost his job at the Ministry of Works, Power, and Water during 1995—reportedly because he circulated the petition at the Ministry during work hours. There are reports that other employees lost their government jobs for participating in the petition drive.

The US State Department also reports Ahmed Shamlan, a local newspaper columnist, was reportedly suspended from his job for signing the petition, and a doctor at Salmaniyah Hospital was stripped of his department chairmanship, but retained his job. Other signers, like Munira Fakhro, a member of the University of Bahrain faculty, were dismissed from their positions. Abdul Amir Al-Jamri, a prominent Shi'ite cleric, longtime opposition activist, and one of the petition's original signers, was placed under house arrest on April 1. He remained there until his release on September 25. It should be noted, however, that Al-Jamri has been accused of committing a variety of security-related crimes.[28]

Sheik Isa stated on December 16, 1994, Bahrain's National Day, that he was "continuously encouraging" the Consultative Council, and that, "this march indicates serious trends towards laying the foundation and then proceeding to develop the general march of public participation in the country." Little happened for several years, but Sheik Isa announced on June 2, 1996, that the Majlis would soon be expanded to serve the community and country more effectively. He indicated that the number of members in the Council would be expanded to include representatives of all sections of society, that the Council had demonstrated that it was ready to initiate major recommendations and present them to the government, and that its committees and their functions should be expanded. Sheik Isa spoke at a Council meeting during its fourth term in office, and the Prime Minister Sheik Khalifa bin Salman Al Khalifa and the Crown Prince and Commander-in-Chief Sheik Hamad bin Isa Al Khalifa both attended the meeting.[29]

It is unclear how this situation will develop. The search for a stronger popular role in government inevitably interacts with Bahrain's sectarian and economic problems. Any broadening of popular representation might help undercut Bahrain's Shi'ite extremists and develop a broader degree of consensus. At the same time, any election that included Bahrain's anti-government opposition movements would lead to an almost inevitable clash over the sharing of the nation's wealth and the future role of foreign labor. Creating a popularly elected body might also present problems in defining who is eligible to vote, present problems in debating control over government revenues at a time when hard policy decisions are required, and highlight the difficulty of carrying out political reform without economic reform.

Bahrain's Economy

As is the case with all Gulf states, there are a wide range of different estimates of the trends in Bahrain's economy. One such estimate of the recent trends in Bahrain's economy is summarized in Table Eleven. These estimates are based on data developed by the Economist Intelligence Unit and the *Middle East Economic Digest*, and portray a low rate of recent growth in Bahrain's real GDP and per capita income. The World Bank estimates that Bahrain's GNP was $4.11 billion in 1994. Recent State Department estimates of Bahrain's economic performance are higher and indicate that Bahrain's GDP totaled around $4.3 billion in 1994 and $4.36 billion in 1995, and the CIA estimates that Bahrain's GDP had a purchasing power equivalent of $7.1 billion in 1995.[30]

Chart Five shows a longer term estimate of the trends in Bahrain's GDP, central government spending, military spending, oil revenues (total exports), and arms imports based on the US State Department data. The trends in this chart indicate that Bahrain's economy has been sharply affected by dropping oil revenues and the resulting lack of economic growth.

Chart Six provides further insights into these trends. It shows that the US State Department estimates that Bahrain's rapid population growth, comparatively low world oil prices, and static domestic economy have led to a sharp decline in Bahrain's per capita income since the mid 1980s. Separate studies by the World Bank indicate that Bahrain's GNP per capita dropped by an average of 3.8% per year during 1980–1992, and that its GNP dropped by 0.9% per year during the more recent period of 1985–1994.[31]

Bahrain's own data are considerably more favorable. The Bahrain Center for Studies and Research estimates that Bahrain's GDP was $4.8 billion in 1994, using 1989 dollars, and notes that no official figure was published for 1995 as of May, 1996. Bahraini experts also estimate that the annual average growth rate of Bahrain's GNP per capita dropped by only 0.36% during 1982–1992 and 0.4% during 1984–1995. Bahrain calculates and that there was a slight net average annual increase in GDP of 0.87% during 1982–1992, and of 0.58% during 1984–1995.

These differences are significant, but much depends on the period chosen, and the extent to which it includes the worst years in terms of cuts in oil-related revenues. For example, the World Bank estimates that Bahrain's GDP per capita dropped by an annual average of 5.8% during 1981–1985, and 0.6% during 1986–1990, but rose by 3.3% during 1991–1993.[32]

TABLE ELEVEN   Recent and Projected Trends in Bahrain's Economy

Recent Economic Activity*	1990	1991	1992	1993	1994
Production (barrels per day)	42,192	42,740	41,370	40,753	—
Gas Production (million meters[3] per day)	22.6	22.4	25.9	26.8	—
Petroleum Product Export Receipts ($US current billions)	2.939	2.73	2.61	2.43	
GDP ($US current billions)	3.94	3.98	3.97	4.28	4.21
Per Capita GDP ($US current)	7,805	7,667	7,401	7,651	7,256
Annual Change in Per Capita GDP (%)	-0.8	-1.8	-3.3	-0.6	-5.2
Total Government Revenue ($US current billions)	—	1.361	1.361	1.542	1.59
Total Government Expenditures ($US current billions)	—	1.42	1.53	1.71	1.79
Budget Balance ($US current millions)	—	-58.0	-191	-164	-196

Recent and Projected Economic Trends**	1993	1994	1995	1996
Real GDP Growth in Percent	3.1	-2.5	-1.0	0.5
Consumer Price Inflation in Percent	2.0	2.5	3.0	3.0
Petroleum Exports in $ Billions	2.4	2.2	2.3	2.5
Total Exports in $ Billions	3.8	3.3	3.6	3.8
Total Imports in $ Billions	—	3.8	4.0	—
Current Accounts in $ Millions	-627	-782	-716	-617

Notes: *Adapted by Wayne A. Larsen, NSSP, Georgetown University, from the EIU, Country Profile, *Bahrain/Qatar, 1995–1996*, pp. 10, 19. Oil receipts = $2.43B in 1993, over 60% of government spending.
**Adapted from Economist Intelligence Unit, *Bahrain, EIU Country Report*, 1st Quarter, 1995, London, Economist Press, p. 1; and *MEED*, November 24, 1995, p. 26.

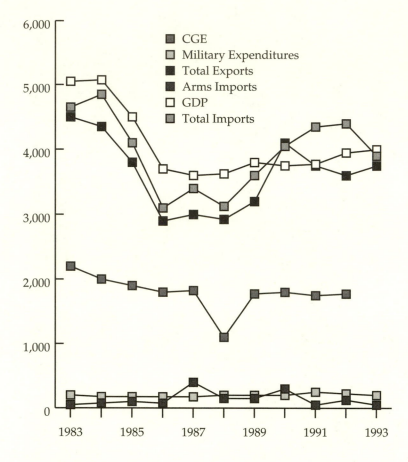

CHART FIVE   Bahrain Gross Domestic Product, Central Government
Expenditures, Military Expenditures, Total Exports, Total Imports, and Arms
Import Deliveries: 1983–1993 (Constant $93 Millions). *Source:* Adapted by
Anthony H. Cordesman from ACDA, *World Military Expenditures and Arms
Transfers, 1993–1994,* ACDA/GPO, Washington, 1995.

Regardless of which set of estimates is correct, the key factors shaping
the trends shown in Bahrain's economy and exports have been oil and
war. Bahrain experienced its first massive oil boom in the early 1970s—a
boom which increased Bahrain's oil revenues from 6 million Bahraini
Dinars in 1965 to 111 million Bahraini Dinars in 1975, and 320 million in
1980. This oil boom continued until the early 1980s, but Bahrain then
went through a series of major economic crises. The first economic crisis
occurred as a result of the Iran-Iraq War—fear of an Iranian victory and

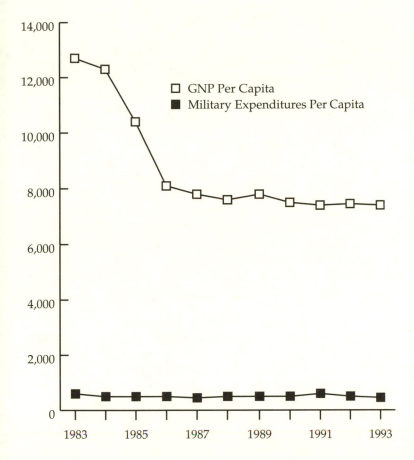

CHART SIX Bahrain GNP Per Capita Versus Military Expenditures Per Capita
(Constant $93). *Source:* Adapted by Anthony H. Cordesman from ACDA, *World
Military Expenditures and Arms Transfers, 1993–1994,* Washington, ACDA-GPO,

the tanker war in the Gulf led to a sharp decline in trade in the Gulf. As
a result, Bahrain's real growth declined by an annual average of 6.5%
during 1985–1987.

Bahrain's economy began to recover once the Iran-Iraq War ended
in August, 1988. Bahrain had 5.9% growth in 1988 and 2.5% growth in
1989, and experienced major growth in the first seven months of
1990s. However, Bahrain was then affected by the political and economic impact of Iraq's invasion of Kuwait. Bahrain had to cancel or
delay a number of its major public works projects and industrial development projects. The Bahraini government estimates that Bahrain

lost $2 billion during 1990–1991 because of capital outflows and reduced investment.[33]

Bahrain's economy seemed to strengthen briefly in early 1992. According to some outside projections, Bahrain's economic growth reached 3.1% in 1993, and Bahrain's own estimates indicate that the GDP grew by 8.2%. Bahrain, then however, faced a new drop in oil prices. Independent estimates indicate that Bahrain's GDP dropped to –2.5% in 1994, and –1.0% in 1995, and will only reach 0.5% in 1996. These projections are summarized in Table Eleven. Once again Bahrain has more favorable projections, and estimates that Bahrain's GDP grew by 2.3%. Other projections indicate that the GDP had no growth in 1994 and a maximum of 1% growth in 1995.[34]

Outside estimates also indicate that Bahrain's external debt rose from $52 million in 1994 to $56 million in 1995, its trade balance had a deficit of $500 million in 1994 and $400 million in 1995, and its balance on current account dropped from –$130 million in 1994 to –$300 to –$450 million in 1995, with a forecast deficit of $350 million in 1996.[35] Bahrain does not yet have serious public debt and balance of payments problems, but its trade balance deteriorated sharply since 1994 and its external debt ratio climbed from 48% in 1988 to 67% in 1994.

If such outside estimates are correct, they indicate that Bahrain is falling behind the level of growth needed to both sustain economic development and deal with a population growth rate that the CIA estimates was 2.58% in 1995, and which the World Bank estimates was 2.59%, with a natural increase of 2.58%.[36]

Further, a number of outside experts indicate that Bahrain's economic problems are limiting its ability to pursue an orderly pattern of development, and are increasing the gap between rich and poor. According to such sources, many Bahraini merchant families have become extremely rich, and some members of Bahrain's emerging middle class have also grown wealthy in spite of the "boom and bust" impact of external crises and shifts in oil prices. In contrast, Bahrain's Shi'ites, however, have had fewer benefits from Bahrain's developments than its Sunnis, and a number of Sunni families have lost their wealth during Bahrain's recession. While much of Bahrain now has the character of a well-developed modern urban state, many outside experts feel there are still a number of poor, largely Shi'ite rural villages and urban areas.

Bahraini official sources, however, again paint a different picture. They project a total average annual population growth rate of 3.6% during 1981–1991, and a native population growth rate of 2.9%. According to Bahraini projections, population growth rate has not substantially exceeded Bahrain's GNP and GDP growth rates since 1992. US and World Bank data would generally agree with such figures, but they ignore the long period between 1981 and 1990 when population growth clearly did exceed the changes in GNP/GDP by an annual average of well over at least 3%.[37] Further, many analysts believe that successful development only occurs when the increase in GNP/GDP is at least two percent higher than the rate of population growth.

Oil, Gas, and the "Post-Oil Economy"

There is less debate over another major aspect of Bahrain's economy. Bahrain is the first Gulf state which is being forced to move towards a "post-oil economy." Bahrain has been exploiting its limited oil reserves since 1932. It is still an oil exporter, but its reserves are now limited and its production has been reduced to token levels by Gulf standards. Bahrain now has proven recoverable oil reserves of only 350 million barrels. As Table Twelve shows, this total gives Bahrain far less than one percent of the world's total oil reserves and Bahrain has produced at the rate of a little over 40,000 barrels per day in recent years.[38] Even this level of production required a major workover of Bahrain's oil field and gas injection system and currently can only be sustain for a maximum of 25 years.[39]

Most of Bahrain's domestic oil production is converted to refined oil products by the Bahrain Refinery, a joint 60/40 venture between the government of Bahrain and Caltex Petroleum Corporation. This refinery exports about 94% of Bahrain's domestic oil production—largely to the Indian sub-continent and the Pacific Rim. The Bahrain Refinery plays a critical role in Bahrain's economy, and is heavily dependent on Saudi oil. It has a capacity of 245,000 barrels a day, and it can only function near its capacity because it gets 80% of its oil from Saudi Arabia. The Saudis provide Bahrain with roughly 200,000 barrels of light crude oil per day at market prices.[40]

Bahrain also obtains oil income from the sale of crude oil from the Abu Sa'afa field, which is operated by Saudi Aramco and lies in Saudi waters, but which is shared jointly by Bahrain and Saudi Arabia. The field's production capacity is 140,0000 barrels per day, and Bahrain receives 100,000 barrels per day for sale on the international crude oil market. The income from the Abu Sa'afa field provided 36% of the revenue of Bahrain's government in 1994.

The end result has been the steady decline in Bahrain's oil trade as a share of GDP shown in Table Thirteen. These limits to Bahrain's oil wealth are critical to its economic stability and development. At the same time, petroleum and petroleum products still accounted for about 64% of Bahrain's $3.5 billion in exports during 1994, and little change is projected in this percentage through 1996.[41] Oil also still accounted for 64% of export receipts, 54% of its government revenues, and 16% of its GDP.

TABLE TWELVE Comparative Oil Reserves and Production Levels of the Gulf States

Comparative Oil Reserves in 1994 in Billions of Barrels

Country	Identified	Undiscovered	Identified and Undiscovered	Proven	% of World Total
Bahrain	—	—	—	.35	
Iran	69.2	19.0	88.2	89.3	8.9
Iraq	90.8	35.0	125.8	100.0	10.0
Kuwait	92.6	3.0	95.6	96.5	9.7
Oman	—	—	—	5.0	NA
Qatar	3.9	0	3.9	3.7	0.4
Saudi Arabia	265.5	51.0	316.5	261.2	26.1
UAE	61.1	4.2	65.3	98.1	9.8
Total	583.0	112.2	695.2	654.1	64.9
Rest of World	—	—	—	345.7	35.1
World	—	—	—	999.8	100.0

(continues)

TABLE TWELVE (continued)

Comparative Oil Production in Millions of Barrels per Day

Country	1995 Actual	1995 OPEC Quota	DOE/IEA Estimate of Actual Production 1990	1992	2000	2005	2010	Maximum Sustainable 1995	2000	Announced Capacity in 2000
Bahrain	—	—	—	—	—	—	—	—	—	—
Iran	3,608	3,600	3.2	3.6	4.3	5.0	5.4	3.2	4.5	4.5
Iraq	600	400	2.2	0.4	4.4	5.4	6.6	2.5	5.0	5.0
Kuwait	1,850	2,000	1.7	1.1	2.9	3.6	4.2	2.8	3.3	3.3
Oman	—	—	—	—	—	—	—	—	—	—
Qatar	449	378	0.5	0.4	0.6	0.6	0.6	0.5	0.6	0.6
Saudi Arabia	8,018	8,000	8.5	9.6	11.5	12.8	14.1	10.3	11.1	11.1
UAE	2,193	2,161	2.5	2.6	3.1	3.5	4.3	3.0	3.8	3.2
Total Gulf	—	—	18.6	17.7	26.8	30.9	35.0	23.5	28.2	28.2
World	—	—	69.6	67.4	78.6	84.2	88.8	—	—	—

Source: Adapted by Anthony H. Cordesman from estimates in IEA, *Middle East Oil and Gas*, Paris, OED/IEA, 1995, Annex 2 and DOE/EIA, *International Energy Outlook, 1995*, Washington, DOE/EIA, June, 1995, pp. 26–30, and *Middle East Economic Digest*, February 23, 1996, p. 3. IEA and DOE do not provide country breakouts for Bahrain and Oman. Reserve data estimated by author based on country data.

TABLE THIRTEEN   Economic Dependence of Middle Eastern States on Oil
                  Production

Oil Exporter	Trade in Fuels as a Percent of GDP*				Share of Total Exports 1993
	1970	*1974*	*1984*	*1993***	*1993*
Gulf					
Bahrain***	140	105	72	67	90
Iran	20	47	7	15	90
Iraq	3	2	9	2	35
Kuwait	62	80	47	40	80
Oman	78	70	47	30	95
Saudi Arabia	46	90	37	33	99
Gulf Cooperation Council	50	85	35	35	95
Other Middle East					
Algeria	15	30	22	20	85
Egypt	5	2	6	7	45
Syria	6	8	7	14	42
Total Middle East and North Africa					
Percent	25	60	20	30	90
Total Value of Exports in $ Current Billions	10	90	100	110	80

Notes: *Mineral fuels, including petroleum and products, natural gas, and natural gas liquids.
**Estimate.
***Includes fuel processed from Saudi Arabia.
Source: Adapted by Anthony H. Cordesman from World Bank, *Claiming the Future,* Washington, World Bank, 1995, p. 17.

Saudi Arabia has since agreed to a change in the present sharing arrangement for a limited period that gives Bahrain all 140,000 barrels per day from the Abu Sa'afa field. If Saudi Arabia was to agreed to continue to give Bahrain all 140,000 barrels per day in the long-term, this would be an important option that would help Bahrain transition to a post-oil economy.

Bahrain also has 48 trillion cubic feet of gas reserves, and is producing about 272 billion cubic feet of gas per year. It has gas reserves of approximately 14 trillion cubic feet in its Khuff field, and this field is estimated to have 50 years of life at its current rate of production. As Table Fourteen shows, however, these gas reserves are very small. Bahrain has no plans

TABLE FOURTEEN   Gulf and World Gas Reserves and Production

| Nation | *Reserves in 1995* | | *Percent World Supply* | *Production in 1993 (BCM)* |
	TCF	*BCM*		
Bahrain	—	—	—	—
Iran	741.6	21,000	14.9	60.0
Iraq	109.5	3,100	2.2	2.75
Kuwait	52.9	1,498	1.1	5.17
Oman	—	600–640	—	—
Qatar	250.0	7,070	5.0	18.4
Saudi Arabia	185.9	5,134	4.2	67.3
UAE	208.7	5,779*	4.2	31.63
Gulf	1,548.6	—	31.1	185.25
Rest of World	3,431.7	104,642	68.9	—
World Total	4,980.3	148,223	100.0	—

Note: *Other sources estimate 6,320–7,280 BCM for Abu Dhabi only.

Source: The reserve and production data are adapted by Anthony H. Cordesman from IEA, *Middle East Oil and Gas,* Paris, OECD, IEA, 1995, Annex 2.

to export gas and intends to utilize it as its low-cost energy base for future non-oil related economic growth.[42]

Diversification and Other Areas of Economic Activity

Bahrain has reacted to these limits to its oil and gas income by making active efforts to diversify its economy—an effort that has been reinforced by the decline of its agriculture, fishing and pearling industries. Agriculture and fishing now account for less than 2% of Bahrain's GDP.

Agriculture and Fishing.   Bahrain now has virtually no profitable agriculture, although it was once a major date producer. Bahrain's cultivated area has been reduced from around 6,000 hectares in 1971 to less than 1,500 hectares today. This area is divided into about 10,000 plots that range from a few square meters to four hectares. Most land is under the control of about 800 owners and much of the land is under the control of a few absentee owners—including members of the government. There are probably fewer than 2,000 people employed as farmers today—largely employees working on three year contracts for absentee landlords, and many may no longer be Bahraini.[43]

Water consumption during the summer months can exceed Bahrain's capacity of 70 million gallons a day and can force water rationing. These water problems already limit the production capacity of some industrial activities like Bahrain's paper mill, and peak water demand is expected to reach 100 million gallons a day by 1998 and 126 million gallons a day by 2005. Water has become so expensive that there would be little or no agricultural activity in Bahrain if water was priced at its market value, and much less use of water for parks and landscaping.[44]

Bahrain cannot change this situation in ways that make added agricultural activity economic. It has some of best natural springs in the Gulf, but current demand for water is depleting Bahrain's natural water resources, and the country is increasingly dependent on desalination. At present, Bahrain gets at least 60% of its water through desalination. Further, Bahrain already allocates 60% of its water to domestic consumption, 36% to industry, and only 4% to agriculture—which makes it difficult to reallocate water more efficiently except through domestic conservation.[45]

Bahrain's pearling and fishing industries were once its leading source of employment. Bahrain now, however, has no pearling vessels in spite of a major rise in the value of natural pearls. Bahrain's fishing industry declined to fewer than 1,000 fishermen as early as the 1970s. The government began to attempt to revitalize the fishing industry in 1981, and provided modern fishing boats and equipment. These efforts raised output to 9,200 tons in 1989, but pollution hurt the shrimping industry, and major oil spills further limited output in 1983 and 1991. Fishing continues, but it is scarcely a growth industry and now involves high technology and only a limited number of jobs.[46]

Diversification in Modern Economic Activity. At the same time, economic change has created many high paying jobs, and has urbanized virtually all of Bahraini society. At least 89% of Bahrain's population now lives in cities and suburbs, and well over 90% relies on urban jobs.[47] It is scarcely surprising, therefore, that Bahrain has made significant efforts to diversify into more modern areas of economic activity.

Bahrain has had some significant successes. Bahrain now has two major industrial complexes which do not depend on oil-related revenues: The first is the Aluminum Bahrain (ALBA) aluminum smelter, which was built with Saudi aid. The second is the Arab Shipbuilding and Repair Company (ASRY).[48] These two industries have given Bahrain the largest non-oil industrial output of any Southern Gulf country. This output reached a total of 17% of Bahrain's GDP in 1994, while Oman's non oil industrial output was only 6% of total.[49]

ALBA alone accounted for 10% of Bahrain's GDP in 1994, and 27% of the manufacturing sector's contribution to the GDP. It has been particularly successful in recent years—partly because of a recovery in aluminum prices in 1994, and partly because of well-judged expansion programs. ALBA's smelter capacity was nearly doubled to 450,000 tones per year in 1993, and it became the world's third largest operating smelter. This doubling was completed shortly before aluminum reached a five year high of $2,150 a ton. It helped Bahrain to increase aluminum exports by 24% in 1994 in 1994, reaching a value of $558 million.[50]

ALBA uses the latest smelter technology, and has one of the lowest cost smelters in the world. This smelter is being further expanded to 500,000 tons per year at a cost of $140 million, making it the largest smelter outside the USSR. ALBA is also expanding aluminum billet production and is considering plans for coke production, but its smelter capacity cannot be expanded significantly beyond 500,000 tons a year unless new sources of cheap power become available, and there are limits to its hiring capacity if it is to keep efficiency at the present 220 tons per employee—a level of efficiency typical of European plants.

Bahrain is actively seeking to expand its aluminum extrusion and anodizing capacity. The Bahrain Aluminum Extrusion Company has a capacity of 13,500 tons per year and is studying plans to expand to 21,000 tons per year. The Bahrain Alloys Manufacturing Company is considering construction of a 20,000 ton per year alloy plant. The total output from Bahrain's aluminum plants is already sold through 1996. Bahrain, however, must expand into the manufacturing sector if its aluminum is to further diversify its economy and create large numbers of new aluminum-related jobs. One example of this activity is Aluwheel, which produces about 350,000 alloy wheels a year.[51]

ASRY is the largest ship repair facility in the Gulf and is one of Bahrain's most labor intensive industries, although much of its labor is foreign.[52] It has two floating docks capable of handling carriers of up to 120,000 tons and is one of the few dockyards in the world modern enough to comply with the ISO 9002 standard. Although a global depression in the shipping industry, and fiercely competitive freight rates, have led to intense competition in the shipbuilding and repair industry, dock occupancy at the ASRY has been relatively high by world standards, and the yard is well suited to serve the oil tanker industry. ASRY revenues reached an all-time high of $68.2 million in 1994 (a 18.5% increase over the previous year), and operating profits reached $7.5 million. ASRY is currently investing $87 million on expansion over the next two to three years, and is expanding its docks and the depth of its shipping channels. This expansion will only produce a relatively limited increase in employment and profitability, however, unless there is a major increase in freight rates.

Bahrain is diversifying into other areas. These activities include a $136 million urea plant, a paper mill, a battery plant, and the expansion of

Bahrain's international airport. The government has also sought to encourage investment in small to medium sized projects, and to further strengthen its strong service and banking sectors.

Shipping and Banking. All of these efforts have made some progress, and have significant future potential. The present economic climate in the Gulf and political unrest in Bahrain have, however, led to a loss of profitability in the service sector and a shortage of private investment capital. Private indebtedness has risen by over 60% since 1991. In June, 1994, the Bahrain Monetary Agency had to ask private banks to reduce their supply of private credit to private citizens, but banks were forced to resume extensive lending to consumers in loans in June, 1995.

Bahrain has plans to create a $220–340 million new port and industrial estate to supplement Mina Sulman. This modernization is necessary to react to the changes taking place in Gulf shipping. In the past, Bahrain's good port facilities, and proximity to Saudi Arabia, Qatar, and Kuwait, gave it a strong trading advantage and resulted in substantial entrepot activity. However, the creation of modern high capacity ports in neighboring states has virtually ended this entrepot activity. There has also been a shift in the traditional pattern of shipping in the Gulf, which was largely center on Bahrain, Shipping companies are off-loading cargoes in Port Rashid in Dubai for transshipment to other ports in the Gulf and this has further diminished Bahrain's mercantile role in the region.

Bahrain's banking industry is also encountering problems. In the past, Bahrain has been able to offer foreign business a better social climate and more stable political environment than most other Gulf states. This helped create a strong banking industry. Bahrain has experienced a sharp contraction of its offshore banking operations as a result of recent wars and the "oil glut" that began in the mid-1980s, however, and the development of oil and gas resources in the UAE has shifted banking, investment, and insurance activity to Abu Dhabi and Dubai. Other investment activity has moved to the Levant or is now managed from outside the region. Although Bahrain is still an important Gulf financial center, its banking industries face serious limits to their probable future expansion. As a result, Bahrain's non-oil income is projected to be relatively constant, with a total of BD 242 million ($645 million) in 1994, BD 237 million in 1995, and BD 245 million in 1996.[53]

In short, Bahrain has made very real progress in diversification, although it has not been able to create new jobs at the rate required. Its problems in finding investment capital have also led to limits in key aspects of its infrastructure like the electric power and water. Bahrain currently uses 980 megawatts of 984 megawatts capacity, and is only able to support growth by obtaining 250 megawatts of additional capacity from

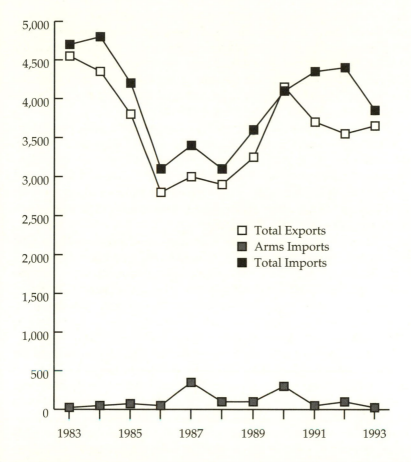

CHART SEVEN   Bahrain's Trade Balance During 1983–1993 (in Constant $1993).
Source: Adapted by Anthony H. Cordesman from ACDA, *World Military Expenditures and Arms Transfers, 1993–1994,* Washington, ACDA-GPO, 1995, Table II.

ALBA's 800 megawatt plants—a strategy that inevitably limits the expansion of ALBA. Plans for a new power and desalination plant of 260 megawatts and 30 million gallons capacity were announced in May, 1996, with the plant to become operational in 1999. [54]

Population and Shifts in Per Capita Income

These economic problems make the previous uncertainty over the Bahrain's level of per capita income and the distribution of its wealth even more important. Bahrain's per capita income is still relatively high by the standards of the developing world, but it has been dropping steadily in constant dollars, and is now substantially lower than it was in 1983. If US estimates are right, Bahrain's GDP per capita reached $12,740 in 1983, in constant 1993 dollars. It dropped to about $8,300 in 1985, and now approaches $7,000. The World Bank estimates that Bahrain's per capita income totaled $8,030 in 1993, and $7,500 in 1994.[55]

These figures compare with a current average per capita income of about $8,000 in the Southern Gulf states, with a high of about $17,000 in the UAE and a low of $5,900 in Oman.[56] The effects of this drop in Bahrain's per capita income have been made worse by the decline in the value of the US dollar because oil is priced in dollars, while most of Bahrain's imports come from Europe and Asia where local currencies have risen in value relative to the dollar.[57]

Even if Bahrain's much favorable estimates are correct, Bahrain still faces significant future demographic pressures. As has been mentioned earlier, Bahrain has long had a high rate of population growth. Its total population was only 230,000 when its oil boom began in early 1970. It rose to 350,000 by 1980, and some Western estimates indicate that Bahrain's total native and foreign population rose by an average of 3.4% during 1981–1993. This growth raised Bahrain's population to 503,000 by 1990, and to 572,000 by 1995—a total well over twice Bahrain's population at the time when the oil boom began.[58] Bahraini data are similar. They indicate that Bahrain's total population increased by 3.6% during 1981–1991, and that the native population increased by 2.9% during this period. They also indicate that Bahrain's population totaled 568,100 in 1994.

Chart Eight provides a conservative World Bank estimate that projects Bahrain's population growth through 2035. The World Bank estimates that Bahrain's population will grow from 503,000 in 1990, and 572,000 in 1995, to 639,000 by the year 2000, 770,000 by 2010, and 903,000 million by 2020. In the process, Bahrain's total number of young men in the group reaching job age (15–19 years) will rise from a total of 22,000 in 1995 to 31,000 in 2000, 37,000 million in 2005, 40,000 million in 2010 and then level off. The number of young men needing jobs will still, however, be at least 44,000 by the year 2030.[59] This is a major demographic burden, and one that will steadily increase the demand for jobs and economic diversification.

Further, a number of observers feel Bahrain faces three other demographic problems with its labor force:

- Bahrain's labor policies gave its citizens a wide range of services and job protection rights, but these same policies discouraged them from taking lower paying jobs and often made them more expensive to

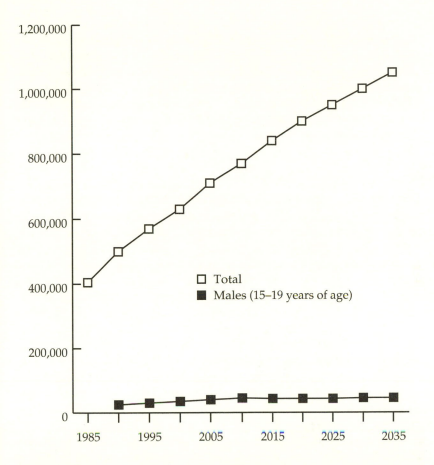

CHART EIGHT   Estimated Trends in Bahrain's Population During 1990–2035. *Source:* Adapted by Anthony H. Cordesman from World Bank, *World Population Projections, 1994–1995,* Washington, World Bank, 1994, and material provided by the CIA.

employ than foreign labor. As a result, at least 58% of Bahrain's labor force was foreign by 1995, in spite of unemployment among the native labor forces, particularly among Bahrain's younger Shi'ites.

- Employment in Bahrain came to reflect a split where about 90% of the jobs in government were held by native Bahrainis versus only 30% of the jobs in the private sector. As is typical of most Southern Gulf states, this added to Bahrain's economic problems because many government and state organizations over-staffed and created jobs with little real function or economic output.[60]

• Bahrain did not extend all privileges equally to parts of its "foreign" population that were effectively native citizens. Only a modest percentage of the population can trace their roots back to families that were living in Bahrain in 1921, and excluding many families who came to Bahrain after that date from citizenship created a source of discrimination affecting Shi'ites, although the government has recently taken significant measures to reduce the problems of such "non-citizens."[61]

Government Budgets and the Economy

It is not surprising that the government's efforts to deal with these economic, demographic, and labor problems have forced Bahrain into growing budget deficits—deficits which have serious potential consequences in a nation where direct government expenditures account for 19% of the GDP and where much of the economy is government owned.

Bahrain must also cope with the legacy of a welfare system it can no longer easily afford and which has been a key factor in easing its sectarian divisions. Bahrain's government made consistent efforts to improve Bahrain's social services and living standards after the oil boom in the early 1970s. The poorer sections of the population, which are largely Shi'ite, benefited from this new prosperity in the form of greatly improved government services; the extension of power, water, and utility systems to villages; the building of hospitals and clinics; government subsidies on staple foods; and educational scholarships at home and abroad.

The government opened Bahrain University during this period, and made inexpensive higher education available to all segments of the nation. These government expenditures and services benefited Bahrain's poor and Shi'ites. For example, educational benefits also opened up opportunities for Bahrain's Shi'ites and Shi'ite students of Persian origin quickly became the upper quartile in examination results.

The end of the oil boom has changed this situation. Bahrain has had annual budget deficits every year after 1984. Its accumulated deficit has grown from only BD 45 million in 1990, to BD 138 million in 1992, BD 203 million in 1993, and BD 329 million in 1994. Its annual deficits reached BD 65 million in 1993 and BD 74 million in 1994, and there is little prospect that Bahrain will have a balanced budget before the year 2000. According to the US Embassy in Bahrain, its accumulated deficit reached $1.05 billion in 1995 and $1.35 billion in 1996.

Recent projections indicate that government revenues are expected to drop from BD 620 million in 1994, to BD 520–530 million in 1995 and 1996. Most of this decline is due to a reduction in oil-related revenues, which is forcing the government to reduce expenditure by about 5% from the 1994 level during 1995 and 1996. As a result, expenditures will have to be held to about BD 644 million in spite of budget deficits. This has a major impact on an economy where salaries for government employees account for about 50% of outlays, and 30% goes to other recurrent costs.

Further, some government estimates have projected deficits as high as BD 122 million in 1995 and BD 114 million in 1996—in part because of reduced subventions by Kuwait and Saudi Arabia. Recent rises in oil prices may cut such deficits, as may increases in Saudi aid. If such projections are accurate, however, Bahrain will have an estimated accumulated deficit of BD 450 billion in 1995 and BD 560 million in 1996.[62]

The end result of these deficits has already been cuts in social services and education that compound Bahrain's unemployment problems, and are occurring at a time when some estimates indicate Bahrain's economy may find it difficult to generate even half the new jobs over the next five years that will be required to employ Bahrainis enter the labor market.

At the same time, Bahrain has had to concentrate its remaining government expenditures on maintaining its remaining social services—leaving less money for the kind of new investment that helps create new jobs. The share of capital investment in the budget has had to be cut by 2 to 5% per year since the early 1990s, while the cost of simply maintaining existing services (recurrent expenditures) has increased by a total 128%. This shift in the budget has prevented the kind of investment in the water and power sectors necessary to create the infrastructure for growth, and investment in economic activities that create new jobs.

Economic Factors and Internal Stability

Bahrain's government has responded to these problems by making significant efforts to stimulate and diversify its economy, and there is little doubt that Bahrain's problems would be much worse if the government had not taken strong steps to reduce Bahrain's dependence on the oil sector. At the same time, outside studies of Bahrain's economic performance indicate that these government efforts have not yet been able to meet Bahrain's needs.

The US State Department, for example, has issued estimates that indicate Bahrain's economy has not diversified enough to reduce dependence on petroleum related income. In fact, these estimates indicate that activity in key private sector activities like construction has dropped from 10.5% of GDP in 1984 to only 6% in 1994. The State Department estimates that real economic activity is contracting at a time when Bahrain needs about 4–6% growth simply to sustain the living standards of its growing population. As a result, Bahrain's economic problems, a lack of job opportunities for native Bahrainis, the economic problems of its poorer Shi'ites, and Iranian interference in the situation, are now the main threat to Bahrain's stability and security.

Much of this threat is the result of factors the government cannot control, such as Bahrain's declining oil wealth and cuts in world oil prices which have depressed economic activity throughout the Gulf. No actions by Bahrain's government could have diversified the economy quickly enough to sustain growth, support the present level of welfare and state investment, and support the present dependence on foreign labor. Further, Bahrain's neighbors have been slow to recognize the scale of aid Bahrain will need in the future, and have failed to emphasize native employment within the GCC states.

Bahrain, however, is also to blame. Like the other Southern Gulf states, Bahrain did emphasize welfare over development and privatization, and adopted labor and social policies which tended to discourage native employment. The government has long had a policy of Bahrainisation, but this policy has not been matched by action and the government has been slow to recognize the true urgency of major reductions in Bahrain's foreign labor force, slow to change Bahrain's education system to emphasize job skills. It has been slow to effectively implement laws and incentives that force the employment of native labor.

The government has created one of the most liberal climates for private enterprise foreign investment in the developing world, but it also relied too much on market forces in a troubled and uncertain corner of the world. It was been slow to recognize that it might also need to create major incentives for privatization and foreign investment.

As a result, Bahrain faces problems of a kind that that threaten most Southern Gulf regimes. Barring a major sustained increase in real oil prices that is far greater than the increase currently projected by OPEC, the IEA, or DOE, Bahrain can only deal with the growing structural economic problems created by the decline in its oil wealth if it makes concerted efforts to:

- Rigorously enforce legislation like the Labor Law for the Private Sector (Decree Number 23 for 1976), and regulations limiting and controlling foreign visas. Accelerate its efforts to reduce the number of foreign workers, with priority for reductions in servants and in trades that allow the most rapid conversion to native labor.
- Eliminate economic disincentives for employers in hiring native labor, and create new disincentives for hiring foreign labor. Bahrain's young and increasingly well-educated population needs to replace its foreign workers as quickly as possible, and it will only develop a work ethic and suitable skills once it is thrust into the labor market by ensuring that foreign labor cannot compete.

- Reduce those aspects of state subsidies and welfare that distort the economy and discourage the native population from seeking jobs.
- Conduct a popular education program to limit population growth, with careful attention to the higher birth rate among its poorer citizens.
- Ensure water, electricity, motor gasoline, foods, and services are priced at market levels and replace subsidies with jobs and economic opportunities. Ensure that employers are charged for any unreimbursed government-provided services and infrastructure used by foreign labor.
- Continue to restructure the educational system to focus on job training and competitiveness. Create strong new incentives for faculty and students to focus on job-related education, sharply down-size other forms of educational funding and activity, and eliminate high overhead educational activities without economic benefits. Emphasize educational opportunities and scholarships for poorer Shi'ite and Sunni citizens, and expand vocational programs even further.
- Unify and reform the structure of the national budget to ensure that all of the nation's revenues and foreign reserves are integrated into the national budget and into the planning process. Provide for expanded public review of the budget, allowing both Sunnis and Shi'ites to play a serious role in reviewing the budget's structure and management of funds.
- Tax domestic capital holdings and property above a given value and ensure that all income from the foreign investments and property of wealthier Bahrainis is subject to progressive taxes.
- Selectively tax earnings and sales with progressive taxes to reduce budget deficits, but structure such taxes to encourage local investment over consumption, and to create added disincentives for the expatriation of capital.
- Ensure that all income from enterprises with state financing is reflected in the national budget and is integrated into the national economic development and planning program.
- Freeze and then reduce the number of civil servants, and slowly restructure and down-size the civil service to shift native labor to more productive areas of activity.
- Establish market criteria for all major state and state-supported investments. Require detailed and independent risk assessment and projections of comparative return on government investment. Down-size the scale of programs to reduce investment and cash flow costs and the risk of cost-escalation.
- Create new, market-driven incentives for privatization to increase the efficiency of investments in downstream and upstream operations, to create real jobs and career opportunities for native workers,

and to open investment opportunities to a much wider range of investors.

- Manage privatization in ways ensuring an opportunity for all native citizens to share in the privatization process. Privatization must not be conducted in a manner that benefits a small, elite group of investors and discourages popular confidence and willingness to invest in Bahrain.
- Create new market-driven incentives for foreign investment. Bahrain already offers foreign companies and investors one of the freest economies in the developing world, but it is going to have to provide added incentives in light of the present unrest in Bahrain and competition from other countries.
- Convince Bahrain's people that Bahrain's wealth is being spent in ways that broadly benefit Bahrain's people and not members of the royal family or ruling elite. This requires full transparency in the budget, accounting measures that refute the charges of corruption and favoritism made by the government's hard-line opponents, and a clear policy regarding how much of Bahrain's future income will go to royal accounts.
- Place national security spending on the same basis as other state spending. Integrate it fully into the national budget, including investment and equipment purchases. Replace the present emphasis on judging purchases on the basis of initial procurement costs and technical features with a full assessment of life cycle cost—including training, maintenance, and facilities—and with specific procedures for evaluating the value of standardization and interoperability with existing national equipment and facilities, those of other Gulf states, and those of the US and other power projection forces.
- Develop mid and long-term economic plans that cover the period five and ten years in the future, and which explicitly address the issues of job creation, income distribution, education, and the role of foreign labor. Oman has already shown that five year plans must be supplemented by longer-term plans that provide a warning of the possible implications of present trends and problems and which examine a range of long-term solutions. Bahrain needs to confront the issues it faces, rather than deny them, and examine the possible implications of "worst case" trends. It also needs to do everything possible to focus public debate on Bahrain's development needs.

At the same time, Bahrain needs and deserves more aid from its neighbors. Saudi Arabia has talked of increasing Bahrain's share of oil from the Bahraini-Saudi Abu Sa'afa oil field to include all of the oil from the field. This would be an important step, but its unclear whether such aid will be provided, and whether any such increase is likely to be offset by further cuts in the Saudi subvention. Bahrain needs aid to avoid cutbacks in social services, including the welfare programs that help low income and unemployed Bahrainis. More aid is needed to fund education and job opportunities. The plentiful government scholarships available in the 1980s need to be revived and the government needs support to fund the vigorous new vocational training program it announced in June, 1995.

More broadly, Bahrain neighbors need to take a hard look at the implications that Bahrain's economic and demographic pressures have for other Southern Gulf states. Bahrain's current economic, demographic, and foreign labor problems are symptoms of problems that will eventually affect all Southern Gulf countries. They are problems which require a systematic restructuring of all Southern Gulf societies and economies. Bahrain may be the first post-oil economy in the Gulf, but virtually all Gulf economies face a future where oil and gas cannot provide the present level of prosperity, and where no amount of diversification can provide a level of economic growth that can both sustain the present level of per capita wealth and the present level of dependence on foreign labor.

Foreign and Native Labor, Sunni and Shi'ite

Bahrain faces serious demographic challenges which are closely linked to its economic ones. Bahrain's total population is now over 576,000. Roughly 65% of this population is native Bahraini, and this native population is divided between Sunnis and Shi'ites. Estimates differ over the relative proportion of each branch of Islam in the native population—and there are no official statistics—but Bahraini experts estimate that the native population is about 35% Sunni and 65% Shi'ite. The CIA estimates that the native population is about 70% Shi'ite and 30% Sunni, and a few experts feel that the percentage of Shi'ites is even higher.[63]

Virtually all sources agree that Bahrain's population growth rate has averaged well over 3.5% during the last decade, and that the native population has grown by around 3%. This population growth has consistently been higher among the foreign population. According to US estimates, foreigners grew from 122,000 in 1981 to 187,000 in 1992, or by about 67%. In contrast, Bahrain's native population grew by only 52.5% during the same period. Precise figures are not available on the relative growth of native Sunnis and Shi'ites, but virtually all observers agree that native Shi'ites have long had a higher birthrate than its Sunnis, and that poor native Shi'ites have an exceptionally high growth rate for cultural and religious reasons.[64]

In short, demographic factors have shifted the composition of Bahrain's population in two important ways. First, in favor of foreign labor, and second, in favor of native Shi'ites. US estimates indicate that the balance of Bahrain's native population has shifted from one which was almost evenly split between Sunni and Shi'ite in the 1950s to one that is now about 70% Shi'ite.[65]

The split between Sunni and Shi'ite is complicated by other divisions. The native Sunni population is composed the Al Khalifa family, other tribal Arabs, and Sunnis of Persian origin known as "Hawala." Indigenous Arab Bahrainis are known as "Baharna." About 13% to 15% of Bahrain's Shi'ites of Persian origin, and are known as "Ajam." About 3,000–5,000 Shi'ites—largely of Iranian origin—do not have full citizenship or passports—although they are second and third generation residents. These residents are called "Bidoon"—which means "without." They cannot legally buy land, start businesses, or obtain government loans. Bidoon and other Bahraini citizens who speak Farsi instead of Arabic have difficulties in gaining employment and promotion in Bahrain. Bahraini Arabic-speaking Sunnis have been favored in government and the private sector, and in commercial legal disputes. According to some US experts, even those Bidoon who do speak unaccented Arabic have had problems getting jobs.

Discrimination or Non-Discrimination Against Bahrain's Shi'ites

Shi'ite critics of the government, and some outside observers, have charged that there has been a systematic process of institutionalized discrimination but the truth seems more complex. The fact that Bahrain's Shi'ites are generally poorer than its Sunnis does not mean that Bahrain has engaged in systematic discrimination.

There is no doubt that the distribution of political and economic power has tended to favor Bahrain's Sunnis. Political power has long been concentrated in the Khalifa family, which is Sunni, and in the hands of senior Sunni members of the government.[66] Bahrain's wealth has been heavily concentrated in its Sunni elite, and there still are only a relatively limited number of wealthy Shi'ites.

Similar ethnic concentrations of power and wealth exist in the US, however, and market forces did much to ensure that private investment and government expenditures went to firms managed by Bahrain's wealthier citizens during the oil boom, whether Sunnis or Shi'ite. Sunnis, many of which came from Iran, also made up a considerable majority of Bahrain's leading merchant families. Their economic wealth and ties to the government gave them a natural advantage in obtaining government contracts, and exploit government-related investment trade opportunities.

Sunnis dominated Bahrain's middle class before the oil boom and had a larger cushion of wealth to deal with Bahrain's recession. In contrast, some Shi'ites who entered the middle class during the oil boom lost much of their wealth and dropped out of the middle class. It is also natural that those who make up a large proportion of Bahrain's poor suffered most from the decline in Bahrain's oil wealth and its cutbacks in spending.[67]

Bahraini government experts respond to charges of discrimination by noting that Bahraini law and social services do not discriminate against Shi'ites, and that the government has expanded the number of Shi'ites in the Cabinet and has ensured that Shi'ites have equal representation in the Majlis. They also note that the government began to improve its treatment of the Bidoon in 1995, in part because they refused to take part in the recent demonstrations against the government. It granted many passports for the first time, and offered more economic privileges as well. It is unclear, however, that the Bidoon will remain as passive if other forms of Shi'ite unrest grow stronger.

Many outside observers do feel that there is both conscious and unconscious discrimination against Shi'ites. Cultural, linguistic, family, and religious factors have an inevitable impact. At the same time, many of these observers believe that the problems faced by Bahrain's Shi'ites are more problems faced by all of Bahrain's poor citizens than the result of overt discrimination. These problems include the higher vulnerability of the poor, higher birth rates, the lack of a modern work ethic, inferior education, language difficulties, and cultural factors.

A Developing Pattern of Sectarian Violence?

One thing is clear. There is tension and sometimes conflict between Sunni and Shi'ite. Further, sectarian divisions created problems long before the current recession. Bahrain's large number of Shi'ites and Iranians was a factor that helped lead the Shah of Iran to renew his claim to Bahrain in 1968. Religious divisions also helped lead to the break up of Bahrain's constituent assembly. This assembly was created in 1973, but broke up in 1975—largely because of left wing political extremism led by Shi'ite politicians.

Shi'ite challenges to the government were relatively limited between 1975 and 1979—although some Shi'ite exile groups did exist and Bahrain's internal security forces kept Shi'ite opposition movements under close surveillance. They became much more serious, however, after the fall of the Shah of Iran. As has been discussed earlier, Khomeini seems to have actively sponsored the creation of pro-Iranian Shi'ite cells in Bahrain and anti-government indoctrination of the Bahrain Shi'ite clergy being educated in Iran. There is considerable evidence that Iran sponsored a coup attempt in Bahrain in 1981, and that the Iranian embassy was smuggling arms into the country. This coup attempt was broken up by Bahrain's Public Security Force before any fighting began, but the effort to organize it revealed increased friction between the ruling family and some of Bahrain's younger Shi'ites.[68]

Suppressing the coup attempt did not solve Bahrain's problems. Many of Bahrain's Shi'ite clergy and a large numbers of other students were trained in Iran, and many were indoctrinated with pro-Khomeini or pro-revolutionary doctrine. Pro-Iranian political parties like the Islamic Front for the Liberation of Bahrain and the Hizbollah (Party of God) continued to be active, often with the support of exile groups.

Two new arms caches were discovered in 1984, and as many as 30 people were arrested. A new and relatively well organized opposition movement called the Islamic Front began to form cells in the Shi'ite villages in 1986, and had organized some cells to conduct guerrilla and sabotage operations in 1987. This led to 60–100 arrests in 1988. Similar annual levels of arrests took place throughout the 1980s. Many Shi'ites were arrested and detained under a 1974 State Security Measure, while others were exiled or were not given passports.[69]

Foreign Labor and Shi'ite Unemployment

Bahrain's economic problems and reliance on foreign labor added a new dimension to Bahrain's sectarian problems during the 1990s. The percentage of native Bahrainis dropped from around 83% of the total population in 1971, 70% in 1981, and then to around 66% in 1993. By 1995, about 34% of the total population—and 66% of the total work force—was foreign. The total ethnic mix had shifted to the point where 12% of the total population was Asian, 7% was Iranian, and 6% was a mix of other groups.[70] Estimates differ sharply by source, but one source indicates that in 1993, Bahrain's native work force consisted of 64,000 males and 13,000 females (total 77,000) while the expatriate work force consisted of 114,000 males and 21,000 females (total 135,000).[71]

This high population of foreign workers increasingly competed with the poor Shi'ites for job opportunities for both skilled and low skilled labor. The government's efforts to reduce this competition also did as much to contribute to the problem as to solve it. Efforts to limit foreign labor were undercut by a growing trade in illegal or "free visa" visas—which currently sell for around $1,350 a head.[72] The government was very slow to improve its job training and recruiting efforts. Further, Bahraini Shi'ites—both of Arab and Persian origin—were not permitted to join the armed forces and were discriminated against for senior positions in the civil service. This presented special problems in an economy where over 68% of all workers are in government and service jobs, versus 2.0% in agriculture and 29.8% in industry.[73]

Bahrain's income was unevenly distributed, and its Sunnis generally had substantially higher incomes than its Shi'ites.[74] This gave many Sunnis the skills, capital, and influence to survive the oil recession and grow even wealthier. Some Sunnis also suffered, but a disproportionate part of Bahrain's emerging Shi'ite middle class lost much of its wealth in the recession and became substantially worse off. As a result, Bahrain's economic problems had a disproportionately heavy impact on its Shi'ites.

At the same time, the high birth rate in the lower income portion of the population increased the number of Shi'ites trying to enter the labor market with few qualifications and few opportunities. Further, Bahrain's urban development did not extend evenly to its poorer, largely Shi'ite rural areas. For example, World Bank studies indicate that only 57% of rural Bahrainis had access to safe drinking water, versus 100% for urban Bahrainis.[75]

Outside estimates indicate that up to 25% of Bahrain's poor Shi'ites faced serious economic and employment problems by 1994. According to US estimates, at least 15% of Bahrain's native work force was unemployed in 1994–1995 versus only 6.6% in 1981, and 75% of this unemployment was contained in the part of the work force that was under 30 and overwhelmingly Shi'ite. It should be noted, however, that Bahrain's numbers are very different. Bahrain estimates that direct unemployment of native workers was only 14.8% in 1991, and that the rate of unemployment dropped to 7.3% in 1995. Bahrain basis this estimate on a manpower pool of 184,227 native workers and 13,394 unemployed.

Research by the ILO also found that the Bahraini government had failed to create an effective educational and job development base for Bahrainis of both Sunni and Shi'ite background, and that the Ministry of Labor had failed to make effective efforts towards encouraging "Bahrainisation." Business and technical education at the secondary school level was particularly weak and unrelated to job skills, and only 25% of those who succeeded in completing a technical education found jobs in their area of specialty. The ILO found the Ministry of Education was poorly organized to educate Bahrainis for Bahrain's labor market.[76]

It is important to note, however, that Bahrain's problems impacted on its Sunnis as well as its Shi'ites. Many Sunnis found themselves locked into dead end jobs in government and state industry. Some Sunnis experienced downward mobility and others found they had increased problems in competing with foreign labor. Sunnis as well as Shi'ites felt the government was slow to react, tended to understate or deny some of Bahrain's social problems, favored a wealthy power elite, and failed to broaden the base of political power. Much of this criticism was probably more the product of the impact of war and low oil revenues than any action of the government, but the government became the natural target of popular resentment.

New Tensions Arise in the 1990s

It is not surprising, therefore, that both Sunni and Shi'ite opposition groups began to attack the government and press for "reform." As many as 300 Sunni and Shi'ite notables submitted a petition calling for the reactivation of Bahrain's National Assembly in November, 1992. These pressures helped lead the Amir to set up the Consultative Council in 1992, but this did not meet the demands of many members of opposition groups. The speeches of anti-government clerics began to receive broad attention. Cassettes of such speeches began to circulate, and once isolated Shi'ite protests began to take on the character of a popular movement. At the same time, a number of prominent Sunnis and Shi'ite continued to call for elections and legal reforms.[77]

This raises an important point about the forces for political change in Bahrain. The recent debate over reform has created four organized movements pressing. Two are mixed groups of Shi'ites and Sunnis and are pressing for peaceful reforms like bringing back the National Assembly. Two are religious and Shi'ite in character. As has been mentioned earlier, the Bahrain Freedom Movement claims to be peaceful and pressing for democratic reforms and equality, rather than Shi'ite religious causes. The Islamic Front for the Liberation of Bahrain is more open about sponsoring demonstrations and creating incidents.

Bahrain is not, therefore, completely polarized into Sunni and Shi'ite, or government conservatives and religious radicals, and there is no one, united opposition. It is likely that the majority of Bahrainis do not support radicalism or violence, or wish to see the country divided along religious lines. Most Bahrainis who criticize the government still seek relatively limited economic concern or are seeking a better economic position rather than Islamic change. As has been discussed earlier, there are also a wide range of moderate reforms and evolutionary changes that can deal with Bahrain's problems without violence or civil conflict.

Nevertheless, there has been some polarization along sectarian lines. In January and March, 1994 Shi'ite gatherings occurred at the Al-Mumin mosque in Manama that used the commemoration of the death of the Iranian Grand Ayatollah Golpayegani to protest their political and economic situation. These demonstrations were dispersed by the security forces and the mosque was closed temporarily. In April, the security police arrested 14 Shi'ite students, following a fight between Sunni and Shi'ite students, and held them for two months without trial. In July and

September, security forces used tear gas to break up large Shi'ite protest demonstrations at the Ministry of Labor and Social Affairs, which became violent. They detained and sometimes arrested the leaders and protesters—although most were later released without charge.

In November, 1994, the security forces arrested Sheik Ali Salman and 12 of his followers for inciting violence against male and female foreigners who had worn brief running clothes while taking part in a marathon race. Ali Salman is a 28 year old Shi'ite cleric who had returned to Bahrain in 1992, after theological training in Qom. He is one of almost 100 Najaf (Iraq) and Qom (Iran) trained clerics in Bahrain, and was virtually unknown to the Arab Shi'ites outside his own village prior to his arrest. He had been deported by the government for subversive activities before he had gone to Qom, and had been allowed to return to Bahrain 18 months earlier upon his written agreement to desist from any further anti-government activities. His arrest was due in part to the fact he had broken this agreement.

Nevertheless, the arrests led to demonstrations and violent protests in Manama and several Shi'ite villages. Protests took place in the main *souq* in Manama, and demonstrations occurred against the annual summit meeting of the leaders of the GCC, which took place in Manama in December, 1994. The largely Pakistani and Baluchi security police responded by using rubber bullets and considerable force. The protesters responded by using stones and Molotov cocktails to attack police stations, public security vehicles, and branches of the national bank of Bahrain. Three demonstrators and one policeman were killed, and the police arrested 500–600 Shi'ites.

Security Developments in 1995 and 1996

New demonstrations and riots took place in 1995. In mid-January the police arrested several hundred more demonstrators. According to some reports, several civilians and two policemen were killed. There were no demonstrations during the holy month of Ramadan, but during the Eid Al Fitr, immediately following Ramadan, demonstrations recommenced with an escalation in the level of violence. New protests also took place when the security forces attempted to arrest opposition leaders like Abdelwhahhab Hussein and Sheik Abdul Amir al-Jamri. Once again civilians were injured and several were killed.

Demonstrations and violence continued during March, along with attacks on power substations and power transformers. "Protest bombs" exploded in numerous locations around the island as demonstrators used burning tires to ignite propane tanks. These "bombs" were noisy, but caused no damage. Other actions were more dangerous. Western expatriates were harassed: Some houses were burned out and others were petrol-bombed in areas off the Budiya Highway. Westerners' cars were torched. Some Eastern expatriates were threatened and there were isolated attacks upon them and their property. As a result, some expatriates moved from areas of frequent rioting to safer non-Shi'ite areas elsewhere on the island.

The government was forced to react. On April 1, security forces arrested Sheik Abdul Amir al Jamri, a Shi'ite cleric educated in Najaf in Iraq and a former member of the National Assembly. This arrest led to a confrontation that resulted in the arrest of 18 members of the Sheik's family, the shooting of two of his neighbors, 50 injured and the arrest of several hundred others. Another policeman was killed and several were wounded in early April, along with at least one foreigner. The summer vacation of University of Bahrain was extended for a week.[78]

By May, the incidents appeared to threaten both Bahrain's political stability and its long-standing reputation as a secure regional business center that was well disposed towards Western investment and foreign workers. Majid Jishi—the Minister for Public Works, Electricity, and Water—issued an estimate that put the cost of recent sabotage at $2.3 million.[79] The government stepped up its efforts to arrest and interrogate those involved in the demonstrations and protests—although estimates that as many as 5,000 people were arrested or detained seem sharply exaggerated. The interrogation of these detainees—most of whom were in their teens and early twenties—led to the progressive detention of the majority of the leaders of what proved to be a loose federation of Arab Shi'ite village protesters. Approximately 700 remained in detention in August, 1995.

These arrests helped bring a temporary end to much of the violence, but some observers feel that the protesters changed character during this period. Incidents in December 1994, took place in the poorest Arab Shi'ite rural villages—village areas with most of Bahrain's growing untrained and unemployed high school drop-outs. By April, 1995, however, more city-dwelling Shi'ites of Persian origin became involved, and sectarian confrontations began to take place in Bahrain's schools and Bahrain University.

Some of the opposition escalated from attacks on government officials to attacks on the Al Khalifa family. At the same time, organized radical opposition groups like the Islamic Front for the Liberation of Bahrain and the Islamic Movement for the Liberation of Bahrain continued to insist that they only sought reform and the restoration of the 1973 constitution and the National Assembly. The Islamic Movement for the Liberation of Bahrain now operated out of London, and consistently took this position. So did Bahrain's two secular left-wing movements—the Bahrain Popular Front and National Liberation Front.

Bahrain was able to obtain support from its neighbors. The ministers of the interior of the GCC held a special meeting in Manama on April 18, 1995, to show their support for the government. The government had less success, however, in its efforts to negotiate with Shi'ite leaders. It summoned older village leaders for talks with the Amir, but these leaders proven unable to control the more radical members of a generation of 15–25 year old demonstrators. The government then turned to the Shi'ite clergy. A leading Arab Shi'ite businessman (who has since been appointed Minister of Labor in the new Cabinet) acted as a spokesman within the Shi'ite community in negotiations between the government and the Shi'ite Mullahs during April, 1995. The result was that a group of 12 Shi'ite clergymen issued a statement on April 19, that had been formulated with the concurrence of the Prime Minister. These 12 clergy included a number of popular leaders, but they only included about 25% of the 42 clerics the government had been contacted. More than half of those the government contacted refused to sign.

This statement was read in all Shi'ite mosques on April 21, 1995. It called for an end to the violent demonstrations and destruction of government property. It also called for dialogue, respect for holy places and private property, the release of those in detention, and the degree of Sunni and Shi'ite unity that would allow Bahrainis to act as a "single family." This statement was welcomed by the majority of the Arab Shi'ites, and led to another temporary decline in violence. However, it did little to produce a lasting peace or come to grips with the underlying issues involved.

During May and June, the government had to deploy additional security forces, although it did not make any use of the armed forces.[80] The government was forced to deploy the security forces to prevent new uprisings on June 9—the Shi'ite festival of Ashura. A number of Shi'ites were killed during the various riots and protests, and hundreds more were arrested. Members of the Shi'ite clergy complained of arbitrary arrests and shootings—particularly about actions by the security services in the village of Diraz. Opposition estimates of those killed by the security services rose to 14, although this figure may well be sharply exaggerated and cannot be confirmed. Some Sunni clerics began to join in the Shi'ite criticism of the government, and one accused the Al Khalifa family of corruption. Some Bahrainis also began to boycott Indian and other Asian markets, some Asians living near poorer Shi'ite villages were beaten, and a few Asians were killed.[81]

The government responded on June 26, 1995 by making the first major changes in the cabinet in 20 years. All ministers resigned, and the Amir dropped five ministers, and brought more Shi'ites into the cabinet. The Development and Industry Minister, Information Minister, Education

Minister, Commerce and Agriculture Minister, and Minister of State for Legal Affairs were replaced. However, the key posts of Defense, Foreign Affairs, Finance and National Economy, Interior, and Transport did not change, and seven posts in the 16 man cabinet continued to be held by the Al Khalifa family.[82] The Prime Minister also announced after the changes in the cabinet that Bahrain's internal and external security would continue to be the nation's first priority, and that the government would continue to deal swiftly and vigorously with any further breakdown in law and order.

The government made more changes in personnel and ministerial realignments during the third quarter of 1995, and the Amir met with many of the clergymen detained in past arrests, including Sheik Abdul Amir al-Jamri.[83] Nevertheless, the violence continued. The death of a 15 year old Shi'ite youth during interrogation in the first week of July led to a short but fierce response from the Shi'ite villagers which led to heavy police action and some shooting. Incidents in late July led to the burning of two liquor stores, and small demonstrations.[84] On November 1, 1995, the government had to take action to prevent "illegal gatherings" after supporters of the opposition assembled at Bani Jamara, following the end of ten day a hunger strike by opposition leaders. Sheik Abdel-Amir al-Jamri had called the strike after claiming that the government had failed to make good on its promises.[85]

New protests over unemployment began in December, 1995 and security forces arrested three men for planting percussion bombs. The security forces fired tear gas at crowds in January, 1996 after the fourth anti-government protest in two weeks. The protest occurred at al-Deeh—about five miles from Manama—after the Islamic Front for the Liberation of Bahrain falsely claimed that a 17 year old boy had been killed in a traffic accident by a member of the Al-Khalifa family.[86]

Further clashes occurred on January 16, 1996, and Sheik Al-Jamri was again arrested at his home. The government arrested a number of other opposition leaders—including Abdul Waha Hussein, Jamil Abdil Wahab, Abdul Amir Abdul Wahab, and a number of others. On January 17, a small bomb exploded in a toilet in the Meridian Hotel. The bomb was timed to explode during an energy conference in the hotel, and marked a significant escalation in attacks affecting foreign businessmen in Bahrain. Another attack struck the Diplomat Hotel. This led some foreign businessmen to cancel trips and others to leave Bahrain.[87]

New riots, protests, and bombing incidents also took place during the festival of Eid al-Fitr at the end of Ramadan. Shi'ite opposition leaders urged their followers to boycott the festival and spend it in support of religious ceremonies The security forces responded by deploying near Shi'ite mosques on February 20, the first day of Eid, and carried out at least 20 arrests in the villages of Karzakan and Malkhiyeh outside Manama. Shi'ites responded by treating the end of the Eid as a day of mourning and holding mass meetings of families of "martyrs." Roads were barricaded, new tire bombs were set off and a branch of the National Bank of Bahrain in Karzakan was set on fire on February 23, 1996. The government responded with new arrests of suspected rebels and Shi'ite religious leaders in villages like Qafool, Jannossan, Dair, Daih, Karzakan, Malkhiyeh, and Jedhafs.

On February 24, a bomb wrecked the car of a top newspaper editor only about 200 yards from the main US Navy base at Juffair, marking the first major incident close to a US military facility. This was the fifth bombing since the beginning of 1996, and came after another car bomb had exploded prematurely on February 14.[88]

In spite of new security crackdowns, violence reached new levels. Fire bombers began to pour gasoline on the floor of some of the targets they attacked. On March 14, 1996, the fire-bombing of an Asian restaurant killed seven Bangladeshis. Bombers started a fire in a Western-patronized sports club in A'ali on March 15, another fire in the four star Baisan Hotel on March 19, and bombed an automobile showroom in Zenji village on March 21. These bombings took place in spite of major security sweeps through Shi'ite areas in Sitra, Sanabis, and Daih. Shi'ites also demonstrated by closing the market in Jadhafs, limiting their spending in Sunni markets, and staging school sit-ins.

The death penalty was then implemented for the first time since 1977. On March 26, 1996. Isa Ahmed Hassan Qamber, a 29 year-old Shi'ite, was shot by firing squad after having led an ambush which killed a Police Sergeant, Ebrahim Rashid Abdul Karmi Al-Saidi. The other members of his group had received prison sentences.

In spite of security efforts to seal off the major Shi'ite areas of unrest, the execution sparked another series of demonstrations and riots.[89] On April 15, the State Security Court sentenced 10 opposition activists to one to five year prison sentences. Another 11 people were imprisoned for taking part in anti-government demonstrations on April 23, and five bombs gutted two stores and damaged five more on May 4.[90]

As has been discussed earlier, Bahrain announced on June 3, 1996 that it had uncovered evidence that Iran was supporting a new conspiracy by hard-line Shi'ite extremists against the government. It reported that it had uncovered an organization known as the military wing of the Bahrain-Hezbollah which had been plotting, "since early 1993 to undermine Bahrain's security" and which, "was planning to overthrow the rule of Bahrain's government by force and establish a pro-Iran rule . . . the movement's main aim is to stage an armed revolution to overthrow the Bahrain government and replace it with a pro-Iranian regime."[91]

The Bahraini government reported that the organization was founded in Qom in 1993, and that the goal was to create an organization of at least 3,000 members. It reported that the Bahrain-Hezbollah was organized into five wings: Military, political, financial, information, and women's. It had a military training committee headed by Adel Al-Shoalah, who escaped arrest; a Financial Committee and Committee of Coordination Affairs head by Ali Ahmad Al-Kazem Abd Ali; a Women's Recruitment Committee; and an Information Committee head by Khalil Sultan, who also escaped arrest. The government found some weapons, and the organization was evidently intending to import more.

Iran denied any support of the Bahrain-Hezbollah, but the Bahraini government announced that it had made 44 arrests in the conspiracy and televised confessions by six of those who had been arrested. These confessions indicated that those arrested had direct contact with Iranian officials, that the suspects had been asked to gather data on the US forces in Bahrain, and several of the conspirators had been trained by pro-Iranian Hezbollah in Lebanon and had been given training in using light, medium, and heavy weapons; in using explosives and bomb-making techniques, and of making bombs . . . We had training on booby traps and explosives." Bahrain's Interior Minister, Mohammed bin Khalifa Khalifa, also announced that many of the detained suspects had been recruited 18 months before riots began in December 1994.[92]

These charges and arrests marked a major new watershed in the tensions between the government and its hard-line Shi'ite opposition. They also indicated that Bahrain was likely to face continuing violence from such opposition and that it would have at least some Iranian support.

The Role of the Government and Social Unrest

Western criticism of Gulf governments often focuses on the role of the ruling families, the lack of democracy, and vague charges of special privilege and "corruption." An examination of Bahrain, however, raises different issues. There is no doubt that Bahrain's ruling elite has special privileges and has a great deal of the nation's wealth, but it is far from clear that "corruption" is any worse in Bahrain than in most Western states, or that concentration of wealth is the primary factor causing political unrest.

The primary causes of unrest in Bahrain are economic problems that are largely the result of external factors like war and changes in world oil prices. Population growth and over-dependence on foreign labor compound these problems, as does the government's over-reliance on paternalism and failure to respond to Shi'ite protests about economic and social discrimination. So does the fact that Bahrain's technocrats and planners have been slow to recognize the need for fundamental economic reforms, changes in education, and efforts to reduce dependence on foreign labor, rather than problems in the structure of Bahrain's government.

Similarly, it has been argued that Bahrain's problems cannot be explained solely in terms of Islamic extremism and/or the actions of radical regimes like Iran. Iran has exploited Bahrain's problems. Most outside observers agree that Iran has provided growing support for Bahrain's extremist opposition movements. At the same time, few feel that Iran has been a primary cause of Bahrain's problems. Since December, 1994, the government has increasingly blamed "a foreign power" for Bahrain's disturbances, but many Western observers feel that the Bahraini government has exaggerated Iran's role in order to use it as a scapegoat. As a result, the government's willingness that to admit the largely domestic nature of the present disturbances may be a key factor shaping its ability to take appropriate action.[93]

It is important to recognize that Bahrain has already made important progress in a number of areas. Key industries like ALBA and ASRY already employ large numbers of Shi'ites, and Bahrain can point to growing progress in Bahrainisation in the hotel and banking industries. Officials like Abdel Nabi al Shoa'la, the Shi'ite Minister of Labor, have stressed the need for Bahrainisation and new job training efforts. They have set a goal of a 5% annual reduction in foreign labor and replacing many of the 130,000 low-paid Asian workers in Bahrain. They have also created programs that call for the creation of 35,000 new jobs for Bahrainis in the next five years, for added vocational training.[94]

At the same time, Bahrain's programs need more emphasis and funding, and some of the fundamental economic, political and social problems of a significant percentage of the population are not being dealt with on the grounds that the government will not negotiate or act under duress from militants. Few Western observers inside or outside of Bahrain agree with the governments unemployment figures. Some estimates suggest that direct unemployment continues to run as high as 30% in some Shi'ite villages, direct unemployment for poorly educated young Shi'ite men is higher, and disguised unemployment may total as high as 45%.[95]

The practical question is whether the government will recognize the true scale of the reforms required and that security measures and repression will create steadily growing mid and long-term problems if major structural reform does not occur and if the government does not act aggressively to coopt moderate members of the Shi'ite opposition into a national effort to deal with Bahrain's problems.

It is also important, however, that Bahrain's neighbors recognize that Bahrain's sectarian and foreign labor problems are another reason it needs more external aid than it has been promised to date. Although the leaders of the other Southern Gulf states have provided considerable political support, they have not yet provided the level of financial support Bahrain needs.[96]

Bahrain's Military Forces

Bahrain's Defense Forces are subordinate to the ruling Amir, Sheik Isa bin Sulman Al Khalifa, and the Prime Minister, Sheik Khalifa bin Sulman Al Khalifa. They are under the command of the Crown Prince, Sheik Hamad bin Isa Al Khalifa. The Minister of Defense is Sheik Khalifa bin Ahmed Al Khalifa. The Chief of Staff is Sheik Abdullah bin Sulman Al Khalifa.

Bahrain's forces have expanded in three major phases since the early 1980s. The first phase comprised planning, construction of military installations, and training of personnel. The second phase involved the purchase of Bahrain's first modern heavy weapons and developing the administrative and management aspects of the military forces. The third phase, which is still underway, is concentrating on the acquisition and absorption of modern military technology.

Bahrain's Military Expenditures

Chart Nine shows that Bahrain has spent about four to eight percent of its GDP on defense, and 10 to 20 percent of its central government expenditures, but the resulting military expenditures are low relative to those of other Gulf states. This is true even if Bahrain's military efforts are compared to those of its smaller neighbors. Qatar has spent about 50 percent more annually on its military forces than Bahrain. Oman—which also has significant economic and military expenditure problems—has spent about five to eight times more than Bahrain.[97]

There are some differences over the exact size of Bahrain's recent military expenditures. ACDA estimates that Bahrain spent $108 million on military forces in 1978, $143 million in 1979, $157 million in 1980, $215 million in 1981, $281 million in 1982, $166 million in 1983, $148 million in 1984, $151 million in 1985, $161 million in 1986, $160 million in 1987, $187 million in 1988, $196 million in 1989, $216 million in 1990, $237 million in 1991, $252 million in 1992, $251 million in 1993, and $256 million in 1993.[98] The IISS has issued slightly different estimates. It estimates that Bahrain's military expenditures were $183 million in 1989, $201.9 million in 1990, $193.9 million in 1991, $237.6 million in 1992, $244.1 million in 1993, and $248.1 million in 1994.[99]

These figures only reflect a limited rise during the Gulf War. Unlike Kuwait and Saudi Arabia, there was little Bahrain could do to expand

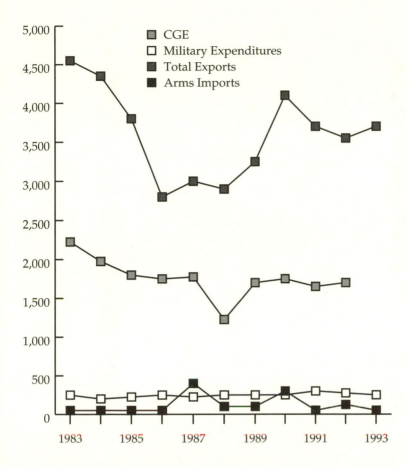

CHART NINE   Bahrain Central Government Expenditures, Military Expenditures, Total Exports, and Arms Import Deliveries: 1983–1993 (Constant $93 Millions). *Source:* Adapted by Anthony H. Cordesman from ACDA, *World Military Expenditures and Arms Transfers, 1993–1994,* ACDA/GPO, Washington, 1995.

its forces in time to respond to the Gulf War. The war did, however, cost Bahrain's economy nearly $2 billion during 1990–1991 because of the collapse of trade and tourism and forced Bahrain to spend over $50 million beyond its defense budget to help UN Coalition forces.[100] The US embassy estimates that Bahrain is currently spending about 18% of its total Central Government Expenditures ($248 million) on military forces and 10% on its Ministry of the Interior, versus about 2% on development.

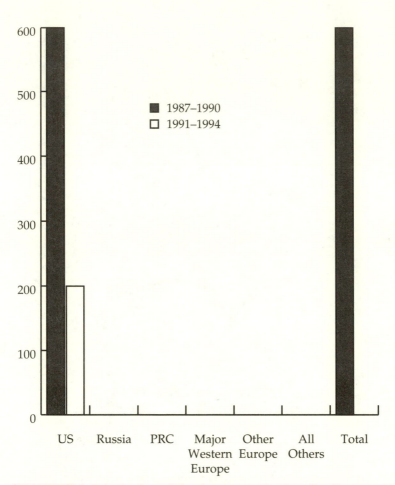

CHART TEN   Bahrain Arms Sales Agreements by Supplier Country: 1987–1994
($Current Millions). *Source:* Adapted by Anthony H. Cordesman from work by
Richard F. Grimmett in *Conventional Arms Transfers to Developing Nations, 1987–
1994,* Congressional Research Service 95-862F, August 4, 1995, pp. 56–57.

Bahrain's Arms Imports

As Table Fifteen shows, Bahrain has made some significant arms orders
since the Gulf War. Nevertheless, it has spent comparatively little compared to other Gulf states. ACDA estimates that Bahrain imported $20
million worth of arms in 1979, $40 million in 1980, $40 million in 1981, $5
million in 1982, $30 million in 1983, $40 million in 1984, $60 million in
1985, $40 million in 1986, $290 million in 1987, $100 million in 1988, $90

TABLE FIFTEEN   Key Bahraini Equipment Developments

- 60 M-60A3s on order from the US
- 25 YPR-765 AIFVs from the Netherlands, and plans to upgrade the engines on its Panhards by the year 2000
- Ordered nine fire units of the US Multiple Launch Rocket System
- Considering the purchase of the Matra Mistral or Hughes Stinger short-range air defense missile
- Improved Hawk battery
- US loan of an FFG-7 frigate—equipped with the Standard air defense missile and Phalanx close-in defense system
- 14 ex-US Army AH-1E Cobra attack helicopters in 1994. According to some reports, it ordered 16 additional AH-1Es in 1995
- Proposing to transfer Bahrain's F-5C/Ds to the US Navy, where they could be used as aggressor aircraft, for 18 F/N or F-16A/B aircraft.
- Seeking the Aim-120 Advanced Medium Range Air-to-Air Missile (AMRAAM), three Sharpshooter target designation systems and LANTIRN

million in 1989, $290 million in 1990, $50 million in 1991, $130 million in 1992, $60 million in 1993, and $80 million in 1994.[101]

Bahrain has long been heavily dependent on the US and Western Europe for arms. ACDA estimates that Bahrain took delivery on $120 million worth of arms during 1979–1983—including $10 million worth of arms from the US, $40 million from France, $40 million from West Germany, $10 million from Italy, and $20 million from other countries.[102] Bahrain took delivery on $505 million worth of arms during 1984–1988. This included $250 million worth of arms from the US, $60 million from France, $2.5 million from the PRC, $5 million from the UK, $180 million from Germany, and $5 million from other countries. ACDA estimates that Bahrain took delivery on $270 million worth of arms during 1992–1994—including $260 million worth of arms from the US, and $10 million from other West European countries.[103]

Data on the cost of Bahrain's more recent arms imports are summarized in Chart Ten, and it is striking that Bahrain has spent less on arms imports during the four years since the Gulf War than it did during the four years before it. Bahrain only purchased $200 million worth of new arms agreements during 1991–1994, all from the US. This total compares with $600 million worth of new arms sales agreements during 1987–1990—the period before the Gulf War. Similarly, Bahrain took delivery on $300 million worth of arms during 1991–1994, the period during and after the Gulf War—virtually all from the US. It took delivery on $800 million worth of arms during 1987–1990.[104]

Reporting by the US Defense Security Assistance Agency shows that Bahrain's annual arms imports from the US have varied sharply by year.

TABLE SIXTEEN   US Foreign Military Sales (FMS), Commercial Arms Export Agreements, Military Assistance Programs (MAP), and International Military Education and Training (IMET) Programs with Bahrain: FY1985–1994 (Current Millions)

	1985	1986	1987	1988	1989	1990	1991	1992	1993	1994
Foreign Military Financing Program										
Payment Waived	—	—	—	—	—	—	0	1.0	0.5	0
DoD Direct	—	—	—	—	—	—	—	—	—	—
DoD Guarantee	—	—	—	—	—	—	—	—	—	—
FMS Agreements	185.3	96.0	361.5	41.1	85.2	90.0	74.3	17.4	102.1	40.0
Commercial Sales	0.7	2.3	3.0	3.1	4.9	2.5	0.7	0.8	—	—
FMS Construction Agreements	—	8.1	3.2	1.7	—	—	—	—	0.6	—
FMS Deliveries	8.5	53.6	162.7	32.1	26.2	254.8	60.1	106.5	72.4	72.1
MAP Program	—	—	—	—	—	—	—	—	—	—
MAP Deliveries	—	—	—	—	—	—	—	—	—	—
MAP Excess Defense Articles Program	—	—	—	—	—	—	—	—	—	—
MAP Excess Defense Articles Deliveries	—	—	—	—	—	—	—	—	—	—
IMET Program/ Deliveries	—	—	—	—	—	—	—	0.1	0.1	0.1

Source: Adapted from US Defense Security Assistance Agency (DSAA), "Foreign Military Sales, Foreign Military Construction Sales and Military Assistance Facts as of September 30, 1994," Department of Defense, Washington, 1995.

They did not surge as a result of the Gulf War, but have risen significantly in the mid-1990s as the result Excess Defense Articles made available through the US FY1995 and FY1996 security assistance programs. Bahrain obtains virtually all of its US equipment through the FMS program and rarely buys commercially. Table Sixteen shows that Bahrain has made little use of foreign military financing and US military construction services. Bahrain has only had limited amounts of International Military Education and Training (IMET) in the past, but this total will increase to $150,000 in FY1997.[105]

US experts believe that the current round of deliveries of equipment will meet Bahrain's major weapons needs through the year 2000, with the exception of a need to phase out its remaining F-5s and replace them with F-16s. They believe Bahrain already faces problems in financing the roughly $43 million annually needed to operate its US-supplied equipment, and that Bahrain should concentrate on training, readiness, sustainment, and maintenance.

Bahrain's Military Forces and Manpower

Bahrain's forces remain small, and Bahrain faces manpower as well as funding problems. In 1995, Bahrain's military forces totaled about 10,700 men, including a number of Pakistanis, Jordanians, and Sudanese.[106] At the same time, Bahrain's total male manpower pool between the ages of 15 and 49 was only about 211,000. The CIA estimated that there were 117,000 males between the ages of 15 and 47 fit for military service. Only 4,346 males reach the age of 15 each year, and become eligible for military service.[107]

The IISS estimates that there are 25,600 males between the ages of 13 and 17, 20,800 between the ages of 18 and 22, and 40,800 between the ages of 23 and 32.[108] Military service is not a popular career, and few native Shi'ites are allowed into the armed forces—at least half of Bahrain's officers, NCOs, and technicians are native. Bahrain is, however, heavily dependent on foreign contract personnel for support.

Chart Eleven shows the trends in Bahrain's military manpower, and Table Seventeen shows how Bahrain's military forces compare to those of the other Gulf states.

The Bahraini Army

In 1996, Bahrain's army had 8,300 to 8,500 men. It was forming an armored brigade with two tank battalions and a reconnaissance battalion, and had a mechanized infantry battalion with two mechanized battalions, and one motorized infantry battalion. Bahrain had a special forces

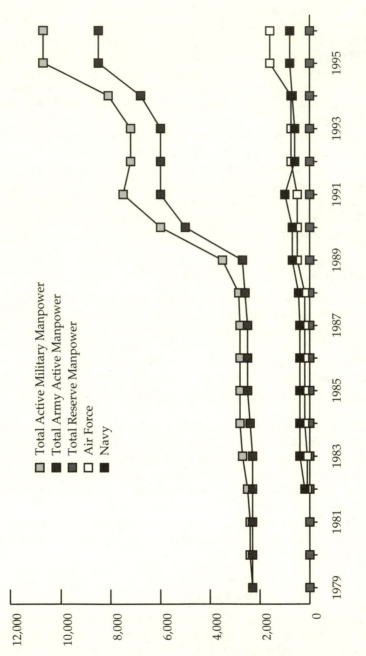

CHART ELEVEN Trends in Bahrain's Military Manpower: 1979–1996. *Source:* Adapted by Anthony H. Cordesman from various editions of the IISS, *Military Balance.*

TABLE SEVENTEEN   Gulf Military Forces in 1996

	Iran	Iraq	Bahrain	Kuwait	Oman	Qatar	Saudi Arabia*	UAE	Yemen
Manpower									
Total Active	320,000	382,500	10,700	16,600	43,500	11,100	161,500	70,000	39,500
Regular	220,000	382,500	10,700	16,600	37,000	11,100	105,500	70,000	39,500
National Guard & Other	100,000	0	0	0	6,500	0	57,000	0	0
Reserve	350,000	650,000	0	23,700	0	0	0	0	40,000
Paramilitary	135,000	24,800	9,250	5,200	4,400	0	15,500	2,700	30,000
Army and Guard									
Manpower	260,000	350,000	8,500	10,000	31,500	8,500	127,000	65,000	37,000
Regular Army Manpower	180,000	350,000	8,500	10,000	25,000	8,500	70,000	65,000	37,000
Reserve	350,000	450,000	0	0	0	0	20,000	0	40,000
Tanks	1,350	2,700	81	220	85	24	910	133	1,125
AIFV/Recce, Lt. Tanks	515	1,600	46	130	136	50	1,467	515	580
APCs	550	2,200	235	199	7	172	3,670	380	560
Self Propelled Artillery	294	150	13	38	6	28	200	90	30
Towed Artillery	2,000	1,500	36	0	96	12	270	82	483
MRLs	890	120	9	0	0	4	60	48	220
Mortars	3,500	2,000+	18	24	74	39	400	101	800
SSM Launchers	46	12	0	0	0	0	10	6	30
Light SAM Launchers	700	3,000	65	48	62	58	650	36	700
AA Guns	1,700	5,500	0	0	18	12	10	62	372
Air Force Manpower	20,000	15,000	1,500	2,500	4,100	800	18,000	3,500	1,000
Air Defense Manpower	15,000	15,000	0	0	0	0	4,000	0	0

(continues)

TABLE SEVENTEEN   (continued)

	Iran	Iraq	Bahrain	Kuwait	Oman	Qatar	Saudi Arabia*	UAE	Yemen
Total Combat Aircraft	295	353	24	76	46	12	295	97	69
Bombers	0	6	0	0	0	0	0	0	0
Fighter/Attack	150	130	12	40	19	11	112	41	27
Fighter/Interceptor	115	180	12	8	0	1	122	22	30
Recce/FGA Recce	8	0	0	0	12	0	10	8	0
AEW C4I/BM	0	1	0	0	0	0	5	0	0
MR/MPA**	6	0	0	0	7	0	0	0	0
OCU/COIN	0	18	0	11	13	0	36	15	0
Combat Trainers	92	200	0	11	22	0	66	35	12
Transport Aircraft**	68	34	3	4	14	5	49	20	19
Tanker Aircraft	4	2	0	0	0	0	16	0	0
Armed Helicopters**	100	120	10	16	0	20	12	42	8
Other Helicopters**	509	350	8	36	37	7	138	42	21
Major SAM Launchers	204	340	12	24	0	0	128	18	87
Light SAM Launchers	60	200	0	12	28	9	249	34	0
AA Guns	0	0	0	12	0	0	420	0	0
Navy Manpower	38,000	2,500	1,000	1,500	4,200	1,800	17,000	1,500	1,500
Major Surface Combatants									
Missile	5	0	3	0	0	0	8	0	0
Other	2	1	0	0	0	0	0	0	0
Patrol Craft									
Missile	10	1	4	2	4	3	9	10	7

(continues)

TABLE SEVENTEEN (continued)

	Iran	Iraq	Bahrain	Kuwait	Oman	Qatar	Saudi Arabia*	UAE	Yemen
Other	26	7	5	12	8	6	20	18	3
Submarines	2	0	0	0	0	0	0	0	0
Mine Vessels	3	4	0	0	0	0	5	0	3
Amphibious Ships	8	0	0	0	2	0	0	0	2
Landing Craft	17	3	4	6	4	1	7	4	2

Notes: Does not include equipment in storage. Air Force totals include all helicopters, and all heavy surface to air missile launchers.

*60,000 reserves are National Guard Tribal Levies. The total for land forces includes active National Guard equipment. These additions total 262 AIFVs, 1,165 APCs, and 70 towed artillery weapons.

**Includes navy, army, national guard, and royal flights, but not paramilitary.

Source: Adapted by Anthony H. Cordesman from International Institute for Strategic Studies *Military Balance* (IISS, London), in this case, the 1995–1996 edition; *Military Technology, World Defense Almanac, 1994–1995*; and Jaffee Center for Strategic Studies, *The Military Balance in the Middle East, 1993–1994* (JCSS, Tel Aviv, 1994).

unit, an artillery brigade with one heavy and three light field artillery battalions and one multiple rocket launcher battery, and two mortar batteries. It also had an air defense battalion with two surface-to-air missile and one air defense gun battery.

Bahrain deployed a small company or battalion-sized element to King Khalid Military City as part of the GCC's Peninsular Shield Force. Bahrain's tank and infantry battalions are the size of regiments in several other Arab countries and total 500 to 1,000 men.[109]

Army Equipment and Support Capability

Bahrain's army has a mix of British, French, and US equipment. The trends in its armored weapons are shown in Chart Twelve. In 1996, Bahrain had 81 M-60A3 tanks, and 22 AML-90 armored infantry fighting vehicles. It has another 48 M-60A3s on order from the US and may receive a total of 60. The order for these new tanks was placed in January, 1995. Bahrain is considering upgrading the engines of its M-60A3s to the new 785 HP version.[110]

Bahrain's other armored vehicles include 10 AT-105 Saxons, 110–115 M-113As and 100–111 Panhard AML-M-3/VTT APCs—plus 20 Ferret, Shorland, and Saladin armored cars in its security forces. Bahrain has ordered 25 YPR-765 AIFV's from the Netherlands, and plans to upgrade the engines on its Panhards by the year 2000. It is also getting M-548A1 tracked cargo carriers as part of the US FY1995 Security Assistance Program.

This mix of different types of other armored vehicles makes it difficult for Bahrain to develop coherent armored tactics and presents support and maintenance problems because of a lack of standardization. Bahrain has also been unable to afford all of the support equipment it needs for mobile armored warfare, including fuel tankers, water tankers, and mobile workshops.[111]

The trends in Bahrain's artillery strength are shown in Chart Thirteen. In 1996, Bahrain had 8 105 mm and 28 M-198 155 mm towed artillery weapons, and 13 used M-110A2 203 mm self-propelled howitzers it acquired from the Netherlands. It also had nine 81 mm mortars, ten 81 mm mortars, 15 BGM-71A TOW and TOW-2 anti-tank guided weapons, 30 106 mm M-40A1 and six 120 mm recoilless rifles, and large numbers of LAWs and other rocket launchers.[112]

Bahrain has recently taken delivery on nine fire units of the US Multiple Launch Rocket System as a force multiplier.[113] The MLRS offers about 16 times as much firepower as a 155 mm gun and has the range to cover most of Bahrain. It also provides Bahrain with considerable firepower in any confrontation with Qatar over the Fasht-e-Dibal and Hawar Islands. Bahrain has also sought the US Army Tactical Missile System (ATACMS),

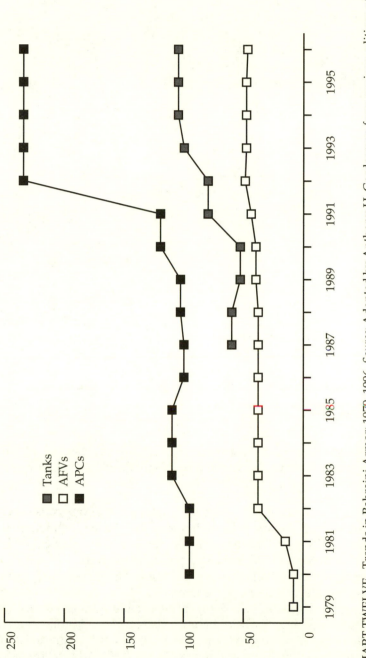

CHART TWELVE Trends in Bahraini Armor: 1979–1996. *Source:* Adapted by Anthony H. Cordesman from various editions of the IISS, *Military Balance.*

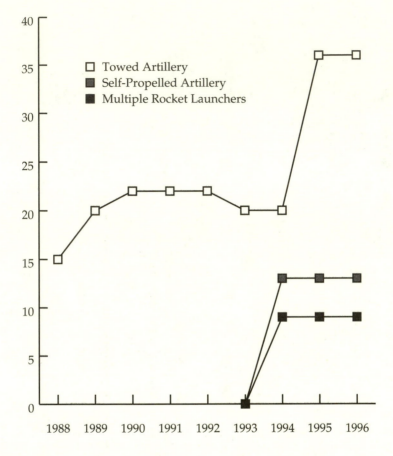

CHART THIRTEEN   Trends in Bahraini Artillery: 1979–1996. *Source:* Adapted by Anthony H. Cordesman from various editions of the IISS, *Military Balance.*

but is unlikely to receive this system for cost reasons and because such an arms transfer might be termed a violation of the Missile Technology Control Regime (MTCR).[114] Bahrain will also receive 25 surplus US 89 howitzers as part of the FY1995 Security Assistance program.

The army operates Bahrain's air defenses. These included approximately 10 Crotale launchers, more than 40 RBS-70 surface-to-air missile fire units (160 missiles), and 18–20 man-portable Stinger surface-to-air missile launchers (400 missiles). Bahrain also had 10–15 radar-guided 35 mm Oerlikon air defense guns, and 10–15 obsolescent, unguided 40 mm anti-aircraft guns.[115] Bahrain will receive 2 AN/TSQ-72 battalion defense systems as part of the FY1995 Security Assistance program.

Bahrain is considering purchases of the Matra Mistral or Hughes Stinger short-range air defense missiles, but it badly needs longer range systems to defend its army and to provide land-based support for the air defense of Bahraini territory. Bahrain needs at least one medium surface-to-air missile battery, and links to an effective command and control system and sensor net like that of Saudi Arabia. Bahrain can only afford such a system, however, if it is paid for out of Saudi or US aid.

The US agreed to provide Bahrain with an Improved Hawk battery with eight launchers in January, 1995.[116] This IHawk battery well be delivered in the second quarter of 1997, as part of the US FY1995 Security Assistance Program. It will help strengthen Bahrain's air defenses, but it may not be adequate for the future because of Bahrain's exposed forward position in the Gulf and need for theater ballistic missile defenses. The ideal solution would be to provide an advanced air defense system like Patriot. The permanent sitting of such a unit would greatly extend the lethality and area coverage of Bahrain's air defenses, and provide a limited ballistic missile defense capability. In fact, the US deployed a Patriot battery to Bahrain in August, 1992, because of rising tension with Iraq. Bahrain cannot afford to buy a system as expensive as Patriot, but has made proposals to lease one and procuring such a system for Bahrain is a key priority for GCC, Saudi or US aid.[117]

Readiness and Warfighting Capability

Bahrain's army is all-volunteer, relatively well paid, has good privileges and housing. It is manned largely by Sunnis and carefully screened foreigners. Nevertheless, it has many qualitative problems. The army has suffered from the loss of a number of Jordanian officers and personnel that served in the army as a result of Jordan's support of Iraq during the Gulf War.[118] Many of its combat elements are still in the process of transition into full combat capability and are dependent on foreign advisors. It also needs better communications and command and control equipment, and better support equipment.

The army is reaching near saturation in equipment and needs to focus on training, sustainment, and maintenance—particularly preventive maintenance. It needs more technical training, to create a strong NCO corps, and improve its interoperability with US forces and other Southern Gulf states. It is gradually developing combined arms and joint warfare capabilities, but needs extensive additional exercise experience. It also needs to supplement the relatively high peacetime reliability and operational readiness of its armor in peacetime garrisons with the ability to keep equipment operational under high tempo warfighting conditions.

The army is capable of suppressing any uprising or coup by any foreseeable radical element in the nation's Shi'ite majority. Bahrain does, however, face serious problems in covering all of its territory with its small land forces and limited firepower. The army also has a number of training, maintenance, support, and logistic problems. It is heavily dependent on foreign technicians, and often lacks the expertise to manage and coordinate its efforts properly.

The Bahraini Navy

Bahrain is slowly building up its naval forces. The Bahraini navy totaled 300 men in early 1988, and about 700 men in early 1996. Its naval forces are based largely in Manama and Mina Sulman, and include 6 combat ships. Bahrain has shown that it can operate the more advanced sensors, weapons systems, and communications gear on its ships, although it is dependent on foreign naval advisors and technical support. Bahrain is also getting considerable support from the US Middle East Force, which uses the island's harbor and wharfage facilities. The US Navy has long had close relations with Bahrain's Navy, relations which have become even closer as a result of the US build-up in the Gulf in 1987–1988, and the Gulf War. Bahrain has excellent commercial shipbuilding and repair capabilities.

Equipment and Support Capabilities

Bahrain's largest operational combat ships are two Al Manama-class Lurssen 62-001 63 meter missile corvettes, commissioned in 1987 and 1988. They displace 632 tons fully loaded, and are armed with two twin MM-40 Exocet missile launchers—the MM-40 is a sea-skimming missile with a maximum range of 70 kilometers (40 miles) at Mach 0.9 and a 165 kilogram warhead. They are also armed with one dual-purpose Oto Melara 76 mm gun, two twin Breda 40 mm guns, two 20 mm guns, and two triple 234 mm torpedo tubes. They can carry a SA-365F helicopter armed with anti-ship missiles, but these are planned and are not yet embarked.[119]

Bahrain also has four Ahamd el Fateh-class Lurssen TNC(FPB)-45 missile fast patrol boats commissioned during 1984–1989. These ships displace 259 tons fully loaded, and are armed with two twin MM-40 Exocets, a 76 mm gun, two twin Breda 40 mm guns, and three 7.62 machine guns.

In January 1995, the US has offered Bahrain the loan of an ex-Oliver Hazard Perry-class FFG-7 frigate—the former *USS Jack Williams*. Some of Bahrain's warfighting problems should be solved in the next few years. The ship is equipped with the Standard air defense missile and Phalanx close-in defense system, and is due to be delivered in September, 1996.[120]

The ship will be loaned to Bahrain as an Excess Defense Article during FY1996. Bahrain will also get 60 Standard missiles as part of the FY1995 Security Assistance Program.

This loan may solve some of Bahrain's naval air defense problems if its navy can obtain the required funds and manpower to make the *Jack Williams* fully operational. The ship has a 200 man crew and requires a major expansion of Bahraini naval manpower. However, Bahraini crews for the *USS Jack Williams* began training in the US in late 1994.[121]

Bahrain's smaller combat ships include two Lurssen FPB-38 (Al Riffa-class) gun boats with twin Breda 40 mm guns and mine launchers, commissioned in 1982. These ships displace 205 tons fully loaded. Other ships and boats include two Al Jarim-class Swift FPB20 fast-attack craft armed with 20 mm guns, and four Ajeera-class 420 ton support ships which are built to a modified LCU design, can carry 200 tons of supplies, and have a bow ramp and 15 ton crane.[122]

Readiness and Warfighting Capabilities

Bahrain's current naval forces are probably adequate to meet current threats, although they could not halt an Iranian amphibious operation without US aid, and Bahrain cannot hope to fund, man, or maintain a naval force that secure Bahrain fully against outside infiltration of arms or military personnel.

The US has offered Bahrain several excess US minesweepers but Bahrain lacked the funds and manpower to take up the US offer.[123] This may be just as well; the surplus US minesweepers are obsolescent and have limited capability against modern types of mines. Bahrain does have a priority for improved maritime surveillance, but this is more for internal security than direct naval operations against a potential threat like Iran or Iraq.

Bahrain's navy also has the same needs to improve its manpower, sustainability, maintenance, and training as its other forces. It now is more a patrol forces than a combat force, and it must operate jointly with Bahrain's air force, other Gulf forces, and/or US and British forces to operate against any significant Iranian or Iraqi threat.

Bahrain has a separate 1,000 man Coast Guard under the Ministry of Interior, with 250 men assigned to seagoing duties. This force is equipped with one 30 meter patrol boat, eight 20 meter patrol boats, 15 small patrol boats, one support craft, one landing craft, one Tiger-class hovercraft, 10 small open fiberglass boats, and eight diver support boats. According to one report, four more US landing craft are on order.[124] This force has a number of British advisors and seems to be effective, but is more a police and customs force than a military force.

The Bahraini Air Force

Bahrain's air force has developed rapidly in recent years. This build up is reflected in Chart Fourteen. Bahrain acquired its first modern combat aircraft—four F-5Es and two F-5Fs—in 1986. Today, Bahrain has a 1,500 man air force with 24 combat aircraft and 10 armed helicopters. It is operating F-16Cs and F-16Ds, and US experts feel that Bahrain's air force has achieved a high standard of performance.

Equipment and Support Capabilities

In 1996, Bahrain's main combat aircraft consisted of eight F-16C and four F-16Ds that it had purchased in 1990, plus eight F-5Es and four F-5Fs.[125] Bahrain also had 10 AB-212 helicopters, armed with SS-12 missiles, machine guns, and rockets. Its transport aircraft included 4 Bo-105 helicopters, one S-70A, and one UH-60L(VIP) helicopter. Two C-130s were in the process of delivery as US excess defense equipment. Two to three of its AB-212s were equipped with Bendix 1400 long range maritime radars. Bahrain had one B-727, one Gulfstream II, and one Gulfstream III in its Amiri Flight.

Bahrain ordered its F-16s from the US in January, 1987 and June, 1988. It did so as part of a $400 million arms package that included a total of 16 F-16C/D fighters, Sidewinder air-to-air missiles, AGM-65 Maverick air-to-surface missiles, AN/A LE-40 chaff dispensers, and spares, support, and training. It also bought an AN/ALQ-131 electronic countermeasure pod.

After the Gulf War, Bahrain considered ordering 8–12 Apache AH-64A attack helicopters, and 500 Hellfire missiles from the US. The AH-64 had important advantages for Bahrain because the AH-64 offered excellent firepower against any small amphibious ships or light armored attacks, could be rapidly dispersed, and could operate off of Bahrain's smaller islands. Cost was a major consideration, however, and Bahrain decided to order 14 ex-US Army AH-1E Cobra attack helicopters in 1994. It obtained six AH-1P Cobras in 1995 as US Security Assistance, and 10 AH-1Es in 1996.[126] These deliveries will eventually give Bahrain a total of 24 Cobras plus 6 surplus training Cobras to use as wartime spares.

These developments will give Bahrain a total force of 12 F-5s, 16 F-16s, and 14–30 AH-1Es by the late 1990s. This is, however, a limited air force for the Southern Gulf state which is most exposed to Iranian and Iraqi air and sea power.

Bahrain's air force sorely needs to replace its F-5s and convert to an all F-16 force. The F-5 is aging and Bahrain cannot afford to maintain two different types of fighters, particularly since the maintenance burden imposed by its aging, limited performance F-5s now equals or surpasses

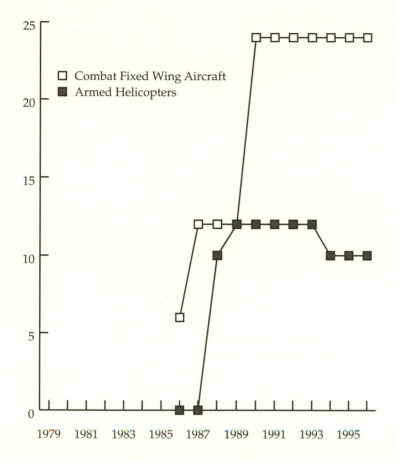

CHART FOURTEEN   Trends in Bahraini Combat Air Strength: 1979–1996.
Source: Adapted by Anthony H. Cordesman from various editions of the IISS,
Military Balance.

that of an F-16. Such a conversion is necessary if Bahrain is to make cost-
effective use of its pilots and support facilities, and to provide effective air
defense and attack capabilities. The F-5E/F simply is not advanced
enough to meet the threat posed by Iran or Iraq's most advanced French
and Soviet-supplied fighters.

Bahrain is currently seeking more F-16s, and is considering a swap
that would transfer Bahrain's F-5C/Ds to the US Navy, where they
could be used as aggressor aircraft. One option would give Bahrain 18
F-16N aggressor aircraft that the US Navy used to imitate the tactics

and air-to-air combat techniques of Warsaw Pact pilots. A cheaper alternative would give Bahrain a no-cost lease of USAF F-16A/B aircraft, along lines similar to the no-cost lease package that the US has given Jordan. Both the F-16Ns and F-16A/Bs would need substantial upgrading. The F-16s would need improved avionics, radars, and wing components, and would present support problems. Only 14 of the 18 aircraft could be made operational because a different support line would be required from the USAF support provided to Bahrain's existing F-16C/Ds, and four of the F-16Ns would have to be held in reserve as spares.[127] British Aerospace has also proposed the sale of Hawk 100 trainer-light attack aircraft to Bahrain, but Bahrain has not taken action on this proposal.

Bahrain is seeking the Aim-120 Advanced Medium Range Air-to-Air Missile (AMRAAM) to improve its beyond-visual-range air combat capabilities, and the Three Sharpshooter target designation system and Low Altitude Navigation and Targeting Infrared (LANTIRN) system to improve its attack capabilities. Release of the AMRAAM is still being evaluated, but Bahrain is already scheduled to receive laser guided bomb pods for its F-16s which have many of the features of the export version of these pods. Both AMRAAM and the laser guided bomb pods and LANTIRN are important force multipliers, and could help Bahrain compensate for its lack of aircraft numbers.[128]

Most of Bahrain's aircraft are based at Sheik Isa Air Base—a large modern air base on the main island which is currently being expanded and modernized, and which is being equipped to allow joint operations by the Bahraini Air Force and US power projection forces.

Bahrain's command and control system has been improved by the creation of a modern underground operations center at Sheik Isa Air Base. Bahrain has Cossor SSR and Plessey Watchman air traffic control radars, and Bahrain now seems to have secure digital, voice and Teletype links to Saudi Arabia and US ships. This system is not, however, adequate to deal with either Bahrain's air defense or maritime surveillance needs

Bahrain will only have adequate warning of an Iranian or Iraqi attack, however, if it receives information from an airborne warning and air control platform like the US or Saudi AWACS, and if it is fully integrated into Saudi Arabia's air defense system. There are plans to provide for such integration as part of the Saudi Demon-I and Demon-II air C4I/BM improvement programs and Al Yamamah II program. Both Hughes and Ferranti have made proposals for such integration, and it would provide a major improvement in regional air defense capability, and US air reinforcement capability, particularly if the Saudi-Bahrain system was integrated with that of Kuwait and the UAE.

Readiness and Warfighting Capability

Bahrain's air force has trained good native pilots and has impressed US experts with its proficiency. Bahrain has also shown that it has sound modernization plans and can effectively operate advanced fighter aircraft, although the operation of Bahrain's combat aircraft is dependent on foreign technical support. Bahrain's readiness is limited, however, by its need for funds or aid to standardize on the F-16. Bahrain can only generate low fixed and rotary-wing sortie rates and is only beginning to acquire the capability to support complex air operations with the reaction times and precision required.

Like the army, Bahrain's air force needs to focus on training, sustainment, and maintenance—particularly preventive maintenance. It needs more technical training, to create a strong NCO corps, and improve its interoperability with US forces and other Southern Gulf states. It is gradually developing combined arms and joint warfare capabilities, but needs extensive additional exercise experience. It also needs to supplement the relatively high peacetime reliability and operational peacetime readiness of its aircraft with the ability to fly higher fighter and helicopter sortie rates under high tempo warfighting conditions.

More broadly, Bahrain's war fighting capability is limited by the fact that it cannot deal with an Iranian or Iraqi threat except as part of a force that includes US and/or Saudi C⁴I/BM support and combat aircraft. Bahrain is too small and too close to large potential threats to fight alone, and would confront massive diseconomies of scale it tried to do so. Bahrain's air force is doing what it can, but its success will be dependent on the support of allies and progress in collective defense.

Bahrain's Internal Security Forces

The Ministry of Interior is responsible for public security, and its Public Security Force (police) and Security and Intelligence Services (SIS) are responsible for maintaining internal order. The Bahrain Defense Force (BDF) defends against external military threats, and did not play an active role in internal security. It made itself available to deploy in support security mission in late 1995, and it has held cooperative exercises with Saudi forces designed to demonstrate that it could count on Saudi support.

Bahrain has significantly improved the effectiveness of its internal security forces since the Shi'ite-Iranian coup attempt in December, 1981. Bahrain has quietly consulted with both Britain and the United States regarding both internal security assistance and defense against Iran, and discussed contingency plans for Saudi military assistance. The army, police, and special forces will undoubtedly support the Ruling Family in a civil disorder, particularly if it is Shi'ite. In addition, Bahrain could call upon Saudi forces in the event of a major coup attempt or civil crisis.

Bahrain has recently improved some aspects of its treatment of its Shi'ite majority, its controls over foreign labor, and the quality of its surveillance over radical elements. At the same time, the need to deal with Shi'ite unrest has led to steadily harsher measures since 1994, and has created growing resentment of the security forces, the government, and the Al Khalifa family.

The Public Security Force

The Public Security Force numbers some 11,000 personnel and comes under the Ministry of the Interior.[129] This force appears large, but over 1,000 are assigned to the Coast Guard, and another 4,000 are assigned to tasks like providing guards for commercial premises, banks, embassies, and schools. Bahrain has no private security guards. The Security and Intelligence Services (SIS) have a British director—Ian Henderson—and British and Pakistani advisors in technical areas. It has a large Pakistani and Indian component and is armed with light weaponry and has three Bell 412 and helicopters. The Public Security Force is supported by elite security, counter-terrorist, and intelligence units. The manpower in these forces is heavily Sunni or foreign, but includes a number of Shi'ites.[130]

The Public Security Force controls virtually all public activity and the criminal justice system is administered in ways that favor internal security.[131] The efforts of the internal security forces are reinforced by other government activity. The Ministry of the Interior controls the Office of the Public Prosecutor which has broad powers to investigate and arrest as part of "investigatory detention". The State Security Act of 1974 allows detention without trial for periods of up to three years—sometimes in Al-Jaw (Qala'a) Security Prison—and those arrested may be tried in a special Security Court. Until recently, however, such detentions and trials have been limited and have generally dealt with Bahrainis with close links to Iran.

In the past, the government has preferred to exile citizens or offer amnesty in return for political cooperation. About 150–250 Bahrainis now live in exile. Some of these exiles are legitimate peaceful opponents of the regime, but others are organized into groups like the Committee for the Defense of Human Rights, the Bahrain Freedom Movement, the Bahrain Human Rights Organization. These groups claim to be human rights or liberal political organizations but seem to be Shi'ite religious groups that are largely fundamentalist in character. According to Bahraini government sources, they may receive funds from Iran, Islamist extremists, and other radical sources.

Rising Internal Violence

As is the case with all of the Southern Gulf states, there is a sharp difference of view between the Bahraini government and the human rights experts in the US State Department over the extent to which Bahrain's security forces have or have not created human rights problems. The US State Department reports that the security forces have become increasingly repressive in dealing with protests, individuals who speak out against the government, and such movements in response to the escalating violence of Shi'ite protests and bombings. Since mid-1995, there have been reports of some killings during the suppression of riots and arrests, and reports of deaths and torture of those held in confinement. It is not possible, however, to verify such reports.[132]

The State Department reports that the security forces have used tear gas, rubber bullets, and occasionally, live ammunition on dozens of occasions to disperse various gatherings. It indicates that protesters involved called for the re-establishment of an elected parliament and the release of prisoners; objected to Al-Khalifa rule; denounced police brutality; protested over foreigners in the security forces and in the labor force; and demanded increased employment opportunities. After each of these incidents, suspected leaders and active participants were arrested, generally for participating in or inciting violence.

The State Department also reports that police and security forces killed seven demonstrators while trying to control arson attacks and other civil disturbances during the first half of 1995. In one case, the police may have beaten a boy to death. Four of the deaths occurred when police used force on crowds of antigovernment demonstrators. On January 12, an unidentified man was killed in the village of Diraz after police opened fire on demonstrators. On January 26, Hani Ali Al-Safi was shot and killed during a similar confrontation with police in the village of Sitra. Also on January 26, Abdul Ridha Mansur Al-Hajji died of injuries sustained 10 days earlier in a demonstration that was broken up by police in the village of Bani Jamrah.[133]

An unidentified man was shot and killed by security forces during another demonstration in Bani Jamrah on April 1. On May 4, Nidal Habib Al-Nashabah reportedly was shot and killed by security forces during a demonstration in Diraz. On May 24, a 10-year-old boy, Muhammad Shihab Al-Fardan, from the village of Karzakkan, died under suspicious circumstances. Opposition press releases claim that the boy was arrested, tortured, and killed by security forces. The government, however, stated publicly that the boy died after falling from a building that was under construction. On July 9, a 15-year-old boy died in police custody reportedly after being beaten during interrogation at the police station in the village of Khamis.

The State Department estimates that approximately 2,700 people had been arrested, and 2,000 people were being held in detention at the end of 1995. An estimated 261 people remained in detention at the end of 1995, and that no police or security forces officials have been prosecuted for any offenses against demonstrators or the opposition.[134]

These are important issues, but many of the charges in the State Department's human rights report are taken from reports by hard-line opponents of the government, and are not verified independently by the State Department. The actions of Bahrain's security forces must also be put in the context of the extremism and violence the security forces have had to deal with. The same US State Department reporting that describes repressive actions by the security forces also reports that domestic unrest by Shi'ite Muslim youths involved hundreds of acts of arson during the first half of 1995, and resulted in the deaths of 11 people, including 7 demonstrators, 2 policemen, and 2 expatriate laborers. If the State Department is correct, this may have led to the arrest of more than 2,700 people during that period, almost all for committing acts of violence.

Two police officers were killed by demonstrators in 1995. On March 22, Ibrahim Rashid Abdul Karim Al-Saidi was murdered by a group of protesters near his home in the village of Nuwaidrat. A second policeman was killed in the village of Sitra in April when demonstrators threw a Molotov cocktail into his vehicle. Two expatriate laborers were killed after being trapped in buildings that had been set ablaze by demonstrators.[135]

The activities that led to detention, questioning, warning, or arrest have often included such minor actions as painting anti-regime slogans on walls; joining antigovernment demonstrations; possessing or circulating anti-regime writings; preaching sermons with a distinct anti-regime political tone; and harboring or associating with persons committing more serious acts. In many cases, such suspects were released with a warning.

Under proceedings used by the Criminal Court, police may detain a suspect for up to 7 days of questioning before filing charges.[136] However, most of those who were detained for more than a few days were held for committing illegal or violent acts like skirmishing with police, breaking windows, damaging cars or other property, burning electrical substations, tires, cars, palm groves, banks, stores, schools, sports clubs, furniture, and auto showrooms.[137]

Even in these cases, only a few of those who have been arrested have faced serious penalties. In keeping with tradition, the Government released 175 prisoners by Amiri decree on the March Eid Al-Fitr holiday, including several self-described political detainees. Another 2,000 were released during the course of the year. By the end of 1995, only 50 Bahrainis had been tried in the Security Court; fewer than 750 were tried in criminal courts, and the remainder were released without charge.

Security and Religion

Until recently, the Bahraini government has not reacted by suppressing religious activity as distinguished from suppressing active opposition and demonstrations. The US State Department reports that Sunni and Shi'ite sects have been subject to governmental control and monitoring, but there was no interference with routine worship, preaching, religious courts, Islamic charitable foundations, mosque construction, religious education, or other religious activities.[138]

Public religious events, including the large annual marches by Bahraini Shi'ite, are permitted—although they are closely watched by the police. There were no restrictions on the number of Bahrainis permitted to make pilgrimages to Shi'ite shrines and holy sites in Iran, Iraq, and Syria, although very few Bahrainis made pilgrimages to Iraq. Religious study in and pilgrimages to Iran were strongly discouraged, and the government monitored travel to Iran and scrutinized those who pursued religious study there. However, travel to Iran for pilgrimages, business trips, tourism, and family visits was common.[139]

On April 24, 1996, however, the Amir decreed that an Islamic High Council would be set up to screen preachers in the mosques and issue rulings on religious issues. The measure was not specifically targeted against the Shi'ite opposition, but it was clear that the government intended to exert much closer control over any religious activity with political content.[140]

The government also faces a conflict between the conservatism of its more extreme Shi'ite opposition and its need to create a modern and diversified economy. Conservative Shi'ites and some conservative Sunnis object to the government's efforts to achieve economic diversification by actively pursuing the development of tourism. They claim that the social impact of the facilities required to attract tourism and serve tourists—such as hotels, night clubs, billboards, and video stores—is seriously eroding the cultural, religious and scholarly traditions of Bahraini society.

According to Western observers in Bahrain, this feeling is reflected in the response of some young Bahrainis who refuse to take employment in such establishments, and the "torching" of video shops during the recent demonstrations is a violent manifestation of such resentment towards the impact of foreign movies on public morality. Bahrain's long and well respected history as a center of religious thought, scholarship and writing is in direct contrast to the new openness and permissiveness that is daily thrust in front of society.

This conservative resentment includes the spreading use of satellite TV, particularly the music channels and the uncensored movies which go far beyond acceptable norms of public viewing in Bahrain. The fact that the TV programs are available 24 hours a day is also resented as "destroying young minds," "wasting time," and failing to leave time for piety or prayer. There are complaints that Bahrainis are subject to criticism when they visit other Gulf states.

Secularization is a major area of concern for both conservative Sunni and Shi'ite religious leaders in Bahrain and is frequently the subject of their sermons. Such religious figures feel that Bahrain is being bombarded with Western custom which are seeping insidiously into Bahrain's Islamic culture and destroying it from within. They also make charges that there is wide-spread corruption at all levels of government

Bahrain has a long history of tolerance, and the importance of such views should not be exaggerated. At the same time, some Western experts living in Bahrain do feel that the criticisms of such religious conservatives, fundamentalists and extremists reflect the fears of a significant number of Bahraini who are afraid of where their nation is headed and who question the value of what Bahrain's society will provide for the children of the next generation.

One observer with long experience in Bahrain puts it this way:

> For them, such values are fundamental but not fundamentalism. They simply consider rapid secularism to be too high a price to pay for economic diversification. This is the growing concern in Bahrain today as a society grapples with the socio-economics changes being pressed upon them by their political leaders. It seems to force upon society the need to isolate themselves from the national leadership and increased their resentment in their inability to control or influence the society in which they live. When added to poverty and discrimination, the social contract between the government and the governed becomes increasingly fragile. Perhaps herein lie the real roots of Islamic fundamentalism.

The Impact of the Security Forces

The net result of all these internal security actions is unclear. In spite of steadily tighter controls, violence has tended to escalate from small "tire bombs" in unpopulated areas, and scattered acts of sabotage and arson, to attacks on Asians, more important facilities, and Westerners and officials. Being arrested has become something of a status symbol for younger

Shi'ites and a significant number of Shi'ites now feel that the government will not respond effectively to their demands without active dissent or violence. The Islamic rhetoric of Shi'ite dissenters has become more extreme, and some younger Shi'ites have begun to talk of "martyrdom." Repression without cooption and reform rarely does more than drive violence and dissent inwards and towards more extremist action.

Further, opposition groups—particularly opposition groups based abroad in Damascus, Beirut and London—have stepped up their political attacks on the security forces. They have sharply protested the role of British advisors in the government, and the security services. They charge that these officers were opponents of increased democracy, provided leadership in the operation of the security services, and participated in human rights violations. These allegations have sometimes focused on Ian Henderson, because of his role as Chief of the SIS. US experts who monitor the political and human rights situation in Bahrain believe these charges are exaggerated, and that Henderson has played a role in moderating the actions of the security services and limiting any use of the armed forces.

The Role of the Courts and the Rule of Law

Like other Gulf countries, Bahrain's civil legal system does not provide the same protection of individual rights as is common in Western countries. This has not led to extensive abuses of the rule of law in the past because Bahrain has preferred to coopt or exile opponents. In recent years, however, Bahrain has often held political prisoners incommunicado and/or in detention. It has made increasing use of its Special Security Court, and the State Security Act of 1974. This law allows prisoners held for security reasons to be held for up to three years without trial. The act is so broadly defined that the public prosecutor can hold virtually anyone in detention for such reasons.

The Security Court is composed of the Supreme Court of Appeals, but trials held by the Security Court are different from the normal proceedings of civil trials and often are not public. A number of reports indicate that the government intervenes directly in such trial procedures. At least several hundred persons have been arrested and held for security reasons since 1994 under conditions which bring them under the potential jurisdiction of the Security Court, but only a limited portion seem to have had their cases subject to any kind of review.

The government has also used the courts, exile, and revocation of citizenship for internal security purposes. The Ministry of Interior controls the Office of the Public Prosecutor, whose officers initially determine whether sufficient evidence exists to continue to hold a prisoner in investigatory detention. In the early stages of detention, prisoners and their attorneys have no recourse to any authority outside the Ministry of Interior.

The government uses exile and the revocation of citizenship to punish individuals suspected of, or convicted of, anti-regime activity. The State Department reports that four deportations took place in 1995. The Government deported Sheik Ali Salman Ahmed Salman, Sheik Hamza Al-Sitri and Sheik Haydar Al-Sitri to the United Arab Emirates on January 15. They traveled onward to London the next day. Sheik Adel Al-Sho'ala was deported on January 18. He is believed to be in Damascus. The Government reportedly deported these four clerics because they instigated an attack on a charity marathon in November 1994 in which several participants were beaten and stoned, and because they encouraged anti-government rioting. According to the émigré groups, as many as 500 Bahrainis continue to live in exile. This figure includes both those prohibited from returning to Bahrain and their family members who voluntarily live abroad with them.[141]

Once again, such actions must be kept in perspective. The government has had constant provocation and is dealing with very real security problems. It has been careful to avoid sweeping abuses of its powers, it has often restricted arrests to house arrest and the Amir has often pardoned those brought up on security charges. Nevertheless, such a use of the rule of law is a double-edged sword. It allows the opposition to charge that all uses of the legal system for security purposes are repressive and illegitimate, and to broaden its attacks on the government. It also inevitably means that there are cases of real repression that can be used for propaganda purposes inside and outside the country. Like the other Southern Gulf states, Bahrain needs to adopt a more open and credible rule of law and one where security cases do not become a mid or long-term embarrassment to the government. This does not mean copying the West, but it does mean change.

The Ministry of Information and the Ministry of Labor and Social Affairs

The Ministry of Information plays a major internal security role by controlling the local media, and exercising informal censorship over all domestic media. It controls imports of foreign media, and sometimes prevents foreign critics from entering the country. Bahrain does not, however, restrict access to foreign TV broadcasts or limit all criticism. Academic debate is allowed as long as the legitimacy of the regime or government is not directly challenged. There are some indications, however, that the Ministry of Information failed to exercise proper control over the handling of information during the recent demonstrations, and that this led to the replacement of the Minister of the Information in the June, 1995 reshuffling of the cabinet.[142]

The Ministry of Labor and Social Affairs supervises foreign labor. Foreign laborers are not permitted to engage in political activity or strikes, and disputes tend to be resolved in favor of Bahrainis. The government has tried to limit the abuse of foreign laborers and maintain a reasonable minimum wage, but working conditions are often poor and unskilled laborers often go without pay for long periods.

No labor unions are permitted as such. All legal worker representation is part of the trade-oriented Joint Labor-Management Consultative Committees. The labor members of these councils elect the 11 members of a General Committee of Bahraini workers. Committees have been set up in a total of 16 major companies with a total of around 19,500 employees, These organizations represent about 70% of Bahrain's indigenous workers. Major strikes do not occur, but intensive negotiations take place and small strikes and walk outs are permitted and often result in wage increases.

The government also controls passports and exit visas through the Directorate of Immigration, under the authority of the Ministry of the Interior. About five percent of the indigenous population—largely of Shi'ite Arab and Persian origin—have been denied passports and external travel privileges. It conducts security checks at Bahrain's airports and harbors, and sometimes arrests Bahrainis and other potential security risks as they transit through immigration.

Strategic Interests

Bahrain plays an important strategic role in the Gulf, and is an important Western strategic asset in preserving stability in the Gulf and the security of the world's oil imports. It allows the US use of its airfields and ports, and permits the US to maintain a small headquarters and some prepositioned stocks. Its military forces are relatively small, but their capabilities are expanding steadily, and Bahrain's geographic position makes it critical to any attempt to develop collective regional efforts aimed at setting up air defense, missile defense, and maritime defense systems.

Bahrain's Role in Western Power Projection

Bahrain furnished extensive naval and air facilities to the US and Britain during the Gulf War. In September, 1990, Bahrain accepted US F/A-18, A-6, EA-6 and AV-8B air units, and British Tornado units, and provided fuel for US and British land, naval, and air forces during both "Desert Shield" and "Desert Storm."

Bahrain's air force was relatively new and just absorbing deliveries of F-16s. Nevertheless, the Bahrain Air Force flew a total of 266 combat sorties. It used its new F-16s to fly 166 defensive and offensive counter-air sorties, averaging 4–6 sorties per day. It used its F-5s to fly 122 interdiction sorties, averaging about 3–4 sorties per day. It attacked targets like radar sites, Silkworm sites and artillery positions. Bahrain also contributed a 200-man infantry company to Joint Forces Command (East) in support of the Coalition during Desert Storm and the liberation of Kuwait.[143] Bahrain deployed a squadron of fighter aircraft to Kuwait when Iraqi forces moved towards the Kuwaiti border in October, 1994.[144]

On October 22, 1991, Bahrain signed a ten year bilateral agreement, expanding the US military presence in Bahrain. The agreement allowed the US to increase its prepositioning in Bahrain, called for more joint exercises and training, allowed the US to set up a JTME (USCENTCOM headquarters), and increased US access to Bahraini ports and airfields. On July 1, 1995, Bahrain agreed to allow the US to create the headquarters for its new 5th Fleet in Bahrain, with an Admiral, a headquarters contingent, and roughly 1,500 US military personnel and dependents based in Bahrain. This agreement also expanded the area available for US use from 10 acres of administrative buildings to 23.[145]

The importance of these steps has been demonstrated four times since the Gulf War Bahraini and US cooperation has had three tangible effects since the Gulf War:

- Bahrain supported the US in October, 1994, when Iraq moved two Republican Guard divisions and three additional divisions to positions near its border with Kuwait. The US had to rush in additional forces to the Gulf, beginning on October 9, to supplement the 13,000 US personnel already in the theater. These forces initially included the 18,000 men in the 1st Marine Expeditionary Force, 16,000 troops from the US army 24th Infantry Division, 306 fixed wing aircraft (including A-10s, F-16s, RF-4Cs, F-15Es, F-15Cs, F-111s, EF-111s, F-117s, JSTARS, F/A-18s, B-52s, and E-3As, 58 helicopters (including 54 AH-64s), two batteries of Patriot missiles, and a carrier battle group. The US also decided to deploy another 73 fixed wing combat aircraft. Bahrain served a critical naval and air staging point during this build up.
- Bahrain supported the US in its build-up in the Gulf in late August, 1995, when there were indications that Iraq might again be deploying forces to invade Kuwait. It deployed a total of 12 prepositioning ships from Diego Garcia and other locations to the Gulf, with enough armor, artillery, food, fuel, water, vehicles, and other equipment to sustain a 16,500 Marine Corps MEF (Forward), and a 15,000–17,000 man US Army Corps in combat.[146]

- In October, 1995, Bahrain allowed the US to base 18 USAF F-16 fighter jets in Bahrain to make up for the "gap" created in the US presence in the Gulf when the US had to rotate one carrier out of the Gulf without immediately replacing it with another.[147] According to one report, the US and Bahrain are also discussing allowing the US to preposition equipment for one US Army brigade and additional USAF equipment. The pact also calls for the US to "consult" Bahrain if its security is threatened.
- Bahrain and the US cooperated again in January 1996, when US intelligence concluded that Iraq had brought five armored divisions to sufficient readiness to deploy to Kuwait with only five hours notice. The US deployed 12 prepositioning ships—enough to equip a Marine Division and a US Army Brigade—into the Gulf. The US did not send troops, but this move allowed the US to deploy up to 20,000 troops on short notice, and the US deployed additional combat aircraft and ships to Bahrain and Kuwait.[148]

In spite of Bahrain's limited resources, Bahrain relies heavily on US combat equipment, and Bahraini land and air forces are largely interoperable with US forces. Between FY1950 and FY1990, it purchased $874.8 million worth of US Foreign Military Sales (FMS), and took delivery on $545.2 million worth.[149] Since the Gulf War, it has purchased $197.9 million worth of US Foreign Military Sales (FMS), and taken delivery on $239.6 million worth.[150]

Bahrain receives about $200,000-$400,000 a year worth of IMET military training assistance from the US.[151] Bahrain cannot, however, finance the level of military modernization it needs and would greatly benefit from added military aid—much of which might be accomplished through the transfer of excess US defense articles or Saudi funding of the Bahraini portion of GCC and other southern Gulf collective security efforts.

Cooperation with Other Southern Gulf States

Bahrain recognizes that it cannot obtain security against the potential threats from Iran and Iraq without aid from its Southern Gulf neighbors. It is a strong supporter of the Gulf Cooperation Council and works closely with Saudi Arabia. It recognizes the benefits of collective efforts to improve southern Gulf air defense, maritime defense, and rapid reaction efforts.

One key problem limiting Bahrain's collective security efforts is its dispute with Qatar. Bahrain needs diplomatic help and good offices in resolving this dispute. At the same time, this dispute is only part of the issue. The Gulf Cooperation Council has rarely been able to transform good intentions into substantive progress in creating regional military capabilities. At the same time, Bahrain, Kuwait, Saudi Arabia, and the US have only begun to create fully interoperable military capabilities in the Upper Gulf.

Some of the most critical aspects of Bahrain's security will thus be dependent on whether Bahrain's neighbors recognize the need to move forward by:

- Creating an effective planning system for collective defense, and truly standardized and/or interoperable forces.
- Integrating its C^{4}I and sensor nets for air and naval combat, including beyond-visual-range and night warfare.
- Focusing on deploying its forces to support the joint land defense of the Kuwaiti/Northwestern Saudi borders and reinforcing other Gulf states like Oman in the event of any Iranian amphibious or air borne action.
- Creating joint air defense and air attack capabilities.
- Creating joint air and naval strike forces.
- Establishing effective cross reinforcement and tactical mobility capabilities.
- Preparing fully for outside or over-the-horizon reinforcement by the US and other Western powers.
- Setting up joint training, support, and infrastructure facilities.
- Creating common advanced training systems that develop a brigade and wing-level capability for combined arms and joint warfare, and which can support realistic field training exercises of the kind practiced by US and Israeli forces.
- Improving its capability to provide urban and urban area security and to fight unconventional warfare and low intensity combat.

Bahrain's movement towards standardization on US equipment is improving its interoperability and standardization, and with Kuwaiti and Saudi forces as well as with US forces. Its future military progress, however, will depend heavily on the extent to which Bahrain can move forward in procuring interoperable and/or standardized equipment to provide the capability to perform the following missions:

- Heavy armor, artillery, attack helicopters, and mobile air defense equipment for defense of upper Gulf.
- Interoperability and standardization with US power projection forces.
- Interoperable offensive air capability with stand-off, all-weather precision weapons and anti-armor/anti-ship capability.

- Interoperable air defense equipment, including heavy surface-to-air missiles, beyond-visual-range/all-weather fighters, AEW & surveillance capability, ARM & ECM capability. (Growth to ATBM and cruise missile defense capability)
- Maritime surveillance systems, and equipment for defense against maritime surveillance, and unconventional warfare.
- Mine detection and clearing systems.
- Improved urban, area, and border security equipment for unconventional warfare and low intensity conflict.
- Advanced training aids.
- Support and sustainment equipment.

At the same time, Bahrain must be careful to avoid the mistakes of most other Southern Gulf states, and much of its overall capability to rationalize its forces will be limited by the failure of its neighbors to rationalize their military procurements and eliminate the waste of funds on:

- Unique equipment types and one-of-a-kind modifications.
- "Glitter factor" weapons; "developmental equipment and technology.
- Non-interoperable weapons and systems.
- Submarines and ASW systems.
- Major surface warfare ships.
- Major equipment for divided or "dual" forces.
- New types of equipment which increase the maintenance, sustainability, and training problem, or layer new types over old.

Internal Development and Internal Security

The most serious strategic challenge Bahrain faces is not overt external threats, but rather the need to come to grips with its internal economic and social problems, and with the risk that Iran and possibly Iraq will exploit Bahrain's internal divisions.

Bahrain's highest priority is to carry out the internal reforms necessary to give it lasting stability. Unless Bahrain makes substantial changes in its labor policies or receives significant levels of external economic aid, it will find it very difficult to reform its economy, rapidly reduce its dependence on foreign labor, and slowly coopt its Shi'ite majority into a more stable society. It is clear, however, that Bahrain's government must be perceived as making every possible effort to achieve rapid economic and social reform. It must also be perceived as making a steady increase in the number of Shi'ite officials, actively trying to increase Shi'ite jobs and wealth, and reducing corruption, nepotism, and favoritism.

These reforms have been discussed earlier, and include efforts to:

- Rigorously enforce legislation like the Labor Law for the Private Sector (Decree Number 23 for 1976), and regulations limiting and controlling foreign visas. Accelerate its efforts to reduce the number of foreign workers, with priority for reductions in servants and in trades that allow the most rapid conversion to native labor.
- Eliminate economic disincentives for employers in hiring native labor, and create new disincentives for hiring foreign labor. Bahrain's young and increasingly well-educated population needs to replace its foreign workers as quickly as possible, and it will only develop a work ethic and suitable skills once it is thrust into the labor market by ensuring that foreign labor cannot compete.
- Reduce those aspects of state subsidies and welfare that distort the economy and discourage the native population from seeking jobs. Bahrain must steadily replace subsidies with jobs.
- Conduct a popular education program to limit population growth, with careful attention to the higher birth rate among its poorer citizens.
- Ensure water, electricity, motor gasoline, foods, and services are priced at market levels and replace subsidies with jobs and economic opportunities. Ensure that employers are charged for any unreimbursed government-provided services and infrastructure used by foreign labor.
- Continue to restructure the educational system to focus on job training and competitiveness. Create strong new incentives for faculty and students to focus on job-related education, sharply down-size other forms of educational funding and activity, and eliminate high overhead educational activities without economic benefits. Emphasize educational opportunities and scholarships for poorer Shi'ite and Sunni citizens, and expand vocational programs even further.
- Unify and reform the structure of the national budget to ensure that all of the nation's revenues and foreign reserves are integrated into the national budget and into the planning process. Provide for expanded public review of the budget, allowing both Sunnis and Shi'ites to play a serious role in reviewing the budget's structure and management of funds.
- Tax domestic capital holdings and property above a given value and ensure that all income from the foreign investments and property of wealthier Bahrainis is subject to progressive taxes.
- Selectively tax earnings and sales with progressive taxes to reduce budget deficits, but structure such taxes to encourage local investment over consumption, and to create added disincentives for the expatriation of capital.

- Ensure that all income from enterprises with state financing is reflected in the national budget and is integrated into the national economic development and planning program.
- Freeze and then reduce the number of civil servants, and slowly restructure and down-size the civil service to shift native labor to more productive areas of activity.
- Establish market criteria for all major state and state-supported investments. Require detailed and independent risk assessment and projections of comparative return on government investment. Down-size the scale of programs to reduce investment and cash flow costs and the risk of cost-escalation.
- Create new, market-driven incentives for privatization to increase the efficiency of investments in downstream and upstream operations, to create real jobs and career opportunities for native workers, and to open investment opportunities to a much wider range of investors.
- Manage privatization in ways ensuring an opportunity for all native citizens to share in the privatization process. Privatization must not be conducted in a manner that benefits a small, elite group of investors and discourages popular confidence and willingness to invest in Bahrain.
- Create new market-driven incentives for foreign investment. Bahrain already offers foreign companies and investors one of the freest economies in the developing world, but it is going to have to provide added incentives in light of the present unrest in Bahrain and competition from other countries.
- Convince Bahrain's people that Bahrain's wealth is being spent in ways that broadly benefit Bahrain's people and not members of the royal family or ruling elite. This requires full transparency in the budget, accounting measures that refute the charges of corruption and favoritism made by the government's hard-line opponents, and a clear policy regarding how much of Bahrain's future income will go to royal accounts.
- Place national security spending on the same basis as other state spending. Integrate it fully into the national budget, including investment and equipment purchases. Replace the present emphasis on judging purchases on the basis of initial procurement costs and technical features with a full assessment of life cycle cost—including training, maintenance, and facilities—and with specific procedures for evaluating the value of standardization and interoperability with existing national equipment and facilities, those of other Gulf states, and those of the US and other power projection forces.
- Develop mid and long-term economic plans that cover the period five and ten years in the future, and which explicitly address the

issues of job creation, income distribution, education, and the role of foreign labor. Oman has already shown that five year plans must be supplemented by longer-term plans that provide a warning of the possible implications of present trends and problems and which examine a range of long-term solutions. Bahrain needs to confront the issues it faces, rather than deny them, and examine the possible implications of "worst case" trends. It also needs to do everything possible to focus public debate on Bahrain's development needs.

It is also clear that such action must be taken by the Al Khalifa family, in conjunction with ministers and the "government." Popular opinion in Bahrain has evolved to the point where the Amir and Prime Minister are now held responsible for Bahrain's progress or non-progress. There is also a popular perception that some members of Bahrain's ruling family favor such reforms—along with many of its technocrats and military— but that other members are slow to perceive the seriousness of the problem and the need for change. This perception of divisions and inaction within the Ruling Family could lead to even more serious crises between Sunni and Shi'ite.

A repressive attempt at preserving the status quo is doomed to failure. The other Southern Gulf states can probably continue to defer coming to grips with issues relating to foreign labor, expanding the non-petroleum sector, and power sharing for at least another few years. Bahrain cannot. If it does not aggressively pursue reform, and take draconian measures to replace foreign labor with native Bahrainis, it will create an unbridgable gap between its political and economic elite and its poorer Shi'ites.

Bahrain has reason to move carefully in broadening political participation. Rushing to create a National Assembly and holding elections is likely to accomplish little in a nation with such divisions and so little political experience. Bahrain must focus on first things first. It must offer its Shi'ites new opportunities, restructure its economy, and improve the distribution of its wealth.

At some point, however, Bahrain will need to provide its citizens with some form of popular representation and well as representation in making decisions about the national budget and the course of Bahrain's development. Bahrain can only achieve stability if power is more balanced between its ruling Sunni elite and Shi'ite majority, and decision making is carried out on a more collective basis. The past benevolence of the government cannot substitute for economic change and broader based institutions of government, in which open political debate and peaceful dissent are essential instruments of peaceful change.

3

Oman

Oman was once one of the great sea powers of the Arab world. It ruled an empire that included an enclave in British India (today's Pakistan), and Zanzibar and Mombassa in East Africa. This empire broke up in 1856, however, and Zanzibar and most of Oman's African possessions became a separate state. The introduction of European steamships in 1862 made it impossible for Omani shipping to compete on many routes, and Oman's trade rapidly declined. Further, an almost constant series of dynastic battles took place within the ruling al-bu-Said dynasty during the period from 1866 to 1915. This fighting sharply undercut the power of the Sultans, and they gradually lost control over both part of Western Oman and the Dhofar region in the south.[152]

Britain's role in the area increased as Oman's power declined, and the power of tribal groups increased relative to the Sultan. Britain declined to intervene when one Omani Sultan asked for British aid in 1895, but it became involved in the struggles between the Sultan, the Ibadhi Imam, and various tribal groups in 1915 when these threatened the stability of the country. From 1915 to 1920, a British political agent helped broker a peace between Sultan Taimur and rebels who threatened Muscat. This peace was signed at Seeb in September, 1920, and created a compromise that effectively limited the Sultan's control over both the Imam and tribal affairs.

The situation grew worse after 1932, when Said bin Taimur, Sultan Qabus's father, came to power. Although Said had been educated in India and initially seemed likely to lead Oman forward, his efforts to obtain revenue through oil concessions led him to sign an agreement with the Iraq Petroleum Group in 1937 that ignored the fact that the Imam had control over much of the territory involved and other portions were in areas Oman disputed with the Emirates and Saudi Arabia. The end result was that the Imam proclaimed his independence, canceled the concessions, and turned to Saudi Arabia. Sultan Taimur was left without power and revenues and gradually became an isolationist who rejected virtually every form of change—including foreign travel, eyeglasses, and higher education.

Sultan Said's lack of leadership and refusal to modernize Oman's military forces made Oman increasingly vulnerable to both internal and outside threats. In 1950, Saudi forces advanced into northwestern Oman and occupied the Buraymi Oasis that Oman shared with Abu Dhabi. Efforts to resolve the disputed lasted dragged on until 1954, and by that time, Sultan Taimur's refusal to share the growing wealth from Oman's oil concessions helped cause an open rebellion by Oman's western tribes.

The resulting tribal struggle was called the "Imamate Opposition." It had its roots in the long struggles between the Sultans, Imam, and tribes, and involved differences over both religion and the Sultan's political authority. It was catalyzed by a charismatic new leader, Ghalib bin Ali, who became Imam of Oman's Ibadhi sect in 1954.[153] Ghalib turned to the Arab League and Saudi Arabia, and applied to the Arab League for recognition of western Oman as a separate country. Saudi Arabia backed Ghalib with money and arms, and attempted to use the rebellion to annex both the Buraymi Oasis and part of Western Oman.

The British and the Sultan responded with attacks by the British-led Trucial Oman Scouts. The Trucial Oman Scouts drove the Saudis out of the Buraymi Oasis in November, 1955. Britain also deployed troops to Nizwa and other towns and villages. Ghalib bin Ali was forced to resign as Imam, although his brother Talib fled to Saudi Arabia and reorganized the tribal forces with Saudi support.

Talib invaded Oman in early 1957, and Ghalib again proclaimed himself Imam in June, 1957. The tribal forces, however, were no more successful than before. The British used the Tribal Oman Scouts and British troops based in Aden to drive Ghalib bin Ali's forces into the Jebel Akhdar mountains in July, Britain then used the RAF to bomb the rebels while it helped to train and equip the Sultan's forces. When this effort to build up the Sultan's forces failed—partly due to poor leadership and partly due to the Sultan's alienation of the tribes in the area—Britain sent troops back into the area. British troops, the RAF, and the Sultan's forces attacked the Imam's positions in the Jebel Akhdar in August, 1957. British troops and the RAF then continued to aid the Sultan's forces until the Ghalib's forces finally collapsed in early 1959—partly because of military defeats and partly because of payments to Ghalib's forces to desert him.

The Birth of Modern Oman

The Dhofar rebellion which followed the suppression of the Imamate rebellion, proved to be a different and grimmer story, and triggered events that led to the birth of modern Oman. The Dhofar region includes the southern third of the country. It has a narrow coastal plain extending from Raysut past Salalah. This coastal plain and the hills immediately above it are watered by the Monsoon rains, but the area to the west rapidly becomes an arid desert with rough terrain that ends in the sand sea of the Empty Quarter. Dhofar shares a common border with Yemen, but it is isolated from the rest of Oman by a near desert to the north.

Dhofar was annexed to Oman in 1879, but its people spoke a different dialect and tribal character. For the next eighty years, the Sultans made no attempt to develop Dhofar, or share any of Oman's revenues with the area. This lack of concern led to low level rebellion that began in 1963. The rebels came to include an increasing number of radicals as time went by, and drew on Marxists outside Dhofar for ideological, financial, and military support. By 1965, the Dhofar rebels controlled much of the countryside, and in June, 1965, they began to attack government strong points and installations.

The Dhofar rebellion became an even more serious military problem in 1967, after Britain evacuated Aden. A new Marxist radical state emerged from the fighting called the People's Democratic Republic of Yemen. This state quickly began to provide arms and support to the Dhofar rebels, who were initially divided into the Dhofar Liberation Front (DLF), National Democratic Front for the Liberation of the Occupied Arabian Gulf (DLF), and Popular Front for the Liberation of Oman (PFLO). On June 11, 1970, the Dhofar rebels started a new offensive in the south and soon came to control virtually all of southern Oman, except for its main port city of Salalah.

This success led the British to help the Sultan's son, Qabus bin Sa'id Al Sa'id, in carrying out a coup on July 23, 1970. The Sandhurst-trained Qabus soon proved to be an effective and modern leader. He granted the Dhofaris a considerable degree of autonomy, and rapidly "Omanized" the armed forces. He offered the rebels amnesty, and a significant number of DLF and PFLO rebels joined him. These defections helped lead the remaining rebels to form a new hard-line Marxist organization called the Popular Front for the Liberation of Oman (PFLOAG) in February, 1972.

Sultan Qabus also created a mix of highly effective light infantry forces, and recruited tribal militias from the Dhofar region called *firquats*. Sultan Qabus also made effective use of British advisors and troops, including elements of the SAS. He went on the counter-offensive and began to attack PFLOAG positions and the PDRY with artillery and air power. He also sent Omani and SAS commando teams into the border area and Hauf to attack Dhofar rebel artillery positions and sanctuaries.

In December, 1973, the Sultan obtained further aid from the Shah of Iran, who sent an entire brigade of troops to Oman in 1973. At the same time, more of the Dhofar rebels joined the Sultan because of the actions of the Marxist extremists that came to dominate the PFLOAG, and who alienated many Dhofaris with experiments like the collectivization of children. By 1974, Oman was able to secure a series of defensive positions only 50 miles from the border with the PDRY called the Hornbeam line.

In 1975, the Sultan obtained additional support from Jordan, and his forces began to sweep the last areas near the border. Sources differ over the nature of Omani attacks on the PDRY. According to some sources, Iranian aircraft and Omani ships attacked the town of Hauf in the PDRY on October 17, 1975, and the PFLOAG withdrew from its last positions in Oman. According to others, the British Special Air Services (SAS) attacked Hauf on several occasions to pressure the PDRY to halt its support for the rebels.

By the end of 1975, Oman had secured a new series of positions about 25 miles from the PDRY border called the Damavand line. These victories effectively ended the rebellion. The Sultan declared the end of the rebellion on December 11, 1975. Jordanian troops left Oman in 1976, and Iran removed most of its forces in January, 1977—although some Iranian troops remained in the area until 1979. Most British troops left in March, 1977. By this time, however, several thousand people, including many women and children, had died in the fighting.

Oman's Strategic Importance

In the years that have followed, Oman has become one of the success stories of the developing world. It has created a modern educational system, developed a modern infrastructure, become an oil exporter, developed its country-side, and turned Muscat into a large, modern city. Much of Oman's new wealth has also reached its poorer citizens.

Oman has cooperated with the West and its neighbors in maintaining the security of the Gulf. In 1981, Oman and was the first Southern Gulf state to formally offer the US the basing facilities and transit rights needed to improve its power projection capabilities. Oman provided the US and Britain with strong support during the "tanker war" with Iran in 1987–1988, the Gulf War, and the US build-up in Kuwait in October, 1994.

Oman has played an important role in the Gulf Cooperation Council (GCC). Sultan Qabus has been a leader in calling for cooperation in military matters and in stating that the alliance must go beyond political and economic cooperation. In 1990, he was the first leader to call for strong, unified GCC forces. He has also played an important role in resolving the difference between Southern Gulf states, and in encouraging the Arab-Israeli peace process.[154]

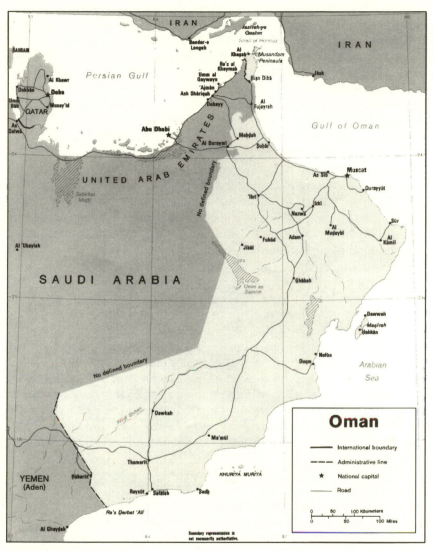

MAP THREE   Oman

Oman is of considerable strategic importance for other reasons. Oman plays a major strategic role in ensuring the maritime security of the Gulf because of its location at the Strait of Hormuz—which separates Iran from Oman's Musandam Peninsula. The shipping channels through the Strait of Hormuz link the Persian Gulf and the Gulf of Oman, and are one of the world's most important strategic water ways. Roughly 17% of the world's oil production transited through the Strait in 1990, and this percentage could nearly double by the year 2010. The Strait is one of the world's most critical maritime chokepoints.

The geography of the Strait of Oman makes Iran a continuing potential threat. The Strait is about 60 to 100 kilometers (40 to 60 miles) wide and Oman's Musandam Peninsula faces Iran across the Strait, while both Oman and Iran have long coasts on the Gulf of Oman. Iran's main naval base at Bandar-e Abbas, and smaller bases on the islands of Qeshm, Larak, and Jazireh are all just across the Strait from Oman's small naval base at Ghanam (Goat) Island.

The main east-west shipping channels through the Strait pass just south of the mid-point in the Strait and Iran's 12 mile limit, and north of Oman's Qu'oin islands (As Salmah, Didamar, and As Salamah Wabanat-uha). These shipping channels are 30–35 kilometers long and 8–13 kilometers wide. They are divided into inbound and outbound channels about two kilometers wide, with depths of 75 to 200 meters—although a shallower route exists to the northeast of the Qu'oin Islands which is about 45–80 meters deep. Further, the Musandam Peninsula is separated from the rest of Iran by the UAE, and the Peninsula has very rough terrain and few significant airports. Its northern islands are vulnerable to an Iranian amphibious operation, and it is difficult for Oman to reinforce.

Oman is the only Gulf state with a coast and ports on the Indian Ocean. It has a total of 2,092 kilometers of coastline. Its coastline on the Gulf of Oman about is 1,700 kilometers long and is located on the Gulf of Oman. The Gulf of Oman is an arm of the Arabian Sea that is bordered on the north by Iran and on the south by Oman. It is about 565 kilometers (350 miles) long and 320 kilometers (200 miles) wide. Like the Strait of Hormuz, the Gulf of Oman is a critical petroleum shipping route.

Oman's External Security

Oman has been at peace since the end of the Dhofar War over twenty years ago. At the same time, Oman faces significant strategic challenges from Iran. Its relations with Saudi Arabia are sometimes tense, and more correct than friendly. South Yemen strongly supported the Dhofar Rebels against Oman, and a long period of tension followed along Oman's border with Yemen. Omani and Yemeni relations have improved significantly in recent years, but are still a subject of concern.

The Threat from Iran

The same geography that helps give Oman strategic importance makes Iran a potential security threat. Control of the shipping channels through the Strait would give Iran added leverage over a large part of the world's oil traffic as well as many of the Gulf's imports. As a result, Iran has tended to challenge Oman when Iran's rulers have felt it could seek hegemony in the Gulf.

In 1977, the Shah unilaterally asserted joint control over the entire Strait of Hormuz. Iranian ships attempted to enter Omani waters in 1980—during the Iran-Iraq War—and only turned back when Oman deployed naval forces that were backed by the threat of British and US intervention.

In 1987, Iran began to deploy long range Silkworm anti-ship missiles at three sites which can attack ships moving through the Strait. Iran has since bought new weapons systems that can threaten the Strait and shipping moving through the Gulf of Oman, including new land and sea-based anti-ship missile systems, submarines, and "smart" bottom mines which pop to the surface when ships with a given size or noise profile sail over them. Iran is digging tunnels to provide secure sites for its long range Scud C missiles in sites along its southern coast, and is expanding its naval facilities at Jask and Chah Bahar in the Gulf of Oman.[155]

Oman could face a serious challenge from Iran if Iran should actively attempt to exert hegemony in the Gulf, control the Strait of Hormuz, or expand its naval presence in the Gulf of Oman. Like Bahrain and the Eastern Province of Saudi Arabia, Oman is one of the natural focal points for any struggle for control of the world's oil resources and the Gulf, and could become involved in any future conflict or tensions between a revanchist Iraq and Iraq's neighbors and the West.

An Iranian land invasion of Oman is less likely than challenges by sea or from the air. Nevertheless, Oman's Musandam region is directly across the Strait of Hormuz and Iran could deploy forces to the Musandam quickly by sea or air and with little warning. The Musandam peninsula is a separate enclave of Oman separated from the rest of country by the UAE. These separation could presents significant problems in deploying Oman's forces, which would have to pass through Fujayrah, or move by air or sea. The Musandam also has very rough terrain; it has a fjord-like coast, and its rugged mountains reach heights of 1,800 meters.

Like most other Southern Gulf states, Oman has chosen to deal with this Iranian threat through dialogue, rather than follow the US in attempting to isolate Iran. Oman holds regular conversations with Iranian officials, and there have been exchanges of visits between senior Omani and Iranian military officers. The Omani and Iranian navies have exchanged visits and port calls. Oman encourages trade with Iran, although this trade has only limited volume. Oman hopes that its attempts at "constructive engagement" will preserve its military options and may well prove to be a more practical method of dealing with Iran than the US focus on "dual containment."

At the same time, Oman blames Iran for trying to organize a coup attempt in Oman in 1994. Oman has given priority to improving its naval forces, cooperating closely with the US Navy and other Southern Gulf navies, and structuring its military planning to counter Iranian action. There is no question that Oman sees Iran as its principal potential military threat and continues to be concerned about Iranian support for Islamic extremists in Oman.

Oman and Iraq

Oman has taken a somewhat similar approach to dealing with Iraq. Oman strongly supported the Coalition and US operations in the Gulf during the Gulf War. At the same time, it does not feel that sanctions are certain to drive Saddam Hussein from power and feels that opening a dialog with Iraq is preferable to isolation. In late October 1995, Oman welcomed a call by the UAE for reconciliation with Iraq and lifting the embargo. At the same time, Oman has not attempted to "tilt" towards Iraq in an effort to counterbalance Iran. It has insisted that Iraq must first comply will all UN resolutions as the price for the lifting of sanctions.[156]

Oman and Yemen

Oman also faces potential threats to its land borders. Oman is one of the larger Southern Gulf states, with a total territory of 212,460 square kilometers—an area slightly smaller than the state of Kansas. Like most Gulf states, Oman has a legacy of local conflicts which affect both its security and its ability to develop effective collective security arrangements with its neighbors.

Oman may still face a threat from Yemen. A long Yemeni-backed civil war took place in Oman's Dhofar region in the 1960s. Dhofar has a 288 kilometer border with Yemen, and accounts for a third of the country. It also presents significant defense problems. Its coastal plain extends from Raysut in the west to beyond Salalah. It is only eight kilometers wide at maximum, but it is relatively highly populated because it receives rain during June to September from the monsoons. The terrain then rises sharply to a rocky plateau with hills of up to 1,500 meters. The edge of the plateau receives some rain, but the plateau then becomes a virtual desert which ends in the Empty Quarter. Patrolling and defending these hilly, desert areas is difficult because of the terrain and poor lines of communication.

During the 1980s, Oman faced a direct military challenge from the PDRY over the control of potential oil fields in their undemarcated border area. This confrontation did not lead to fighting, as did the border clashes between Yemen and Saudi Arabia. However, in October 1987, battalion or company sized Omani and Yemeni forces fought in the area, and Oman launched air strikes against PDRY forces. The President of the PDRY visited Oman to try to defuse the situation in 1988. Even so, there were further clashes, although none went beyond exchanges of fire between small patrols.

Relations eased significantly after a civil war in the PDRY brought a more moderate regime to power, and after the PDRY's unification with the YAR in 1991. Oman was able to negotiate a demarcation of its 288 kilometer border area in October, 1992, and the German firm Hansa Luftbild was awarded a contract to carry out a detailed survey of the border, including printing new maps. Oman and Yemen then opened their first border crossing in 1993, and agreed to build a road and construct an Omani city at the border to facilitate the transfer of goods and people.

Oman and Yemen have since remained friendly. In 1995, Oman's Minister of State and Governor of Dhofar Mosalem Bin Ali al-Bousaidi greeted Yemeni officials at Habrout, about 1,300 km (780 miles) south of Muscat, where each country has set up its own post on the 308 km (184 miles) long border.[157] Nevertheless, a new civil war took place in Yemen in May–July, 1994, and it is all too possible that there will be new political upheavals in Yemen. No border settlement in the Gulf ever seems to be "final" and there is a continuing risk that Yemen may make claims to Omani territory.

Oman and Saudi Arabia

Oman has a 676 kilometer long border with Saudi Arabia, and there is a long history of tension between the two countries. Saudi Arabia made claims to parts of Western Oman beginning in the 1930s. These claims affected the Western Hajar, Al Joof, Dhahira area, and Dhofar. They led to continuing tension between Saudi Arabia and Oman, and finally to actual conflict in the 1960s. Saudi Arabia occupied the Buraymi Oasis, backed a rebellion against the Sultan in Western Oman, and made attempts to annex part of Oman territory. These Saudi efforts were only halted when the British-led Trucial Oman Scouts reoccupied the Buraymi Oasis, British-backed Omani forces put down the rebellion in Western Oman, and Sultan Qabus restored political stability and unity to Oman.

Sheik Zayed bin Sultan al Nuhayyan of Abu Dhabi was able to negotiate an agreement between Oman, the UAE, and Saudi Arabia over the Buraymi Oasis dispute in 1975. This agreement gave Oman control over the Buraymi Oasis while allowing free access between Abu Dhabi and the Oasis. Oman felt, however, that Sheik Zayed mistakenly ceded territory that belonged to Oman.

Saudi Arabia returned some of the disputed territory to Oman in 1977. However, Saudi officials sporadically indicated that Saudi Arabia still had claims to part of Oman, and tension continued to exist between Oman and Saudi Arabia over ownership of Western Oman, until the early 1990s. It was only on May 21, 1992, that Oman and Saudi Arabia began to reach a more final agreement on the demarcation of most of their borders. They then signed documents agreeing to a full demarcation of their entire border area on July 10, 1995.[158]

These border agreements seem to resolve the main security disputes between Oman and Saudi Arabia, but there is still tension and rivalry between the two countries. Omani officials view Saudi Arabia as a nation which is attempting to dominate the Arabian Peninsula and the Southern Gulf, and which is blocking broader military cooperation in the Gulf Cooperation Council (GCC). Saudi officials see Oman as a rival influence in Gulf affairs, and one which has tried to use the GCC to obtain military aid and expand its military and strategic influence. There is a cultural clash between the outward-looking Omanis, who belong to the relatively tolerant Ibadhi Muslims, and the inward-looking Saudis who are conservative Wahhabis, and some Omani officials blame Saudi Arabia's support of fundamentalism and toleration of Omani Sunni religious extremists for the internal security problems Oman experienced in 1974.

Oman and the UAE

Oman has improved its relations with Abu Dhabi and Dubai, and there is an agreed Administrative Line between the UAE and Oman in the far north. However, part of Oman's 410 kilometer border with the UAE is not demarcated. There are potential problems between the two countries because of the competing claims and allegiances of members of the Shihuh tribes which affect the border areas of Oman near Dibba in the Southern Musandam.

Oman has had one near clash with Ras al-Khaimah. Sheik Saqr of Ras al-Khaimah attempted to take control of part of Oman in 1977, and to place drilling rigs in Omani waters. Oman used military force to take back its territory. Oman reached a border settlement with Ras al-Khaimah but only after Sheik Zayed, the president of the UAE and its most powerful ruler, strongly backed Sultan Qabus against Sheik Saqr.[159]

Oman has had broader claims to UAE territory in the past, and for many years sent ambassadors to each of the smaller Emirates within the UAE, rather than recognized Abu Dhabi as the center of federal authority in the UAE. Some experts in the Gulf feel Oman has never totally abandoned its ambitions to include part of the UAE in its territory, and that Oman might try to absorb the Western Emirates if the UAE should break up after the death of Sheik Zayed of Abu Dhabi.

Such concerns may be exaggerated, but they have been raised by both UAE and Saudi officials. Further, the UAE has phased nearly 6,000 Omanis out of its armed forces in spite of protests by Sultan Qabus, and rejected an appeal by Sultan Qabus for compensation for the financial impact that forcing Omani's to leave UAE military service had on Oman.

Oman and Qatar

Oman has good relations with Qatar and the two states have pursued common diplomatic initiatives in improving relations with Iran and Israel. Both states have sometimes cooperated in trying to limit Saudi influence in the Gulf Cooperation Council, and Sultan Qabus of Oman played an important role in quietly mediating Qatar's dispute with Bahrain, Saudi Arabia, and the UAE over the selection of a Saudi Secretary General of the GCC in 1995.

Oman and Israel

Oman was one of the first Gulf nations to establish relations with Israel. Oman's Foreign Minister met with Shimon Peres when he was Israel's Foreign Minister, and then after Peres became Prime Minister. There have been a number of meetings between Omani and Israeli officials. Israeli businessmen travel regularly to Oman, and Yousef Bin Alawi Bin Abdullah, Oman's Minister of State for Foreign Affairs, agreed to establish a trade office with Israel in October 1995.[160]

Oman has long seen improved relations with Israel as a way of resolving a long-standing regional crisis that has weakened the development of the Arab world. It also sees improved relations with Israel as a way of strengthening its influence outside the Gulf, of improving relations with the US, of asserting itself relative to Saudi Arabia, and of expanding trade and investment ties to one of the most rapidly developing nations in the Middle East.

Oman's Internal Security

Oman is currently one of the most stable Gulf nations. It is not, however, immune to the need for change or to internal security problems. There is no clear successor to Sultan Qabus. Oman is slowly evolving towards more representative institutions, but it still lacks any elected body. Most significant, it has demographic problems and problems with foreign labor, and has had problems with internal unrest and Islamic extremism.

The Role of Government and the Royal Family

The Sultanate of Oman has been ruled by the Al Bu Sa'id family since the middle of the 18th century. The current monarch, Sultan Qabus Bin Sa'id Al Sa'id, has proved to be a highly effective leader in balancing Oman's different tribal, regional, and ethnic interests, and created a broadly based political leadership that included several ministers who were once Dhofar rebels. His government has maintained the internal security of Oman in the years that followed the end of the Dhofar rebellion. It has encouraged well-planned economic development, and has made good use of Oman's limited oil resources.

The Sultan has steadily liberalized Oman, although Oman still has censorship, strict immigration controls, and does not have political parties. He has also established a modern structure of government that consists of a Council of Ministers, a Majlis, and various specialized councils and ministries. The Council of Ministers is the highest authority in the government and derives its power from the Sultan. Oman is divided into 59 Wilayets (districts), most of which are under the jurisdiction of the Ministry of the Interior. A Wali or governor heads each Wilayet, and the Majlis has members from each Wilayet.[161]

The Sultan created a State Consultative Council (SCC) in 1981, which was Oman's first attempt at moving towards popular rule. The SCC had 55 appointed members, and met three times a year. While it had no formal power to veto the Sultan's actions or legislation, debate was relatively free and often vigorous. Unlike his father, Sultan Qabus followed an earlier Omani tradition of consensual decision-making, broadening the base of discussion to include planners, technocrats, and the nation's emerging business class.[162]

Citizens have indirect access to senior officials through the traditional practice of petitioning their patrons, usually the local governor, or Wali, for redress of grievances. The Sultan appoints the governors and the royal court regularly reviews their treatment of such petitions. The Sultan also makes an annual 3-week tour of the country, accompanied by his ministers, to listen directly to his subjects' problems. Omani citizens also have the right to petition the Sultan in the case of need and if a Ministry does not deal with the citizen's request or complaints. These petitions are reviewed nightly and it is traditional that action be seen to be taken the next day.

In 1991, the Sultan created a popular assembly or Majlis al-Shura. Its mandate is to review and debate legislation on economic development, education, social services, and medical services before it becomes law. It has broader representation than the SCC, and excludes government officials. The SCC included 11 government officials of under secretary rank who sat in the SSC in their official capacity. The Majlis is structured to give additional representation to rural areas. Its members are chosen by Oman's governors, rather than the Sultan, and approved after the Sultan's endorsement.[163]

In 1994 the Sultan expanded the number of Majlis seats to 80 from the original 59, a move which allocated two members for districts with a higher population. The Omani government selected the Council members from several nominees elected in caucuses of prominent persons in each district. In 1994, four women were nominated for Majlis seats; two of them were selected to serve. The Majlis now meets four times a year in plenary session, and has seven committees focusing on key policy issues.[164]

The Majlis has no formal legislative powers, and the Sultan issues all laws by decree.[165] However, the Majlis serves as a conduit of information between the people and the government ministries. It is empowered to call Ministers to account—except for the ministers involved in finance, foreign affairs, and security—and to regularly review legislation. No serving government official is eligible to be a Council member. The Council may question government ministers, review all draft laws on social and economic policy, and recommend legislative changes to the Sultan, who makes the final decision.[166]

Economic and social development is carried out through five year plans that are generated by technocrats in the government and reviewed and debated by the Sultan, Council of Ministers, and Majlis. The 1991–1996 five year plan has just been completed and is in its initial implementation stage. Oman has also developed detailed analyses of its economic options through the year 2020, and the new 1996–2000 plan is beginning to be implemented.

National security and foreign policy decisions are made by the Sultan. International treaties, agreements, and charters must be approved by the Sultan and then become law from their date of publication in the Official Gazette. Oman is a member of the Arab League and Islamic Conference Organization, and a founder of the Gulf Cooperation Council. It is a member of many other regional organizations, and served a two year term on the Security Council of the United Nations that began on January 1, 1994.[167]

Oman has one of the most effective governments in the Gulf. There may, however, be problems with the succession. The Sultan is now 55 years of age. He has no wife and no formal heir has been designated. This potential risks posed by this situation were highlighted when the Sultan was involved in a serious accident on September 11, 1995. The accident killed one of his most senior advisors, Qays al-Zawawi.

Western experts have speculated over the succession, and have named several possible candidates. These names include the Sultan's uncle, Deputy Prime Minister for Security and Defense, Sayyid Fahr Bin Taymur, but he may be too old for the job. Other names include Deputy Prime Minister for Cabinet affairs, Sayyid Fahd Bin Mahmud, and the Secretary General of the Ministry of Foreign Affairs, Sayyid Haytham Bin Tariq. There is no evidence to indicate that any of these names will ultimately be Sultan, although some reports indicate that Sultan Qabus has formed a family council to deal with the succession issue.[168]

Ethnic, Political, and Population Issues

Like all the Southern Gulf states, Oman faces problems with population growth and foreign labor. Oman carried out its first national census in December, 1993. This census produced an estimated population of 2,017,591, and was used to expand the Majlis to 80 members. About 26% of this population (537,060) was expatriate—largely South Asian. The estimated population growth rate was very high—ranging from 3.5% to 3.9% per year.

Oman's most recent statistical handbook shows a total population of 2,018,074, of which 1,483,226 (73%) are native Omanis, and 534,848 are foreign. About 25% of this total lives in the Muscat area. The CIA estimates that Oman's population was 2,125,089 in July, 1995.[169]

Oman's native population is largely Arab, with some small Baluchi, Zanzibari Arabs, and South Asian elements. The population is largely Islamic, with about 75% of its members from the Ibadhi sect, and the rest largely Sunni with a small number of Shi'ites and Hindus. Oman is more linguistically diverse than the other Gulf states. The official language is Arabic, but Swahili, Farsi, Baluchi, and various Indian dialects are common.[170]

In spite of this ethnic diversity, Oman does not seem to suffer as much from the religious, ethnic, and class divisions as most other Gulf states. The regional divisions between Muscat, Western Oman, and Dhofar now seem to have relatively little political importance. The government seems to be broadly popular among all ethnic and regional groups, and the Sultan seems to be one of the most popular leaders in the Gulf.

There have, however, been security problems. In 1994, the Omani government announced that it had discovered a "secret religious movement" which had unidentified foreign support. This movement consisted largely of Omani Sunnis that had received religious training in Saudi Arabia and/or had links to Wahhabi groups in Saudi Arabia. There was no evidence of deliberate Saudi government sponsorship, but Omani security officers found that a number of those involved had been educated in Saudi Arabia, had live in Saudi Arabia, and/or were receiving at least indirect support from Saudi religious groups.

The government detained well over 200 people—including two junior Ministers—in connection with an alleged plot to destabilize the country. Some of these detentions were preventive and involved people whose names had simply appeared on lists prepared by the plotters. Other arrests involved Omanis involved in a serious plot against the Sultan.

The Omani government charged 131 of these suspects with sedition and tried them in secret before the State Security Court. Some were given long prison sentences and a few were sentenced to death. As is generally the case in Oman, the treatment of the prisoners was merciful. The death sentences were later commuted and all remaining prisoners were released in November 1995, as the result of an amnesty the Sultan granted on the 25th anniversary of his rule. The Sultan had previously refused the resignation of a senior minister whose family had been implicated in the plot.[171]

The Sultan has since given speeches warning about the dangers of Islamic extremism. He has attacked "stagnation . . . fanaticism based on a lack of knowledge among the Muslim youth about the true facts of their religion . . ." and, "alien ideas, masquerading as beneficial promises." He has stated that Islam, ". . . rejects exaggeration and bigotry, because it is the religion of liberality," and that, "extremism under whatever guise, fanaticism of whatever persuasion would be hateful poisonous plants in the soil of our country that would not be permitted to flourish." Oman has placed added restrictions on the activities of non-Muslims, and the security forces have increased surveillance of the Muslim clergy.[172]

Oman also faces structural demographic and employment problems that could eventually reach the crisis level. There are no rules as to what level of population growth a given nation can sustain, but Oman's recent and projected economic growth is better suited to a population growth rate of 2–2.5% than its current 3.5% to 3.9% per year. Some 46% of Oman's population is now under 15 years of age, and the CIA estimates that Oman's population growth rate was as high as 3.71% in 1995.[173]

Chart Fifteen shows that a conservative World Bank estimate of Oman's population growth that is based on the assumption that Oman's annual rate of natural increase will steadily drop from 3.86% a year in 1990 to 2.08% by 2035. This estimate still projects that Oman's population will grow from 1.52 million in 1990 and 1.88 million in 1995, to 2.3 million by the year 2000, 2.8 million by 2005, 3.3 million by 2010, and 4.5 million by 2020. Chart Sixteen shows that Oman's rate of population increase is much

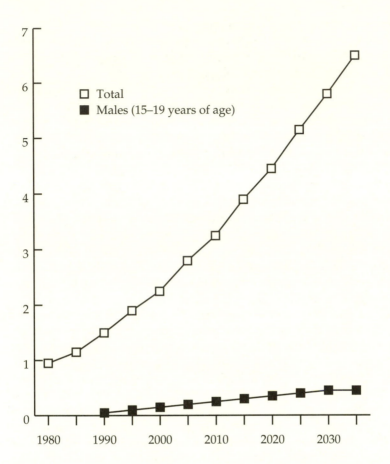

CHART FIFTEEN   Estimated Trends in the Omani Population During
1990–2035 (in millions). *Source:* Adapted by Anthony H. Cordesman from World
Bank, *World Population Projections, 1994–1995,* Washington, World Bank, 1994,
and material provided by the CIA.

faster than that of any other small Gulf country, although these countries
have some of the fastest growing populations in the world.[174]

This kind of population growth creates a high demand for new jobs.
The total number of young men reaching job age (15–19 years) will rise
from 73,000 in 1990 and 96,000 in 1995 to 120,000 in 2000, 183,000 in 2010,
and 255,000 in 2020. The growth of the population at younger ages will
be even steeper. Male children of four years of age or less will rise from
147,000 in 1990 and 184,000 in 1995 to 223,000 in 2000, 257,000 in 2010,
and 293,000 in 2020.[175]

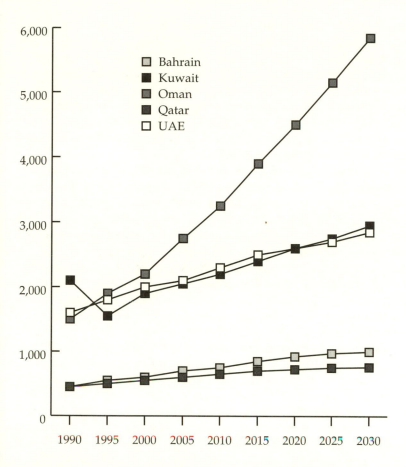

CHART SIXTEEN   Estimated Trends in Population of the Smaller Gulf
Cooperation Council States During 1990–2030 in 1,000s. *Source:* Adapted by
Anthony H. Cordesman from World Bank, *World Population Projections,
1994–1995,* Washington, World Bank, 1994, and material provided by the CIA.

These demographic problems are complicated by the fact that Oman is
highly dependent on government jobs and foreign labor. The civil service
alone employed 81,453 personnel in 1993, of which only 66% were
Omani. The government as a whole employed 98,342 personnel, of which
65% were Omani, and public corporations employed 4,540 more personnel. The government reports that it issued a total 484,672 labor cards for
non-Omanis in 1993—compared with only 351,606 in 1990. About 2% of
this work force is other Arab, 1% is Western, 0.1% is African, and 96.7% is
Asian (58% Indian).

Virtually all of Oman's workers compete for jobs with Omanis and they have an advantage in such competition. Foreign workers will accept lower salaries and native Omanis often lack the training and work ethic to be equally efficient. Some 14% of these foreign workers are sales workers, 15% are service workers, 15% are production workers, 15% operate transport equipment and 26% are laborers.[176] The oil companies (65%) and commercial banks (78%) are heavily Omanized, but many other private sector activities are not. For example, only 25% of the insurance sector and 20% of the hotel sector is Omani.

This dependence on low-cost foreign labor has almost inevitably led to growing tensions over jobs between native Omanis and the foreign work force. Many younger native Omanis face problems in finding employment because of competition from foreign labor. As is the case in all other Southern Gulf countries, this situation is also made worse by government policies that make it easier to hire and fire foreign labor and because foreigners do not necessarily receive the same benefit packages. There is also some resentment of the role of foreigners—particularly the British—in holding key jobs and positions.[177] Coupled with Oman's high population growth rate and limited economic diversification, this dependence on foreign labor is creating a growing political problem.[178]

Sultan Qabus is attempting to deal with this problem though a slow process of "Omanization," which is reflected in Oman's 1996–2000 Five Year Plan. The plan estimates that Oman had 266,000 native workers at the end of 1995 versus 207,000 expatriate workers. It estimates that 174,000 more Omanis will reach working age by the year 2000, and that 110,000 will want to enter the labor force. This creates an estimated demand for 376,000 native Omani jobs by 2000, of a total labor force that Oman estimates will rise from 739,000 in 2000 to 903,000 in 2000. As a result, the labor force will change from 35% to 42% Omani.[179]

This pattern of Omanization is shown in more detail in Table Eighteen, and raises some serious questions about Oman's plans. Although the overall rate of Omanization does increase, the total number of foreign workers in Oman would increase from 473,000 to 527,000. About half of these foreign workers are also projected to take semi-skilled and unskilled jobs. This indicates that Oman will still have a remarkably high number of foreigners performing unskilled labor—a luxury for a developing country with Oman's estimated future wealth. The rate of Omanization is relatively low for skilled manual workers and skilled office workers, and the rate of total increase in skilled office workers indicates that Oman will have little success in improving the efficiency of these now over-staffed white collar jobs. Oman will make little progress in Omanizing its most skilled jobs, which inevitably means a large outflow of capital and diminished opportunities for Omanis in highly paid positions.

TABLE EIGHTEEN Omanization During 1995–2000

Category	Omani Workers		Expatriate Workers		Percent of Omanization	
	1995	2000	1995	2000	1995	2000
Specialists/University Graduates	19,000	30,000	43,000	52,000	30.6	36.5
Technicians	15,000	24,000	16,000	25,000	45.5	49.0
Skilled Office Workers	35,000	44,000	19,000	24,000	64.8	64.7
Skilled Manual Workers	77,000	104,000	28,000	43,000	73.3	70.7
Semi-Skilled Office Workers	6,000	9,000	85,000	107,000	6.7	7.8
Semi-Skilled Manual Workers	1,000	16,000	22,000	15,000	4.3	51.6
Other Semi-Skilled and Unskilled Workers	113,000	149,000	256,000	261,000	30.5	51.6
Total	266,000	376,000	473,000	527,000	36.0	41.6

Source: Adapted by Anthony H. Cordesman from Sultanate of Oman, Ministry of Development, *Basic Components and Main Indicators of the Fifth Five Year Plan (1996–2000)*, Muscat, Government of Oman, January 1996, pp. 57–64.

A close look at other data in Oman's five year plan also indicates that an unrealistically large amount of Omanization will take place between 1998 and 2000. Expatriates will peak at 604,000 in 1998 and drop to 527,000 in 2000. This kind of sudden improvement in the out years of a five year plan raises inevitable questions about its credibility.[180] In short, the pace of Omanization is unlikely to meet popular expectations, is too slow to reduce the high cost of expatriate labor to the Omani economy, and may still be unrealistic.

Oman's Economy

Oman faces major challenges in economic development. Its high population growth rate, dependence on foreign labor, and dependence on oil and gas revenues present major problems in creating enough jobs and per capita income for its growing population. While Oman does not face the same problems that Bahrain faces in shaping a post-oil economy, it faces significantly greater challenges than Qatar, Kuwait, Saudi Arabia, and the UAE.

The Broad Patterns in Oman's Economy

The recent trends in Oman's GDP, central government spending, trade balance, and military efforts are shown in Table Nineteen. The longer term trends are shown in Chart Seventeen.[181] These trends represent vast progress over the primitive economy that existed when Sultan Qabus took power from his father in July, 1970. Although Oman began exporting oil in 1967, no significant effort had been made to modernize its economy for nearly a century. Almost all of its population was illiterate and there were only three schools in the country. Medical services were limited to two small hospital/clinics, and the mortality rate was high. There was little development, only a few homes in Muscat had electricity, and there were only 10 kilometers of paved roads in the entire country.

Since that time, Oman has used its oil and gas revenues wisely. It has greatly improved education, human services, and the nation's infrastructure. Oman began a major development effort in 1971, and was able to establish the infrastructure for growth by 1975. It had built airports at Seeb and Salalah, new ports at Mutrah and Raysut, greatly expanded the school system and begun the education of women. It had also introduced postal, telecommunications, and television services. In 1976, it began to implement the first of a continuing series of five year development plans.

Today, Muscat is a sprawling modern city, and most of Oman's towns and villages have modern urban services. Oman has a well developed road system, and Oman's ports, telecommunications, and utilities are

TABLE NINETEEN   Key Economic Indicators in Oman

Trends: 1990–1994*	1990	1991	1992	1993	1994
Production (1,000s of barrels per day)	684	708	741	779	—
Oil Exports (1,000s of barrels per day)	628	643	691	732	—
Oil Export Receipts ($ US current billions)	4.13	3.22	4.64	4.21	—
GDP ($ US current billions)	10.53	10.18	11.48	11.68	—
Annual Real Change in GDP (%)**	7.5	9.2	6.8	–7.9	—
Per Capita GDP ($ US current)	7,022	6,447	7,006	7,126	—
Annual Real Change in Per Capita GDP (%)**	3.9	3.7	2.9	–4.3	—

Projected Trends: 1995–1996*** (Millions of Omani Rials)	1994	1995	1996
GDP	4,348.8	4,653.3	—
GDP Growth (Current Prices)	1.2%	7%	—
Total Exports	2,131	2,260	—
Total Imports	1,543	1,550	—
Trade Balance	588	710	—
Current Account	–355	–160	—
Government Revenues			
Oil	—	1,352.4	1,473.0
Gas	—	65.0	58.0
Other	—	429.6	403.0
Total	—	1,847	1,934.0
Government Revenues			
Defense & Security	—	667.0	699.0
Civil Ministries	—	828.9	854.0

(continues)

TABLE NINETEEN   *(continued)*

Projected Trends: 1995–1996*** (Millions of Omani Rials)	1994	1995	1996
Other	—	218.2	216.0
Total Current Expenditure	—	1,714.1	1,769.0
Capital Expediture	—	427.5	367.0
Equity Participation & Subsidies to Private Sector	—	17.4	16.0
Total	—	2,159.0	2,152
Deficit	496	312	218

Notes: *Adapted by Wayne A. Larsen, NSSP, Georgetown University, from the EIU, Country Profile, *Oman/Yemen, 1995–1996,* pp. 12, 21.
**Measured in constant dollars.
***From Omani government data and *Middle East Economic Digest,* May 3, 1996, pp. 10–12.

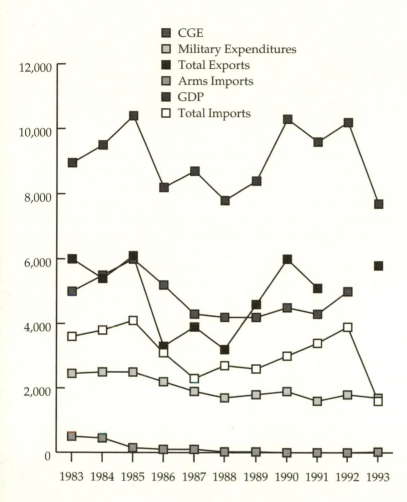

CHART SEVENTEEN   Oman's Gross Domestic Product, Central Government
Expenditures, Military Expenditures, Total Exports, Total Imports, and Arms
Import Deliveries: 1983–1993 (in Constant $93 Millions). *Source:* Adapted by
Anthony H. Cordesman from ACDA, *World Military Expenditures and Arms
Transfers, 1993–1994,* ACDA/GPO, Washington, 1995.

modern and well developed. Oman's recent five year plans have
expanded electrical output and the infrastructure in the interior, and
reduced Oman's dependence on oil. A quarter century has changed virtually every aspect of Oman's economy and society.[182]

Oman has options to reduce its dependence on oil revenues.
Tourism, natural gas, and minerals all have considerable potential.

Pipelines through Oman to ports in the Indian Ocean could provide the Southern Gulf with a secure means of bypassing the Strait of Hormuz. At the same time, Oman remains dependent on oil and gas to fund most of its development. Petroleum products provide about 80 percent of its government revenues and 37% of its GDP. About 87% of Oman's $5 billion in exports in 1994 came from sales of petroleum. Oil alone accounted for 76% of Omani exports in 1995, and its only other major export was fish.[183]

Table Twenty shows the trends in Oman's dependence on fuel exports, and provides a very rough indication of the extent to which Oman is reducing the share of fuel exports as a percent of its total economy. Much of the reduction in the share of fuel exports shown in Table Twenty, however, is misleading. It is largely the result of the growth of service industries dependent on fuel exports for the income that makes them possible.[184]

It is scarcely surprising, therefore, that Oman's economic growth has fluctuated sharply with oil prices, and has failed to keep up with its population growth. The growth of Oman's GDP dropped from 9.2% in 1992 to 1.3% in 1993, and 0.5% in 1994. It has since begun to rise, but projections of 4% growth in 1995 now seem optimistic. Low oil prices have not only meant a significant drop in the crude oil sector, but a drop in other key sectors like construction and government activity and an imbalance in trade and a drop in foreign reserves.

Oman's current per capita income is far higher than it was in 1970. Even though Oman's GDP has been hurt by the drops in oil prices during the 1980s and early 1990s, the World Bank estimates that per capita income rose by an average of 4.1% per annum during 1980–1992 in constant 1992 dollars. Oman was the only Southern Gulf state to experience a rise in real GDP during this period. Nonetheless, Oman's present per capita GDP is only about $6,000, and Oman has the same problems with the poor distribution of income between rich and poor that exist in all of the Southern Gulf states.[185]

While Oman probably has the best economic planning of any state in the Gulf, and has developed a series of excellent five year plans, low oil prices have also helped to deprive it of capital. Oman has run budget deficits since the early 1980s, and has had to finance these deficits by issuing bonds and drawing down on its reserves.[186] Oman's budget deficit in the first six months of 1995 was 74.2 Omani Rials ($193 million), and the total deficit for the year was projected at 312 million Omani Rials ($810 million). Oman has tightened its fiscal policies, and hopes to reduce or eliminate its budget deficits by 1996/1997.[187] However, the end result is heavily dependent on oil revenues, and Oman's ability to finance its budgets and development plans is uncertain.

TABLE TWENTY　Economic Dependence of Middle Eastern States on Oil
　　　　　　　　　Production

Oil Exporter	Trade in Fuels as a Percent of GDP*				Share of Total Exports 1993
	1970	1974	1984	1993**	1993
Gulf					
Bahrain***	140	105	72	67	90
Iran	20	47	7	15	90
Iraq	3	2	9	2	35
Kuwait	62	80	47	40	80
Oman	78	70	47	30	95
Saudi Arabia	46	90	37	33	99
Gulf Cooperation Council	50	85	35	35	95
Other Middle East					
Algeria	15	30	22	20	85
Egypt	5	2	6	7	45
Syria	6	8	7	14	42
Total Middle East and *North Africa*					
Percent	25	60	20	30	90
Total Value of Exports in $ Current Billions	10	90	100	110	80

Notes: *Mineral fuels, including petroleum and products, natural gas, and natural gas
liquids.
**Estimate.
***Includes fuel processed from Saudi Arabia.
Source: Adapted by Anthony H. Cordesman from World Bank, *Claiming the Future,*
Washington, World Bank, 1995, p. 17.

Oman's Oil Industry

Oil and gas are the keys to Oman's economic development and stability. Oman only began to exploit its oil resources in 1962, but it has fueled most of Oman's development and growth since that time and will play a critical role in its economy until well beyond the year 2000. Oman may have reduced its dependence on oil from 67% of its GDP in 1975 to 49% in 1990, and 38% in 1993 on paper, but oil exports still fund most government expenditures and much of its investment in economic growth.[188]

Oman estimates that oil production will produce 6,504 million Omani Rials, or 75.5% of total government revenues, during the period of 1996–2000 covered in its new five year plan. This total compares with 7,453 million Omani Rials during the 1991–1995 plan, or 73.9% of total government revenues. The 1996–2000 plan assumes that Oman's oil revenues will increase by an average real rate of 0.8% per year during 1996–2000. It also assumes that oil revenues will equal 2,123 Omani Rials or 32% of the GDP in 2000. This compares with 1,890 Omani Rials or 35% of the GDP in 2000.[189]

Most of Oman's proven oil reserves are located in Oman's northern and central regions. There is some debate over the size of Oman's reserves, but recent Omani discoveries have raised Oman's oil and condensate reserves by 270 million barrels, and probably give it a total of a little over 5 billion barrels.[190] The Yibal, Natih, Fahud, al-Huwaisah, Lekhwair, and Shibkah fields in the north contain an estimated combined total of 1.8 billion barrels of reserves. Most of the crude oil found in this region is light, with gravities in the 32–38° API range. Heavier oil is found in the southern region, near the 400-million barrel Amal Eastern High field, which contains 19° API crude.[191]

Oman had produced a total of about 3.3 billion barrels of oil by the end of 1990, and has a moderate reserve-to-production ratio of 18/1.[192] All of Oman's oil is blended and is exported through Muscat. Omani oil goes largely to Asian markets.[193]

Petroleum Development Oman (PDO) holds over 90 percent of the county's oil reserves and accounts for about 95 percent of production. PDO is a consortium comprised of the Omani government (60%), Shell (34%), Total (4%), and Partex (2%). However, Shell operates most of the country's key fields, including Yibal and Lekhwair. Occidental, Elf, Japex, and IPC account for the balance of Oman's oil production. MPM announced in early 1995 that 20 percent of PDO's concession will be auctioned by the end of the year. Oman hopes this will increase upstream competition and bring new technology into the oil sector. (The concessions on offer probably will include tracts near the Saudi and Yemeni borders as well as offshore areas in the Gulf of Oman.)[194]

Oil Reserves and Production Plans

Chart Eighteen and Table Twenty-One show that Oman is a small oil power by Gulf standards.[195] As of 1994, Oman had estimated proved oil reserves of only 4.5–5.2 billion barrels, with probable additional reserves of 2 billion barrels. Total crude oil and condensate production has risen from 740,000 barrels per day in 1992, 776,000 barrels per day in 1993, 805,000 barrels per day in 1994, 857,000 barrels per day in 1995, and remained at over 850,000 barrels per day in mid 1996.[196]

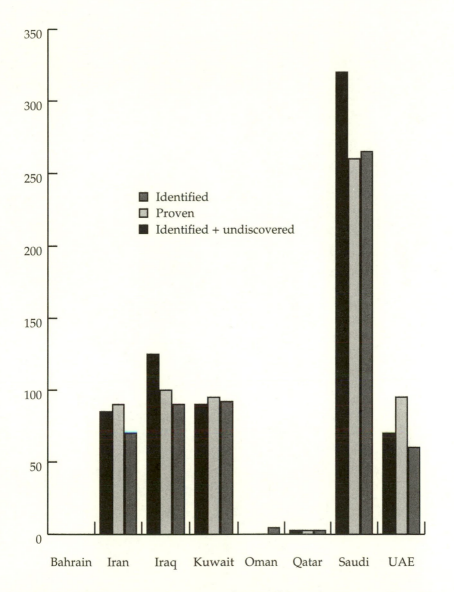

CHART EIGHTEEN   Total Oil Reserves of the Gulf States (in Billions of Barrels).
Source: IEA, *Middle East Oil and Gas,* Paris, OECD, IEA, Annex 2, and data
provided by Bahrain and Oman. Bahrain's reserves are only 350 million barrels
and do not show up on the chart because of scale.

TABLE TWENTY-ONE   Comparative Oil Reserves and Production Levels of the Gulf States

Comparative Oil Reserves in 1994 in Billions of Barrels

Country	Identified	Undiscovered	Identified and Undiscovered	Proven	% of World Total
Bahrain	—	—	—	.35	
Iran	69.2	19.0	88.2	89.3	8.9
Iraq	90.8	35.0	125.8	100.0	10.0
Kuwait	92.6	3.0	95.6	96.5	9.7
Oman	—	—	—	5.0	NA
Qatar	3.9	0	3.9	3.7	0.4
Saudi Arabia	265.5	51.0	316.5	261.2	26.1
UAE	61.1	4.2	65.3	98.1	9.8
Total	583.0	112.2	695.2	654.1	64.9
Rest of World	—	—	—	345.7	35.1
World	—	—	—	999.8	100.0

(continues)

TABLE TWENTY-ONE (continued)

Comparative Oil Production in Millions of Barrels per Day

Country	1995 Actual	1995 OPEC Quota	DOE/IEA Estimate of Actual Production 1990	1992	2000	2005	2010	Maximum Sustainable 1995	2000	Announced Capacity in 2000
Bahrain	—	—	—	—	—	—	—	—	—	—
Iran	3,608	3,600	3.2	3.6	4.3	5.0	5.4	3.2	4.5	4.5
Iraq	600	400	2.2	0.4	4.4	5.4	6.6	2.5	5.0	5.0
Kuwait	1,850	2,000	1.7	1.1	2.9	3.6	4.2	2.8	3.3	3.3
Oman	—	—	—	—	—	—	—	—	—	—
Qatar	449	378	0.5	0.4	0.6	0.6	0.6	0.5	0.6	0.6
Saudi Arabia	8,018	8,000	8.5	9.6	11.5	12.8	14.1	10.3	11.1	11.1
UAE	2,193	2,161	2.5	2.6	3.1	3.5	4.3	3.0	3.8	3.2
Total Gulf	—	—	18.6	17.7	26.8	30.9	35.0	23.5	28.2	28.2
World	—	—	69.6	67.4	78.6	84.2	88.8	—	—	—

Source: Adapted by Anthony H. Cordesman from estimates in IEA, *Middle East Oil and Gas*, Paris, OED/IEA, 1995, Annex 2 and DOE/EIA, *International Energy Outlook, 1995*, Washington, DOE/EIA, June, 1995, pp. 26–30, and *Middle East Economic Digest*, February 23, 1996, p. 3. IEA and DOE do not provide country breakouts for Bahrain and Oman. Reserve data estimated by author based on country data.

Recent Omani exploration programs have resulted in annual reserve increases that have offset production depletions. In March 1995, official Omani calculations raised the country's proven oil reserves to 5.0 to 5.23 billion barrels. According to this official estimate, about 500 million barrels of new reserves were discovered in 1994. Some of these "newly" discovered reserves were known previously, but were considered unproved or uneconomical to develop. Horizontal drilling and enhanced oil recovery (EOR) projects have led to reclassification of some of these reserves.[197]

Even with these discoveries, however, Oman will not be able to sustain its long term oil production. Even the new estimate of reserves gives Oman less than 0.5% of the world's total oil reserves.[198] Oman has only 17 years of proven reserves at its current rate of production of 850,000 barrels per day.[199] As a result, Oman is making aggressive attempts to expand its oil resources, develop downstream operations, create ties to foreign oil companies and develop its gas resources. The Omani government invested 749 million Omani Rials in crude oil projects during its 1991–1995 five year plan, and the private sector invested 621 million Omani Rials. These investments totaled 32% of all government investment (capital formation) during 1991–1995, 40% of all private investment and 35% of all investment.[200]

The Ministry of Petroleum and Minerals (MPM) announced plans in 1995 to spend $4 billion in oil exploration and development over the next 5 years. Roughly 18 percent of this amount was targeted for exploration, 44 percent for the development and installation of production facilities, and the remaining 38 percent for operating expenses.[201]

The 1996–2000 development plan calls for the Omani government to invest 865 million Omani Rials in crude oil projects, and for the private sector to invest 815 million Omani Rials. This will be 25% of all government investment (capital formation) during 1996–2000, 21% of all private investment and 23% of total investment. Total investment in oil will increase by 23% over total investment in oil during the previous 5 year plan.[202]

These efforts may well discover new oil reserves, and such discoveries will be critical to Oman's economic development. At the same time, Oman's oil assets are scattered over a wide area and most new discoveries have been smaller pockets at greater depths. Oman already has 47 gathering stations, 12 production stations, 1,800 wells in 75 fields, and a 2,700 kilometer pipeline network. Oman will need 5,000–6,000 new wells to meet its future production goals.

The use of advanced technology has become increasingly important to Oman's oil sector, and Oman is making steadily greater use of such technology. It now carries out 3-D seismic surveys, which allow for greater resolution of geological structures than the 2-D surveys that were initially used to map Oman's oil resources. Oman is now extensively using infill drilling, simplified well designs, production automation, and secondary recovery and EOR techniques. It is shifting to horizontal drilling and will use this in over 70 percent of all future wells. Horizontal wells can result in a 300 percent increase in well productivity with only a 50 percent increase in cost.[203]

Oman has had considerable success. Oman's largest producing oil field is at Yibal, which supplies approximately one-quarter of PDO's total production. An ongoing drilling program at Yibal has resulted in over 75 new wells since 1991, many of which are horizontal. Production at Yibal rose from 140,000 barrels per day in 1986 to roughly 170,000 barrels per day in 1994. With the recent completion of four gathering centers, the $200-million Shuaiba Phase 2 project is commencing and will involve drilling 96 more wells.

Oman completed a $300-million water injection project at PDO's Lekhwair oil field in 1992. Production at the field subsequently increased from 26,000 barrels per day in 1992 to over 100,000 barrels per day in 1993. In addition to new production and injection facilities, the Lekhwair project involved drilling over 200 wells and the construction of four gas pipelines. The lines to connect Lekhwair to the Yibal gas plant will be needed as production of associated gas increases.[204]

Occidental is currently producing 30,000-barrels per day of 42° API crude oil from its Safah field on the Omani-United Arab Emirate border. The Safah field has estimated recoverable reserves of about 120 million barrels. In addition, Oxy has active exploration efforts in the area. Elf is producing 46° API crude oil from its small Sahmah and Ramlat fields. However, the company estimated in mid-1994 that Sahmah's reservoir was 80 percent depleted. After coming on-line in 1980, Sahmah's output has fallen from 13,000 barrels per day in 1992 to about 6,000 barrels per day in 1994. In 1990, Japex began production of 7,500 barrels per day from its small Daleel field. In late 1994, the company was attempting to boost production with 10 new horizontal wells. However, well productivity is low, and the horizontal wells are anticipated to add only 2,000 barrels per day.[205]

Refining and Downstream Projects

Oman now has limited refining and downstream operations. In 1982, Oman constructed its first refinery at Mina al-Fahal. Subsequently, the 50,000-barrel per day plant was expanded to 85,000 barrels per day. MPM proposed selling the refinery in late 1993, but this proposal has not yet received government approval.[206]

Oman is attempting to expand both its domestic and international downstream operations. In April 1995, Neste-Borealis, a Finnish-Norwegian venture, signed a letter of intent to study the feasibility of constructing a 260,000 ton per year ethylene plant and two polyethylene plants. The proposed $700-million complex would take five years to build and would have the capacity to produce 65,000 barrels per day of polypropylene for export, possibly to Asia.[207]

Oman formed the Oman Oil Company (OOC) in the late 1980s, in an effort to promote Oman's interests in overseas downstream operations. OOC's first agreement occurred in 1991, when it assisted the government of Kazakhstan in its negotiations with foreign oil companies, namely Chevron. In 1993, OOC obtained an exploration tract in Atyrau in western Kazakhstan. OOC's most significant activity in Kazakhstan is its participation in the Caspian Pipeline Consortium (CPC), which includes Kazakhstan and Russia. The consortium is planning to build a 1.5-million barrels per day export pipeline to transport oil from Kazakhstan's large Tengiz oil field to the Black Sea.[208]

There are problems in this project because Chevron is developing the field separately under the Tengizchevroil joint venture, and would be the proposed pipeline's major supplier. Chevron has so far refused to enter the consortium because of a disagreement with Oman over financing and equity ownership. Oman had agreed to provide the $100 million capital necessary for the first phase of a pipeline. However, Chevron wants participation in this first phase and will not commit to using the proposed line, which ultimately would run through Russia. In June 1995, there were indications that Kazakhstan might eject Oman from CPC in an effort to placate Chevron—although some experts believe Oman has firm legal status as a member of the CPC and that Russia firmly supports Oman's participation.[209]

The Oman Oil Company (OOC) is also involved in several overseas refinery projects. In India, OOC has a 26% stake in a Hindustan Petroleum venture to build a 120,000-barrels per day refinery on India's west coast. OOC has a share in a Bharat Petroleum project to construct a 120,000-barrels per day refinery in Madhya Pradesh. This venture will include a 400-mile crude oil pipeline linking the refinery to a coastal terminal. Both refineries are expected to come on-line by 1999 and will cost OOC approximately $2.7 billion for its share of the finances. Oman hopes to supply roughly 60,000 barrels per day of crude oil to each refinery.

The OOC agreed in October 1994 to provide the financing for the construction of a 100,000-barrels per day refinery in Sindh in Pakistan. The OOC had considered minority stakes in two refineries in Thailand. In May 1995, however, OOC dropped out of its plans for a 25 percent share in a Caltex venture to build a 130,000-barrels per day refinery at Rayong. However, OOC is still evaluating an investment with Sukhotai Petroleum to construct a 130,000-barrels per day refinery.[210]

Oman's Emerging Gas Industry

Gas is an important source of future revenue. Gas currently only produces about 122.1 billion cubic feet of gas per year, which provides about 3% of the revenue of Oman's government versus 77% for oil. However, Oman has nearly doubled its estimated gas reserves since 1992, as the result of an extensive exploration program and gas is likely to be a major source of future earnings.

The Energy Information Agency (EIA) of the US Department of Energy (DOE) estimates that Oman currently has proven reserves of 22–25.3 trillion cubic feet (tcf), with recoverable reserves of at least 14.5 tcf. About one-third of this amount is associated gas, most of which is located in the Natih and surrounding fields.

The International Energy Agency (IEA) uses somewhat different calculations, but estimates that Oman has proved reserves of 600 billion cubic meters and ultimate reserves of 640 billion cubic meters. At least 200 billion cubic meters of these reserves can be used to support LNG exports. The IEA estimates that Oman has an annual export potential of 6.2 million tons of LNG and can sustain this production from 2000 to 2020 and beyond.[211]

Neither the DOE or IEA estimates rank Oman among the world's top 20 nations in gas reserves. Chart Nineteen and Table Twenty-Two show Oman's ranking, and indicates that Oman has only about 2% of the worlds reserves. At the same time, all recent estimates indicate that Oman can be a significant LNG exporter, and support a petrochemical industry. There are also indications Oman may have substantially larger gas reserves in areas that are still to be explored. Omani estimates of Oman's reserves already have reached 27.4 trillion cubic feet, with 11 to 14 trillion cubic feet in Oman's central fields. Some experts feel that Oman has potential reserves of 33–35 trillion cubic feet.[212]

Investing in Gas Development. As a result, Oman is making a massive increase in its investment in natural gas and LNG projects. The Omani government invested 143 million Omani Rials in natural gas and LNG projects during its 1991–1995 five year plan, and the private sector invested 23 million Omani Rials. These investments totaled only 6% of government investment (capital formation) during 1991–1995, 1.4% of private investment and 4.3% of total investment.[213]

In contrast, Oman's 1996–2000 development plan calls for the Omani government to invest 1,504 million Omani Rials in natural gas and LNG projects, and for the private sector to invest 928 million Omani Rials. This effort will account for 44% of total government investment (capital formation) during 1996–2000, 24% of total private investment and 33.4% of total investment.[214]

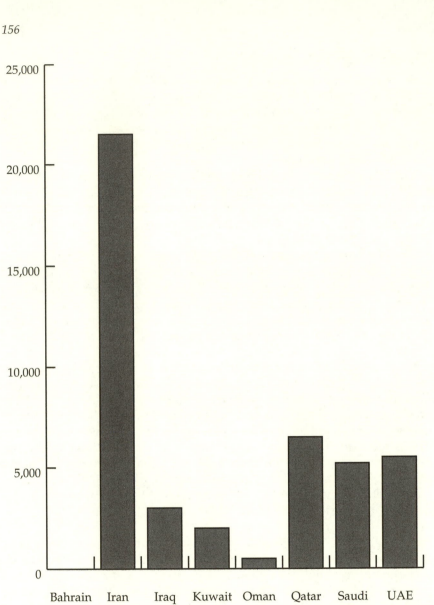

CHART NINETEEN Total Gas Reserves of the Gulf States (in Billions of Cubic Meters). *Source:* Adapted by Anthony H. Cordesman from IEA, *Middle East Oil and Gas,* Paris, OECD, IEA, 1995, Annex 2, and data provided by Bahrain and Oman. Bahrain's reserves are too small to show on the chart because of scale.

TABLE TWENTY-TWO   Gulf and World Gas Reserves and Production

Nation	Reserves in 1995		Percent World Supply	Production in 1993 (BCM)
	TCF	*BCM*		
Bahrain	—	—	—	—
Iran	741.6	21,000	14.9	60.0
Iraq	109.5	3,100	2.2	2.75
Kuwait	52.9	1,498	1.1	5.17
Oman		600–640		
Qatar	250.0	7,070	5.0	18.4
Saudi Arabia	185.9	5,134	4.2	67.3
UAE	208.7	5,779*	4.2	31.63
Gulf	1,548.6	—	31.1	185.25
Rest of World	3,431.7	104,642	68.9	—
World Total	4,980.3	148,223	100.0	—

Note: *Other sources estimate 6,320–7,280 BCM for Abu Dhabi only.

Source: The reserve and production data are adapted by Anthony H. Cordesman from IEA, *Middle East Oil and Gas*, Paris, OECD, IEA, 1995, Annex 2.

Total Omani investment in LNG projects will rise from 60 million Omani Rials in 1991–1995 to 2,355 million Omani Rials during 1996–2000.[215] The cost of this investment will be a major factor shaping Oman's future budget deficits and the high capital cost of its 1996–2000 five year plan (7,283 million Omani Rials versus 3,886 million Rials for the previous five year plan).[216]

Gas Development Plans.   The development of Oman's gas reserves may not be easy in spite of this investment. Over 10 tcf of Oman's non-associated gas is located in deep geological structures, many of which are beneath active oil fields. Oman's only producing non-associated gas field is the offshore Bukha field, bordering Iranian territorial waters.

Oman has, however, already made considerable progress. It began the development of its gas resources in the late 1970s. It built gas pipelines and processing facilities to utilize, rather than flare, associated gas. A 580-million cubic foot per day (mmcf/d) gas treatment plant at Yibal was constructed in 1985, and just under 200 mmcf/d was processed through the MPM gas system for domestic use in 1992.[217]

A consortium of Vancouver-based IPC, Bermuda-based Transworld Oil, and South Africa-based Engen developed the Bukha gas field, which came on-line in mid-1994. Its production is currently limited to 44 mmcf/d by an underwater export pipeline connecting the field to Ras al-Khaymah in the United Arab Emirates. Oman and Iran agreed to consider jointly developing the 1-tcf Hengam gas field in 1993, but no progress followed.

Since that time, Oman has examined two major gas export projects, and has already moved forward with one. The first project is an $8.2-billion, 6.2 million ton per year LNG plant. The project is under development by the Oman Liquefied Natural Gas Company (OLNGC) which is comprised of the Omani government (51%), Shell (34%), Total (6%), Mitsubishi (3%), Mitsui (3%), Partex (2%), and Itochu (1%).

In October 1994, the Omani government committed much of the country's gas resources to this LNG project. The proposed plant will be supplied with an estimated seven tcf of non-associated gas from the recently discovered Saih Nihayda, Saih Rawl, and Barik gas fields. Under the plan, gas will be shipped via a $600-million, 250-mile pipeline to the plant at al-Ghalilah, about 125 miles from Muscat.

The Omani government plans to borrow about $5.1 billion of the total project cost, and about $2.25 billion of this cost has already been underwritten by a consortium of eight banks. If there are no financing difficulties, the plant will come on-line in 2000. Contract awards for the plant construction are expected in mid-1996. There were indications in June 1995, that a Mitsui-Flour Daniel consortium was a leading candidate but plans to finance the first $3.5 billion of the project were still being finalized in December, 1995.[218]

OLNGC currently is looking for LNG buyers, including Japan, Thailand, and other Asian countries. In March 1995, Korea Gas Corporation signed a contract to receive three million tons per year for 25 years, beginning in 2000. In December, it also agreed to provide the necessary LNG tankers, relieving Oman of the burden of buying the tankers and saving it an estimated $1 billion. After additional customers are found, OLNGC anticipates that LNG and associated condensate sales could add an additional 20 percent of revenues on top of Oman's oil revenue base.[219]

Oman also hopes that its gas and LNG projects will provide resources for industrial development in Oman. It is setting up a one billion dollar fertilizer plant at Sur, with a capacity of about 1.7 million tons per year. It has plans for a gas-fed 360,000 ton per year aluminum smelter, a 1,300 megawatt power plant, and a desalination plant at Sohar, and is studying the feasibility of a major ethylene cracker and polyethylene plant. It hopes that gas development will trigger other industrial projects and create an industrial center around the gas and fertilizer plants at Sur.[220]

The second project is much more uncertain and may be canceled. This project is a gas pipeline to India. In September 1994, Oman signed an agreement with India to build a 600-mile underwater pipeline to carry Omani gas from Ras al-Jifan to Gujarat on India's western coast. The pipeline would face major technical challenges. It would have to move through waters some 3,000 meters deep and be the deepest pipeline in the world. It would cost an estimated $5 billion to support potential exports worth $50-billion in natural gas sales over the project's lifetime.

In 1994, a feasibility study was completed by a consortium comprised of McDermott, Bechtel, ETPM, and Saipem and Snamprogetti. Construction of the 11,500-foot deep pipeline was originally set to begin in mid-1995. Plans for the pipeline project indicated that the first phase could supply 1 Bcf per day by 1999, and a second 1-Bcf pipeline might be built by 2001. In March 1994, the Oman Oil Company signed a deal to build a 5,000-megawatt (MW) power station fueled by gas from the proposed Omani pipeline to supply western and southern India with electricity.[221]

In April 1995, however, Omani officials announced that more time was necessary to overcome the technical problems associated with the depth of the pipeline, which would be over four times deeper than the world's present deepest underwater pipeline. Many experts also believe that Oman does not have the gas resources to support both its LNG projects and a pipeline to India, and Oman already has a tentative commitment to provide gas for a smaller pipeline to Sharjah.[222]

The Growing Need for Diversification

The Omani government is conscious of Oman's dependence on oil and gas, and plans to diversify the economy as part of its 1996–2000 development plan. These shifts are shown in Table Twenty-Three, and the government plans to cut the oil sector's share of the GDP from 35% to 32% during 1995–2000. It also plans to cut the share of government from 23% to 11%, while it raises the share of commodity production from 12% to 16% and of other services from 40% to 42%.

Such plans are credible in broad terms, but they need close attention. At present, Oman's non-oil sector is heavily oriented towards services—only some of which contribute to development and true economic growth. Agriculture and fishing have declined in importance in recent years to only about 3.3% of the GDP, and little progress is really planned to increase the share of mining—which is only 0.26% of the GDP. Manufacturing is only about 5% of the GDP.

The service sector accounted for 54% of the GDP in 1995, and Oman's current plans indicate that it will still be 53% in 2000. Government services account for 13% of the GDP in 1995, and will still be 11% in 2000. The government sector has grown in recent years, in spite of recent budget deficits, and Omani sources indicate estimates that the government sector grew from 16% of the GDP in 1990 to 19% in 1993.[223]

Oman is also over-dependent on service industries. Much of Oman's service industry is productive and works in areas like tourist-related

TABLE TWENTY-THREE   Diversification of Oman's GDP (Millions of Current
                      Omani Rials)

Sector	1990	1995	2000	Average Annual Growth 1991–1995	1996–2000
Oil					
Crude Petroleum	—	1,833	1,909	–2.6	0.8
Natural Gas	—	57	214	3.4	30.1
Total	2,144	1,890	2,123	–2.5	2.3
Non-Oil					
Production					
Mining	—	17	27	7.8	9.0
Agriculture & Fishing	—	131	169	2.5	5.2
Manufacturing	—	242	445	12.9	13.0
Electricity & Water	—	58	103	8.0	12.2
Construction	—	178	334	11.5	13.4
Total	402	626	1,077	9.2	11.5
Services					
Government	—	696	714	3.9	0.5
Other	—	2,173	2,816	8.7	5.3
Total	2,005	2,869	3,530	7.4	4.2
Total Non-Oil	2,407	3,495	4,607	7.7	5.7
Imputed Banking Services	–91	–166	–132	5.0	2.5
Customs Duties	33	42	62	5.2	8.0
GDP	4,493	5,311	6,660	3.4	4.6

Source: Adapted by Anthony H. Cordesman from Sultanate of Oman, *Basic Components and Main Indicators of the Fifth Five Year Plan (1996–2000),* Muscat, Ministry of Development, January 1996, pp. 7, 13–15, 28–29.

hotels, restaurants, and construction. At the same time, many Omanis and expatriates seem to work in service jobs with limited or no productivity, whose main function is to market and service imports, or work in government. Oman's service sector is also very large for an economy in its state of development. This raises the issue of whether Oman is diversifying in the right areas.

Privatization and Foreign Investment

Privatization and foreign investment are important keys to Oman's future and Oman will need major outside investment to stimulate its economic development and maintain economic stability during the coming decade.[224] Oman intends to pay for much of its development plan with oil revenues. Oil is projected to provide 74% of state revenues during 1996–2000, based on an estimated average oil output of 880,000 barrels a day and an average real sale price of $15 per barrel.[225]

However, Oman cannot meet its investment needs with either government investment or total domestic savings. There is a nearly 46% gap between national savings and Oman's projected investment needs during 1996–2000, and the cost of this gap during 1996–2000 is estimated to total 3.3 billion Rials versus 1.3 million Rials during 1991–1995.

The 1996–2000 plan requires major government expenditures to support the cost of privatization. It also puts a heavy emphasis on the development of Oman's natural gas reserves to provide a revenue-generating substitute for the anticipated decline of its oil exports. The cost of developing a gas export infrastructure is high, especially when compared to the country's 1994 gross domestic product (GDP) of about $12 billion. Annual expenditures on a proposed $8.2-billion liquefied natural gas (LNG) plant, for instance, will comprise roughly one-quarter of GDP for each of the three fiscal years between 1996 and 1998.

Oman's 1996–2000 development plan calls for private investment totaling 3,862 million Omani Rials to help generate the required capital. This total is more than twice the 1,556 million Rials the private sector invested during the 1991–1995 five year plan, and raises the share of private capital from 40% during the previous plan to 53% under the new plan.

If the new plan is successful, private investment will rise by an annual average of 8.3%, with a 15.2% rise in the oil and gas sector and a 3.8% rise in the non-oil sector. Total private investment will rise from 247 million Rials in 1990, and 409 million Rials in 1995, to 609 million Rials in 2000.[226] The plan also strongly encourages the privatization of the public sector, especially utilities and infrastructure projects, and provides some government funds to support privatization.

Furthermore, Oman is seeking a major increase in foreign investment to offset the cost of economic development. Oman is seeking to increase annual foreign investment from a past level of around 1.1 billion Rials during 1991–1995, to a new peak of around 2 billion Rials by 1998. Its requirements will then drop to around 1.4 billion Rials in 2000.[227]

The government has already taken some steps to encourage this foreign investment. In November 1994, the government revised its investment law and raised the maximum percentage of foreign ownership from 49 percent to 65 percent. Full foreign ownership is now permitted under special conditions.

Oman's Minister of Commerce and Industry, Bin Ali Bin Sultan has strongly encouraged private investors in the European Economic Community (EEC) to set up projects in the Gulf, and held a meeting of such investors in Oman during October 16–18, 1995. The EEC's volume of trade with the GCC states totaled $34 billion in imports in 1994 (80% oil), and the EEC exported $60 billion in goods. Oman is hoping that this trade will be supplemented with increased investment, and that it can reduce oil and gas to only 20% of the GDP by the year 2020.[228]

Studies by World Bank, IMF, and other experts have indicated, however, that additional action is needed. Oman needs to remove bureaucratic barriers to foreign investment, eliminate its public sector deficit, reduce public consumption, privatize many areas of government activity, eliminate monopolies, and be more aggressive in encouraging Omanization and fostering policies that encourage the training of the native work force, a work ethic, and Omani entrepreneurial activity.[229]

Agriculture and Water

Oman is seeking to develop agriculture and fishing—along with tourism—as additional tools in diversifying its economy. However, Oman faces a major imbalance between the sectoral distribution of agricultural output and the sectoral distribution of its labor force.

Agricultural output and fishing account for only 2.5% percent of GDP. While the Omani 1996–2000 five year plan projects that the value of agriculture and fishing will rise by 5% per year, it still leaves agriculture at only 2.5% of the GDP in 2000.[230] These data indicate that Oman has no practical chance of moving forward towards its goal of agricultural self-sufficiency, or even of sustaining its present degree of reliance on native agriculture and food production or per capita output.

Equally important, 45% of Oman's labor force works in agriculture versus 24% in industry (including oil, gas, and mining) and 32% in services (including government and the military).[231] This is a very large share of the labor force in agriculture for so little productivity, and Oman only had 0.04 hectares of cropland per capita and 0.66 hectares of pasture land in 1989–1991. Unless radical changes take place, the fact that too many people already work in these industries means that this will present further problems for effective "Omanization," and population growth will mean that arable land per capita will drop by 15–20% per decade.[232]

Oman also faces major water problems. Oman has only about 0.43 cubic kilometers of internal renewable water resources, which is low, and which amounts to about 1,333 cubic meters per person. Even though Oman receives rain from the Indian Ocean monsoons, some 70% of its annual rainfall of 100 mm evaporates without affecting the soil. It is not surprising, therefore, that Oman has begun to deplete the water resources from its wells in the Batinhah Plain, its most fertile region, and may be depleting the water resources of the Salalah Plain.

Oman has long drawn down on its fossil water by over pumping its acquifers. Oman has tried to solve this water problem with retention dams that will force the water into the soil, and by repairing the 1,000 year old Persian system of underground aqueducts that once provided water in Oman's interior.[233] Desalination is too expensive to be a solution to meeting anything other than civil and urgent industrial needs, and Oman currently allocates nearly 94% of its natural water on agriculture versus 3% for domestic needs and 3% for industry.

Furthermore, Oman's rapid increase in population is causing its natural water resources per capita to drop sharply. The World Resources Institute and World Bank estimate that Omani natural per capita water resources dropped from 4,000 cubic meters in 1960 to 1,333 cubic meters in 1990 and will drop to 421 cubic meters in 2025. As a result, Omani water policy is a problem that needs more government attention.[234] Unless Oman receives outside development aid to help it with water, it will become increasingly dependent on food imports and may find it steadily more difficult to create jobs.[235]

Balance of Trade

Oman has a favorable balance of trade, but is a heavy importer of services and makes extensive factor and remittance payments. As a result, Oman had a trade surplus of 2,885 million Rials during the 1991–1995 five year plan, but a 1,353 million Rial deficit on its balance of external accounts. It had a nearly $1 billion deficit in current accounts in 1995, and is projected to have a $700 million deficit in 1996—in spite of higher oil prices.

Oman hopes to increase its trade surplus under its 1996–2000 five year plan, but this plan may be optimistic. Oman is attempting to counter a planned 32% increase in merchandise imports (7,637 million Rials to 10,063 million Rials) with a 27.2% increase in merchandise exports (10,522 million Rials to 13,384 million Rials). It is not clear where this increase in exports is coming from. Oman refers to major increases in exports of goods other than petroleum products and in re-exports, but does not define their source or content.[236]

The cost of imports of services, factor payments, and remittances is planned to rise by 56.8% during 1996–2000, from 4,328 million Rials to 6,645 million Rials. These costs are driven by a 3.6% annual increase in the cost of foreign services, a 15.7% annual increase in the cost of net factor payments, and a 2.9% increase in remittances by foreign labor. This increase in remittances is caused in part by the 1.7% annual rise in foreign workers discussed earlier, and will rise from an annual level of 314 million Rials in 1990, and 649 million Rials in 1995, to 748 million Rials in 2000.[237]

These trends could end in increasing Oman's trade and budget deficits. At the same time, any such increases seem likely to be moderate and much of the increase in the cost of external transactions is the result of the cost of developing Oman's LNG resources and the privatization of some of its service industries. Unlike a number of other Southern Gulf states, Oman is not straining its balance of payments and external transactions with the cost of non-productive services and imports related to subsidies and welfare payments.

Omani Budgets and Five Year Plans

Oman's government faces significant limits on its ability to sustain its economic growth and increase its real GDP per capita. In addition to a population growth rate of close to 4 percent per year, Oman's public sector resources have been strained by low world oil prices. The Omani government has run a fiscal deficit averaging 10 percent of GDP annually over the past 10 years. While the government cut public sector expenditures slightly in 1994, its ability to rein in public sector spending during the next several years will be of critical importance to Oman's economic future.

At the same time, Oman needs major investments to sustain economic growth. Oman's upcoming five year plan, which begins in 1996 and ends in 2000, has a total cost of 10,090 million Omani Rials or $26.2 billion. Oman cannot continue restructuring and diversifying its economy without the major capital expenditures discussed earlier. As a result, the five year plan for 1996–2000 projects budget deficits for every year until 2000, although these deficits do not, however, reach the levels Oman had to spend during 1991–1995.

However, *if* Oman can control its spending and obtain the foreign investment it desires, the new plan will lead to a major reduction in deficit spending. The 1991–1995 plan had a deficit of 2.25 billion Omani Rials or $5.84 billion. The new plan projects an average deficit that is 75% lower; it is projected to be 538 million Omani Rials or $1.397 billion. It also projects that total government spending will drop from 10.9 billion Rials in 1991–1995 to 10.6 billion Rials in 1996–2000, in spite of the growth of the rest of the economy, and that there will be a 23% drop in the size of the public debt relative to the GNP.[238]

Accelerating the Pace of Reform

Oman has an ambitious economic development program that will almost certainly strain the limits of what it can accomplish—if not significantly exceed them. Oman's 1996–2000 plan may be well focused, but it is unclear that it can succeed without new steps to encourage "Omanization," privatization, and foreign investment.

The plan seems too tolerant of Oman's current rate of population growth, too dependent on foreign labor and calls for too slow a rate of "Omanization." It is striking, for example, that the Omani per capita income has already dropped by an average of 2.5% per year during the 1991–1995 five year plan, and that the new plan calls for only a tenuous 1.2% annual increase during 1996–2000. Per capita GDP is projected to rise form 2,432 Rials in 1995 to 2,580 Rials in 2000, but this rise is in current dollars, and means that Oman's real per capita income will have dropped steadily over a decade.[239]

These problems could interfere with the success of Oman's development and reduce Oman's internal stability. Oman needs to reexamine its current programs, five year plans, and long-term planning efforts, and consider new steps to accelerate or initiate the following reforms necessary to:

- Limit population growth through a strong education program, strong birth control program, and family incentives.
- Force radical reductions in the number of foreign workers, with priority for reductions in servants and in trades that allow the most rapid conversion to native labor.
- Restructure the educational system to focus on job training and competitiveness. Create strong new incentives for faculty and students to focus on job-related education, sharply down-size other forms of educational funding and activity, and eliminate high overhead educational activities without economic benefits.
- Freeze and then reduce the number of civil servants, and restructure and down-size the civil service to focus on productive areas of activity with a much smaller pool of manpower. Cut back sharply on state employees by 2000.
- Reduce those aspects of state subsidies and welfare that distort the economy and discourage the native population from seeking jobs. Carry out those aspects of the 1996–2000 plan that reduce the cost of participation and subsidies for the private sector which do not encourage new privatization.[240]
- Eliminate economic disincentives for employers hiring native labor, and create disincentives for hiring foreign labor.
- Consider tax and other subsidies to encourage replacing foreign labor with Omanis.
- Establish market criteria for all major state and state-supported investments, requiring detailed and independent risk assessment

and projections of comparative return on investment, with a substantial penalty for state versus privately funded projects and ventures. Downsize the scale of programs to reduce investment and cash flow costs and the risk of cost-escalation.

- Further encourage privatization and eliminate monopolies. Create new incentives to invest in local industries and business and disincentives for the expatriation of capital, reduce regulatory barriers, and execute the privatization of infrastructure called for by Oman's former Deputy Prime Minister for Financial and Economic Affairs, Qais al-Zawawi.

- Create market driven incentives for foreign investment in major oil and gas projects, refineries, and petrochemical operations. Avoid offset requirements that simply create disguised unemployment or non-competitive ventures that act as a further state-sponsored distortion of the economy. Remove bureaucratic barriers to foreign investment.

- Fully implement new policies allowing foreign firms to have 65% to 100% shares in projects that develop Oman's economy. Simplify the tax laws affecting foreign investment and reduce special taxes and fees levied on foreign investments and firms with a foreign partner.

- Tax earnings and sales with progressive taxes that reduce or eliminate budget deficits, encourage local investment, and create strong disincentives for the expatriation of capital, including all foreign holdings of capital and property by members of elite and ruling families.

- Shift goods to market prices. Remove distortions in the economy and underpricing of services where they exist. Provide reasonable charges for medical services for all but the poor and shift electricity and water costs to full market prices.

- Alter tax laws that currently tax Omani-owned companies at 5–7.5%. Companies with some foreign ownership are taxed at rates of up to 30%, and companies with over 60% ownership are taxed at a sliding scale of up to 50%. This system deters foreign investment and under taxes some highly profitable Omani-owned firms. It needs to be revised to create more incentives for foreign investment in key industries necessary to Oman's development, to eliminate special taxes on stock-holding companies, and tax Omani owned companies at a more progressive rate.

- Establish a firm rule of law for all property, contract, permitting, and business activity and reduce state bureaucratic and permitting barriers to private investment.

- Ensure that all income from enterprises with state financing is reflected in the national budget and is integrated into the national economic development and planning program.

- Reform the structure of the budget to reduce the amount of money going directly to royal accounts, and ensure that most of the nation's revenues and foreign reserves are fully integrated into the national budget and into the planning process. Clearly separate royal and national income and investment holdings.
- Place national security spending on the same basis as other state spending. Integrate it fully into the national budget, including investment and equipment purchases. Replace the present emphasis on judging purchases on the basis on initial procurement costs and technical features with a full assessment of life cycle cost—including training, maintenance, and facilities—and with specific procedures for evaluating the value of standardization and interoperability with existing national equipment and facilities, those of other Gulf states, and those of the US and other power projection forces.

It is also important that Oman should go forward with its efforts at longer term planning. Oman is virtually the only Gulf country to have seriously examined its long term future and to have projected it to 2020. Oman carried out detailed studies of the long-term trends in key areas like sustained growth, gas development, expanding the private sector, and improving human resources. It then held a conference on these issues in Oman on June 3–4, 1995. This conference examined key reforms like Omanization, new incentives for selected foreign investments, creating medium-sized industrial operations, encouraging export-led growth, improving the educational system, and encouraging joint ventures.[241]

Oman needs to carry out similar exercises at regular intervals, expand them to cover demographic and labor trend analysis, and keep looking beyond a five year time horizon. At the same time, Oman's efforts to examine its future should be a model for all Gulf countries. The Gulf needs to do a far better job of coming to grips with both its long-term opportunities and its long-term limits. Even most academic and research groups in the Gulf rarely look more than five years in the future or objectively examine key problems like foreign labor and human resources.

Omani Military Forces

Oman's military forces are commanded by the Sultan, and senior military officers that are either members of the Sultan's family or members with a long history of proven loyalty to the Sultan. Oman has long focused on creating a cadre of well-educated officers has been able to steadily expand the level of Omanization within its forces. At the same time, Oman retains a number of British advisors and its military modernization has faced serious financial constraints.

The recent trends in Omani military expenditures and arms transfers are shown in Chart Twenty. These trends show that Oman has emphasized civil spending over military spending, and that Oman's arms imports are only a small fraction of its total revenues. Oman has a good cadre of Omani officers and NCOs and excellent British advisors. The Sultan appointed an Omani officer to the post of Commander of the Army for the first time in 1984. Oman again strengthened the role of Omanis in top leadership positions and throughout the officer corps in 1988 and 1990.

At the same time, Chart Twenty shows that Oman's total military expenditures are still a considerable portion of Oman's total budget, and Chart Twenty-One shows that Oman's military expenditures per capita represent a significant amount of its GDP per capita—because of a combination of a relatively static real GDP, a rapidly growing population, and the need to maintain significant levels of military spending.

Omani Military Expenditures

Chart Twenty reflects the fact that Oman's military expenditures have fluctuated with oil prices (total exports), and Oman has faced growing problems in developing its defense capabilities to deal with the threat posed by Iran and other regional security concerns. Oman has gotten little aid from its neighbors. While the other GCC states pledged to provide $1.8 billion in aid over 12 years in September, 1983, this total fell far short of what Oman needed to sustain increased expenditures, and much of this aid was never delivered.[242]

The US provided Oman with major amounts of military aid in the early 1980s to construct and expand the military facilities the US needed for prepositioning and staging its forces, but it only provided comparatively limited amounts of aid in obtaining military equipment and much of this "aid" came in the form of loans. Oman has received comparatively little US military aid in the late 1980s, and this aid dwindled to token amounts in the 1990s. As has been touched upon earlier, total US economic and military assistance rose from $5 million in 1981 to $15 million in 1983, but was only $3.6 million in 1992, and dropped to $1.1 million in 1993, and $0.1 million in 1994—poor compensation for a nation that has provided the US with extensive support over a 15 year period.[243]

Oman's funding problems are so serious that in 1994 the World Bank recommended that Oman make major cuts in its military spending to help compensate for its loss of oil revenues.[244] Nevertheless, Oman has tried to fund a transition from largely infantry forces to a more modern combined arms army during the last decade. Oman increased its annual military expenditures from around $700 million in 1979, to $1,059 million

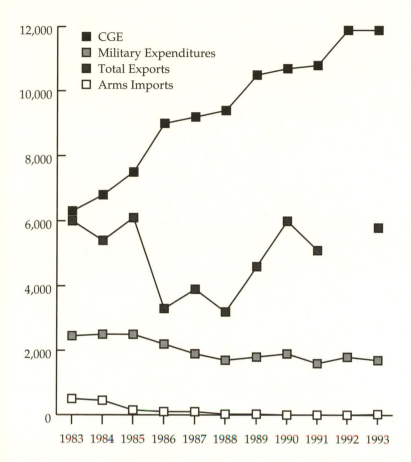

CHART TWENTY Oman's Central Government Expenditures, Military Expenditures, Total Exports, and Arms Import Deliveries: 1983–1993 (Constant $93 Millions). *Source:* Adapted by Anthony H. Cordesman from ACDA, *World Military Expenditures and Arms Transfers, 1993–1994,* ACDA/GPO, Washington, 1995.

in 1980, $1,357 million in 1981, $1,512 million in 1982, $1,744 million in 1983, $1,894 million in 1984, and $1,937 million in 1985. Problems in oil revenues, and diminishing tensions in the Iran-Iraq War then led Oman to cut spending back to $1,731 million in 1986, $1,518 million in 1987, $1,350 million in 1988, and $1,552 million in 1989.[245]

Unlike many of the Southern Gulf states, Oman could not make major increases in military spending because of the Gulf War. Oman only spent $1,707 million in 1990, $1,450 million in 1991, $1,767 million in 1992,

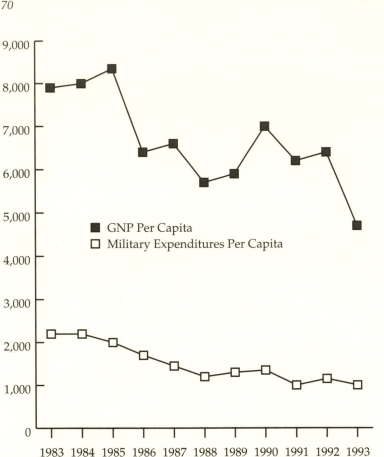

CHART TWENTY-ONE   Oman GNP Per Capita Versus Military Expenditures Per Capita (Constant $93). *Source:* Adapted by Anthony H. Cordesman from ACDA, *World Military Expenditures and Arms Transfers, 1993–1994,* Washington, ACDA-GPO, 1995, Table I.

$1,691 million in 1993, and $1,818 million in 1994.[246] While these figures may appear to be increases over Omani expenditures in 1986, they are reported in current dollars. Real military spending has dropped during most of the 1990s.

Measured in constant 1993 dollars, Omani expenditures peaked at $2,568 million in 1984. They declined to a low of $1,605 million in 1988, rose to $1,765 million in 1989 and $1,861 million in 1990, but dropped back to $1,522 million in 1991 and were $1,806 million in 1992 and $1,380 million in 1993.[247] According to the IISS, they were somewhat higher—at least in current dollars. The IISS estimates them at $1,920 million in current dollars in 1993, $1,900 million in 1994, and $1,590 million in 1995.[248]

At the same time Oman has spent 16 to 22% of its GNP on military forces in recent years, and 35 to 41% of its central government expenditures. This is a high level of national effort for what are modest military expenditures by Gulf standards. It is also one that Oman finds increasingly more difficult to sustain, in spite of recent increases in oil prices. Oman has been forced to consider mothballing some of its aircraft and helicopters, fire some its high-cost British contract pilots, and reduce the readiness of its army and navy.[249]

Oman has allocated 3.3 billion Omani Rials ($8.57 billion) for defense and national security in its fifth five year plan, which covers 1996–2000. This figure amounts to 38% of total expenditure in the plan, versus 42% in the 1991–1995 five year plan. Military spending escalated during the 1991–1995 plan from an estimated level of 2.9 billion Omani Rials ($7.54 billion) to an actual level of 3.6 billion Omani Rials ($8.73 billion). Omani budgets tend to undercost military expenditures and this could occur again in the coming planning period.[250]

Omani Arms Imports

The size of Oman's arms imports have varied sharply by year, although they have consistently reflected the limits posed by Oman's economy. Oman's arms imports have never exceeded $350 million per year and this peak was reached in 1983—when the Iran-Iraq War seemed most likely to threaten Oman in the form of Iranian pressure or attacks on the Musandam Peninsula and Goat Island in the Strait of Hormuz.

ACDA estimates that Oman imported $30 million worth of arms in 1979, $100 million in 1980, $60 million in 1981, $130 million in 1982, $350 million in 1983, $310 million in 1984, $140 million in 1985, $110 million in 1986, $110 million in 1987, $30 million in 1988, $60 million in 1989, $10 million in 1990, $50 million in 1991, $10 million in 1992, $120 million in 1993, and $ 50 million in 1994.[251]

While recent Omani arms expenditures have been limited by Gulf standards, they have still presented financing problems because of the decline in Oman's oil wealth, and oil accounts for 40% of Oman's GDP and 80% of its government expenditures. Oman's GDP is currently around $16.4 billion, and its per capita income is now about $5,000-$6,000, roughly 75% in constant dollars of what is was in the mid-1980s.[252]

The bulk of Oman's arms have come from Europe, many from Britain. ACDA estimates that Oman imported a total of $565 million worth of arms during 1979–1983, with $80 million from the US, $20 million from

France, $430 million from the UK, $10 million from Italy, $5 million from the PRC, and $20 million from other countries.[253] Oman imported a total of $670 million worth of arms during 1984–1988, with $30 million from the US, $20 million from France, $330 million from the UK, $280 million from Germany, and $10 million from other countries.[254]

ACDA indicates that Oman imported a total of $445 million worth of arms during 1985–1989, with $30 million coming from the US, $200 million from the UK, $210 million coming from Germany, and $5 million from other European countries.[255] It indicates that Oman imported a total of only $180 million worth of arms during 1992–1994, with $20 million coming from the US, $150 million from the UK, $5 million from the Middle East, and $5 million coming from other countries.[256]

Other US government data on Omani arms imports before and after the Gulf War are summarized in Chart Twenty-Two. These data indicate that Oman has continued to obtain most of its arms from Britain, but has broadened the range of countries it buys from. Reporting by the Congressional research service indicates that Oman signed a total of $600 million worth of new agreements during 1991–1994, all with major West European countries. This same source reports a total of $300 million worth of major new arms deliveries to Oman during 1991–1994, all of which came from Western Europe.[257]

Oman's recent arms purchases are shown in Table Twenty-Four, They reflect a heavy dependence on British arms, although Oman's recent naval purchases have included buys from the US and Oman has actively sought US equipment when aid was available.

Reporting by the US Defense Security Assistance Agency shows that Oman has spent comparatively little on new FMS sales agreements, although Table Twenty-Five indicates Oman ordered $67 million worth of FMS supplies in FY1990. Oman has not ordered US military construction services. US FMS deliveries reached $42 million in FY1991, but otherwise were under $10 million per year from FY1985–FY1995. Oman imported less than $10 million a year of commercial arms exports between 1985–1995. It has had only token amounts of International Military Education and Training (IMET), and has received virtually no Military Assistance Program (MAP) aid.[258]

Omani Military Manpower and Readiness

The size of Oman's forces relative to those of other Gulf states are shown in Table Twenty-Six. The trends in Oman's manpower are shown in Chart Twenty-Three, which reflects the impact of the Dhofar build-up in the late 1970s, a cut in manpower after the war, and then a steady build-up to reflect the growing threat from the PDRY and Iran.

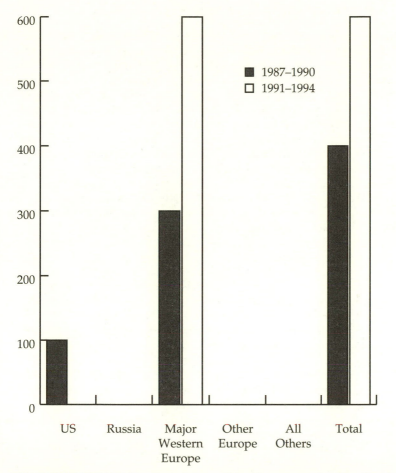

CHART TWENTY-TWO   Omani Arms Sales Agreements by Supplier Country: 1987–1994 ($Current Millions). *Source:* Adapted by Anthony H. Cordesman from work by Richard F. Grimmett in *Conventional Arms Transfers to Developing Nations, 1987–1994,* Congressional Research Service 95-862F, August 4, 1995, pp. 56–57.

Oman's military manpower slowly increased from 15,000 in the early 1980s, to 25,000 in 1985, 25,500 in 1988, 30,400 in 1992, 42,900 in 1995, and 43,500 in 1996. This rate of increase has been limited largely by the size of Oman's military budgets, and a substantial number of Omanis serve in the forces of other Gulf states. Oman has a relatively large manpower base to draw upon by Southern Gulf standards.[259] The CIA estimates the total male manpower pool ages 15–49 is about 383,000, of which 217,735

TABLE TWENTY-FOUR   Key Omani Equipment Developments

- In June 1993, signed an order for 18 Challenger 2 main battle tanks, with the option to buy 18 more. It also ordered four Challenger armored repair and recovery vehicles, two driver training tanks, nine tank transporters, four Alvis Stormer command post vehicles, and a fully logistic support program. The Challenger 2s will be modified to avoid the engine overheating, and have larger radiators, and better air flow. They will have 12.7 mm machine guns instead of 7.62 mm, improved air conditioning, and a GPS system. Oman will receive the L26A1 depleted uranium round. Requirement for a total of 60–80 new tanks.
- Taking delivery on Teledyne Ryan Gold Medallion kits to upgrade its M-60s with 750 HP engines. These kits will be delivered at a rate of 20 per year.
- Ordered 80 Piranhas on May 18, 1994, with an option to buy 46 more and a 25 year support contract. Order includes models with 12/7 mm machine guns, and artillery observation, command, recovery, 81 mm mortar, and ambulance variants. Option for 46 more vehicles.
- Considering modernizing its 56 (CVR(R) series of vehicles, including 37 Scorpion reconnaissance vehicles.
- Examining equipping some of its vehicles with turrets using 120 mm smoothbore mortars.
- Examining purchase of Alvis Stormer APCs and ambulances and South African Mamba light armored vehicles for border surveillance and patrol duties.
- Additional light anti-tank weapons on order from Britain. Plans to buy Thomson-CSF MIRA thermal imaging sights to provide a night firing capability for its Milans.
- Ordered 24 155 mm self-propelled G-6 gun systems from Denel of South Africa.
- Considering purchase of the Vickers 155 mm ultra-lightweight field howitzers to replace its aging and heavy Soviet towed weapons.
- Considering bring its 28 Javelins up to the S-15 Starburst Standard and possibly buying French Matra Mistral light surface-to-air weapons.
- Ordered two additional 1,400-ton, 83 meter, missile corvettes from Vosper-Thorneycroft in late 1991.
- Ordered three Mawj-class (Vigilante JP400) fast attack craft from CMN France in September 1993.
- Examining the possible purchase of mine countermeasures boats, and a hydrographic ship.
- Examining the purchase of several LSTs or LCTs.
- Has expressed interest in obtaining 20 surplus US F-16s.
- Examining proposals for purchases of the E-2C. It is also examining proposals to buy new transport aircraft to replace and supplement its C-130Hs and Skyvans.
- Rapiers are currently being upgraded to the B1(X) standard, with new Mark 2 missile with an IR and proximity fuse.
- Studying the purchase of 25 mm or 35 mm air defense guns to supplement the Rapiers.

TABLE TWENTY-FIVE   US Foreign Military Sales (FMS), Commercial Arms Export Agreements, Military Assistance Programs (MAP), and International Military Education and Training (IMET) Programs with Oman: FY1985–1994 (Current Millions)

	1985	1986	1987	1988	1989	1990	1991	1992	1993	1994
Foreign Military Financing Program Payment Waived	40.0	9.1	—	—	—	—	3.0	0.5	1.0	—
DoD Direct	—	—	—	—	—	—	3.0	0.5	1.0	—
DoD Guarantee	40.0	9.1	—	—	—	—	—	—	—	—
FMS Agreements	0.7	0.2	0.6	5.6	0.8	67.2	0.8	5.5	6.3	1.3
Commercial Sales	5.0	8.8	4.3	3.0	1.0	2.2	2.8	1.5	1.7	0.1
FMS Construction Agreements	—	—	—	—	—	—	—	—	—	—
FMS Deliveries	1.3	0.7	0.3	0.8	0.5	6.1	42.2	5.8	8.0	8.9
MAP Program	—	—	—	—	—	—	—	—	—	—
MAP Deliveries	—	—	—	—	—	—	—	—	—	—
MAP Excess Defense Articles Program	—	—	—	—	—	—	—	—	—	—
MAP Excess Defense Articles Deliveries	—	—	—	—	—	—	—	—	—	—
IMET Program/ Deliveries	0.1	—	—	0.1	0.1	0.2	0.2	0.1	0.1	0.1

Source: Adapted from US Defense Security Assistance Agency (DSAA), "Foreign Military Sales, Foreign Military Construction Sales and Military Assistance Facts as of September 30, 1994," Department of Defense, Washington, 1995.

TABLE TWENTY-SIX Gulf Military Forces in 1996

	Iran	Iraq	Bahrain	Kuwait	Oman	Qatar	Saudi Arabia*	UAE	Yemen
Manpower									
Total Active	320,000	382,500	10,700	16,600	43,500	11,100	161,500	70,000	39,500
Regular	220,000	382,500	10,700	16,600	37,000	11,100	105,500	70,000	39,500
National Guard & Other	100,000	0	0	0	6,500	0	57,000	0	0
Reserve	350,000	650,000	0	23,700	0	0	0	0	40,000
Paramilitary	135,000	24,800	9,250	5,200	4,400	0	15,500	2,700	30,000
Army and Guard									
Manpower	260,000	350,000	8,500	10,000	31,500	8,500	127,000	65,000	37,000
Regular Army Manpower	180,000	350,000	8,500	10,000	25,000	8,500	70,000	65,000	37,000
Reserve	350,000	450,000	0	0	0	0	20,000	0	40,000
Tanks	1,350	2,700	81	220	85	24	910	133	1,125
AIFV/Recce, Lt. Tanks	515	1,600	46	130	136	50	1,467	515	580
APCs	550	2,200	235	199	7	172	3,670	380	560
Self Propelled Artillery	294	150	13	38	6	28	200	90	30
Towed Artillery	2,000	1,500	36	0	96	12	270	82	483
MRLs	890	120	9	0	0	4	60	48	220
Mortars	3,500	2,000+	18	24	74	39	400	101	800
SSM Launchers	46	12	0	0	0	0	10	6	30
Light SAM Launchers	700	3,000	65	48	62	58	650	36	700
AA Guns	1,700	5,500	0	0	18	12	10	62	372
Air Force Manpower	20,000	15,000	1,500	2,500	4,100	800	18,000	3,500	1,000
Air Defense Manpower	15,000	15,000	0	0	0	0	4,000	0	0

(continues)

TABLE TWENTY-SIX (continued)

	Iran	Iraq	Bahrain	Kuwait	Oman	Qatar	Saudi Arabia*	UAE	Yemen
Total Combat Aircraft	295	353	24	76	46	12	295	97	69
Bombers	0	6	0	0	0	0	0	0	0
Fighter/Attack	150	130	12	40	19	11	112	41	27
Fighter/Interceptor	115	180	12	8	0	1	122	22	30
Recce/FGA Recce	8	0	0	0	12	0	10	8	0
AEW C4I/BM	0	1	0	0	0	0	5	0	0
MR/MPA**	6	0	0	0	7	0	0	0	0
OCU/COIN	0	18	0	11	13	0	36	15	0
Combat Trainers	92	200	0	11	22	0	66	35	12
Transport Aircraft**	68	34	3	4	14	5	49	20	19
Tanker Aircraft	4	2	0	0	0	0	16	0	0
Armed Helicopters**	100	120	10	16	0	20	12	42	8
Other Helicopters**	509	350	8	36	37	7	138	42	21
Major SAM Launchers	204	340	12	24	0	0	128	18	21
Light SAM Launchers	60	200	0	12	28	9	249	34	87
AA Guns	0	0	0	12	0	0	420	0	0
Navy Manpower	38,000	2,500	1,000	1,500	4,200	1,800	17,000	1,500	1,500
Major Surface Combatants									
Missile	5	0	3	0	0	0	8	0	0
Other	2	1	0	0	0	0	0	0	0
Patrol Craft									
Missile	10	1	4	2	4	3	9	10	7

(continues)

TABLE TWENTY-SIX (*continued*)

	Iran	Iraq	Bahrain	Kuwait	Oman	Qatar	Saudi Arabia*	UAE	Yemen
Other	26	7	5	12	8	6	20	18	3
Submarines	2	0	0	0	0	0	0	0	0
Mine Vessels	3	4	0	0	0	0	5	0	3
Amphibious Ships	8	0	0	0	2	0	0	0	2
Landing Craft	17	3	4	6	4	1	7	4	2

Notes: Does not include equipment in storage. Air Force totals include all helicopters, and all heavy surface to air missile launchers.

*60,000 reserves are National Guard Tribal Levies. The total for land forces includes active National Guard equipment. These additions total 262 AIFVs, 1,165 APCs, and 70 towed artillery weapons.

**Includes navy, army, national guard, and royal flights, but not paramilitary.

Source: Adapted by Anthony H. Cordesman from International Institute for Strategic Studies *Military Balance* (IISS, London), in this case, the 1995–1996 edition; *Military Technology, World Defense Almanac, 1994–1995*; and Jaffee Center for Strategic Studies, *The Military Balance in the Middle East, 1993–1994* (JCSS, Tel Aviv, 1994).

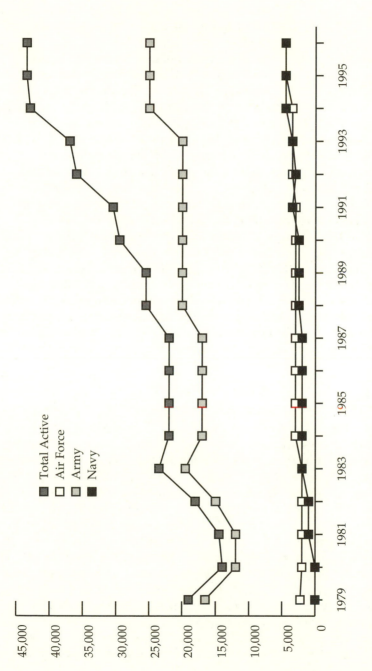

CHART TWENTY-THREE Oman: Military Manning—1979–1996. *Source:* Adapted by Anthony H. Cordesman from various editions of the IISS, *Military Balance,* the JCSS, *Military Balance in the Middle East,* and material provided by US experts.

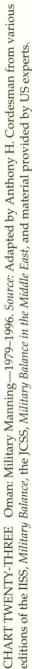

are fit for military service. About 22,000 males reach military age (14 years) each year. The IISS estimates that there are 105,600 males between the ages of 13 and 17, 83,400 between the ages of 18 and 22, and 127,800 between the ages of 23 and 32.

Manpower is also Oman's greatest military strength. Its troops are among the best trained and motivated troops in the Southern Gulf, and Qatar and the UAE have previsouly recruited in Oman to supplement their military manpower pools. Oman is one of the few states in the Gulf to have a professional NCO corps and to give NCOs their proper importance.

At the same time, the Omani manpower pool lacks technical education and Omanis resent performing service jobs like assignments as cooks. Like most Gulf citizens, Omani other ranks also do not like cleaning and low level maintenance work—which is seen as demeaning—although the armed forces have succeeded in training an increasing number of mechanics and other personnel for "hands on" technical work.

About 3,700 of Oman's 43,500 military personnel are foreign. Oman is slowly converting its officer corps to native personnel, but still has nearly 150 British officers and NCOs seconded to the Omani armed forces. It also has limited number of personnel from Jordan and Egypt, and large numbers of Pakistani Baluchis, many of whom are becoming Omani citizens. Oman has established both specialized secondary schools to train its military intake, and a central training center near Muscat. It trains officer and technical personnel in Britain, Germany, France, Jordan, and Saudi Arabia.

The Omani Army

Oman's force structure is significantly different from that of most other Gulf states. Chart Twenty-Three shows that Oman has built up a relatively large army by the standards of the Southern Gulf states, and it is important to note that this manpower is native, and well motivated. In 1996, the Omani Army had about 25,000 highly trained regulars, almost all consisting of native Omanis. Omani soldiers and army officers are respected throughout the Gulf and Omanis often form an important portion of the total military manpower of other GCC states, especially those of the UAE.

At the same time, Oman's army has relatively little heavy and high technology equipment—although Charts Twenty-Four and Twenty-Five show that the Omani Army is slowly expanding its armor and artillery strength. Chart Twenty-Four shows that Oman has limited tank strength and has not mechanized most of its forces. It has chosen instead to put its resources into the other types of armored vehicles that are best suited to its terrain and threats. Accurate data are not available on the trends in Oman's artillery holdings, but Chart Twenty-Five is broadly accurate in showing a recent build-up in weapons strength.

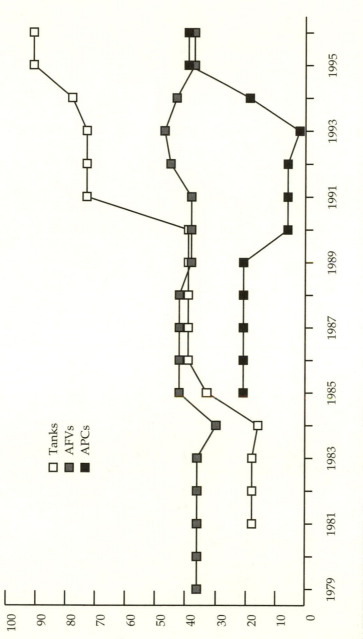

CHART TWENTY-FOUR Oman: Armored Weapons Strength—1979–1996. *Source:* Adapted by Anthony H. Cordesman from various editions of the IISS, *Military Balance,* the JCSS, *Military Balance in the Middle East,* and material provided by US experts.

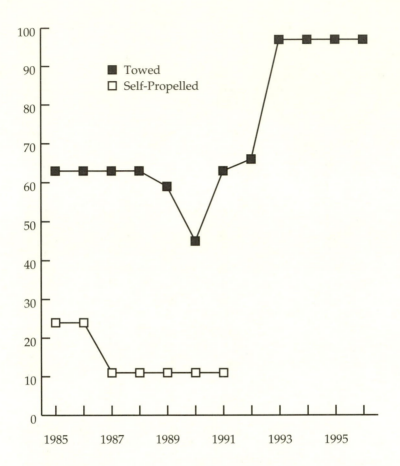

CHART TWENTY-FIVE   Oman: Artillery Weapons Strength—1979–1996.
Source: Adapted by Anthony H. Cordesman from various editions of the IISS,
Military Balance, the JCSS, *Military Balance in the Middle East,* and material
provided by US experts.

Organization and Command Structure

The Omani army is organized under a division headquarters with two
brigade headquarters. Its combat and major support forces were organized largely into regiments about the size of Western battalions. In 1996,
these forces included:

- One armored brigade with two armored regiments with three tank
  squadrons,

- One armored reconnaissance regiment with three armored car squadrons,
- Five Omani and 3 Baluchi infantry regiments,
- One airborne regiment,
- One infantry reconnaissance regiment with 3 reconnaissance companies,
- Two independent reconnaissance companies.
- Two field artillery regiments.
- One medium artillery regiment with two batteries.
- One air defense regiment with two batteries, and
- One field engineer regiment with three squadrons.

Oman had several independent land force units: a royal household force with 6,500 men—including a Royal Guard brigade of 5,000 men, equipped with Fahd 4X4 APCs. It had two special forces regiments with 1,000 men, which is equipped with new inflatable boats and assault rifles. It has a 250 man Royal Flight, and a 150 man royal yacht squadron with two ships: a 3,800 ton yacht with a helipad, and troop and vehicle transport that could deck up to two AS-332C Puma helicopters. There was also a Musandam Security Force with an independent rifle company.[260]

Oman had another brigade in the north, and a Royal Guard brigade to guard the Sultan in Muscat. Oman deployed some of its forces on the Saudi and UAE borders, and some in the Musandam Peninsula. In spite of improved relations with Yemen, it kept a full regiment deployed along the mountainous border area between the two countries. This unit is one of Oman's most effective forces. It has some British officers or advisors, and is located in fire bases and strong points along the border. Oman had reserve ground forces and supplies in Thamarit and Salalah, and considerable helicopter support. The road net and military communications system throughout Oman is surprisingly modern, and Omani infantry forces have considerable mobility.

Army Equipment

The Oman army has long faced severe financial problems in modernizing its forces. In 1996, Oman it had only 24-Chieftain Mark 7 and Mark 15, 43 M-60A3, and 6 M-60A1 tanks, although it had ordered new tanks and armored vehicles.

The Oman army signed an order for 18 Challenger 2 main battle tanks, with the option to buy 18 more, in June, 1993. It also ordered four Challenger armored repair and recovery vehicles, two driver training tanks, nine tank transporters, four Alvis Stormer command post vehicles, nine

Unipower M series tractor trucks and Lohr semi-trailers, and a fully logistic support program.

The Challenger 2s will be modified to avoid engine overheating, a problem exposed during trials in Oman, and will have larger radiators, and better air flow. They will have 12.7 mm machine guns instead of 7.62 mm, improved air conditioning, and a GPS system. Oman will receive the L26A1 depleted uranium round.[261] The first deliveries of these tanks began in late August, 1995, and were complete by the end of 1995.

Oman has an option for 18 more Challengers, and nine more Unipower M series tractor trucks and Lohr semi-trailers, but has not exercised it. It has a requirement for a total of 60–80 new tanks. Oman also is taking delivery on Teledyne Ryan Gold Medallion kits to upgrade its M-60s with 750 HP engines. These kits will be delivered at a rate of 20 per year.[262]

Oman's holdings of other armored vehicles are equally limited. In 1996, its holdings of other armored fighting vehicles included 37 Scorpions, 9 VBC-90s, and 13 Sultans. Oman also had 4 VAB/VCI armored infantry fighting vehicles, and 9 VAB/VCI and 15 AT-105 armored personnel carriers. Some estimates indicate it had 40 Saladin armored cars and 8 other armored vehicles in storage.

Oman is, however, buying more modern light armored fighting vehicles to mechanize its infantry. During 1991–1992, it examined the purchases of CIS BTR 80 8X8, French SMS VAB, Swiss GKN MOWAG Piranha 8X8, and US Cadillac Gage Textron V-300 6X6 families of armored vehicles. It ordered 80 Piranhas on May 18, 1994, plus a 25 year support contract. The order included models with 12/7 mm machine guns, and artillery observation, command, recovery, 81 mm mortar, and ambulance variants. Oman took delivery on 20 Piranas by mid-1995, and deliveries are to be completed by the end of 1996.[263]

Oman has an option to purchase 46 more vehicles—including anti-tank and reconnaissance variants. It is considering modernizing its 56(CVR(R) series of vehicles, including its 37 Scorpion reconnaissance vehicles. Oman is also examining equipping some of its vehicles with turrets using 120 mm smoothbore mortars, and the purchase of Alvis Stormer APCs and ambulances and South African Mamba light armored vehicles for border surveillance and patrol duties.[264]

The Omani army also has 8 TOW-II and 10 TOW launchers mounted on light vehicles, and additional crew portable TOW launchers. It has 32–50 Milan anti-tank guided weapons, including some on VCAC armored vehicles. It has 10 106 mm recoilless rifles and large numbers of 84 mm Carl Gustav rocket launchers. Additional light anti-tank weapons are on order from Britain. It plans to buy Thomson-CSF MIRA thermal imaging sights to provide a night firing capability for its Milans.

The army has long relied on towed artillery weapons. They include 42 ROF light 105 mm howitzers, 12 M-1946 and 12 Type 59-1 130 mm guns, 30 D-30 122 mm howitzers. According to some reports, it also has 12 FH-70 155 mm howitzers, and 25–30 towed 70 mm multiple rocket launchers. This reliance on towed weapons has seriously limited its armored maneuver capability and ability to deploy to other nations in the Gulf.

Oman is, however, converting to self-propelled weapons. It has 12 M-109A2 self-propelled artillery weapons. It has also ordered 24 155 mm self-propelled G-6 gun systems from Denel of South Africa, 12 of which had been delivered by the end of 1995. The G-6 has a maximum range of 39 kilometers, versus 27 kilometers for Oman's M-46s, and developmental rounds exist with ranges over 40 kilometers. The G-6s are being delivered from October, 1995 to April, 1996.[265] Oman's holdings of mortars include 90–100 81 mm, 20 4.29 M-30 107 mm mortars.

Oman has no sophisticated artillery targeting and fire control systems. It is considering ordering UAVs to improve its targeting and reconnaissance capabilities. Oman is also considering purchase of the Vickers 155 mm ultra-lightweight field howitzers to replace its aging and heavy Soviet towed weapons.[266]

Oman has relatively few light air defense weapons. Its holdings include several 20 mm unguided air defense guns (9 on VAB-VDAASs), 4 ZU-23-2 23 mm guns, and 12 Bofors L/60 40 mm guns. It also has 24 Blowpipe launchers, 28–29 Shorts Javelin RBS-70 fire units, and 34 SA-7 light surface-to-air missiles. Oman has, however, bought Oerlikon-Contraves 35 mm GDF towed anti-aircraft guns, which are controlled by Skyguard radars. It is considering bringing its 28 Javelins up to the S-15 Starburst Standard and possibly buying French Matra Mistral light surface-to-air weapons.[267]

The Readiness and Warfighting Capability of the Omani Army

The Omani Army is steadily improving its exercise performance. It conducts exercises with French and US forces. Omani, British, French, and US forces hold a series of joint exercises called Kunjar Hadd in April of each year. The Omani Army has not found it easy to cooperate with the Saudi Army, however, and the refusal of Omani forces to obey Saudi commanders during the Peninsula Shield Exercise in 1992 effectively broke up the exercise.[268]

The Omani Army has proved to be effective in securing its border areas, and is highly effective in defending rough terrain. It has good basic training, and is effective in infantry and mountain combat. It has a strong NCO corps, although one lacking in technical education and training. It is perhaps the only land force in the Gulf with a clear understanding of the need for a proper balance between training, sustainability, maintenance, modernization, and force expansion. It is, however, experiencing growing problems in paying for the proper level of spares, war time reserves, and contract maintenance and is sometimes forced to deadline equipment because of the slow response of Western contractors in providing spares or carrying out repairs that must be done outside of Oman.

There are many areas, however, where the Omani army needs external aid to develop its capabilities. The Omani Army is badly under-equipped by comparison with most other Gulf armies and is only able to conduct limited armored or artillery operations. It is unable to afford proper standardization and interoperability. For example, its tank brigade has to operate three different types of tanks. It also is unable to afford important support equipment like night vision systems and chemical-biological warfare defense protection and decontamination gear.

Oman lacks rapid deployment capability, mobile sustainability and support, and any mechanized operations are dependent on operating from nearby bases. It badly needs added helicopter lift to deal with contingencies in the Musandam and along the Yemeni border.

Omani training is largely at the battalion level and the army would have problems in operating effectively in larger formations. There is a tendency to compartment planning and training by branch. Armored warfare training is largely in the mechanized infantry role, and Oman has had only limited armored maneuver and heavy armored warfare training.

The Omani Navy

Oman's navy must defend a 2,900 kilometer coastline, including the main shipping routes through the Strait of Hormuz. This helps explain why Chart Twenty-Three shows that Oman has built its naval manpower up from 2,000 men in the mid-1980s to 3,400 in 1992, and 4,200 in 1995.[269]

Chart Twenty-Six shows the comparative strength of the Gulf's naval forces, but it is more of an indication of how difficult it is to provide even a crude "head count" of naval strength than an indication of the relative strength of the Omani Navy. Far too many of the ships of the other Gulf navies shown in this chart spend virtually all of their time decorating their home ports and lack combat-effective crews. In contrast, Oman has a long seafaring tradition, and it has had the services of excellent British advisors and officers, as well as training in France.

The Omani Navy is headquartered near Seeb. It has four major combat ships, 9 patrol boats, a support ships used in the patrol role (*al Mabrukah*), and six amphibious vessels and landing craft. It has a ship maintenance and repair facility at Muscat, and naval bases at Ghanam island, Mina Raysut near Salalah, al-Masnaa al-Wudam Alwa (the main base), Alwi,

Khasam, and Muscat. The new naval base at al-Masnaa al-Wudam was begun in 1977, and opened in mid-1988.[270]

Oman is slowly converting to all Omani manned naval forces, and the operational forces of the Navy are virtually all crewed by Omanis. The growth of the navy's size and technical sophistication has, however, meant that Oman is still dependent on British support.

Major Omani Naval Forces

Oman's principal ships consist of four 394-ton Province-class (Dhofar-class) fast attack boats, armed with 1 76 mm Oto Melara L/62 gun, twin 40 mm Breda Compact mountings, and 6–8 MM-40 Exocet missiles. Three of the ships have 2 × 4 Exocet missiles each, and one has 2 × 3. They were handed over to Oman in 1982–1988. The radar and fire control system includes a Racal-Decca TM1226C surveillance radar and Phillips 307 director.[271]

During the late 1980s, Oman planned to order four to six new missile corvettes. It had to cut these plans for financial reasons in 1990–1991, however, and ordered two 1,400-ton, 83 meter, missile corvettes from Vosper-Thorneycroft in late 1991. Oman has also considered a low cost lease for a US Navy FFG-7 frigate, but has had to reject this because it cannot afford the cost of the lease, training and conversion, and support facilities without external aid.[272]

The two new ships Oman has been able to buy from Vosper-Thorneycroft will be armed with an OTO Melara super-rapid, radar-guided 76 mm gun, two 20 mm guns, two nine barrel chaff/IR decoy launchers, and two quad launchers with eight Exocet MM-40 missiles. They will have modern radars (including a 3D surveillance radar), integrated electronic warfare systems and fire control systems—including the Thomson-CSF DR3000 ESM system and Signaal TACTICOS command system. They will be fitted with an octuple Crotale NG ship-to air missile launcher to act as a close-in defense system. Some press reports also indicate there will be provisions for a 16 cell vertical-launch Seawolf missile system, but these are not confirmed.

The first of these two ships, *the Qahir al Amwaj* was launched on September 21, 1994. Sea trials began in May, 1995, and the first ship was transferred to the Omani Navy in February, 1996. The second ship—the *Al Mua'zzar*—was launched on September 26, 1995. The ships have a crew of 61, and has demonstrated speeds in excess of 25 knots. No sonar or underwater defense systems are currently scheduled to be fitted, but they can be added at any time in the next two years and the British Aerospace/Thomson Sintra ASM Active Towed Array Sonar has been selected. No decision has been reached regarding the selection of a helicopter, but the ship can deck a Super Puma sized helicopter.[273]

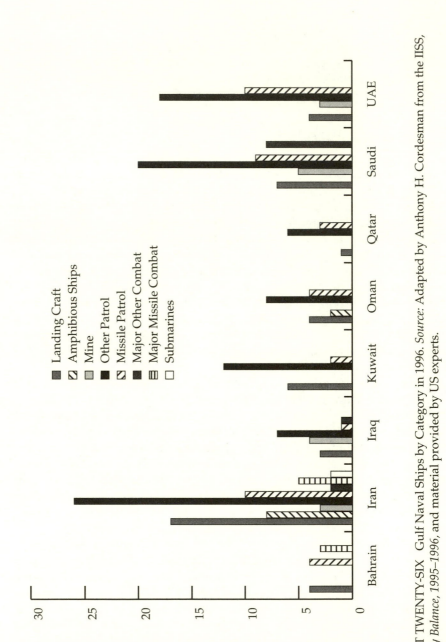

CHART TWENTY-SIX Gulf Naval Ships by Category in 1996. *Source:* Adapted by Anthony H. Cordesman from the IISS, *Military Balance, 1995–1996*, and material provided by US experts.

CHART TWENTY-SIX *(continued)*

	Bahrain	Iran	Iraq	Kuwait	Oman	Qatar	Saudi	UAE
Submarines	—	2	—	—	—	—	—	—
Major Surface Combat								
Missile	3	5	—	—	—	—	8	—
Other	—	2	1	—	—	—	—	—
Patrol Craft								
Missile	4	10	1	2	4	3	9	10
Other	—	26	7	12	8	6	20	18
Mine Vessels	0	3	4	—	—	—	5	3
Amphibious Ships	0	8	0	0	2	0	0	0
Landing Craft	4	17	3	6	4	1	7	4

Oman has one Al Mabrukah-class 900 ton patrol ship with a 40 mm gun. Oman declined the loan of a US Oliver Hazard Perry-class frigate in 1995, but is considering the future purchase of up to four more Qahir-class ships.[274]

The Omani navy has four 153-ton Brooke Marine (Al Wafji -class) 37.5 meter fast patrol boats, two of which are now armed with Exocet. These ships began to be delivered in 1977, however, and are best suited for close in patrol duty. It has four 61-ton (Seeb) 25 meter patrol boats armed with Oerlikon 20 mm guns; one Tyler-Vortex inshore patrol craft, and the Omani police have 8–13 light patrol boats, a dive boat, and 3 watercraft. None of these smaller ships has adequate air defense or modern sensors.[275]

Oman ordered three Mawj-class (Vigilante JP400) fast attack craft from CMN France in September, 1993. France also signed two military cooperation agreements with Oman in 1989, and Omani crews are being trained by Navfco in France and participating in exercises with the French navy. Oman has an option for four more ships, and has negotiated with France for the possible purchase of 6–8 more ships in batches of three.[276]

The first two French-supplied ships—the *Al-Bushra* and *Al-Mansour*—arrived in September, 1995, and the third will arrive in 1996. The Mawj-class ships will replace the Al Wafji-class vessels. They are 54 meter ships that displace 475 tons, and are armed with two 406 mm torpedo tubes, and 76 mm and 20 mm guns. They have surface search radars, modern Celsius Tech fire control systems, Sagem Viper infrared surveillance systems, and chaff launchers. They may be equipped with British Aerospace/Thomson Sintra ASM Active Towed Array Sonar systems. Oman has not yet decided on the IFF and torpedo systems for the ships.

Oman has one of the few GCC navies with some capability for amphibious operations. In addition to the ships in the Royal Yacht Squadron, Oman has one 2,500 ton LST called the *Nasr el Bahr* which can carry 240 troops, seven tanks, and a deck helicopter—although this ship is normally in reserve. It also has the *Al Munassir*, a 2,000 ton LST which can carry 200 troops, eight tanks, and deck a helicopter—although this is now used as a harbor training ship and may not be operational. Its active landing ships include three 230-ton LCMs, and 1–2 130-ton LCUs in service. Oman is examining the purchase of several LSTs or LCTs.[277] Oman is also interested in the mine countermeasure mission, and is examining the purchase of a hydrographic ship.

Oman's support ships include a 5,186-ton support ship, the *Al Mabrukah* training and offshore patrol ship, a 1,380-ton coastal freighter, a diving craft, two harbor craft, a sail training craft, two royal yachts, and a survey craft. The Omani coastguard is considering the purchase of new 35 meter patrol boats.[278]

The Readiness and Warfighting Capability of the Omani Navy

The Omani navy has growing proficiency and held the first GCC-wide naval exercise in 1994.[279] It now hosts key GCC naval exercises like the Taawun series. It has growing proficiency in anti-ship missile warfare and is acquiring the capability to perform technically sophisticated missions. It is also the most "international" of Oman's military services. It has exchanged port calls with the Iranian Navy and visits by the Omani and Iranian naval chiefs of staff.

Like the army, the Omani navy has a strong NCO corps, although one that needs improved technical education and training. It has understanding of the need for a proper balance between training, sustainability, maintenance, modernization, and force expansion. Like the army, however, it is experiencing growing problems in paying for the proper level of spares, war time reserves, and contract maintenance.

The main limitations of the Omani Navy are its lack of larger ships that could directly challenge Iranian ships, a lack of air defense capability, a lack of mine warfare capability, and a lack of maritime surveillance capability, although it has several transports it uses for visual airborne surveillance.

These are missions, however, which the Omani Navy can leave to the US and UK until it can afford far more sophisticated and more expensive missions. Both British and US ships and maritime patrol aircraft routinely support Oman in patrolling the approaches to the Strait of Hormuz, and the US can rapidly supplement Omani forces with over-the-horizon reinforcements. In the interim, the modernization of Oman's navy should allow it to deal with low level contingencies and create some deterrent capability against medium level conflicts even without US reinforcements.

At the same time, Oman lacks the funds it needs to maintain and improve the operating proficiency of its existing ships, and it has had to cut back on the readiness and activity of some of its forces—especially its support ships. Oman also does not have the funds to buy the level of modernization necessary to evolve improved defense capabilities and exercise sovereignty over its waters—a task no nation can delegate to others.

Further, unless Oman receives external aid, it may be forced to rely on outside forces for relatively routine patrol, surveillance, and mine warfare tasks—a function that is not cost-effective for other nations to perform. As a result, the US and Britain need to examine whether moderate direct aid would enable Oman to perform essential naval tasks at a far lower cost than sudden surges in Western power projection efforts.

The Omani Air Force

Chart Twenty-Three shows that Oman is one of the few Gulf countries that devotes enough manpower to its air force to properly support its aircraft. The Omani Air Force has about 4,100 men, almost all Omani citizens.

Oman has experienced problems in getting the skilled manpower it needs for its air force. It is gradually building up a cadre of native pilots, but still has only about 70% of its minimum requirement for pilots. According to one report, Oman only has 24 pilots for its 32 Jaguar and Hawk fighters and some of these pilots are from the RAF. Oman also seems to have only 24 pilots for its 30 helicopters. It does have a technical school, and is trying to improve the technical base of its air force manpower, but its combat and technical training is still limited. Oman is still heavily dependent on foreign support and technicians.[280]

Major Omani Air Units and Equipment

Chart Twenty-Seven reflects the history of the problems Oman has had in building up the Omani Air Force, and that its air force is still very small for a nation the size of Oman.[281] Oman currently has 46 active combat aircraft—with 10 more in storage—and no armed helicopters. The combat aircraft include two attack squadrons (Numbers 8 and 20 Squadrons) with 15 Jaguar S(0) Mark 1 and Mark 2s and 4 T-2s based at Thamarit. The Jaguars are good attack aircraft, but have been in service since 1977–1983, and only have limited visual air-to-air combat capability using guns and AIM-9-P4 infra-red missiles.[282]

Oman's other combat aircraft include a fighter ground attack/ reconnaissance squadron with 12 Hawk 203s and 4 Hawk 103s based at Masirah. Oman withdrew all its obsolete Hawker Hunter FGA-6 and FR-10/T-67 light attack/trainers from service. Oman has a COIN/training squadron with 12 aging BAC-167 Mark 82 Strikemasters, and has Skyvans at a number of bases. Oman's air ordnance is relatively unsophisticated and includes R-550 Magique and AIM-9P air-to-air missiles, and BL-755 cluster bombs.

Oman sought to buy up to two squadrons of F-16 or Tornado fighters during the mid-1980s, and planned to expand Thamarit air base into a fully modern facility to base them. In 1985, however, Britain offered preferential terms for a Tornado sale and Oman ordered eight Tornadoes as part of a $340 million arms package.[283] Oman ran into funding problems, however, and lacked the skilled manpower to operate such a force. As a result, it ordered 2 AS-202-18 trainers, and 16 Hawk trainers from the UK in 1990, at a cost of 150 million British pounds. The 16 Hawks include a mix of 12 Hawk 200 fighter/air defense aircraft and four Hawk 100 two-seat trainer/light attack aircraft. Deliveries began in 1993, and are allowing Oman to retire its aging Hunter FGA-73s or limit them to a training role.[284] Oman is considering the purchase of electronic warfare and mar-

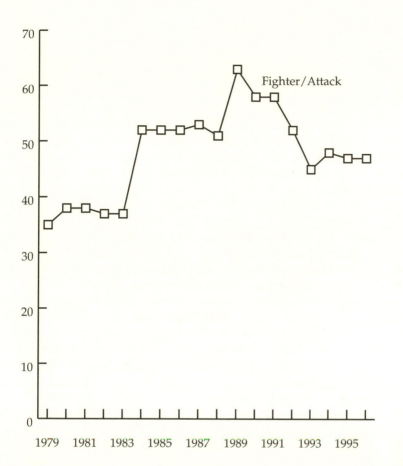

Fighter/Attack

CHART TWENTY-SEVEN   Oman: Fixed Wing and Rotary Wing Combat Air Strength—1979–1996. *Source:* Adapted by Anthony H. Cordesman from various editions of the IISS, *Military Balance,* the JCSS, *Military Balance in the Middle East,* and material provided by US experts.

itime surveillance aircraft, and is examining proposals for purchases of the E-2C.[285]

Oman recognizes that it has a need for modern air defense aircraft, and has expressed interest in obtaining 20 US F-16C/Ds, buying more Jaguars, or buying a new fighter. Oman does not, however, have the money to purchase such aircraft, handle the training and conversion costs, or create new dedicated maintenance facilities and related C^4I/BM capabilities. It can only modernize its air force to defend its air space, provide maritime surveillance, and provide air support for its navy if it receives external aid or can obtain "surplus" US fighters like the F-16A/B or F-18A/B.[286]

Oman has three transport squadrons. One with 3 BAC-111s, and two with 3 C-130H Hercules. Two squadrons with 15 Short Skyvan 3M STOL aircraft are at Salalah and Seeb. Oman has found the Skyvans to have great value in mountain and desert operations. The Omani air force helicopter force includes 3 AB-206 Jet Rangers, 20 AB-205s, 3 AB-212B/Bell 212s, and 5 AB-214s. These aircraft are based at Seeb and Salalah, with detachments at Khasab and Masirah. Oman would like to buy 20–30 Blackhawk or Cougar helicopters to improve its lift capability, but does not have the funds to do so.

The royal flight has two Gulfstreams, one DC-8, two B-747SPs fixed wing aircraft, and 2 AS-332C, 1 AS-332L, and 3 AS-330M armed helicopters. Oman has examined proposals for purchases of the E-2C, but lacks the money and crews to buy and operate the aircraft. It is examining proposals to buy new transport aircraft to replace and supplement its C-130Hs and Skyvans, but again lacks the funds to do so.[287]

Oman does not have any major surface-to-air missile systems in service or on order. Oman's land-based air defenses have undergone two major phases of improvement. The first phase took place during the early 1970s. It provided a mobile British Aerospace system that integrated warning and command and control radars with Oman's Jaguars, Hunters, and BAC-167 Strikemaster aircraft, and with 28 Rapier fire units. Marconi provided early warning radars and communications systems. These Rapiers are now deployed in two squadrons at Seeb, Masirah, and Thamarit. They are currently being upgraded to the B1(X) standard. This will give the Rapier units the new Mark 2 missile with an IR and proximity fuse.[288]

Oman is studying the purchase of 25 mm or 35 mm air defense guns to supplement the Rapiers. Oman bought four batteries of the Oerlikon 35 mm gun with the Skyguard radar with two guns each, to protect its army units. The air force would like similar weapons to protect its air bases but lacks the funds to make such a purchase. Oman also has the Denel 35 mm Englass gun with the GEC-Marconi Apache mobile fire control radar, Blazer self-propelled hybrid weapon system with the TRS-2630 surveillance radar, and G6 with the GEC-Marconi Marksman turret.[289]

The second phase began in 1985. Marconi received a contract to expand and improve the Omani air control and warning system. It provided two long range Martello S713 three dimensional radars, with associated MACE data display and handling systems. These are now operational, and are linked to two improved Sector Operations Centers (SOCs), two improved Control and Reporting Centers (CRCs), one regular CRC, and one new CRC. The improved CRCs are in Muscat and near the border with Yemen. They are linked by a tropospheric scatter communications system and each uses local terminals and repeater systems to expand communications coverage in its area.

Oman is continuing to upgrade its command center, and is seeking to improve its air warning and battle management links to the UAE's C⁴I/BM system. It has obtained other air defense system improvements, and C⁴ equipment from France, and is considering the purchase of additional Martello radars or Lockheed AN/FPS-117s.[290]

Oman shelters its main air bases at Masirah and Thamrait, which have been greatly improved with the deployment of US facilities, air control equipment, terminal buildings, and fuel storage. Oman has additional military airfields and strips at Khasab on the Musandam Peninsula, co-located at the modern international airport at Seeb near Muscat, and Salalah.

The Readiness and Warfighting Capability of the Omani Air Force

The Omani air force has evolved in an environment where the emphasis has been on ground attack and interdiction missions in support of its ground forces. It suffers from a lack of pilots and trained manpower, and lacks the training and communications systems between air and land units to allow the Omani air force to be effective in the close air support mission. It is also experiencing growing problems in paying for the proper level of spares, wartime reserves, and contract maintenance. It is sometimes forced to deadline aircraft because of the slow response of Western contractors in providing spares or carrying out repairs that must be done outside of Oman.

The Omani air force has also lacked the funds it needs to buy modern combat aircraft and heavy surface-to-air missiles, and has had growing problems in funding training and readiness. Oman's limited oil revenues and need for civil investment led to a $20 million cut in readiness and training funds in 1995. There have been reports that the air force has been forced to consider mothballing half of its helicopter fleet in 1996. Its fleet of Agusta AB-204, AB-212, and AB-214 helicopters already suffered from a shortage of trained pilots and shortages of spares, and were flying only about 20 hours each versus a goal of 30 to 40 hours.[291]

The air force also has serious problems with pilot numbers for its fixed wing aircraft. This shortfall is partly a result of the fact that Omani pilots are rapidly promoted and are moved to headquarters or command assignments. It has led Oman to retain a number of expensive British contract pilots, however, and the cost of such pilots has led Oman to begin studying ways to mothball its fixed wing aircraft as well as its helicopters.[292]

The Omani air force has had very limited modernization. It has been able to withdraw all of its obsolete Hunters from service, and shift aging transport aircraft like its Islanders to civilian roles, but it suffers badly from a lack of modern multi-role fighters. It lacks the ability to engage first-line Iranian combat aircraft and it also badly needs medium helicopters to improve its lift capabilities.

The air force has received moderate to good training in visual range air-to-air combat, but it is still dogfight oriented in air-to-air combat at a time when potential enemies like Iran are beginning to emphasize the use of radar vectoring, advanced look-down shoot-down radars, and long range missile combat.

Maintenance and logistics seem to be good, and the Omani air force is virtually the only Gulf air force to have high standards for preventive maintenance except for Bahrain. Oman does, however, lack modern radar or infrared reconnaissance assets and would need foreign assistance to conduct any significant form of electronic warfare.

Omani Paramilitary and Internal Security Forces

Oman has paramilitary forces, but most are of relatively low quality. It has 3,500 men in its tribal forces (Firqat), plus is a small 85 man security force on the Musandam Peninsula called the Shikuk Tribal Militia. These forces are more important in terms of providing the government with a way of subsidizing tribal groups and maintaining internal security than as fighting forces. Oman does, however, have high quality police and internal security forces.

Police and Security Forces

Oman has approximately 7,000–9,000 men in police, coast guard, and border forces. The latter units are reasonably effective and operate some light aircraft, helicopters, and patrol boats. The Police Coast Guard has 400 men, and 15 AT-105 armored personnel carriers, 11–15 coastal and 3 inshore patrol craft, 13 support craft, and 28 speed boats. The air wing of the police has 1 Do-228-100s, 2 CN-235Ms, 1 BN-2T Islander, and 6 Bell 214s, and 3 Bell 205A helicopters. These forces are not capable of sustained combat, but can play a role in counterinsurgency and rear area security operations.[293]

Oman's security apparatus falls under the authority of the Ministry of Palace Office Affairs which coordinates all intelligence and security policy and activity. The Omani internal security service investigates all matters related to internal security. The Royal Oman Police performs regular police duties, provides security at airports, acts as immigration officials, and maintains a small coast guard.

As is the case in all Gulf states, Omani legal and security procedures differ from those of the US. The State Department reports that police usually obtain warrants prior to making arrests but are not required by law to do so. The authorities should obtain court orders to hold suspects in pretrial detention, and there is a system of bail. The police are required to file charges or ask a magistrate judge to order continued detention within 24 hours of arrest. The police do not always follow these procedures, however, and judges may order detentions for 14 days to allow investigation and may grant extensions if necessary.[294]

The police do not routinely notify a detainee's family of such detentions, or in the case of a foreign worker, the worker's sponsor. The authorities do post a list of persons scheduled for trial near the magistrate court building in Muscat. While there have been no reports of incommunicado detention in 1994, the police do not always permit attorneys and family members to visit detainees. Judges occasionally intercede to ensure that security officials allow such visits.

The Legal System and Security Court

As is the case in most Gulf states, there are different processes of law for security cases. The judiciary comprises the magistrate courts, which adjudicate misdemeanors and criminal matters; the Islamic, or Shari'a, courts, which adjudicate personal status cases such as divorce and inheritance; the Authority for the Settlement of Commercial Disputes (ASCD); the Labor Welfare Board; and the Real Estate Committee, which hears tenant-landlord disputes.[295]

The various courts are subordinate to the Sultan. The Sultan appoints all judges, acts as a court of final appeal, and intercedes in cases of particular interest, especially in national security cases. However, there have been no reported instances in which the Sultan has overturned a decision of the ASCD or the magistrate courts.

The State Department reports that Omani trials use very different procedures from those common in the West. The Criminal Code does not specify the rights of the accused. There are no written rules of evidence, or codified procedures for entering cases into the criminal system, or any legal provision for a public trial. Criminal procedures have developed by tradition and precedents in the magistrate courts. In criminal cases, the police provide defendants with the written charges against them, defendants are presumed innocent, and have the right to present evidence and confront witnesses. The police are not required by law to obtain search warrants. There is a widespread belief that the Omani government eavesdrops on both oral and written communications, and Omanis are guarded in both areas. Citizens must obtain permission from the Ministry of Interior to marry foreigners.[296]

The prosecution and the defense question witnesses through the judge, who is usually the only person to question witnesses in court. There are no jury trials. A single judge tries misdemeanors; a panel of three judges tries felonies and security offenses. Magistrate court judges must be citizens. Public prosecutors are senior police officers. They may bring additional charges after defense attorneys have inspected the charge sheet or during trial.

A detainee may hire an attorney but has no explicit right to be represented by counsel. The government does not pay for the legal representation of indigents. Judges often pronounce the verdict and sentence within one day after the completion of a trial. Defendants may appeal jail sentences longer than three months and fines over the equivalent of $1,300 to a three-judge panel. Defendants accused of national security offenses and serious felonies do not have the right of appeal. Death sentences, which are rare, require the Sultan's approval.

It is the State Security Court, however, that tries cases involving national security. Although it is administratively distinct from the other courts, magistrate court judges have presided over trials in the State Security Court.

In 1994 the Omani government detained 200 people in connection with an alleged plot to destabilize the country. The Omani government charged 131 of these suspects with sedition and tried them in secret before the State Security Court. The Court issued verdicts on November 12, 1994. It sentenced two defendants to death and the others from 3 to 15 years in prison. The Sultan later commuted the death sentences to prison terms.[297]

The Omani government tried the detainees for conspiracy to subvert national unity and security and the misuse of Islam. The authorities stated that the police obtained the necessary court orders for the detentions and that formal charges were brought as quickly as possible. However, the lack of public information about the cases has raised questions about the possible arbitrary nature of the arrests and detentions—and the fairness of the trials.

Freedom of Speech, the Media, and Political Association

The US State Department reports that the Omani government restricts freedom of expression and association, and does not guarantee full rights for workers and women.[298] The law prohibits any criticism of the Sultan in any form or medium. The authorities do tolerate criticism of government officials and agencies, but such criticism rarely receives media coverage. The 1984 Press and Publication Law authorizes the Omani government to censor all domestic and imported publications. Ministry of

Information censors may act against any material regarded as politically, culturally, or sexually offensive.

The State Department reports that journalists and writers generally censor themselves to avoid government harassment. Editorials reflect the Omani government's views, although the authorities tolerate some criticism on foreign issues. The Omani government discourages in-depth reporting on controversial domestic issues, and seeks to influence privately owned dailies and periodicals by subsidizing their operating costs. In late August, 1995 all four daily newspapers reported the arrest of the 200 alleged subversives only once—by publishing the dispatch of the government-owned Oman News Agency without further comment.[299]

The government limits the circulation of foreign media. On several occasions in 1994, it prohibited the entry of foreign newspapers. The authorities prevented distribution of the August 6 edition of the London-based Arabic daily *Al-Hayat*, reportedly because it contained some statements regarded as critical of the Majlis Ash-Shura. They also prevented distribution of the November 7 edition of the *Financial Times* because Oman felt it contained a factually incorrect article that was critical of the Omani government's economic policy.

Customs officials sometimes confiscate video cassette tapes and erase offensive material. The Omani government controls the local radio and television companies. They do not air any politically controversial material. The Omani government does not allow the establishment of privately owned radio and television companies. However, the availability of satellite dishes has made foreign broadcast information accessible to the public.

The appropriate Omani government authority, such as the Sultan Qabus University, the police, or the relevant ministry must approve cultural events, including plays, concerts, lectures, and seminars. The State Department reports that most organizations avoid controversial issues for fear the authorities may cancel their events. Academic freedom is restricted, particularly regarding controversial matters, including politics. Professors may be dismissed for going beyond acceptable boundaries.

The law does not guarantee freedom of assembly. The Omani government regards all private associations as illegal unless lawfully registered. The Ministry of Social Affairs and Labor must approve the establishment of all associations and their by-laws. The Omani government uses the power to license associations as the power to control the political environment. It does not license groups regarded as a threat to the predominant social or political views of the Sultanate.

All public gatherings require government sponsorship. The authorities do not always enforce this requirement, and unauthorized gatherings take place without government approval. In 1994 the Omani government increased restrictions on most types of public gatherings.

Oman shows considerably greater religious tolerance than most Gulf states, but has taken steps to limit Islamic extremism and unrest. Islam is the state religion and most Omanis are Ibadhi or Sunni Muslims, although there is a minority of Shi'ite Muslims. The Omani police monitor mosque sermons to ensure that the preachers do not discuss political topics and stay within the state-approved orthodoxy of Islam. Security forces reportedly arrested a mosque preacher in the city of Salalah for his alleged association with an unauthorized Islamic group.[300]

Non-Muslims are free to worship at churches and temples built on land donated by the Sultan. There are many Christian denominations which utilize two plots of donated land on which two Catholic and two Protestant churches have been built. The Omani government does prohibit non-Muslims from proselytizing Muslims. It also prohibits non-Muslim groups from publishing religious material, although imported printed material may be brought into the country.

Members of all religions and sects are free to maintain links with co-religionists abroad and undertake foreign travel for religious purposes. Since 1994, the government has placed restrictions on most types of public gatherings which have resulted in a substantial curtailment of non-Muslim religious celebrations that might cause Islamic unrest. For example, the authorities did not grant permission to the Hindu and Zoroastrian communities to celebrate some of their religious festivals in public.

Foreign Labor and Labor Issues

Like all Gulf countries—and virtually all countries in the Middle East—Oman places tight control on labor organizations and particularly on foreign labor. The current law stipulates that "it is absolutely forbidden to provoke a strike for any reason." It does not provide for the right to collective bargaining. It does require that employers of more than 50 workers form a joint labor-management committee as a communication forum between the two groups. The State Department reports that implementation of this provision is uneven, however, and that the effectiveness of these committees is questionable. In general the committees discuss such questions as living conditions at company-provided housing. They are not authorized to discuss wages, hours, or conditions of employment. Such issues are specified in the work contracts signed individually by workers and employers and must be consistent with the guidelines of the Ministry of Social Affairs and Labor.[301]

Foreign workers constitute 74 percent of the work force and as much as 50 percent of the modern-sector work force. Most earn substantially less than Omanis.[302] The Ministry of Social Affairs and Labor issues minimum wage guidelines for various categories of workers. The minimum wage for nonprofessional workers was about $156 a month (60 Rials). Minimum wage guidelines do not cover domestic servants, farmers, government employees, or workers in small businesses. Many foreigners work in fields exempt from the minimum wage statute. The Omani government is lax in enforcing minimum wage guidelines for foreign workers employed in menial jobs.[303]

The current law defines conditions of employment for some Omanis and foreign workers in ways which tend to discriminate against foreign workers. It covers domestic servants and construction workers, but not temporary workers or those with work contracts that expire within 3 months. Regardless of the size of the company, any employee, including foreign workers, may file a grievance with the Labor Welfare Board, and Omani law prohibits compulsory labor. In most cases, the Board releases the complainant from service and awards compensation for time worked under compulsion. Employers face no other penalty than to reimburse the worker's back wages.

Some foreign workers are not aware of their right to take such disputes before the Labor Welfare Board, however, and others are reluctant to file complaints for fear of retribution by unscrupulous employers. Employers can also withhold letters of release, a document releasing the worker from his employment contract and allowing him to switch jobs. Without the letter, a foreign worker must continue to work for his current employer or face deportation.

Progress in Human Rights

Oman is, however, one of the few Middle Eastern states that is making improvements in the rights of workers. In 1994, the Ministry of Social Affairs and Labor drafted a new labor law, and the Consultative Council recommended some changes. Although consensus on the final draft has not yet been reached, government officials said that the new labor code will be consistent with international labor standards. It will reportedly contain a provision for the establishment of worker committees in the workplace and remove the prohibition against strikes.

Although strikes are still technically illegal, workers do sometimes stage job actions. In general, these disputes are settled without police intervention. In 1994 the Omani government joined the International Labor Organization. The Omani government also received an ILO representative who provided advice on the draft labor law.

Sultan Qabus has stressed the importance of human rights in his speeches, as well as the need to expand the role of women in Omani society, and to reject a restrictive and backward view of Islam.[304] Oman does not commit many of the human rights and security abuses common in the Middle East and the Third World. The State Department reports that there are no known political prisoners, and Oman does not practice exile as a form of punishment.[305] The Omani government does not restrict travel within the country except to military areas. There are no confirmed reports of political or extrajudicial killings, disappearances, or torture. Prison conditions reportedly meet internationally recognized minimum standards.

The State Department also reports that the Omani government took measures in 1994 to address such human rights concerns.[306] The government increased the number of seats on the Consultative Council and allowed women to take part in nominations for Council members. In November, 1994, the Omani government selected two women to serve on the Council. The government also joined the International Labor Organization (ILO) and began to draft a new labor law that addresses worker rights.

Strategic Interests

Oman is one of the best managed states in the Near East and Southwest Asia, although it faces serious challenges because of population growth and limited oil and gas resources. While its population is becoming increasingly politicized, the Sultan has coopted a large number of former rebels, modernized his government, and increased the rate of Omanization. Oman's five year plans have been relatively successful, although development has been seriously restricted by low oil prices the country's limited oil revenues.

Oman's Strategic Ties to the West

Oman has long had strong strategic ties to Britain, and has cooperated with the US since the time of the Dhofar Rebellion. The US provided informal assistance to Oman, Britain, and Iran during their campaigns against the Dhofar rebels. The US supported Oman in its long confrontation with the PDRY, and in dealing with the potential threat posed by Iran after the beginning of the Iran-Iraq War. In return, Oman provided the US and UK with data on tanker and other ship transits through the Strait of Hormuz to the US and UK from its base on Goat Island.

Oman and the US signed a military access agreement in June, 1980. It did so at a time when most other Gulf countries refused to provide the US with such support. Ironically, Kuwait offered Oman a substantial aid payment not to support the deployment of US forces, although the Kuwaiti government reversed its position a decade later, after its invasion by Iraq, and publicly praised the Sultan for his vision.

Since that time, Oman has provided the US with critical contingency and prepositioning facilities. These facilities include airfields and prepositioned equipment at Masirah Island, and airfield facilities at the international airport at Seeb and at Thamrait in Southern Oman, plus additional storage and a dock at Masirah and Ras Musandam naval base (Goat Island).[307] The US Army Corps of Engineers has also upgraded the old 2,000 foot direct runway at Khasab with a 6,500 foot surface air base. These facilities played an important role during the US build-up for Desert Storm, and Oman gave the US considerable support during the US operation in Somalia.

Oman provided US access to its bases and allowed it to build cantonments, hardened shelters, warehouses, and other facilities at Seeb, Masirah, Khasab, and Thamarit air bases, and ports at Muscat and Salalah, in return for $320 million in U S funds to build-up these facilities.[308] The US provided over $199.1 million in FMS credits to Oman between FY1980 and FY1990, and about $853,000 in IMET assistance. During FY1981-FY1985, the US provided support to Oman for the construction of four air bases at Masirah, Seeb, Khasab, and Thamarit that could be used by US air units in rapid deployment to the Gulf.

This construction included facilities for rear area staging and forward deployment, and included improved operations, personnel, storage, and maintenance facilities. The US Navy developed an aircraft maintenance facility, ground support equipment shop, warehouse facility, and ammunition storage facility. The US Army created a staging base at Masirah to support the forward deployment of US Army forces. The US helped provide hardened shelters, dispersal and access pavements, environmentally controlled warehouses, transient billeting, and cantonment support areas at Seeb and Thamarit. The US access agreement is reviewed every five years, and the latest review took place in June, 1995.

The Omani base at Goat Island and other facilities in the Musandam Peninsula are particularly important because they guard the Strait of Hormuz and are only 26 miles from Iran. More than 50 large ships, 60 percent of them tankers, passed through these waters every day during 1986 and 1987. The Musandam Peninsula is a small enclave with a population of about 12,000, and is separated from the rest of Oman by a 40 mile strip of the UAE. Oman has been assisted in developing this region since 1976 by a US firm called Tetra Tech International. It has spent nearly $5,000 per resident in recent years to develop the region.[309]

Oman allowed the US and Britain to use Oman as a staging base and to deploy reconnaissance aircraft during the "tanker war", and allowed the US to stage reconnaissance and air control flights out of Oman during

Operation Praying Mantis—when the US attacked Iranian oil platforms in the Gulf. Oman provided about 950 troops to the Arab Joint Forces Command (East) during the Gulf War. US ability to use the prepositioned equipment in Oman during the Gulf War also saved the US the equivalent of 1,800 C-141 airlift sorties and played a major role in the speed of the US build-up during Desert Shield. Oman contributed a naval vessel to the defense of Kuwait when Iraqi forces moved towards the Kuwaiti border in October, 1994.[310]

Oman has regularly renewed its access agreement with the US, and roughly 20% of all US prepositioned supplies in the Gulf are now located in Oman—largely at Masirah, Seeb, and Thamarit.[311] US ships regularly resupply at Omani ports, and the US has an electronic surveillance center in Oman which plays an important role in covering Iran.[312] The US currently keeps $1.3 billion worth of equipment stored in Oman, and is able to "recycle" much of this equipment—using it for an operation or exercise and then returning it to Oman for future use. The US has used this equipment, and Omani facilities, to support US Air Force operations in Bahrain, Jordan, Kuwait, and Saudi Arabia and major exercises like Bright Star.

Many of Oman's arms are British supplied, and Oman lacks the funds to make major military purchases. Oman did, however, purchase $163.3 million worth of US Foreign Military Sales (FMS) between FY1950 and FY1990, and took delivery on $91.8 million worth.[313] Since the Gulf War, it has purchased $13.2 million worth of US Foreign Military Sales (FMS), and taken delivery on $56.6 million worth.[314] Oman also receives about $400,000 a year worth of IMET military training assistance from the US. It trains between 15 and 20 Omani officers in the US each year.[315]

Oman continues to work closely with Britain, and there are roughly 500 British officers and NCOs seconded or contracted to the Omani forces. British officers play a major role in training the Omani Army. There are British officers and NCOs seconded to the Omani Navy, and some 80 British officers seconded to the Omani air force. The crew training for Oman's new Muheet-class frigates is carried out by the Royal Navy's Flag Officer Sea Training. British SAS personnel have trained the Omani anti-terrorist force and assist in surveillance of the border with Yemen. France provides a limited amount of training for Omani officers. The US and Britain have a joint venture contract for some of the facilities in Masirah.

British forces also make frequent use of Omani facilities, have an intelligence post near Muscat, and use the Omani base at Goat Island in the Strait of Hormuz and a new intelligence post at Qabal in the Musandam Peninsula for a variety of reconnaissance functions. Both US and British forces made use of Omani facilities during the Western intervention in the Gulf in 1987–1988, and again during the Gulf War in 1990–1991.

France signed two military cooperation agreements with Oman in 1989, and now trains part of the Omani Navy. Oman conducts joint exercises with British, French, and US forces. The joint Kunjar Hadd Exercise—held in April, 1995—was part of an annual series of exercises involving Omani, British, French, and US units. Oman regularly holds smaller exercises with British and US forces.

Oman has long openly conducted military exercises with outside powers, including Britain, Egypt, France, and the US. Oman was the first Southern Gulf state to carry out ground force exercises with the US, which began in 1983. It conducts an annual battalion-level amphibious exercise with the US, and holds annual joint exercises involving all of the US military services.

Oman held an exercise in March 1985, called Codename Thunder which involved roughly 10,000 men. It was the largest and most effective exercise that any GCC state has conducted, and Oman has regularly played an important role in GCC exercises ever since. Oman also exercises regularly with British forces. Refueled British RAF Tornadoes have flown non-stop to air bases in Oman, and Oman holds joint exercises with Britain called the "Swiftsword" series. One of these exercises, in December, 1986, involved over 5,000 British service men, and included a 400 man landing by British marines, air drops, and air reinforcements. Some 5,000 Omani troops worked with the British in the role of defenders, while another 2,000 played the role of an anonymous enemy that looked very much like Iran.[316]

Oman's Role in Power Projection and Strengthening the GCC

Oman has played a critical role in helping the US project power to the Gulf and has consistently supported the West in ensuring the security of the Gulf and access to its oil exports. While it has placed some limits on US access to facilities and exercises, it has done so only out of political necessity. Oman has argued, and with considerable justification, that it has provided considerably more support than its received in return in US arms transfers and aid. This has been particularly true in recent years, when the US has not even met its pledges to the Omani government.[317]

It is one of the ironies of current US policy in the Gulf that so little attention is paid to a country that is absolutely critical to the containment of Iran, and which clearly needs external aid to develop the capability to exert its sovereignty of the shipping channels through the Strait of Hormuz and defend its waters and air space. While Oman does not need massive new shipments of arms, it does need external aid to modernize and improve the equipment of all of its military services.

Oman also needs outside aid in resolving its differences with Saudi Arabia, and in encouraging the integration of Oman's military forces into collective defense structures that can cover the entire Gulf.[318] Oman has argued for a 100,000–200,000 man joint Gulf Cooperation Council force, with the chairmanship rotating among the six members. While this concept may not prove practical, the geography of the Persian Gulf, Strait of Hormuz, and Gulf of Oman require Oman to have modern air defenses, maritime surveillance capabilities, and be part of any effort to provide the Gulf with theater missile defenses—all of which will require outside aid. Similarly, Oman requires sufficient land strength and rapid deployment capability to deter any incursions or amphibious operations by Iran and challenges across its border with Yemen.

Finally, Oman suffers from the overall lack of progress in transforming the rhetoric of the Gulf Cooperation Council into substantive progress. In spite of massive GCC-wide spending since the Gulf War, little progress has been made in far too many areas which are critical priorities for cooperative defense. The Southern Gulf states need to develop collective or integrated defense capabilities by:

- Creating an effective planning system for collective defense, and truly standardized and/or interoperable forces.
- Integrating C⁴I and sensor nets for air and naval combat, including beyond-visual-range and night warfare.
- Creating joint air defense and air attack capabilities.
- Establishing effective cross reinforcement and tactical mobility capabilities.
- Setting up joint training, support, and infrastructure facilities.
- Creating joint air and naval strike forces.
- Deploying joint land defenses of the Kuwaiti/Northwestern Saudi borders.
- Preparing for outside or over-the-horizon reinforcement.
- Creating common advanced training systems .
- Improved urban and urban area security for unconventional warfare and low intensity combat.

The Southern Gulf states need to procure interoperable or standardized equipment to provide the capability to perform the following missions:

- Heavy armor, artillery, attack helicopters, and mobile air defense equipment for defense of upper Gulf.

- Interoperability and standardization with US power projection forces.
- Interoperable offensive air capability with stand-off, all-weather precision weapons and anti-armor/anti-ship capability.
- Interoperable air defense equipment, including heavy surface-to-air missiles, BEYOND-VISUAL-RANGE/AWX fighters, AEW & surveillance capability, ARM & ECM capability. (Growth to ATBM and cruise missile defense capability)
- Maritime surveillance systems, and equipment for defense against maritime surveillance, and unconventional warfare.
- Mine detection and clearing systems.
- Improved urban, area, and border security equipment for unconventional warfare and low intensity conflict.
- Advanced training aids.
- Support and sustainment equipment.

And, the Southern Gulf states need to develop coordinated procurement plans to eliminate their current massive waste of resources on:

- Unique equipment types and one-of-a-kind modifications.
- "Glitter factor" weapons; "developmental" equipment and technology.
- Non-interoperable weapons and systems.
- Submarines and ASW systems.
- Major surface warfare ships.
- Major equipment for divided or "dual" forces.
- New types of equipment which increase the maintenance, sustainability, and training problem, or layer new types over old.

Expanding Oman's Strategic Role in the Gulf

Oman already plays an important strategic role in the Gulf. It controls the main shipping channels through the Strait of Hormuz, and is the only Southern Gulf state with ports on the Indian Ocean. A stable, moderate, and friendly Oman is a critical counterbalance to Iran, and to securing access to the Gulf. Oman can also expand its strategic role in the Gulf. It can offer other Southern Gulf states potential access to the Indian Ocean by pipelines to Omani ports that can be made far more secure than ports in the Gulf or Red Sea.

If the GCC could provide suitable protection, these pipelines could stretch from Kuwait in the east to ocean terminal sites at the Gulf of Oman, and even pipelines from the key oil and gas fields in Qatar, Saudi Arabia, and the UAE could have a major strategic effect. Oil tankers, LNG carriers, and product carriers could then load up and head out unhindered through the Arabian Sea and Indian Ocean to their destinations worldwide.

The Gulf states have already done much of the planning involved. Ten years ago, in April 1985, the Secretariat General of The Cooperation Council of The Arab Gulf States (GCC) issued a detailed evaluation of pipeline transportation of crude oil from GCC countries.[319] This technical and economic analysis (which included Iraq) provided: (1) a comprehensive description of the locations of six proposed routes and five terminals using maps, aerial photographs and satellite images; (2) the preliminary engineering designs of the pipeline system; (3) a detailed economic analysis of pipeline transportation, and (4) brief discussions of the environmental impact, socioeconomic implications and the legal and administrative aspects of pipeline operations.

The GCC examined the option of building up to four pipelines, or a network of connected segments, that could provide oil loading facilities at up to four different ports in Oman. These pipelines could originate as far west as the Rumalia oil field in Iraq and Iran. They pumped through pipes varying from 28 to 60 inches. They terminated near ports at the terminal near Sur in Oman, at Ras Ruwais, Dagam, Ras Madraka, and Salalah.

The total investment cost for the longest pipeline was $3.49 billion in 1985 dollars for an engineering construction effort which would take about 36 months. Today, such a pipeline would cost about $7.2 billion in 1995 dollars, although the cost of building the kind of pipelines and ports needed to secure oil exports from the Southern Gulf states would be substantially cheaper because such pipelines would not have to extend to Iraq and Kuwait, and would only have to ship oil and gas from Qatar, Saudi Arabia and the UAE.

There are other options, but all have important limitations. The Iraqi pipeline link to Saudi Arabia, and the Iraqi pipeline through Turkey, might still reduce the vulnerability of oil shipments in a future Iran-Iraq War. Saudi Arabia can already use the pipelines from the Saudi oil fields near the Gulf coast to Janbu to avoid exporting part of its oil through the Gulf. Kuwait can also cheaply build its own pipeline link through Saudi Arabia and reduce its dependence on the Gulf. However, pipelines to the Red Sea have serious limitations. They now provide only limited capacity, and they cannot carry the massive projected increase in Kuwait and Saudi oil production. They do not offer cost-effective ways of shipping Qatari gas or UAE oil. The Red Sea is not a secure area. It has already been mined once. Radical states like the Sudan have Red Sea coasts, and both the Bab el Mandab and Suez Canal are potential strategic bottlenecks. There is only so much oil that can be shipped to ports in the south, and such pipelines tend to be more vulnerable than pipelines through Oman.

History provides little reassurance about the survivability and safety of pipelines directly to the Mediterranean or the Gulf of Aqaba. An Arab-Israeli peace settlement might ease past risks, but reopening the Trans-Arabian Pipeline from Saudi Arabia through Jordan to Lebanon, or creating a new pipeline link to Aqaba still poses the risk of a Syrian cut-off of exports, political turbulence in Jordan, or new violence in Lebanon. Similarly, Iraq and Syria remain as hostile as ever, and trying to reopen the pipeline from Iraq to the port of Banyas in Syria will do nothing to secure oil exports by the moderate Southern Gulf states.

In contrast, oil and gas pipelines through Oman could move oil and gas from Saudi Arabia, Qatar, and the UAE. They would allow Saudi Arabia to exploit its new fields to the Southeast of the Gawar field, and the UAE to ship from its existing pipeline links that extend from fields near the Saudi border. If current speculation about Saudi oil reserves is correct, such pipelines may even be the most cost-effective way for Saudi Arabia to increase its production from fields in the Empty Quarter.

Such pipelines and the related oil field, pumping, and port facilities would be far less vulnerable to Iranian and Iraqi missile and air strikes, and terrorists. They would go to a true "blue water" port or ports on the Indian Ocean. This would greatly ease the US Navy's task in protecting the pipelines, ports, and shipping with carrier task forces, allow the rapid deployment of US aircraft to bases in Oman, severely limit mine warfare capabilities, and allow the US to use its anti-submarine warfare capabilities with maximum efficiency. Limiting ship movements in the Gulf would greatly reduce the risk of accidents as well as military risks.

Such pipelines and facilities will also become steadily less vulnerable as the Gulf Cooperation Council (GCC) states provide improved air defenses, and they can do a far better job of taking advantage of integrated missile and air defenses than oil and gas shipments to and through the Gulf. The collection facilities and most of the pipelines would be located in unpopulated areas, and the ports in Oman could be located in easily securable areas. This would allow GCC counterterrorism operations to be far more effective. Destroyed sections of pipeline can be put back in operation quickly by standby reaction units which can quickly fly in GCC security forces, repair crews and sections of pipe by heavy lift helicopters, with GCC countries sharing the cost.

Oman's Strategic Future

Oman's present external and internal security policies are some of the most successful in the Gulf. At the same time, Oman faces serious future economic challenges and problems with population growth. It must come firmly to grips with the need to "Omanize" the work force, and adopt far stronger policies to provide incentives for both Omani industry and the native Omani work force to both increase the number of jobs and develop an Omani work ethic.

As has been discussed earlier, these problems could interfere with the success of Oman's development and reduce Oman's internal stability. Oman needs to reexamine its current programs, five year plans, and long-term planning efforts, and consider new steps to accelerate or initiate the following reforms necessary to:

- Limit population growth through a strong education program, strong birth control program, and family incentives.
- Force radical reductions in the number of foreign workers, with priority for reductions in servants and in trades that allow the most rapid conversion to native labor.
- Restructure the educational system to focus on job training and competitiveness. Create strong new incentives for faculty and students to focus on job-related education, sharply down-size other forms of educational funding and activity, and eliminate high overhead educational activities without economic benefits.
- Freeze and then reduce the number of civil servants, and restructure and down-size the civil service to focus on productive areas of activity with a much smaller pool of manpower. Cut back sharply on state employees by the year 2000.
- Reduce those aspects of state subsidies and welfare that distort the economy and discourage the native population from seeking jobs. Carry out those aspects of the 1996–2000 plan that reduce the cost of participation and subsidies for the private sector which do not encourage new privatization.[320]
- Eliminate economic disincentives for employers hiring native labor, and creating disincentives for hiring foreign labor.
- Consider tax and other subsidies to encourage replacing foreign labor with Omanis.
- Establish market criteria for all major state and state-supported investments, requiring detailed and independent risk assessment and projections of comparative return on investment, with a substantial penalty for state versus privately funded projects and ventures. Down size the scale of programs to reduce investment and cash flow costs and the risk of cost-escalation.
- Further encourage privatization and eliminate monopolies. Create new incentives to invest in local industries and business and disincentives for the expatriation of capital, reduce regulatory barriers,

and execute the privatization of infrastructure called for by Oman's former Deputy Prime Minister for Financial and Economic Affairs, Qais al-Zawawi.

- Create market driven incentives for foreign investment in major oil and gas projects, refineries, and petrochemical operations. Avoid off-set requirements that simply create disguised unemployment or non-competitive ventures that act as a further state-sponsored dis-tortion of the economy. Remove bureaucratic barriers to foreign investment.
- Fully implement new policies allowing foreign firms to have 65% to 100% shares in projects that develop Oman's economy. Simplify the tax laws affecting foreign investment and reduce special taxes and fees levied on foreign investments and firms with a foreign partner.
- Tax earnings and sales with progressive taxes that reduce or elimi-nate budget deficits, which encourage local investment, and which create strong disincentives for the expatriation of capital, including all foreign holdings of capital and property by members of elite and ruling families.
- Shift goods to market prices. Remove distortions in economy and underpricing of services where they exist. Provide reasonable charges for medical services for all but the poor and shift electricity and water costs to full market prices.
- Alter tax laws that currently tax Omani-owned companies at 5–7.5%. Companies with some foreign ownership are taxed at rates of up to 30%, and companies with over 60% ownership are taxed at a sliding scale of up to 50%. This system deters foreign investment and under taxes some highly profitable Omani-owned firms. It needs to be revised to create more incentives for foreign investment in key industries necessary to Oman's development, to eliminate special taxes on stock-holding companies, and tax Omani owned companies at a more progressive rate.
- Establish a firm rule of law for all property, contract, permitting, and business activity and reduce state bureaucratic and permitting bar-riers to private investment.
- Ensure that all income from enterprises with state financing is reflected in the national budget and is integrated into the national economic development and planning program.
- Reform the structure of the budget to reduce the amount of money going directly to royal accounts, and ensure that most of the nation's revenues and foreign reserves are fully integrated into the national budget and into the planning process. Clearly separate royal and national income and investment holdings.

- Place national security spending on the same basis as other state spending. Integrate it fully into the national budget, including investment and equipment purchases. Replace the present emphasis on judging purchases on the basis on initial procurement costs and technical features with a full assessment of life cycle cost—including training, maintenance, and facilities—and with specific procedures for evaluating the value of standardization and interoperability with existing national equipment and facilities, those of other Gulf states, and those of the US and other power projection forces.

Oman is critical to collective security efforts in the Gulf, the security of Gulf shipping and the movement of oil, and Western power projection into the Gulf region. At present, however, Oman is being asked to give without receiving the aid it needs to play its potential strategic role properly. It is also being asked to take risks relative to Iran that ignore its exposed position and lack of military resources. Oman needs foreign investment and economic and military aid.

Like Bahrain, and the poorer states of the UAE, Oman cannot sustain development with its own resources, or pay for both the guns and butter it needs. Oman requires significant increases in cooperation and support from the West and its richer neighbors to both create stronger military forces and self-sustaining economic growth.

4

Qatar

Qatar is a small peninsular nation that extends to the north from the Arabian mainland. While Qatar has an area of only 11,000 square kilometers. It occupies a strategic position in the central portion of the Southern Gulf. It is an oil exporter, although its reserves are relatively small compared to those of many of its Gulf neighbors. Qatar had proven oil reserves of 3.3–4.3 billion barrels (0.4% of the world's total). Qatar is, however, a major gas power. According to US estimates, Qatar has total produceable gas reserves of approximately 237 Tcf, or 40 billion barrels of oil equivalent.[321] This is about 5% of all the world's gas reserves and Qatar is the third largest nation in the world in terms of total gas reserves. Qatari sources claim that Qatar has reserves approaching 380 trillion cubic feet.

Qatar is one of the founders of the Gulf Cooperation Council (GCC), and Qatari troops fought on the side of the UN Coalition during the Gulf War. The Qatari forces at the battle of Ras al Khafji were among the first Coalition troops to engage Iraqi ground forces. Since the Gulf War, Qatar has steadily expanded its strategic ties to the West and the United States. It is providing prepositioning facilities for a US Army brigade and the support equipment for a division base, and conducts regular exercises with British, French, and US forces.

Qatar is now heavily urbanized, and its population is dependent on the security of its cities, urban services, desalinized water, and food imports. Its main city is the capital, Doha, which is also Qatar's main port. There are also municipalities at Al Doha, Al Khwar, Al Rayyan, Al Wakrah, Ash Shamal, and Umm Salal. Qatar's main oil port is located at Umm Said.

Qatar has few resources other than oil and gas. It has no arable land without irrigation, and only 5% of its land can be used for grazing. Its territory is largely flat, gravel desert with small outcroppings of rock. There is a small amount of cultivated land in the north, which relies on desalinized water. Its oil fields are located both along its western coast—where there are low hills and cliffs—and offshore to the East. The south consists largely of sand dunes and salt flats.

Qatar's strategic position makes Iran its primary potential threat. Qatar has a 563 kilometer coastline, and vulnerable offshore facilities. Qatar has negotiated an off-shore boundary with Iran, but Iran has made claims to offshore areas that contain a large part of Qatar's North Field gas reserves in the past, and Iran is developing offshore gas fields which share at least one reservoir with Qatar's North Field.

At the same time, Qatar has border disputes with Bahrain and Saudi Arabia and some tension exists between Qatar and several of its Southern Gulf neighbors. Qatar's northwest coast comes within 30 kilometers of Bahrain, and the two nations dispute control over the Hawar islands, which are just one mile off of the central part of Qatar's west coast and about eight miles off the coast of Bahrain.

Qatar's land borders are disputed, but most maps show that Qatar's borders with Saudi Arabia now total only 40 kilometers. These borders are the result of concessions that the UAE made to Saudi Arabia in return for Saudi Arabia giving up its claims over Al Buraymi. Qatar and Saudi Arabia agreed to jointly survey and demarcate their border in March 1996, and it may change as a result. Qatar claims it has no boundary with the UAE, and this issue seems to be resolved—but the UAE has made claims to roughly 20 kilometers of territory along Qatar's southern eastern border.

History and Strategic Background

The Qatari peninsula has been inhabited for millennia, but most native Qataris are now descended from a number of migratory tribes that came to Qatar in the 18th century to escape the harsh conditions of the neighboring areas of the Najd and Al-Hasa. Some Qataris are also descended from Omani tribes. The Qataris are mainly Sunni ("Wahhabi") Muslims, although they also include large numbers of "Hawala" Arabs from the Iranian coast. Islam is the official religion. Islamic jurisprudence has been the traditional basis of Qatar's legal system, but is being displaced by a legal system based upon civil statutes.

The key events which have shaped Qatar's modern history are a shift in ruling families that occurred in the late 1860s, the discovery and production of oil, and Qatar's emergence as a fully independent state. The shift in ruling families originated in disputes over the control of the Gulf coast and piracy, both of which began in the 1700s. The Al Khalifa and Al Jalahima branches of the Bani Utub tribe migrated to Qatar in the 1760s, at a time when Qatar was sparsely inhabited. The Al Khalifa and Al Jalahima feuded over control of Qatar, but the Al Khalifas became the dominant family because of family and trading ties to Kuwait. The Al Khalifas settled in the port at Al Zubarah on Qatar's northwestern coast.

Al Zubarah's growing wealth led an Omani Sheik, who ruled Bahrain from the port of Bushehr, to attack the port. The Al Khalifas and several other tribes in Qatar invaded Bahrain in response, and seized control of its islands in 1783. This conquest led most members of the Al Khalifa family to migrate because of Bahrain's superior wealth, shipping, agricultural, and water resources, and the Al Khalifas only maintained a limited presence in Al Zubarah.

From the 1780s to the mid 1800s, the Al Khalifas became involved in a complex struggle to maintain control of both Bahrain and Qatar. The Al Khalifas faced a steadily greater challenge from the Al Thanis, a tribe that had lived in Qatar for nearly 200 years and had migrated from the Najd in the Arabian Peninsula. The Al Thanis trace their lineage to the Al-Ma'dhai clan of the Bani Tamim tribe. They emerged as the leading family in eastern and southern Qatar in the 1850s, after the Al Khalifas migrated to Bahrain and began to compete with Al Khalifas for control over the Qatari peninsula.

This struggle occurred at a time when the British, Turks, Omanis, Iranians, and other Arab families were competing to control the Gulf. It reached a crisis point in 1867, when Al Khalifa forces from Bahrain attacked the ports of Doha and Al Wakrah on Qatar's eastern shore. The British political agent in the Gulf intervened in response and reached a settlement in 1868 which acknowledged the weakening of Al Khalifa control of Qatar and the new role that the Al Thani family had come to play in the peninsula. Under the terms of this settlement, the leading families in Qatar agreed to pay them tribute to be paid to the Wahhabis.

The Al Thanis allied themselves to the Ottomans, who were then expanding their role in the Gulf, as a counterweight to Britain. In 1871, the Al Thanis used the support provided by this alliance to seize power over most of Qatar. They recognized Ottoman suzerainty in 1872, and ceased to pay tribute to the Al Khalifas—who were reduced to controlling the now unimportant port of Al Zubarah. This last Al Khalifa presence in Qatar ended in 1878. Sheik Qassim bin Muhammed Al Thani charged that pirates loyal to the Al Khalifa family were attacking shipping en route to Qatar. He then attacked and destroyed Al Zubarah, leaving little but ruins.[322]

The Al Thani family continued to rule under Ottoman suzerainty until 1893, when the Turks attempted to assert more direct control. The Ottoman representative, Nafiz Basha, was seeking to strengthen his power and attempted to arrest Qassim bin Muhammed Al Thani. Nafiz Basha did so, in part, because Qassim Al Thani had denied the Ottomans a right to set up a customs house in Doha. He also acted, however, because Qassim was seeking to become a ruling Sheik and was inclined to Wahhabi beliefs. The end result was open warfare between the Ottomans and the Qataris. This fighting ended with a Qatari victory in battle.

Ottoman power and influence in the Gulf declined steadily during the early 20th century, and the Ottomans formally renounced suzerainty over Qatar in 1913. Britain recognized Sheik Abdullah bin Qassim Al Thani—Sheik Qassim bin Muhammed Al Thani's son—as Qatar's ruler. In 1916, Britain sought to consolidate its position in the Gulf under the pressure of World War I. British signed a treaty of protection with Qassim's successor, Sheik Abdulla, which was similar to the treaties it had entered into with the other Gulf emirates. Under the treaty's terms, Shiek Abdullah agreed not to dispose of any of his territory except to the United Kingdom and agreed not to enter into relationships with any other foreign government without British consent. In return, the British promised to protect Qatar from all aggression by sea and to lend their "good offices" in case of a land attack.

Oil and Independence

This British-Qatari treaty had limited practical impact in the years that followed because Qatar had little wealth and trade, and was of limited interest to Britain. It was only in the 1930s that Britain began to play a more active role in Qatar—largely because of competition with the US to exploit the Gulf's oil resources. In 1935, Britain signed a treaty with Qatar that granted British protection and aid. As a result, Qatar granted a 75 year concession to the Qatar Petroleum Company—a branch of the British-dominated Anglo-Persian oil company.[323]

However, active development of Qatar's oil resources did not take place for another decade. The Qatar Petroleum Company was owned by Anglo-Dutch, French, and US interests, but the global depression that began in 1929 limited exploration activity. It was only in 1939 that high-quality oil was discovered at Dukhan, on the western side of the peninsula. World War II then delayed any exploitation of the discovery. No major investment was made in oil production until after World War II, and oil exports did not begin until 1949.

This delay in exploiting Qatar's oil resources had a serious impact on Qatar's economy and development. Its traditional sources of wealth were pearling, fishing, and trade. However, the world-wide depression sharply cut demand for pearls, and the introduction of Japan's cultured pearl industry caused a quick collapse in pearling activity throughout the Gulf. Qatar's economy went into a severe depression in the 1930s that did not end until the early 1950s. After that time, Qatar's gradually increasing oil revenues brought prosperity, large-scale immigration, and social change.

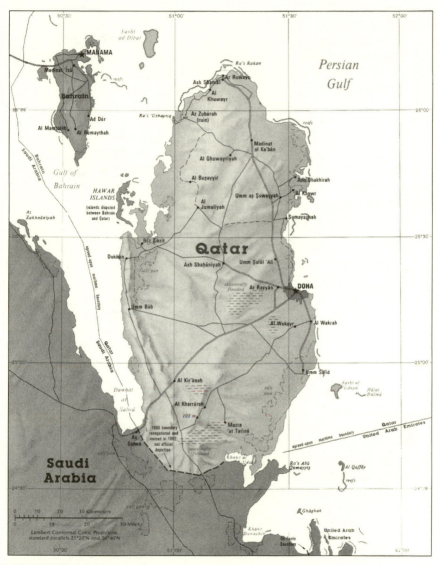

MAP FOUR Qatar

In 1968, however, Qatar began to face a new challenge. The British Government announced it would end the treaty relationships it had with the Gulf emirates, and that it would leave the Gulf in 1971. As a result, Qatar joined the other eight emirates then under British protection (which included Bahrain and the seven Trucial emirates that now make up the United Arab Emirates) in a plan to form a union of Arab emirates.

A provisional federation was established in July, 1968, but it did not last. Bahrain and Qatar were more developed than the other seven sheikdoms that had been part of the British Trucial states. Both sheikdoms were feuding over control of the waters between them, and Qatar saw little reason to join a federation that promised to involve it in at least as many political and economic problems as it would solve. As a result, Qatar chose independence. It declared a provisional constitution—or "Basic Law"—in April, 1972. This "Basic Law" was based on legislation passed in 1962 and on Islamic law. Qatar declared full independence on September 3, 1971, and was promptly admitted to the United Nations and the Arab League.

External Security

Since its independence, Qatar has often pursued a highly independent foreign policy. Unlike many of the other Southern Gulf states, it avoided taking sides in the Cold War, and established diplomatic relations with the USSR and China in 1988. It chose French rather than British arms after independence, and avoided entanglements in Arab issues outside the Gulf. At the same time, Qatar became an early member of OPEC and was a founding member of the Gulf Cooperation Council (GCC) in 1981. Qatar joined the other Southern Gulf states in supporting Iraq during the Iran-Iraq War, and provided the UN Coalition with strong support during the Gulf War.

Qatar has not, however, had peaceful relations with its neighbors. While it has not been the subject of direct Iranian attacks or pressures, it has faced the risk of such threats from its northern Gulf neighbors. Qatar has also had disputes with Bahrain, Saudi Arabia, and the UAE which have had a significant impact in dividing the Southern Gulf states.

Qatar and Bahrain

The struggle between the Al Thani and Al Khalifa families created a lingering dispute between Qatar and Bahrain over control of the Hawar islands, the Fasht-e-Dibal reef, and the Jarada sandbar off Qatar's northwest coast. Some believe that these islands and waters have significant offshore natural gas resources.

Bahrain now has control over the Hawar Islands because of a British decision in favor of Bahrain in 1939. This decision seems to have been based as much on the fact that Bahrain had set up a small military garrison on the largest of the Hawar Islands, as on any effort to adjudicate the legal issues involved.

Qatar feels that Britain decided in Bahrain's favor because the British adviser to Bahrain presented Bahrain's case in Western legal terms, while Qatar argued its case more on the basis of traditional Arab law. Bahrain feels that it has exercised control over the Hawar Islands since the Al Khalifa family first came to power, and that the Hawar Islands are an integral part of its territorial archipelago. It claims that the islands have long been used by Bahraini fishermen, and by senior Bahraini families for hunting and fishing purposes.

Qatar and Bahrain still dispute control over Al Zubarah, on Qatar's northwestern coast. Although the Al Khalifa settlement at Al Zubarah was destroyed in 1878, the Naim tribe in the region continued to maintain ties to the Al Khalifas. This led to new fighting in 1937. The Naim tribe asserted its independence after the British award of the Hawar Islands to Bahrain. Abdullah bin Qassim Al Thani responded by sending an armed force into the area which defeated the Naim. The British political agent supported Qatar and warned Hamad Bin Isa Al Khalifa—then the ruler of Bahrain—not to take military action. Sheik Hamad ceased military action, but imposed an embargo on trade and travel to Qatar which worsened relations between the two countries.

There have since been a number of public and not so public cases in which Bahraini and Qatari troops and ships have entered the disputed islands and waters. One such clash occurred in early 1986, when Qatari forces attacked a Bahraini position on the Fasht e-Dibal. Bahrain had built up a small base on an artificial island on the reef, and was turning the island into a coast guard station. On April 26, 1986, Qatari helicopters fired on construction crews working on the Fasht e-Dibal, and Qatari troops landed by helicopter and arrested the 29 workers on the island. Bahrain indicated in response that its work crews were actually building a GCC facility to monitor tanker traffic, pursuant to an agreement reached in 1992, which was followed up with GCC funds for the project.[324] Both nations then called military alerts, and Bahrain reinforced its positions on Hawar while Qatar reinforced its positions on the Fasht ad Dibal.[325] Qatar continued to occupy the site for over a month, until Bahrain agreed to destroy its facilities on the Fasht ad Dibal.[326] The captured workers were released in May, 1986.[327]

Another clash occurred in June, 1991, when Qatari Navy ships entered the waters off the Hawar Islands and Bahrain responded by sending fighters into Qatari air space. While GCC attempts at mediation succeeded, and a GCC observation team was sent to end the disagreement, this did not prevent further exchanges of accusations and new tension after the Gulf War. Qatar then filed a claim with the International Court of Justice in the Hague in July, 1991. Bahrain refused to accept the court's jurisdiction, though, because it felt that Bahrain had previously entered into an agreement with Qatar whereby both parties together—rather than either one of them unilaterally—might proceed to the Court once a proper form of agreement have been reached between them setting out the terms on which the case might be presented to the court.

In May 1993, Bahrain passed a Territorial Sea Decree pursuant to the United Nations Convention on the Law of the Sea of 1982. This Decree reflected the terms of the United Nations Convention in that it promulgated a territorial sea of 12 miles from the coast and a contiguous zone of 24 miles. Neither the base points nor the baselines referred to in the Decree have been promulgated, but there is no reference in it to islands or reefs. Qatar fielded new documents in February 1994, as part of its earlier proceedings, but did not file a new case.

The International Court of Justice ruled in February, 1995 that it had jurisdiction over the Hawar Islands dispute. It did so on the basis that minutes that Bahrain and Qatar had signed in 1986 set a deadline (six months) beyond which either country could refer the dispute to an international or impartial institution such as the International Court of Justice. Bahrain, in turn, called for bilateral negotiations or GCC mediation. It called for Saudi mediation on the basis of principles that had been laid down in 1978, and Saudi Arabia offered to mediate because of its concern that a decision by the International Court of Justice would open up other boundary disputes to non-Arab courts. Qatar agreed to discuss such mediation, although it felt that Saudi Arabia might be biased in favor of Bahrain, and that if any such mediation took place, it should have to come from an Arab state outside the Gulf.

Relations between Bahrain and Qatar became worse in late 1995 and early 1996. Qatar walked out of the Gulf Cooperation Council meeting in December 1995, because it felt that Saudi Arabia had pushed the GCC into appointing a Saudi as the new Secretary General of the GCC. Qatar's position was that it had not occupied any major posts in the GCC from its beginning, while all of the other Southern Gulf states had had such positions. It also argued that it had put forward its candidate, Abd Al-Rahman Al-Attiya several months before the Saudi's named a candidate, and that the decision of the selection of a Secretary General had to be unanimous because Qatar saw it as a substantial issue and not a procedural one.

This walk out occurred after Sheik Zayed of the UAE had attempted to mediate, and Bahrain, Saudi Arabia, and the UAE felt that they had been insulted by the way in which Qatar carried out its walk out. The resulting tensions went far beyond the past rivalry between Qatar and Bahrain. Bahrain, Saudi Arabia, and the UAE welcomed the deposed ex-Emir of

Qatar, Sheik Khalifa bin Hamad Al-Thani, as if he were a head of state. They did even though Sheik Khalifa openly claimed that he wanted to regain power from Qatar's new Emir, Sheik Hamad bin Khalifa Al-Thani.

Qatar responded by allowing two members of the Bahraini opposition, Mansour al-Jamri and Sheik Ali Salman, to broadcast calls for "democracy" over Qatari state television and by reprinting excerpts of these TV interviews in its newspapers. The media in some Gulf states then printed attacks on Qatar's government, and Saudi and UAE newspapers printed implicit attacks on Emir Sheik Hamad bin Khalifa Al-Thani and his Foreign Affairs Minister, Sheik Hamad bin Jassim Bin Jabr Al-Thani.[328]

Qatar's Emir, Sheik Hamad bin Khalifa Al-Thani, gave an interview in January 1996 in which he stated that the negotiations on over the Hawar Islands, "are in the courts and the Saudis are meditating. . . . Whenever there is a solution between the two countries, we are ready to pull it from the courts." He also stated that the dispute was one in which the former Emir, Sheik Khalifa bin Hamad could not make concessions, "Do you believe that the Qataris will allow him to do that? This cannot be accepted by anyone in Qatar."[329]

These tensions culminated in a coup attempt in February 1996. They only eased in March and April 1996, after Qatar, Bahrain, Saudi Arabia, and the UAE reached the compromise where Qatar accepted the selection of the new Saudi Secretary General in return for an agreement that future Secretary Generals would be selected in alphabetic rotation and serve for no more than two three year terms. This compromise seemed to support Qatar's original position, although it meant that the rotation would now only select a Qatari Secretary General after an official had served from every other GCC nation. Bahrain also indicated that it might accept the jurisdiction of the International Court of Justice over the Hawar Islands dispute.

The improvement in relations, however, was more cosmetic than real. Qatar felt Bahrain had become a tool of the Saudis and had helped sponsor a coup attempt by Sheik Khalifa bin Hamad Al-Thani. Qatar also felt that Bahrain's ruling family had failed to modernized its political leadership and that its conservatism was responsible for most of the Shi'ite unrest in Bahrain. Bahrain, in contrast, felt that Qatar's rulers had violated the normal courtesies between Gulf ruling elites, were deliberately being provocative, and had exploited Bahrain's internal crisis at a particularly sensitive time.

The tragedy inherent in these differences is that the tribal and generational quarrels between Bahrain and Qatar now prevent cooperation between two states whose geography gives them a common strategic interest and which can only achieve security as part of a broader regional security structure. There is also a potential synergy between the economies of Bahrain and Qatar. Qatar needs to reduce its dependence on foreign labor from outside the Gulf, and has a less well-educated native population. Bahrain needs to find jobs for its citizens and could benefit from industries based on Qatar's immense gas resources. Both states could benefit from an integrated approach to power, desalination, and other aspects of their infrastructure. As is so often the case in the Gulf, however, the past is the enemy of future.[330]

Qatar, Saudi Arabia, and the UAE

Qatar has other tensions with its Southern Gulf neighbors. It has long standing territorial disputes with Saudi Arabia and Abu Dhabi. The Al Thani family of Qatar and the Al Nihayan family of Abu Dhabi long disputed control over the Khaur al-Udaid and the territory behind it. The Khaur al-Udaid is a long winding inlet at the base of the eastern side of the Qatari peninsula. This dispute broadened in 1935, when Saudi Arabia asserted its own claims to the area, along with claims to much of Abu Dhabi.[331]

The disputes seemed to have been peacefully resolved in 1965, when there were reports that Qatar had given up its claims to the Khaur al-Udaid in return for territorial concessions at the base of the Peninsula. Qatar also signed a bilateral security agreement with Saudi Arabia in 1982.[332] Qatar had denied that it made such concessions, however, and the full border between Qatar and Saudi Arabia was never fully demarcated.

A new Qatari and Saudi border clash occurred on September 30, 1992. This clash took place at a small outpost at Khofuous, about 80 miles southeast of Doha. Two Qataris and an Egyptian soldier in the Qatari Armed Forces were killed and a third taken prisoner. Qatar's access to the main road to the UAE was cut off, which had serious economic repercussions. At the same time, Qatar refused to participate in the 1992 series of Peninsula Shield exercises, and Qatar's participation in these exercises has been limited ever since. Another incident took place during September-October 1993, which resulted in several deaths. Five Qatari-Saudi border skirmishes occurred during 1994, as well as a diplomatic row in which Qatar boycotted the November 1994, GCC summit conference.

In December 1994, these incidents led Qatar and Saudi Arabia to consider the formation of a joint committee to investigate the conflicts. A fear of Saudi domination, however, kept Qatar from tying its security closely to Saudi Arabia. As has already been mentioned, the two nations then clashed over the appointment of a new Secretary General to the Gulf Cooperation Council at the Ministerial and the summit meeting of the GCC in December 1995.

Even before walk out, the Saudis felt that Qatar's new Emir, Sheik Hamad bin Khalifa Al-Thani—and his Foreign Affairs Minister, Sheik Hamad bin Jassim bin Jabr Al-Thani—were deliberately disrupting efforts to strengthen the GCC and were deliberately challenging Saudi leadership in the Gulf. The GCC meeting made Saudi and Qatari relations far worse and brought tensions to the crisis point.[333] As a result, Saudi Arabia joined Bahrain and the UAE in receiving visits by the Emir's deposed father—Sheik Khalifa bin Hamad.

Sheik Khalifa posed a potential threat to Emir Hamad because he still had links to a number of Qatari leaders and had retained control over at least $2.5 billion of private and state assets, and some estimates go as high as $5 billion to $7 billion. He had all the resources necessary to fund a major coup attempt.[334]

It is not clear what the UAE's attitudes were towards Sheik Khalifa's effort to regain. Nevertheless, the UAE did receive Sheik Khalifa bin Hamad and a massive entourage on December 21, 1995. Sheik Khalifa announced that he would set up "temporary quarters" in the UAE until he returned to power in Doha and established a headquarters in the Gulf Suite of the Intercontinental Hotel in Abu Dhabi. His entourage occupied nearly 70 rooms in the hotel and included a number of Qatari officers and some foreign mercenaries.

Sheik Khalifa attempted to win further outside support by pledging that he would improve relations between Qatar and its neighbors if he resumed power. He visited Cairo and Damascus. He indicated during his trip to Syria that he supported the Damascus Declaration and received at least some support from the Syrian press.[335]

Qatar's new Emir, Hamad bin Khalifa Al-Thani, responded by indicating that Qatar would not participate in the 1995 series of Peninsula Shield exercises, which were to be held in Saudi Arabia during March 2–20. He visited Saudi Arabia, Jordan, and Oman to demonstrate that he too had influence in other Arab states, and gave an interview indicating that he hoped to solve Qatar's border disputes with Saudi Arabia in a "brotherly way."

Emir Hamad also clarified his position on the selection of a new Secretary General of the GCC by stating that, "If people thought what happened in Muscat was a result of the border (dispute with Saudi Arabia), that is not right at all . . . We don't mind the secretary general being a Saudi . . . (but) All six countries have to agree on this issue. We don't mind Saudi Arabia coming in with its candidate. The way they . . . did it was not a way we can accept. It was a way that did not happen before in the GCC."[336]

What happened next is hotly debated by the Gulf states. Qatar's leadership feels that Bahrain, Saudi Arabia, and the UAE allowed Sheik

Khalifa bin Hamad to prepare a coup attempt. They claim plotters planned to combine a force of Qataris loyal to the deposed Emir with a force of up to 2,000 Yemeni and other Arab mercenaries which were assembling on the Saudi side of the border. They claim that these forces were being organized under the leadership of a French officer who had commanded Sheik Khalifa bin Hamad's personal guard and had been one of the leaders of the French special forces that suppressed the uprising in the Grand Mosque in Mecca. They accuse Bahrain, Saudi Arabia, and the UAE of allowing the deposed Emir to prepare forces in their countries, to plan on staging two Transall transports through their territory to move the forces involved, and even of being ready to provide air cover for the coup.

It is clear that Qatar took the risk of a coup seriously enough to mobilize the Emiri Guard on February 17, 1996. It is also clear that these events led to over one hundred arrests on February 20—including the arrest of sixty army and police officers. Qatar issued a warrant for the arrest of Sheik Hamad bin Jassim bin Hamad—Qatar's former Minister of Economy and Trade—who the government accused of masterminding the coup attempt.[337]

Although Qatari officials feel that a major coup attempt was underway, and that assassination attempts were planned against Qatar's leaders, Bahrain, Saudi Arabia, and the UAE deny that such a coup attempt ever reached the point where Sheik Khalifa bin Hamad assembled any significant forces on their soil and deny that a major recruiting effort ever took place. They accuse Qatar of making false charges to deliberately embarrass them and provide an excuse for its arrests of Emir Hamad's opponents.[338] The other two Southern Gulf states took differing attitudes. Oman responded by denouncing the coup attempt, while Kuwait remained silent.

US intelligence did not detect a build-up for the coup attempt at the time, but several senior US officials have since concluded that a coup attempt was being mobilized. The US and France carried out amphibious and naval military training exercises with Qatar in March 1996, and the US encouraged the Southern Gulf states to resolve their differences peacefully and conduct a summit meeting over the crisis—although Bahrain and Saudi Arabia felt this US action indicated the US was biased in favor of Qatar.[339]

Quiet diplomacy followed—which involved extensive intervention by Oman's Sultan Qabus—and Qatar and its neighbors reached the compromise discussed earlier. On February 17 1996, Qatar agreed to attend the GCC ministerial meeting in Riyadh in March, 1996, and to host the next GCC meeting in December.[340] In March, Qatar and all the other GCC states agreed that the Secretary General of the GCC would now be selected from each Gulf state in alphabetic order and that a Secretary General could only serve for a maximum of two three year terms.

Foreign Ministers Sheik Hamad bin Jassim bin Jabr Al-Thani visited Saudi Arabia to discuss the mechanics of resolving the dispute over the Secretary General. A day later, Emir Sheik Hamad bin Khalifa Al-Thani received the new Saudi Secretary General, Jamil al-Hejailan, in Doha. During this period. Bahraini, Saudi, and UAE support for Sheik Khalifa bin Hamad declined sharply. Bahrain took the more flexible stand regarding the jurisdiction of the International Court described earlier. And, Saudi Arabia and Qatar announced they were forming a joint commission to survey their border and reach a final resolution of any boundary disputes.[341]

These actions did not, however, end the tension between Qatar's ruling elite and that of Saudi Arabia and the UAE—any more than they ended the tensions between Qatar and Bahrain. Qatar felt it confronted aging ruling elites and a Saudi government determined to dominate the Southern Gulf states. It felt that the Saudi leaders also resented Qatar's leaders because the Saudis wished to enforce an unrealistic ultra-conservative political and social orthodoxy on the states of the Arabian peninsula to help protect their own control over the Saudi people. The Saudi and UAE ruling elites felt that Qatar's ruling elite was irresponsible and deliberately seeking to enhance Qatar's status at the expense of GCC unity and political stability. A major generational quarrel between leaders had been added to the long-standing border disputes and rivalries between ruling families.

Qatar's Cooperation with the West

Qatar has compensated for tensions with its neighbors by strengthening its strategic relations with the US and Europe. Qatar did not begin to develop security arrangements with the US until the tanker war of 1987–1988, and only began to develop close security arrangements during the Gulf War. Considerable tension existed over Qatar's purchase of smuggled Stinger missiles from Afghanistan during March, 1988 to November, 1990.

Since that time, relations have steadily improved. Qatar permitted US and Canadian air units to stage out of Qatar during the Gulf War. Qatar deployed a 1,600-man mechanized battalion with 25 tanks, 60 other armored vehicles, and 3–5 artillery weapons. This force successfully deployed to the upper Gulf and fought well at the Battle of Khafji, and in Joint Forces Command (East). Qatar also committed 700 men, 21 fighters, and 12 armed helicopters from its small air force. Qatari Mirage F-1s flew 41 interdiction sorties, with a maximum of about 5 sorties per day. Qatari

Alphajets flew two sorties.[342] The US opened a Military Liaison Office in Doha in October, 1994.[343]

On June 22, 1992, Qatar negotiated a bilateral Defense Cooperation Agreement with the US that offers the US access to Qatari air and naval facilities. A warehouse is now under construction in Doha that will preposition US equipment. Qatar signed a security agreement with Britain in June, 1993. Qatar provided basing facilities for US aircraft that were deployed as part of Operation Vigilant Warrior, and agreed to help offset US costs for the operation.[344]

In March 1995, Qatar formally agreed to the prepositioning of the heavy equipment for one US Army mechanized brigade in Qatar—including up to 110 US M-1A2 tanks—and to host the support base for a full division with nearly 4,000 vehicles. It signed a comprehensive agreement with the US regarding prepositioning and other issues during Secretary Perry's visit in April, 1996. It supported the rotational forward basing of 34 USAF fighters in Qatar in May 1996, which were used to help enforce the no-fly zone in Iraq.

The Qatari air force and other elements of Qatar's military forces have begun to conduct joint air exercises with the US, and the US and Qatar now hold regular bilateral cooperation meetings. Qatar has also held amphibious and naval exercises with the US and French navies and the US Marines.[345]

Qatar's Relations with Iraq and Iran

Qatar has sought to improve its political relations with Iraq and Iran. In the process, Qatar has made it clear that it favors negotiation over sanctions, and political and economic containment. This creates a partial split between Qatar, many of its neighbors, and the US in dealing with the northern Gulf states. Oman does follow somewhat similar policies, but Kuwait and Saudi Arabia feel that Qatar has been too quick to improve relations with Iraq and Bahrain, Saudi Arabia and the UAE feel Qatar has been too quick to improve relations with Iran. The US supports "dual containment."

Qatar has advocated that the UN sanctions on Iraq should be eased for humanitarian reasons and that all the Southern Gulf states should attempt a dialogue with Saddam Hussein's government. Qatar has kept its Baghdad Embassy throughout the Gulf War and its aftermath, although it has scarcely been pro-Iraqi. It has continued to support the enforcement of the UN sanctions affecting Iraq's military capabilities, and senior Qatari officials see Iraq as a significant security threat to the region.

Qatar has maintained an ongoing dialogue with Iran, and members of the Qatari royal family regularly visit Iran to hunt. Senior Iranian officials like the Minister of Defense have visited Qatar, and Qatar even politely rejected an Iranian offer of a defense pact when Iranian Defense Minister Mohammed Furuzadeh visited Qatar in April 1996.[346]

Qatari officials believe this dialogue has had major benefits in easing potential tensions over Qatar and Iran's mutual claims to the off-shore gas resources in the Gulf. They note that when Qatar detected that the exploration efforts of a Iranian-contractor had strayed into Qatari waters, Qatar quietly called the problem to the attention of the Iranian government and then allowed Iran to withdraw the drilling effort without incident. Qatar has also discussed a project to obtain fresh water from Iran's Karun River by financing a $13 billion pipeline under the Gulf, and joint oil and gas projects with the Iranian government, although the cost of these projects makes it uncertain that they will go forward.

Once again, however, Qatari officials recognize the potential threat Iran poses to Qatar and the region. Observers are quick to note that to Qatar, dialogue with Iran does not mean trust, and that the Iranian threat has been a major factor behind Qatar's efforts to improve its military relations with the US. Qatar has also supported the UAE against Iran in the dispute over Iran's seizure full control of the islands of Abu Musa and the Tunbs.[347]

Qatar's Relations with Israel

Qatar has steadily improved its relations with Israel since the Gulf War, and has supported the Arab-Israeli peace process. Qatar is encouraging trade and investment with Israel, and hopes that Israel will become a major customer for Qatari gas exports. Israeli Prime Minister Shimon Peres visited Qatar and Oman in April, 1996. Qatar hosted the second visit of an Israeli Prime Minister to the Gulf region, even though 69% of its native population opposed relations with Israel. It has also signed an agreement with Israel and Enron to go forward with gas exports.[348]

These Qatari and Omani initiatives have played an important role in easing the tensions between the Arab world and Israel and in aiding the peace process. They have, however, received mixed reactions from their neighbors. Most of the other Southern Gulf countries question whether Oman and Qatar should have been so quick to improve relations with Israel. Once again, the Southern Gulf is divided on basic aspects of security policy.

Government and Internal Security

Qatar is a monarchy ruled by the Al-Thani family, which also makes up much of its cabinet. The extended Al-Thani family has over 5,000 members. It has also maintained close ties to merchant families like the Darwish and Al Mana who have played an particularly strong role in Qatar's history since Indian merchants were forced out in the late 1800s. This history helped make Qatar the only Gulf state without a large foreign merchant class until oil led to a massive influx of foreign merchants in the 1950s. Even today, Qatari law strongly favors the economic rights and privileges of citizens over non-citizens. As a result, Qatar has an extended mix of leading families, rather than a clear separation between the separate ruling elite and the native population.

The Role of the Royal Family

Succession within the Al Thani family has involved a complex series of power struggles between and within branches of the ruling family. Under the Basic Law of 1970, the Emir must be chosen from and by the adult males of the Al Thani family, but there are no formal procedures for determining who shall rule. The exact powers that can be assumed by a given Emir vary according to ruler, although custom establishes a number of practical limits on the ruler's power.

The present Emir, Sheik Hamad bin Khalifa Al Thani, assumed power in June, 1995 as the result of the kind of "family coup" that has occurred several times in Qatar since the Al Thani family first took power. For example, Sheik Abdullah bin Qassim Al Thani experienced continuing problems with other members of the royal family during the 1920s and 1930s. He attempted to avoid future succession disputes by grooming his second son—Hamad bin Abdullah Al Thani—for the succession. Hamad died in 1948, however, and this triggered a struggle for the rulership between Ali bin Abdullah (Abullah's son), and his nephew Khalifa bin Hamad Al Thani.

Sheik Ali bin Abdullah won this struggle and ruled as ruler from 1949–1960. At the same time, he showed little interest in the details of governing the country, and stepped down from power on October 24, 1960. When he did so, he violated an arrangement he had made in 1949 to make his nephew Khalifa bin Hamad Al Thani his successor. He instead appointed his own son—Ahmad bin Ali Al Thani—as ruler. Khalifa had to settle for being designated the heir of the new ruler.

Like his father, however, Sheik Ahmad showed little interest in the day-to-day exercise of government. Beginning in the 1960s, Khalifa took over the actual task of ruling. He built upon his power as Prime Minister, and his previous experience in positions as the minister of foreign affairs, finance and petroleum, education and culture, and police and internal security.

By April 1970, when Qatar declared its constitution, Sheik Khalifa bin Hamad controlled virtually every aspect of government. This arrangement did not, however, give Qatar a strong and authoritative head of state. Khalifa could not act as a head of state at a time when Qatar and Bahrain were contemplating the possible creation of a federation which was to include Bahrain and Qatar as well as the emirates that now make up the UAE.

These problems seem to have grown worse when Qatar decided on full independence in 1971, and the Gulf states began to compete actively for influence and power. Sheik Ahmad bin Ali had become so distant from day-to-day rule that he declared Qatar's independence on September 3, 1971, from a villa in Switzerland, rather than his homeland. On February 22, 1972, Sheik Khalifa deposed Sheik Ahmad and became Qatar's new ruler. Sheik Ahmad bin Ali Al-Thani spent the rest of his life in Dubai, or his villa on Lake Geneva, and died in 1977.

This change in power triggered a sometimes acrimonious debate over the allocation of Qatar's petroleum wealth, ministries and control over government contracts between the branches of the royal family. These issues came to a head in 1977, when Khalifa designated his son, Sheik Hamad bin Khalifa, as Crown Prince, rather than Khalifa's younger brother Sheik Suhaim. Sheik Hamad had graduated from Sandhurst in 1971, and was an admirer of both Winston Churchill and Gamel Abdel Nasser.

The Qatari government issued statements that the designation of Sheik Hamad was made, "with the consent of the Royal Family, local notables and religious leaders in accordance with local custom." Other sources indicate, however, that the appointment caused considerable tension between members of the royal family. Suhaim sought Saudi support for his claims in an effort to overturn the decision.

There were reports of an attempt to assassinate Khalifa or some other leader of the GCC in September, 1983. There were also reports in August, 1985 that Sheik Suhaim had plotted a coup against Khalifa and Hamad, and had funded a cadre of armed supporters in the northern part of the country. While it is impossible to confirm the accuracy of these reports, Suhaim died suddenly from a heart attack in 1985, and his sons accused Isa Ghanim Al Kuwari of delaying medical aid. Subsequently, his supporters were imprisoned when they tried to kill Isa Ghanim Al Kuwari.[349]

New reports of rivalries within the Al Thani family surfaced during Qatar's 1986 border confrontation with Bahrain. According to these rumors, Sheik Nasr bin Hamad—another younger brother of the ruler—had been shot in a family quarrel. There is, however, no evidence that this incident took place.

Recent Changes in Qatar's Leadership

From 1977 onwards, Sheik Hamad gradually began to assume power although Sheik Khalifa bin Hamad Al Thani continued to rule as Emir. By the mid-1980s, Sheik Hamad had become the effective ruler of Qatar, in much the same way Khalifa had replaced Ahmad. Sheik Hamad controlled the armed forces in his role as Minister of Defense. He also reorganized the Council of Ministers in July 1989 to appoint more of his supporters to office.[350]

On June 27, 1995, Sheik Hamad bin Khalifa formally took power as ruler. Emir Hamad acted while his father was away in Zurich—reportedly for medical treatment. Sheik Hamad announced that he had acted with the support of the Royal family, noble tribes and families, and people of Qatar. Hamad's brother and the Deputy Prime Minister and Minister of the Interior—Abdullah bin Khalifa Al-Thani—immediately pledged his support as did most other members of the family. Sheik Hamad also had the support of each of the heads of Qatar's armed forces, and was able to withdraw the troops he had deployed to secure Doha and the Rayyan Palace within 24 hours. The US, other Western states, Iran, and most Arab states soon recognized Hamad as Emir.[351]

One significant member of the royal family who did not pledge support to Hamad was Khalifa's second son—Sheik Abdul Aziz bin Khaliah Al Thani. Sheik Abdul Aziz was the ex-Minister of Finance, and was in Paris when the coup occurred. This may have contributed to the fact that Sheik Khalifa kept control over billions of dollars worth of personal funds and further billions worth of Qatar's foreign reserves.

As is usually the case with developments within the Al Thani family, the exact reasons for Hamad's actions are unclear. The new Emir confined himself to stating that, "circumstances forced me to act," and conditions "led me forcefully and with all regret to take a decision . . . and assume the role of successor to my father who will remain the cherished father of all . . ." Hamad seems to have acted because of growing tensions with his father and because of Khalifa's plans to shift power to other members of the Al Thani family. Khalifa had moved away from his office in the Emiri Diwan several months earlier to his private Rayyan Palace. He and Hamad had evidently argued over investment policy and foreign policy, and over the trip Sheik Khalifa was on when he was deposed.[352]

The change may also have had "generational" causes. The new Emir was 45, while his father was 63. Sheik Hamad was a Sandhurst graduate and was the first Western-educated leader to come to power in the Gulf since Sultan Qabus. He had more liberal public policies than his father and more experience with the West and the shifts in power in the region. It was Hamad who led Qatar during the Gulf War. Sheik Hamad also had been more aggressive than his father in pursuing the development of Qatar's oil and gas resources, in modernizing Qatar's armed forces and bureaucracy, in seeking privatization and outside investment, in creating a Qatari stock market, and in pursuing an independent foreign policy. He is also seen as the driving force behind Qatar's diplomatic dialogue with Iran and Iraq.[353]

At the same time, Sheik Hamad was perceived in Bahrain and Saudi Arabia as being a stronger nationalist than his father, and as more interested in pursuing Qatar's territorial claims and asserting an independent foreign policy, thus becoming the main source of the growing friction between Qatar and Bahrain and Saudi Arabia.

It is interesting to note that Hamad sealed the border with Saudi Arabia when he took power, put Qatar's forces on alert, and sent at least some troops south to the border area. Hamad also sent the then Minister of Interior Abdullah and Foreign Minister Hamad bin Jassim to explain his reasons for taking power. Despite an initial silence lasting two days, Saudi Arabia recognized Hamad as early as June 28, 1995. It also did so although Sheik Khalifa had reacted to the coup by stating that he remained the "legitimate Emir," would return to Qatar "whatever the cost," and had Saudi backing in his efforts to return.[354]

The Emirship Under Sheik Hamad

Since he has taken power, Sheik Hamad has made it clear that he supports the eventual creation of democratic institutions. He has largely ended the censorship of Qatar's five newspapers—papers usually avoid personal attacks on Qatari officials. He has promised to hold municipal elections, and to allow all native male Qataris to vote. He has stated that these elections will be the first step in moving towards an elected national assembly. He has tolerated plays satirizing Gulf regimes. He has supported a Qatari version of the Wahhabi faith which is far more tolerant and liberal than the Saudi version.

Sheik Hamad and his Foreign Minister have been the leading actors in expanding Qatar's strategic ties to the US as a counterbalance to dependence on Saudi Arabia and the GCC. He is seen as the leader in opening up a dialogue between Qatar and Israel, and pursuing an independent dialogue with Iran and Iraq in an effort to maintain peaceful relations between Qatar and its northern Gulf neighbors. Sheik Hamad asserted that he would continue to expand Qatar's ties to the US, support the peace process and expand Qatar's dialogue with Israel, and maintain a dialogue with Iran and Iraq, on the day after he took power. He also indicated that Qatar would support the GCC and abide by all UN Resolutions—including those affecting Iraq.[355]

The new Emir appointed an 18 man cabinet on July 11, 1995—and changed the rules for the succession.[356] Sheik Hamad made himself Prime Minister, in place of his father, but kept his previous positions of Minister of Defense and supreme commander of the armed forces. He appointed his brother Abdullah as Deputy Prime Minister and Abdullah kept his post of Minister of the Interior. He kept nine posts for the Al Thani family and retained the Minister of Foreign Affairs and Finance and leading technocrats like the Ministers of Energy.

Emir Hamad also appointed four new members of the cabinet—three from outside the family. He made Sheik Mohammed bin Khalid Al-Thani Minister of State for Cabinet Affairs, Ali Said al-Khiyreen Minister of Health, Najeeb Mohammed Al-Nuami Minister of Justice, and Ahmad Abdullah Al-Mahmoud Minister of State for Foreign Affairs. He also made Sheik Ahmad bin Saif Al-Thani, the former Minister of Justice, Minister of State.

Sheik Hamad fired his father's long time aide, Isa bin Ghanem Al-Kawari, and replaced him as Court Minister with Abdullah bin Khalifa Al-Attaya, the former Foreign Minister. He replaced many senior civil servants—including the heads of the civil service department, and religious courts and the undersecretaries of the ministries of information, interior, and municipal affairs.

According to some reports, Sheik Hamad also amended the succession on July 11, 1995, to go to his eldest son, Sheik Mashall. According to such reports, the succession must go to one of the sons of the Emir under the new law, or to a crown prince chosen by the Emir from within the Al Thani family if the Emir has no sons. The previous rules had simply stated that the post of Emir "shall be on a hereditary basis in the Al-Thani family."[357]

At the same time, the conflict between Sheik Hamad and his father remains unresolved. In spite of the events of February and March 1996, Khalifa bin Hamad Al Thani continues to state that he is the legitimate ruler instead of Hamad and that he intends to return to power.[358]

Foreign Affairs Minister, Sheik Hamad bin Jassem bin Jabr Al-Thani has responded by stating that Sheik Khalifa, "will never rule again in Qatar . . . This thing is finished . . . We are looking forward. This is something of the past. He knows and we know that we cannot return to the past. All the ruling family in Qatar and all the Qatari citizens are with Sheik Hamad . . . There are two kinds of people who are asking the questions. One is making a noise and the other doesn't know the situation in Qatar. Sheik Hamad has been ruler for years in fact and not a few months. Sheik Khalifa will never be ruler in Qatar again. . . . It is our view that he can come any time to Qatar as father for all of us. The father of our Emir is welcome. We thank all of the countries that have received and welcomed him. For us, we would like to see him pass through Qatar."[359]

The Minister of Foreign Affairs has also, however, confirmed that Sheik Khalifa held much of Qatar's foreign reserves in his personal accounts—which are reported to be worth up to three billion dollars. He stated that,

"There is cash in the name of the previous Emir, but this cannot affect our progress and our projects. Our country is a rich country. All the projects we are doing have been studied and are feasible."[360]

The practical question is whether Khalifa and Hamad can reconcile, whether their confrontation leads to a long struggle for power, and whether the other Gulf states will continue to exploit these tensions to put pressure on Qatar or actively seek to put Khalifa back in power.[361]

Government by Consultation

The most important officials in the Qatari government are the Emir, Prime Minister, and Minister of Defense—although the appointment of a new crown prince may create another major position. The Emir is technically an absolute ruler, but his power is limited by a tradition of rule by consensus. This custom of rule by consensus often leads to extensive consultations between the Emir, leading merchant families, religious leaders, and other notables on important policies. Qatar has interlocking family networks, and citizens have the right submit appeals or petitions to the Emir and his officials. Any citizen has the right to appeal personally to the Emir if he feels that Qatar's officials have failed to deal with an issue, and these arrangements provide a wide range of informal avenues for the expression and redress of grievances.

Qatar is also evolving from a traditional society into a modern welfare state, and modern government departments have been established to meet the requirements of social and economic progress. Qatar's laws reflect this mixture of old and new. The Basic Law of April, 1970 institutionalizes many of the local customs rooted in Qatar's conservative, Wahhabi heritage. It is important to note, however, that the Wahhabi traditions of Qatar are more liberal than those of Saudi Arabia and are much more tolerant of foreign customs and other branches of Islam. For example, women can drive and alcohol is permitted in private clubs.

The Basic Law grants the Emir preeminent power, other provisions of the law include respect for the sanctity of private property, freedom from arbitrary arrest and imprisonment, and punishment of transgressions against Islamic law. The Emir cannot violate the Shari'a (Islamic law) and must consider the opinions of leading notables and the Wahhabi religious establishment. The position of the leading families and religious leaders is also institutionalized in the Advisory Council, an appointed body that assists the Emir in formulating policy.[362]

There are few signs of organized political activity, and Qatar does not have political parties or any elected representative body. At the same time, the new Emir is planning municipal elections as the first step in moving towards the creation of a national assembly. His power is also subject to a number of additional constraints, and the media is increasingly free to criticize the government.

Qatar has a growing number of sophisticated businessmen and technocrats whose opinions must be also considered. While Qatar does not have labor unions, the government must take account of its history of labor unrest, especially protests by native Qataris over the use of low cost foreign labor. Qatar has had to expel foreign workers on several occasions in response to protests by native workers, and the government has learned it must either be sensitive to the demands of native workers or compensate them with welfare payments and privileges.

The influx of expatriate Arabs has also introduced ideas that challenge the traditional political structure of Qatar's society. There has been no serious challenge to Al Thani rule, and nothing approaching a broadly based political movement has yet emerged. No prominent notables have emerged to challenge the regime, as Hamad Al-Attyya and Nasir Al-Misnad did during the protests in the 1960s. There have, however, been some protests. For example, nineteen Qataris signed a petition calling for greater political freedom and constitutional reform in December, 1991. Some of the signatories are still reported to be under travel restriction as a result of their petition, and the government's actions indicate the petition may have significant popular support.[363]

Demographics and Dependence on Foreign Labor

The main internal threat to Qatar's stability seems to be the fact that only a small portion of its population now consists of native citizens, and Qatar's dependence on foreign labor. In 1970, Qatar had only 111,000 residents, of which about 45,000 were native. This total rose to 200,000 by the mid-1970s and 369,000 in 1986. By 1986, some 84% of the population was concentrated in the area around Doha, and 88% was urbanized. The rapid development of Qatar's economy had also shifted its demographics to the point where 67% of the population was male, and expatriate workers, mostly South Asian and Arab, outnumbered Qataris by a ratio of 4 to 1.[364]

In 1995, Qatar's total population was about 560,000–600,000, with a growth rate of 2.74%, and a fertility rate of about 4.63 children per mother. The growth rate and fertility rate for native Qataris was much higher than that for the total population, but detailed statistics are not available. According to Qatari estimates, only about 130,000–147,000 residents were native Qataris. About 35% of the total population, and 50% of the native population, is under 15 years of age.

Although such data are uncertain, some sources indicate that the ratio of foreigners to native Qataris dropped from about 4:1 to 3:1 in the early 1990s. This drop was partly the result of a relatively high birth rate among native Qataris, and increase in life span. The World Bank estimates the population growth rate among native Qataris as averaging 5.8% for 1980–1992 and projects a growth of 4.2% for 1992–2000.[365]

The drop, however, was largely the result of a temporary decline in foreign workers in the early 1990s, and a recession in local business produced by low oil prices. This recession led many firms to lay off expatriate staff to cut costs during the early 1990s. When the economy began to recover in 1994, however, the expatriate population began to grow accordingly—particularly workers from Egypt and South Asia. The number of Americans in Qatar also increased sharply. As a result, "Qatarization" has so far had little—if any—impact.

Today, over 80% of Qatar's total population, and over 82% of the 104,000 man work force, is non-Qatari.[366] While Qatar is 95% Muslim, it is ethnically divided into 40% Arab, 18% Pakistani, 18% Indian, 10% Iranian, and 14% other nationalities. The Iranian and Shi'ite minority is particularly important. Many Qataris of Iranian extraction occupy positions of the highest importance in the private sector, but they are rarely found in senior decision making positions in the government. Qatar's few Shi'ites are permitted to practice their faith, but not to carry out public ceremonies that are disapproved of by the Wahhabi sect.[367]

Further, the current structure of Qatar's work force has been distorted by subsidies, the growth of government, and the growth of a largely nonproductive service sector. About 7.8% of Qatar's labor force is involved in subsidized agriculture and fishing (about 4 times the percent that agriculture contributes to the GDP. Roughly 26.8% of the labor force is involved in productive industry, including the oil and gas sectors. A total of 65.4% is employed in the government and services sector.[368]

The Government does continue to try to reduce the number of foreigners by offering government jobs only to Qatari citizens. It is trying to strengthen its "Qatarization" program and all joint venture industries and government departments now have legal and financial incentives to place Qatari nationals in positions of greater authority. Qatar has tightened the administration of its foreign manpower programs, and enforced stricter entry and immigration rules and regulations. The government has only had real success, however, in Qatarizing senior positions. Growing numbers of foreign-educated Qataris, including many educated in the United States, are returning to Qatar to assume key positions formerly occupied by expatriates.

The Qatari government also recognizes that its combination of welfare payments, cultural traditions, and a weak educational system have failed to develop a strong work ethic. It is seeking to reduce subsidy payments and programs that now virtually guarantee all university and high school graduates a government job. It is seeking to reform its educational system, and focus on job-related skills and a more demanding curriculum, although it is meeting resistance from its largely Egyptian teachers.

So far, however, these measures have largely affected government-related, white collar jobs and have only had a limited impact on overall employment. This presents growing problems given Qatar's demographics. Chart Twenty-Eight shows that a conservative World Bank estimate projects that Qatar's population will grow from 486,000 in 1990, and 544,000 in 1995, to 598,000 by the year 2000, 646,000 by 2025, 693,000 by 2010, and 769,000 by 2020. The total number of Qatari young men reaching job age (15–19 years) is projected to rise from 15,000 in 1990 and 20,000 in 1995 to 23,000 in 2000, 29,000 in 2010, and then remain at 29,000–32,000 through 2020.[369]

Wealthy as Qatar may be today, it must sharply reduce its current expenditures on foreign labor to preserve its standard of wealth, and it must create meaningful jobs for its growing number of young citizens. Qatar must also sharply reduce its dependence on foreign labor if it is to ensure that it maintains its identity as a nation.

Economic Security

Qatar is a wealthy state, even by Gulf standards, and is likely to remain so. However, Qatar has far less real export income and per capita wealth than in the past, and it remains an oil and gas-dominated economy. Given the demographic and foreign labor problems, Qatar must be much more careful about its finances and how it manages its economy, and much will depend on the efficiency with which it manages its gas resources

There are a wide range of estimates of the size of Qatar's economy. The CIA estimates that Qatar's GDP had a purchasing power equivalent of $10.7 billion in 1994. Industrial production, including oil and gas, accounted for 50% of the GDP and had a growth rate of 1.9% per year. Qatar's exports were worth $3.13 billion. Roughly 75% of these earnings came from exports of crude oil. The rest came from exports of steel products and fertilizers. Qatar had roughly $1.75 billion worth of civil imports, largely manufactured goods, machinery, and food. About 16% of its trade came from Japan, 11% from the UK, 10% from the US, 7% from Germany, and 5% from France.[370]

Table Twenty-Seven shows the short term trends in Qatar's economy. It shows that striking shifts take place in Qatar's annual GDP and per capita income as the result of shifts in its oil production and world oil prices. Charts Twenty-Nine and Thirty show the longer term trends in Qatar's economy and real per capita income. Chart Twenty-Nine shows that Qatar's total central government expenditures are relatively low as a percent of GDP for a Gulf state, and that exports have normally been

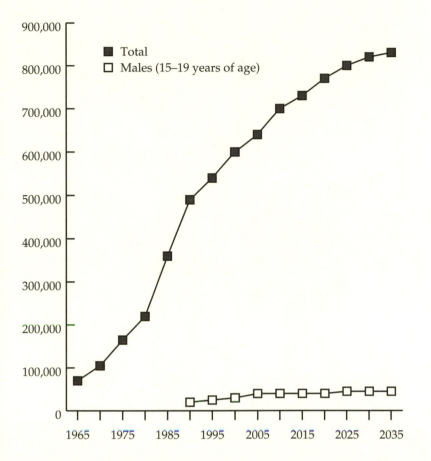

CHART TWENTY-EIGHT   Estimated Trends in the Qatari Population During 1990–2035. *Source:* Adapted by Anthony H. Cordesman from World Bank, *World Population Projections, 1994–1995,* Washington, World Bank, 1994, and material provided by the CIA.

substantially larger than central government expenditures. It also shows that military expenditures and arms imports have been a relatively limited portion of the total GDP.

Chart Thirty shows the longer term decline in Qatar's per capita income resulting from population growth and lower oil prices and export revenues. It shows that Qatar's wealth is both finite and declining relative to its total population. Qatar only has about half the real per capita export income it had when oil prices reached their peak in the 1970s and early 1980s.

TABLE TWENTY-SEVEN   Key Economic and Budget Indicators in Qatar

EIU Estimate*	1990	1991	1992	1993	1994
Production (1,000s of barrels per day)	396	390	400	420	—
Oil Export Receipts ($ US current billions)	2.96	2.817	3.2	2.594	—
GDP ($ US current billions)	7.36	6.88	7.47	7.19	—
Annual Change in GDP (%)	13.4	-6.5	8.6	-3.7	—
Per Capita GDP ($ US current)	15,021	13,766	14,370	12,843	—
Annual Change in Per Capita GDP (%)	6.4	-8.4	4.4	-10.6	—

MEED Estimate (Qatari Rials in Millions)**	1993/1994	1994/1995	1995/1996	1996/1997
Budgeted Revenues	10,373	8,360	9,204	10,800
Actual Revenues	10,645	9,690	10,500	na
Budget Expenditures	13,070	11,830	12,731	13,750
Actual Expenditures	13,435	11,647	12,500	na
Budget Current Expenditures	10,368	9,509	10,507	11,530
Actual Current Expenditures	11,533	9,835	10,500	na
Budgeted Capital Expenditures	2,708	2,321	2,223	2,220
Actual Capital Expenditures	1,902	1,812	2,000	na
Budgeted Deficit	2,703	3,470	3,527	2,930
Actual Deficit	2,790	1,957	1,960	na

Notes: $1 = 3.64 Qatari Rials.
*Source: Adapted by Wayne A. Larsen, NSSP, Georgetown University, from the EIU, Country Profile, *Bahrain/Qatar, 1995–1996*, pp. 34, 36.
**Middle East Economic Digest, May 10, 1996, p.3.

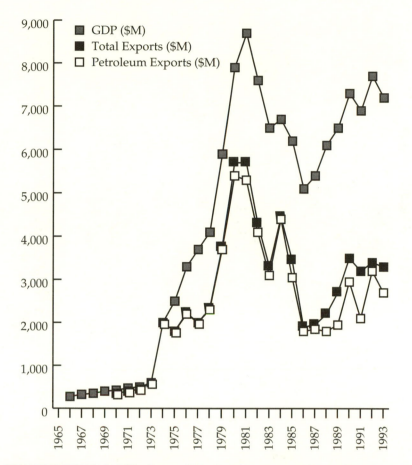

CHART TWENTY-NINE   Qatar: GDP, Total Exports, and Petroleum Exports in Current US Dollars. *Source:* Adapted by Anthony H. Cordesman from International Energy Agency (IEA), *Middle East Oil and Gas,* Paris, 1995, pp. 284, 294, and based on IMF, *International Financial Statistics,* IMF, *World Economic Outlook,* May, 1995, and OECD, *Main Economic Indicators.*

Dependence on Oil and Gas

Like the other Southern Gulf states, Qatar's economy depends almost solely on oil and gas revenues. Oil and gas, and related products account for roughly 84–85% of Qatar's export earnings and 72–75% of its government revenues.[371] Qatar's only other natural resource is fish, but agriculture and fishing together account for less than 2% of Qatar's GDP, and most of this income comes from a growing commercial fishing industry.

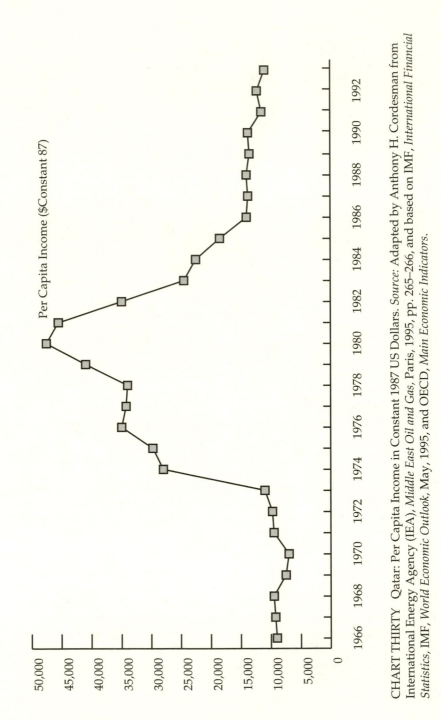

CHART THIRTY Qatar: Per Capita Income in Constant 1987 US Dollars. *Source:* Adapted by Anthony H. Cordesman from International Energy Agency (IEA), *Middle East Oil and Gas*, Paris, 1995, pp. 265–266, and based on IMF, *International Financial Statistics*, IMF, *World Economic Outlook*, May, 1995, and OECD, *Main Economic Indicators*.

Almost all of Qatar's food is imported. Qatar has no arable land, irrigated land or permanent crops, and only 5% of its territory is suitable for light grazing.

Even the limited agricultural production that does take place is extremely wasteful since there is very limited freshwater resources and agriculture must rely on desalinized water, foreign labor, and subsidies. Water is a problem for other reasons. Current estimates indicate that Qatar's groundwater and acquifers will be depleted by 2000, and Qatar is steadily increasing its dependence on large-scale desalination facilities.[372]

Qatar is just beginning to exploit the full downstream potential of its oil and gas resources, attempt to create new jobs for its native labor force, and to encourage private investment outside the service industries. Most of its heavy industrial projects, are based in Umm Said. They include a refinery with a 50,000–60,000 barrels per day capacity, a fertilizer plant for urea and ammonia, a steel plant, and a petrochemical plant. These industries use gas for fuel. Most of them are joint ventures between European and Japanese firms and the State-owned Qatar General Petroleum Company (QGPC).

As a result, Qatar's future economic development depends on maintaining and increasing oil and gas exports, increasing exports of petroleum-related products, and developing gas or petroleum fueled industries.

To put this issue in perspective, Qatar's oil and gas resources produced an economic boom after 1974, when Qatar's oil production and revenues increased dramatically after the oil boycott and rises in oil prices that followed the October War. This boom transformed Qatar from one of the world's poorest countries to a nation with one of the world's highest per capita incomes. This boom ended in the early 1980s, however, and the drop in world oil prices and demand from 1982 to 1989, resulted in a near recession. This recession was made worse by the fact that OPEC (Organization of Petroleum Exporting Countries) cut Qatar's crude oil production quotas.

Oil revenues dropped from $5 billion in 1980–1981 to $4 billion annually in 1982–1985, and then $2 billion annually in 1986–1988.[373] Qatar felt the economic impact of each drop in oil prices, and has sometimes been slow to adjust government spending to match the decline in its income. This resulted in budget deficits after the early 1980s. The decline in oil prices during 1986 was especially hard on Qatar's government. Qatar lost $1 billion in oil export receipts in that year alone.

Qatar's GDP dropped significantly in constant dollars between 1980 and 1992, almost solely because of a drop in real oil prices. Its annual per capita GDP dropped from $34,560 in 1983 to $19,290 in 1986, and $15,190 in 1993. While these figures would be higher if measured using an estimate of the purchasing power equivalent of the GDP, and recent increases in oil and gas revenues have increased Qatar's GDP and GDP per capita, oil wealth is relative even in Qatar.

Unless oil and gas prices rise significantly higher than the US and IEA now project, per capita oil and gas earnings could drop by a further 10% to 20% during the next decade. They could also do so in spite of Qatar's gas projects.[374] Qatar has dealt with some of these issues by limiting its budgets, and by reducing government capital spending to increase the share of the remaining budget that can be allocated to public welfare programs. In the mid to long term, however, Qatar will also have to emphasize privatization, and reductions in its birth rate and reliance on foreign labor.

The Current "Recession"

Qatar already must deal with the combined impact of a recent drop in oil prices, limited oil production, the cash flow crisis created by the fact that the ex-Emir still holds much of Qatar's foreign reserves, the impact of deficit spending, and the high cost of developing Qatar's gas resources.

Oil prices began to recover in 1989, and oil production rose to around 400,000 barrels per day. As a result, oil export revenues increased to $3 billion in 1990. This increase in revenues still left Qatar in the equivalent of a "recession", however, and Qatar was forced to cut real spending steadily after 1991.[375] During the country's 1994/1995 fiscal year, which began in April 1994, government revenues fell by 19% and spending fell by 9.5%, relative to the previous year. This led to the progressive tightening of Qatar's budgets shown in Table Twenty-Seven.

The problems caused by lower oil revenues were compounded by the struggle between the Emir Hamad and his father that began in 1995. Although no reliable data are available, Sheik Khalifa seems to have been left with much of the nation's cash reserves when he was deposed from power. According to various estimates, these assets total from $2.5 billion to $7.5 billion in liquid assets. This range is substantially less than the $17 billion referred to in some reports, but it still involves a very substantial amount. It also seems to have limited the total ready reserves available to the new government to $694 million in December, 1996—with an additional $787 million in foreign assets.[376]

Further, the cost of planned oil and gas development could mean that the Qatari government will face cash flow problems for the next half decade. Qatar has financed nearly $5 billion worth of oil and gas and infrastructure projects since 1993, and another $550 million for the government. Qatar has had to increase its medium and long-term debt to fund some of its LNG projects. Qatar's foreign debt rose from $1.3 billion in 1992 to $3.2 billion in 1994.

Qatar had a deficit of 1,957 million Rials in 1994/95 and 1,960 million Rials ($593 million) in 1995/96, in spite of higher oil prices and reaching 470,000 barrels per day in 1995/96. Oil and gas development costs, are a major reason that Qatar has projected deficits of 2,950 million Rials ($811 million) for 1996/97 and 3,530 million Rials ($971 million) for 1997/98. These are substantial deficits compared to total budgets of 13,750 million Rials ($3,781 million) for 1996/97 and 12,750 million Rials ($3,506 million) for 1997/98.[377]

The key question is whether and when the country's large, liquefied natural gas (LNG) projects will generate enough revenues to end Qatar's problems. With proper management, tight fiscal controls, and moderate economic reforms, this recovery could occur as early as the year 2000. Much will depend, however, on world gas prices and how efficiently Qatar can bring its gas production on-line and market its output.

Oil Resources

Qatar is a relatively small oil power in comparison with many of its Gulf neighbors. Chart Twenty-Nine has already shown the limits to Qatar's oil export earnings. Chart Thirty-One shows the trends in Qatar's oil production, oil exports, and exports of refined products. It shows that Qatar's oil production had dropped from a 1979 high of 508,000 barrels per day to an estimated 413,000 barrels per day in 1994, and that Qatar produced at a monthly rate of 395,000 to 415,000 barrels per day during 1991–1994.[378]

In 1995, commercial sources estimated that Qatar had proven oil reserves of 3.3–4.3 billion barrels (0.4% of the world's total).[379] The US Department of Energy (DOE) has recently issued slightly different estimates. As of January 1995, the DOE estimated Qatar's proven recoverable oil reserves to be 3.7 billion barrels. This estimate was slightly higher than those made in the 1980s and took into account the potential for enhanced oil recovery (EOR) techniques to improve oil recovery rates.[380]

At the same time, the DOE made adjustments for the fact that increased production levels following the August 1990 Iraqi invasion of Kuwait had led to overworked offshore reservoirs and structural damage to Qatar's offshore fields. Maintenance activities in 1994, which were aimed at increasing reservoir pressure through EOR techniques, were only partially successful. They caused average monthly production to fall to 350,000 barrels per day during the month of October 1994, and only produced benefits which promise annual average production of slightly more than 400,000 barrels per day. Production did, however, rise to a 10 year high of 470,000 barrels per day in 1995. Qatar also had low domestic demand and was able to export nearly 97% of its total oil production.[381]

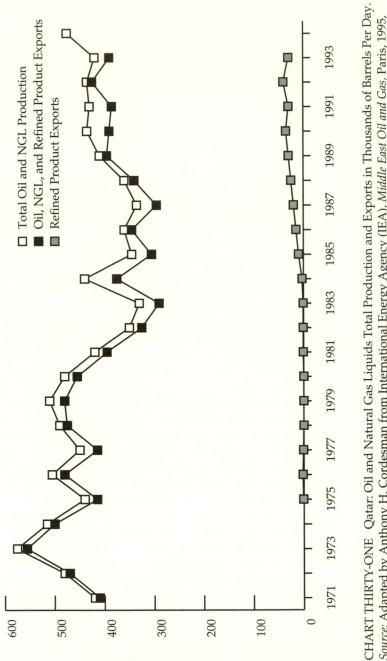

CHART THIRTY-ONE Qatar: Oil and Natural Gas Liquids Total Production and Exports in Thousands of Barrels Per Day. *Source:* Adapted by Anthony H. Cordesman from International Energy Agency (IEA), *Middle East Oil and Gas*, Paris, 1995, pp. 307–317.

The International Energy Agency has similar estimates of Qatar's oil reserves. It estimates identified oil reserves at 3.9 billion barrels, and shows no estimate for probable undiscovered reserves. As Chart Thirty-Two and Table Twenty-Eight show, this makes Qatar a small oil power by the standards of Iran, Iraq, Kuwait, Saudi Arabia, and the UAE.

Qatar's commercial oil production currently comes from one onshore and three offshore fields. The Dukhan oil field is Qatar's oldest, largest, and only onshore field. It contains an estimated 2 billion barrels of recoverable 42° API crude oil. The field is divided into four structures: Khatiyah, Fahahil, Jaleha, and Diyab.

While offshore output declined noticeably in the 1990s, onshore production from Dukhan rose from 190,000 barrels per day in 1991 to an estimated 270,000 barrels per day in 1994. This increase was due partly to the October 1992 start-up of the Diyab structure, which is located on the field's southern flank. Diyab currently produces about 50,000 barrels per day. Production from this structure is transported to the newly-upgraded, Jaleha production facilities. The Diyab structure is the key reason that Qatar has been able to maintain oil production levels over 400,000 barrels per day. Wintershall, the operator of the offshore block adjacent to the Dukhan field, believes that the field extends offshore. However, exploration of this block is limited by the pending case between Qatar and Bahrain over ownership rights of the surrounding islands and reefs.[382]

Along with the Id al-Shargi PSA, Occidental has been awarded a 5-year, $1.9-million technical, service contract to conduct a 3-D seismic survey of the Dukhan field. Both Occidental and QGPC hope to add 10,000 barrels per day to Dukhan's current production within 3 years. Also, QGPC eventually plans to bring 40,000 barrels per day of condensate, on-stream from Dukhan's gas cap. Additionally, US-based Western Geophysical is conducting 3-D, seismic work on the Bul Hanine and Maydan Mahzam fields in the hope of maintaining their outputs, in spite of rising water and gas contents in their maturing reservoirs.[383]

Qatar's offshore production began in 1964, over 15 years after the Dukhan field came on-stream. Qatar has three primary producing offshore oil fields: The 12,000 barrel per day Id al-Shargi field, the 40,000 barrel per day Maydan Mahzam field, and the 90,000 barrels per day Bul Hanine field. These fields have estimated recoverable reserves of 220, 690, and 550 million barrels, respectively. Production from these fields peaked at 320,000 barrels per day in 1973, before falling to about 140,000 barrels per day in 1994. Output from all three fields is tied to production facilities at Halul Island, which lies roughly 30 miles offshore east of Doha.[384]

Qatar shares revenues with the United Arab Emirates (UAE) from the off-shore field al-Bunduq. Production from al-Bunduq is transported to the UAE's Das Island for export, and the field's production and reserves

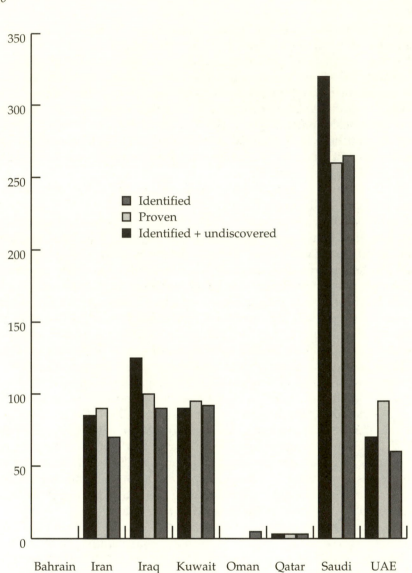

CHART THIRTY-TWO Total Oil Reserves of the Gulf States in Billions of Barrels. *Source:* IEA, *Middle East Oil and Gas,* Paris, OECD, IEA, Annex 2, and data provided by Bahrain and Oman. Bahrain's reserves are only 350 million barrels and do not show up on the chart because of scale.

TABLE TWENTY-EIGHT   Comparative Oil Reserves and Production Levels of the Gulf States

Comparative Oil Reserves in 1994 in Billions of Barrels

Country	Identified	Undiscovered	Identified and Undiscovered	Proven	% of World Total
Bahrain	—	—	—	.35	8.9
Iran	69.2	19.0	88.2	89.3	8.9
Iraq	90.8	35.0	125.8	100.0	10.0
Kuwait	92.6	3.0	95.6	96.5	9.7
Oman	—	—	—	5.0	NA
Qatar	3.9	0	3.9	3.7	0.4
Saudi Arabia	265.5	51.0	316.5	261.2	26.1
UAE	61.1	4.2	65.3	98.1	9.8
Total	583.0	112.2	695.2	654.1	64.9
Rest of World	—	—	—	345.7	35.1
World	—	—	—	999.8	100.0

(continues)

TABLE TWENTY-EIGHT *(continued)*

Comparative Oil Production in Millions of Barrels per Day

Country	1995 OPEC Actual	1995 OPEC Quota	DOE/IEA Estimate of Actual Production 1990	1992	2000	2005	2010	Maximum Sustainable 1995	2000	Announced Capacity in 2000
Bahrain	—	—	—	—	—	—	—	—	—	—
Iran	3,608	3,600	3.2	3.6	4.3	5.0	5.4	3.2	4.5	4.5
Iraq	600	400	2.2	0.4	4.4	5.4	6.6	2.5	5.0	5.0
Kuwait	1,850	2,000	1.7	1.1	2.9	3.6	4.2	2.8	3.3	3.3
Oman	—	—	—	—	—	—	—	—	—	—
Qatar	449	378	0.5	0.4	0.6	0.6	0.6	0.5	0.6	0.6
Saudi Arabia	8,018	8,000	8.5	9.6	11.5	12.8	14.1	10.3	11.1	11.1
UAE	2,193	2,161	2.5	2.6	3.1	3.5	4.3	3.0	3.8	3.2
Total Gulf	—	—	18.6	17.7	26.8	30.9	35.0	23.5	28.2	28.2
World	—	—	69.6	67.4	78.6	84.2	88.8	—	28.2	—

Source: Adapted by Anthony H. Cordesman from estimates in IEA, *Middle East Oil and Gas*, Paris, OED/IEA, 1995, Annex 2 and DOE/EIA, *International Energy Outlook, 1995*, Washington, DOE/EIA, June 1995, pp. 26–30, and *Middle East Economic Digest*, February 23, 1996, p. 3. IEA and DOE do not provide country breakouts for Bahrain and Oman. Reserve data estimated by author based on country data.

are not applied towards Qatar's OPEC quota, nor are they reported with Qatar's oil data. Since 1989, al-Bunduq has produced about 50,000 barrels per day after a $330-million investment was spent in secondary recovery methods during the mid-1980s.[385]

Efforts to Increase Oil Production

Qatar plans extensive secondary recovery programs in its existing fields, which still have reserves of 1.6 billion barrels, including the use of added gas injection and gas recycling. The state-owned Qatar General Petroleum Corporation (QGPC) plans to allocate over $3 billion before the year 2000 to modernize production facilities and to apply EOR technology at the three offshore fields.

Qatar is also seeking foreign expertise and investment to develop identified discoveries with up to 2.6 billion barrels. Qatar has offered new fiscal terms to foreign partners, and seems to be having considerable success in attracting investment by firms like Occidental. Occidental is already having significant success in rebuilding at least one Qatari oil field, and these efforts should give Qatar both the technology and the investment it needs without putting a strain on its budget.[386]

In September 1994, Occidental signed a $700-million production sharing agreement (PSA) to apply EOR techniques to the Id al-Shargi field. By 2002, the company hopes to raise production of the Id al-Shargi's 29° API oil from its current 12,000 barrels per day to roughly 90,000 barrels per day. This will be accomplished by drilling horizontal wells and conducting pressure maintenance programs on the Arab C and D and Shuaiba formations in the field.[387]

In October 1994, Maersk started commercial production at a new field named al-Shaheen near Halul Island. Initial output was 10,000 barrels per day of 33° API crude oil. One of the horizontal wells drilled at al-Shaheen is almost 13,000-feet long and is the longest of its kind ever drilled. The company is considering plans to construct separate export facilities for its production rather than utilizing those at Halul Island.

In 1994, Elf Aquitaine and Agip renegotiated improved cost recovery allowances for their PSA involving work on a potential 80-million barrel field at al-Khaleej. After increasing their profit share from 30 to 50 percent, both companies are planning to invest $50 million in infrastructure additions before anticipated production of 30,000 to 50,000 barrels per day of 29° API oil begins in late 1995.[388]

As a result, Qatar should sustain production well above 400,000 barrels per day, and possibly even reach the goals of 600,000 barrels per day in the year 2000, that Energy and Industry Minister Abdullah bin Hamad Al-Attiya announced in March, 1996. The DOE currently projects that

Qatar can sustain production above 400,000 barrels per day, and that its oil reserves will last another 24 years.[389] The IEA estimates that Qatar's production will rise to 500,000 barrels per day in the late 1990s, and reach 550,000–600,000 by 2000. It estimates that reaching this goal will require $1.6 billion of Qatari investment between 1993 and 2000.[390]

The US Embassy in Qatar does feel, however, that Qatar's oil production and revenues may decline toward the end of the century, and that Qatar's production will not return to earlier peak levels of 500,000 barrels per day.[391] The Embassy feels the major cause for the decline is the gradual depletion of Qatar's oil fields.[392] Qatar may, however, still be able to expand production from its existing fields, and increase production from its new Khaleej oil field, which was discovered in 1991.

Downstream Operations and Refining

Qatar now has limited downstream operations, but they are steadily expanding. Qatari exports of refined product began in 1979, and have risen from 28,000 barrels per day in 1985 to 116,000 in 1993. The IEA estimates Qatar's refining capacity will increase sharply by 1997. The QGPC's North Dome gas field already produces 30,000 barrels per day of condensate, and the QGPC is constructing a 100,000 barrels per day refinery to process this condensate.[393]

In July 1994, QGPC announced plans for a $400 million upgrade of the country's single 63,000 barrels per day refinery at Umm Said. Plans include raising output by 10,000 barrels per day and adding a 30,000 barrels per day condensate processing plant as well as a catalytic cracker. Prospective contractors are expected to arrange their own financing and would be paid with refined products after the scheduled upgrades are completed in early 1998.

Qatar has two large companies using oil and gas feedstocks—QAFCO (Qatar Fertilizer Company) and Qapco (Qatar General Petroleum Company)—and a joint venture called the Qatar Fuel Additives Company (Qafac), which is attempting to integrate methanol and methyl tertiary butyl production. Qatar is considering building a 400,000 ton-a-year ethylene dichloride (EDC) plant to use the ethylene feedstock from the expansion of other Qatari facilities, setting up a melamine fertilizer plant, and a maleic anhydride plant, and using gas to fuel an aluminum smelter.[394]

Qatar's Natural Gas Resources

Qatar's natural gas reserves rank third after Russia and Iran, and the Qatari government believes that the country's economic future is heavily dependent upon developing its vast gas potential. This development, however, is a challenging task. It costs roughly $1.0 billion to bring one million tons of gas export capacity on line, and Qatar has to make hard choices about which project to pursue and when.[395]

According to the EIA, Qatar's North Dome or North Field is the largest non-associated gas field in the world and has gas reserves of 225 to 380 trillion cubic feet, with produceable reserves of about 162 trillion cubic feet. In addition, Qatar's Dukhan field contains an estimated 5 Tcf of associated and 0.5 Tcf of non-associated gas, raising its total gas reserves to approximately 237 Tcf, or 40 billion barrels of oil equivalent.[396] Additional fields may give Qatar a total produceable gas reserve of up to 250.0 trillion cubic feet. This would give Qatar about 5% of all the world's gas reserves and Qatar is the third largest nation in the world in terms of total gas reserves.

According to the IEA, Qatar has even larger reserves. The IEA estimates that Qatar has at least 250 trillion cubic feet (7,070 to 7,170 billion cubic meters) of gas reserves—or around 5% of the world's total supply. About 269 billion cubic meters are located in the associated gas fields at Dukhan and Edd El Shargi/Maydan. A total of over 6,700 billion cubic meters are in non-associated fields at Dukhad Khuff (14.2 billion cubic meters) and North Field/Bul Hanin (6,500+ billion cubic meters).[397] An IEA estimate of the importance of Qatar's gas reserves relative to total Gulf and world gas reserves, is shown in Chart Thirty-Three and Table Twenty-Nine.

Qatari sources claim that Qatar has reserves approaching 380 trillion cubic feet. This estimate is possible, given Mobil Oil's computer models of Qatari reserves.

Qatar is focusing on the development of its offshore North Field to increase its LNG exports and significantly expand the share of petrochemicals in Qatar's total export trade of crude oil, refined products, and LPG. Qatar is also evaluating plans for pipelines to connect Kuwait, Saudi Arabia, Dubai and Oman, and plans for pipeline or LNG shipments to Israel. These plans, however, have a total potential cost of $20.6 billion.[398]

Chart Thirty-Four shows that Qatari gas production has risen sharply in recent years, and that gas exports and the domestic use of gas have only been heavily marketed since 1991. Before that time, most gas was reinjected, flared, or lost. It also shows that the Qatari economy has been boosted by the completion of the $1.5 billion Phase I of the North Field gas development in 1991.[399] Qatar is now producing about 321 billion cubic feet of gas per year, and this total will rise sharply in the future.[400]

The future phases of North Field gas development, involving exports via pipeline and/or gas liquefaction, may cost $5–6 billion, but they will make Qatar a major gas producer.[401] The first phase of North Dome

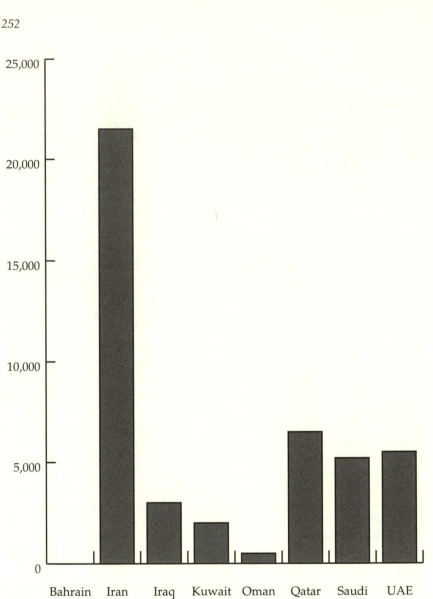

CHART THIRTY-THREE Total Oil Reserves of the Gulf States in Billions of Cubic Meters. *Source:* Adapted by Anthony H. Cordesman from IEA, *Middle East Oil and Gas,* Paris, OECD, IEA, 1995, Annex 2, and data provided by Bahrain and Oman. Bahrain's reserves are too small to show on the chart because of scale.

TABLE TWENTY-NINE   Gulf and World Gas Reserves and Production

Nation	Reserves in 1995		Percent World Supply	Production in 1993 (BCM)
	TCF	BCM		
Bahrain	—	—	—	—
Iran	741.6	21,000	14.9	60.0
Iraq	109.5	3,100	2.2	2.75
Kuwait	52.9	1,498	1.1	5.17
Oman	—	600–640	—	—
Qatar	250.0	7,070	5.0	18.4
Saudi Arabia	185.9	5,134	4.2	67.3
UAE	208.7	5,779*	4.2	31.63
Gulf	1,548.6	—	31.1	185.25
Rest of World	3,431.7	104,642	68.9	—
World Total	4,980.3	148,223	100.0	—

Note: *Other sources estimate 6,320–7,280 BCM for Abu Dhabi only.

Source: The reserve and production data are adapted by Anthony H. Cordesman from IEA, *Middle East Oil and Gas*, Paris, OECD, IEA, 1995, Annex 2.

development began in 1992 and has resulted in current production of 880 million cubic feet per day of natural gas and 40,000 barrels per day of condensate. More than half of this North Dome gas production is now used for domestic industrial consumption. The remainder is reinjected into the Dukhan field as part of continuing secondary recovery efforts.[402]

The IEA estimates that Qatar's capacity to produce LNG will reach 10 million tons by 2000, and reach 12.5 million tons by 2005. It estimates that Qatar can sustain this level for more than a decade and has the capability to reach export levels of 17.5 million tons. The IEA estimates that Qatar's contracted capacity to export LNG will reach 8.4 million tons by 2000, and its spare export capacity will be 1.6 million tons by 2000 and 4.6 million tons by 2005.[403]

The projected total upstream costs for Qatargas' three LNG trains is $900 million, and downstream costs may reach as high as $3 billion. A consortium of Japanese banks will provide the bulk of this downstream financing, mainly through a $2-billion loan which was finalized in June 1994.[404]

Qatar currently has two major LNG projects, Qatar Liquefied Gas Company (Qatargas) and Ras Laffan (Rasgas) in development. These two projects, combined with a possible extension of the current Rasgas venture, have a projected total cost of almost $16 billion, or twice the size of Qatar's economy.[405] Qatar is creating a massive new $1 billion gas port at

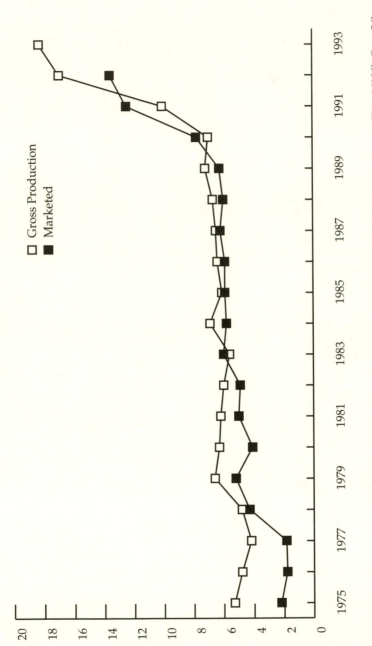

CHART THIRTY-FOUR Trends in Qatari Natural Gas Production in Billions of Cubic Meters. *Source:* IEA, *Middle East Oil and Gas*, Paris, OECD, IEA, 1995, Annex 2.

Ras Laffan, about 14 miles north of Qatar's capital at Doha, and is about to start Phase II of its development of the North Field.

Qatargas is a joint venture among the Qatar Liquefied Gas Company (QGPC), Total, Mobil, Mistsui, and Marubenim. The latter signed a 25 year contract to sell 4 million tons of gas annually to the Chunu Electric Power Company in Japan. A second consortium of Japanese and South Korean companies plans another 2 million ton plant, and a consortium of Mobil and the QGPC is building another 2 million ton plant. The first two major trains will come on line in 1996 and the third in 1999.

Qatargas joint venture (JV) initiated the second phase of North Dome development by beginning work on a project to produce, transport, and market LNG. The Qatargas JV has different upstream and downstream partners, but QGPC holds a 65 percent share in both operations. Total is the chief upstream operator with a 20 percent upstream stake. Mobil, which bought British Petroleum's 10 percent downstream share in 1992, is the primary operator of the downstream side.[406]

Rasgas is Qatar's second largest LNG project, with potential capital investment costs of up to $5 billion. QGPC and Mobil are the JV's partners, with 70 percent and 30 percent shares, respectively. Until late 1994, Rasgas's only confirmed LNG buyer was the Korean Gas Corporation, which had signed a "take and pay" contract to purchase 2.4 million tons per year for 25 years starting in 1998, at an agreed minimum price. However, in November 1994, the Wing Group (China) agreed to receive 2.5 million tons per year with an option for another 2.6 million tons per year. In January 1995, Turkey's Bostas signed a letter of intent to purchase 2 million tons per year with an option to buy another 2 million tons per year. In February 1995, Thailand agreed to receive 2 million tons per year for 25 years starting in 1999, and the Chinese Petroleum Corporation (Taiwan) has also signed an agreement. QGPC currently is discussing other possible contracts with India, Germany, and Trinidad.[407]

In January 1995, Enron signed a letter of intent to develop a $4-billion LNG project which would come on-stream by 1999. Half of the project's 5-million ton/year yield would be sent to Enron's Dabhol Power Company in western India. The rest would be delivered to Mediterranean markets and possibly to Israel, although Qatari Energy Minister Al-Attiya recently stated that Israel is not a likely option.[408]

In January 1995, six Japanese electric utility companies signed a "take and pay" contract to receive 2 million tons of LNG annually for 24 years at an agreed minimum price, starting in 1998. A seventh Japanese utility will receive the same amount for 23 years, starting in 1999. Before the deal's signing, Chubu Electric, which had committed to buy 4 million tons of LNG per year starting in 1997, was Qatargas' only customer. In

June 1994, Chubu extended its contract to take another 2 million tons per year of LNG, making its total 6 million tons per year.[409]

These Korean and Japanese projects have given Qatar "take and pay" contracts for total of about 9.3 million tons of gas. There are about 2.8 million tons worth of gas under contract to South Korea and 6.8 million tons under contract to Japan.

Two non-LNG projects are being developed in the North Dome. In September 1994, Qatar and Pakistan signed a memorandum of understanding to develop a 600-mile, 3.8-billion cubic foot per day (bcf/d) capacity pipeline which could carry 2.4 bcf/d to Pakistan, 0.8 Bcf/d to Dubai, and 0.4 Bcf/d to the northern UAE. The proposed pipeline will run along the Iranian coast and eventually might be extended to India. Partners in the project are Sharjah-based Crescent Petroleum, Trans-Canada Pipelines, and US-based Brown & Root. Total cost of the pipeline is estimated at $3.2 billion.[410]

Qatar is also considering the creation of a GCC gas grid, which—according to Energy Minister Al-Attiyah—would allow regional countries to raise oil exports by substituting domestic consumption of oil with natural gas. Qatar is hoping that increased Kuwaiti gas demand, new power station construction in Bahrain, and the added presence of Arco and British Gas in North Dome development projects will spur the GCC gas grid concept. At present, however, political strains between Qatar and Saudi Arabia and Bahrain may postpone any gas grid development plans for the foreseeable future. Qatar is also examining gas to liquids conversion programs in cooperation with Exxon.[411]

Qatar has, however, experienced some problems in its gas development. In 1994, the Qatar Europe Liquefied Natural Gas Company (Eurogas) LNG JV was canceled because of a pricing disagreement between QGPC and Agip. Elf, another Eurogas partner, was rumored in late 1994 to be seeking part of QGPC's stake in the Rasgas project. Additionally, Elf and Sumitomo recently finished a feasibility study for a new, $5-billion LNG project. The Elf-Sumitomo JV is seeking prospective buyers and is considering destinations such as Turkey, Italy, and other countries in Western Europe for LNG exports.[412]

Investment and Privatization

Qatar was slow to react to the drop in its oil income in the mid-1980s, failed to control subsidies and government expenditures, and failed to tax its citizens. As a result, Qatar has run a deficit virtually every year since 1986—deficits that cannot be related to major expenditures on national security and which are largely a product of the fact that the government has remained reliant largely on oil exports for its revenues—

rather than broadening its tax base. Chart Thirty-Five shows these trends in Qatar's budget, which reflect the same adjustment problems common to virtually all Southern Gulf states.

The new Emir seems committed to improving the management of the nation's resources and development. Qatar has begun to control its government spending, and the 1995/1996 budget that it announced in May, 1995, kept Qatar's budget deficit to Qatari Rials 3,531 million ($969.7 million). The budget included a 7.7% increase in current expenditures—largely to support Qatar's public welfare programs—but cut capital outlays by 4%. This is a feasible short term solution to ease Qatar's financial problems, although Qatar now projects annual budget deficits of up to $1 billion annually through 2005, in part to pay for its massive investment in developing its gas resources.

Chart Thirty-Six shows that Qatar is one of the few Gulf countries to have steadily improved its net liquidity over time. This has helped produce large investment income resources that have supplemented Qatar's export income, although there is some question as to whether the new Emir has access to this liquidity because much of it remains under the control of his father. Chart Thirty-Six shows that this liquidity also helps to offset the cost of Qatar's investments in new gas and gas-related facilities, although Chart Thirty-Seven shows that Qatar has still shown a negative net trade balance because of in transfers in recent years.

Qatar has increased its foreign debt, but largely for investment purposes. Its short term debt has slowly increased from around $400 million in the early 1980s, to between $1.0 and $1.4 billion in the mid-1990s. Its long-term debt has slowly increased from around $200 million in the early 1980s, to around $700 million. This has increased the debt to GDP ratio from under 15% to well over 25%. Service payments, however, remain under $200 million annually, or less than 5% of total exports. This debt burden may not be desirable, but it is affordable.[413] Qatar also has a trade deficit on current account which reached $1.59 billion in 1995 and is projected to be $1.17 billion in 1996.[414]

Qatar is responding to its deficit, debt, and investment problems by actively seeking foreign private investment in its oil and gas operations, and providing investment laws and opportunities that will reduce the cash flow burden of development. Foreign and private investment offers Qatar a more affordable way to make the high cost investments needed to maintain and expand its oil production and develop its massive gas resources. It also offers Qatar access to the necessary technology and management skills, and more effective downstream operations. While the Qatar General Petroleum Company (QGPC), Qatar Liquefied Gas Company (Qatargas), and Ras Laffan (Rasgas) are only beginning major

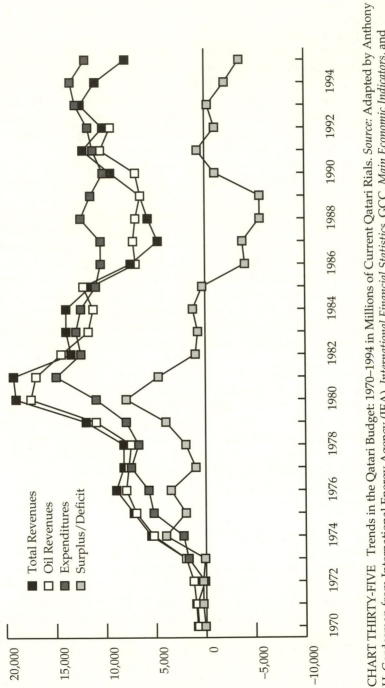

CHART THIRTY-FIVE Trends in the Qatari Budget: 1970–1994 in Millions of Current Qatari Rials. *Source:* Adapted by Anthony H. Cordesman from International Energy Agency (IEA), *International Financial Statistics*, GCC, *Main Economic Indicators*, and Qatar Monetary Agency, *Quarterly Statistical Bulletin.* 1995 is an estimate.

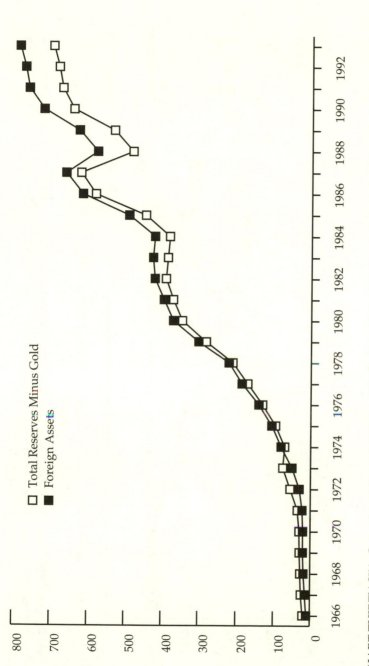

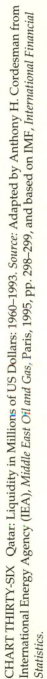

CHART THIRTY-SIX   Qatar: Liquidity in Millions of US Dollars: 1960–1993. *Source:* Adapted by Anthony H. Cordesman from International Energy Agency (IEA), *Middle East Oil and Gas,* Paris, 1995, pp. 298–299, and based on IMF, *International Financial Statistics.*

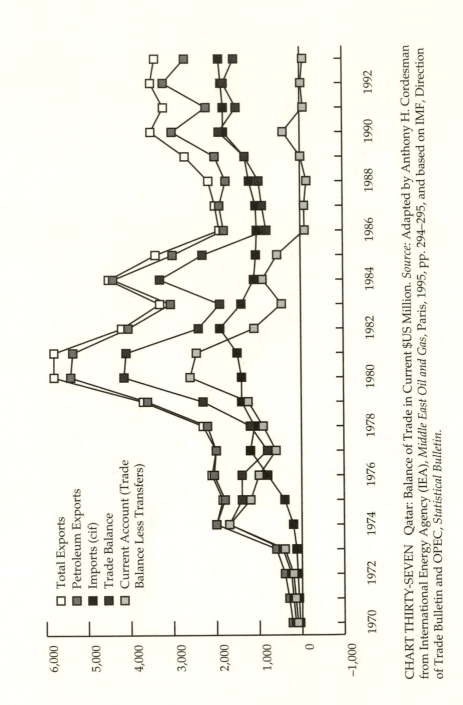

CHART THIRTY-SEVEN Qatar: Balance of Trade in Current $US Million. *Source:* Adapted by Anthony H. Cordesman from International Energy Agency (IEA), *Middle East Oil and Gas,* Paris, 1995, pp. 294–295, and based on IMF, Direction of Trade Bulletin and OPEC, *Statistical Bulletin.*

joint ventures, Qatar seems committed to the kind of investment policies it needs to pursue in the future.

However, even a country with Qatar's potential gas wealth needs to implement further economic reforms. Part of the reason is social. Qatar's dependence on foreign labor threatens its social cohesion, undermines the work ethnic and entrepreneurial skills of its natives, and deprives its steadily growing number of young people of meaningful work. Part of the reason is economic. Unless Qatar makes draconian reductions in foreign labor, its per capita income will drop, and threaten its social stability.

To be specific, Qatar needs to implement many of the same economic and social reforms as the other Southern Gulf countries require. Qatar must:

- Force radical reductions in its number of foreign workers, with priority for reductions in servants and in trades that allow the most rapid conversion to native labor. Shift the remaining dependence on foreign labor to hires from within the Southern Gulf, and create jobs for Bahrainis and Omanis.
- Eliminate economic disincentives for employers hiring native labor, and creating disincentives for hiring foreign labor.
- Reduce those aspects of state subsidies and welfare that distort the economy and discourage the native population from seeking jobs. Create the economic incentives for native Qataris to develop a work ethic. Qatar now has very high subsidies for both natives and foreign labor. Electricity, water, and medical care is free, petroleum products are sharply underpriced.
- Restructure its educational system to focus on job training and competitiveness. Create strong new incentives for faculty and students to focus on job-related education, sharply down-size other forms of educational funding and activity, and eliminate high overhead educational activities without economic benefits. Qatar recognizes this need, but has experienced serious resistance to modernizing its education from its existing staff of largely Egyptian teachers.
- Educate its population to limit population growth.
- Reform the structure of the budget to sharply reduce the amount of money going directly to royal accounts, and ensure that most of the nation's revenues and foreign reserves are integrated into the national budget and into the planning process. Clearly separate royal and national income and investment holdings.
- Ensure that all income from enterprises with state financing is reflected in the national budget and is integrated into the national economic development and planning program.

- Place limits on the transfer of state funds to princes and members of the royal family outside the actual ruling family, and transfers of unearned income to members of other leading families. The Al Thani family is an exceptionally large royal family relative to Qatar's population and economy and this reform has a higher priority in Qatar than in many Southern Gulf states.

- Freeze and then reduce the number of civil servants, and restructure and down-size the civil service to focus on productive areas of activity with a much smaller pool of manpower. Cut back sharply on state employees by the year 2000. End all policies guaranteeing Qatari university and secondary graduates government jobs.

- Encourage privatization. Qatar has set a goal of 25% privatization once its new NGL facilities come on-line and is working with Malaysia to privatize using the techniques that have worked in Southeast Asia. It may, however, be moving too slowly to meet these goals.

- Establish market criteria for all major state and state-supported investments, requiring detailed and independent risk assessment and projections of comparative return on investment, with a substantial penalty for state versus privately funded projects and ventures. Down size the scale of programs to reduce investment and cash flow costs and the risk of cost-escalation.

- Create new incentives to invest in local industries and business and disincentives for the expatriation of capital.

- Create market-driven incentives for foreign investment in major oil and gas projects, refineries, and petrochemical operations. Avoid offset requirements that simply create disguised unemployment or non-competitive ventures that act as a further state-sponsored distortion of the economy.

- Tax earnings and sales with progressive taxes that help reduce or eliminate budget deficits, encourage local investment, and create strong disincentives for the expatriation of capital, including all foreign holdings of capital and property by members of elite and ruling families.

- Establish a firm rule of law for all property, contract, permitting, and business activity and reduce state bureaucratic and permitting barriers to private investment.

- Place national security spending on the same basis as other state spending. Integrate it fully into the national budget, including investment and equipment purchases. Replace the present emphasis on judging purchases on the basis on initial procurement costs and technical features with a full assessment of life cycle cost—including training, maintenance, and facilities—and with specific procedures for evaluating the value of standardization and interoperability with existing national equipment and facilities, those of other Gulf states, and those of the US and other power projection forces.

• Develop effective five and ten year plans. Qatar faces more serious problems in managing its social and economic development than many of its neighbors because of the exceptionally high costs of developing its gas resources. Its present development plans seem relatively sound and conservative, but Qatar needs to develop a very clear picture of its development goals and options. It also needs to develop coordinated plans for its economic, education, labor, and social development.

Qatari Military Forces, Expenditures, and Arms Transfers

Qatar's military forces are under the direction of the Emir and Defense Minister, Hamad bin Khalifa Al-Thani, who is also commander-in-chief of the armed forces. Hamad had reached the rank of Major General before he became Emir. Other members of the Al-Thani family serve as Chief of Staff, Commander of the Air Force and Chief of the Royal Guard. Officers and enlisted men are recruited from members of the royal family, and the leading desert tribes. Pay and privileges are good.

Military Expenditures and Arms Transfers

Chart Thirty-Eight provides a rough estimate of Qatar's level of arms imports relative to its GDP and central government expenditures. This chart indicates that Qatar's GDP and exports are currently adequate to fund its central government budget, total imports, and arms imports, but it is difficult to analyze the size of Qatar's military effort. Qatar is the only country in the Gulf for which ACDA does not provide consistent estimates of annual military expenditures. Other US reports indicate that Qatar increased its annual military expenditures in current dollars from around $260 million in 1978 and $475 million in 1979, to $604 to $780 million annually in 1982 through 1985. ACDA does estimate that Qatar spent $934 million on military expenditures in 1991, $357 million in 1992, $330 million in 1993, and $302 million in 1994.[415]

The IISS reports that Qatar spent $154.2 million in current dollars in 1987, $1.44 billion in 1991, $350 million in 1992, $330 million in 1993, $302 million in 1994, and $326 million in 1995, but these estimates are very uncertain.[416] Qatar seems to have spent about 10% of its GDP on defense in recent years, and 20% of its central government expenditures.[417]

Like Bahrain and Oman, Qatar has spent comparatively little on arms imports—although Chart Thirty-Eight shows that the size of Qatar's arms imports have varied sharply by year. ACDA indicates Qatar's arms imports totaled $20 million in current dollars in 1978, $20 million in 1979, $90 million in 1980, $270 million in 1981, $270 million in 1983, $210 mil-

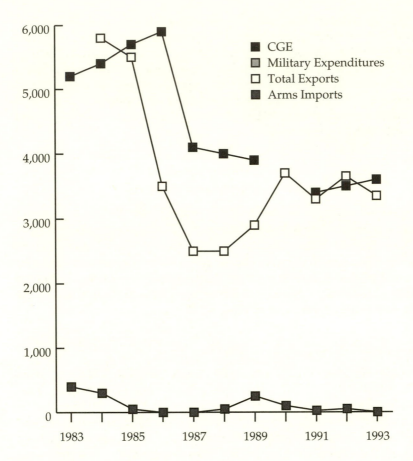

CHART THIRTY-EIGHT   Qatari Central Government Expenditures, Military Expenditures, Total Exports, and Arms Imports Deliveries: 1983–1993 (Constant $93 Millions). *Source:* Adapted by Anthony H. Cordesman from ACDA, *World Military Expenditures and Arms Transfers, 1993–1994,* ACDA/GPO, Washington, 1995.

lion in 1984, $40 million in 1985, $5 million in 1986, negligible in 1987, $30 million in 1988, $180 million in 1989, $100 million in 1990, $20 million in 1991, $40 million in 1992, and were negligible in 1993 and 1994.[418]

Major Sources of Arms

Many of Qatar's arms have come from France, although Qatar has bought arms from a wide range of countries. ACDA estimates that Qatar imported a total of $765 million worth of arms during 1979–1983, with $10 million from the US, $440 million from France, $310 million from the UK, and $5 million from other countries.[419] It imported a total of $360 million worth of arms during 1984–1988, with $10 million from the US, $300 million from France, $20 million from the UK, and $30 million from other countries.[420]

More recent US government data on Qatari arms imports are somewhat conflicting. One source—which is summarized in Chart Thirty-Nine, and which only counts sales and deliveries rounded to the nearest $100 million—indicates that Qatar signed a total of $100 million worth of major new arms agreements during 1987–1990, and $2.0 billion worth of major agreements during 1990–1994—all with major West European states. This same source reports a total of $300 million worth of major new arms deliveries during 1987–1990, and had no major deliveries during 1991–1994.[421]

Another US source indicates that Qatar imported a total of $160 million worth of arms during 1985–1989, with $10 million coming from the US, $100 million from France, $20 million from the UK, and $30 million from Latin America.[422] It also indicates that Qatar imported a total of $50 million worth of arms during 1991–1993, with $10 million coming from France, $20 million from Italy, and $20 million from other sources.[423] Another source indicates that Qatar imported a total of $45 million worth of arms during 1992–1994, with $5 million coming from the US, $10 million coming from France, $20 million from other European countries, and $10 million from other sources.[424]

The one area where all sources seem to agree is that the arms orders Qatar placed during the Gulf War have not yet led to significant deliveries. Qatar seems to control its arms payment schedules carefully, and there are no indications that its arms purchases impose a serious burden on its economy.

Table Thirty shows that Qatar has never been a major importer of US military equipment, and did not place significant new orders as a result of the Gulf War. All US sales to Qatar are cash transactions. Qatar does not make use of the International Military Education and Training (IMET), and has received no recent Military Assistance Program (MAP) aid.[425]

Recent Major Purchases and the Efficiency of the Qatari Effort

Table Thirty-One summarizes Qatar's recent and planned major arms orders by type of equipment. Most of these purchases reflect legitimate military needs, although they reflect Qatar's policy of seeking arms from a wide range of sources with only limited regard to standardization and

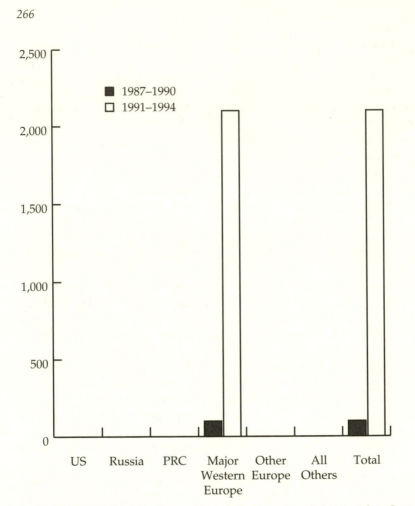

CHART THIRTY-NINE   Qatari Arms Sales Agreements by Supplier Country: 1987–1994 ($Current Millions). *Source:* Adapted by Anthony H. Cordesman from work by Richard F. Grimmett in *Conventional Arms Transfers to Developing Nations, 1987–1994,* Congressional Research Service 95-862F, August 4, 1995, pp. 56–57.

interoperability. This may ultimately present serious problems. Qatar has not developed suitable interoperability and standardization with the forces of its Southern Gulf neighbors. This lack of interoperability and standardization is partly the result of political tensions between Qatar and Bahrain and Saudi Arabia, but it does inhibit the development of effective Qatari military forces.

TABLE THIRTY   US Foreign Military Sales (FMS), Commercial Arms Export Agreements, Military Assistance Programs (MAP), and International Military Education and Training (IMET) Programs with Qatar: FY1985–1994 (Current Millions)

	1985	1986	1987	1988	1989	1990	1991	1992	1993	1994
Foreign Military Financing Program Payment Waived	—	—	—	—	—	—	—	—	—	—
DoD Direct	—	—	—	—	—	—	—	—	—	—
DoD Guarantee	—	—	—	—	—	—	—	—	—	—
FMS Agreements	0.2	0.2	0.1	0.1	0	0	0	2.4	0.3	4.0
Commercial Sales	1.6	0.9	0.3	3.4	0.3	0	1.2	0.6	0.3	0
FMS Construction Agreements	—	—	—	—	—	—	—	—	—	—
FMS Deliveries	0.1	0.1	0.2	0.3	0.5	0	0	0.3	1.0	0.8
MAP Program	—	—	—	—	—	—	—	—	—	—
MAP Deliveries	—	—	—	—	—	—	—	—	—	—
MAP Excess Defense Articles Program	—	—	—	—	—	—	—	—	—	—
MAP Excess Defense Articles Deliveries	—	—	—	—	—	—	—	—	—	—
IMET Program/ Deliveries	—	—	—	—	—	—	—	—	—	—

Source: Adapted from US Defense Security Assistance Agency (DSAA), "Foreign Military Sales, Foreign Military Construction Sales and Military Assistance Facts as of September 30, 1994," Department of Defense, Washington, 1995.

TABLE THIRTY-ONE   Key Qatari Equipment Developments

- Seeking 50 modern tanks to replace its AMX-30s and equip its one armored battalion. The main candidates are the Leclerc, Challenger, and M-1A2.
- Considering re-equipping its four motorized infantry battalions with other armored vehicles that can keep up with its tanks, but has not issued any formal tenders or requests for proposals. It is considering the purchase of AM General high-mobility multi-purpose wheeled vehicles with M-621 20 mm or M-781 30 mm automatic guns for reconnaissance and special operations missions.
- Considering buying 40–50 Giat 155TR 155 mm towed howitzers, Caesar 52 155 mm air transportable self-propelled howitzers, G6 155 mm self-propelled howitzers, and/or VSEL Ultralight 155 mm field howitzers.
- Has bought thermal imaging systems and inertial survey systems to support its artillery operations, and plans to buy artillery observation equipment and UAVs for target acquisition.
- 24 Mistral air defense system launchers and 500 missiles from Matra now deployed. Studying orders for the Stinger or Starburst missile.
- Ordered four Vita-class 350–400 ton fast attack boats to replace its six Barzan-class ships in June 1992. These are 56 meter vessels from Vosper-Thorneycroft equipped with Thomson-CSF sensor and command suite, NCS TACTICOS combat management system, MM-40 Exocet ship-to-ship missiles, an Oto Melara 76 mm gun, and Signal Goalkeeper close-in defense system.
- Purchased 12–15 Mirage 2000-5 fighters from France, along with Magic air-to-air and 50 MICA air-to-surface missiles.
- Planning to upgrade its Westland Commando helicopters, and is considering equipping its Gazelle anti-tank helicopters with laser-range finder sights to improve their daylight attack capability.
- Possibly upgrading its Rolands with Glaive infra-red sights and Thomson-CSF VT-1 hypervelocity missiles.
- Has considered an order for a Hawk MIM-23B surface-to-air missile battery, and two Shahine batteries, but it is unclear if it will make such a purchase.

Qatari Military Forces and Military Manpower

Like the forces of many of the other smaller Gulf states, Qatar's armed forces have evolved out of the palace guard that the Emir had established during the period of British rule as well as small elements drawn from the Trucial Oman Levies (later Scouts) which Britain formed in 1951. Qatar only had a small Royal Guard regiment, a few small security units, a few armored cars, and four light aircraft when it became independent on September 3, 1971. Its forces increased to 5,000 men in the early 1980s, 6,000 men in 1985, 7,500 men in 1992, and 11,100 men in 1995.[426] The relative size of Qatar's military forces are shown in Table Thirty-Two, and the trends in Qatar's military manpower are shown in Chart Forty.

TABLE THIRTY-TWO Gulf Military Forces in 1996

	Iran	Iraq	Bahrain	Kuwait	Oman	Qatar	Saudi Arabia*	UAE	Yemen
Manpower									
Total Active	320,000	382,500	10,700	16,600	43,500	11,100	161,500	70,000	39,500
Regular	220,000	382,500	10,700	16,600	37,000	11,100	105,500	70,000	39,500
National Guard & Other	100,000	0	0	0	6,500	0	57,000	0	0
Reserve	350,000	650,000	0	23,700	0	0	0	0	40,000
Paramilitary	135,000	24,800	9,250	5,200	4,400	0	15,500	2,700	30,000
Army and Guard									
Manpower	260,000	350,000	8,500	10,000	31,500	8,500	127,000	65,000	37,000
Regular Army Manpower	180,000	350,000	8,500	10,000	25,000	8,500	70,000	65,000	37,000
Reserve	350,000	450,000	0	0	0	0	20,000	0	40,000
Tanks	1,350	2,700	81	220	85	24	910	133	1,125
AIFV/Recce, Lt. Tanks	515	1,600	46	130	136	50	1,467	515	580
APCs	550	2,200	235	199	7	172	3,670	380	560
Self Propelled Artillery	294	150	13	38	6	28	200	90	30
Towed Artillery	2,000	1,500	36	0	96	12	270	82	483
MRLs	890	120	9	0	0	4	60	48	220
Mortars	3,500	2,000+	18	24	74	39	400	101	800
SSM Launchers	46	12	0	0	0	0	10	6	30
Light SAM Launchers	700	3,000	65	48	62	58	650	36	700
AA Guns	1,700	5,500	0	0	18	12	10	62	372
Air Force Manpower	20,000	15,000	1,500	2,500	4,100	800	18,000	3,500	1,000
Air Defense Manpower	15,000	15,000	0	0	0	0	4,000	0	0

(continues)

TABLE THIRTY-TWO (continued)

	Iran	Iraq	Bahrain	Kuwait	Oman	Qatar	Saudi Arabia*	UAE	Yemen
Total Combat Aircraft	295	353	24	76	46	12	295	97	69
Bombers	0	6	0	0	0	0	0	0	0
Fighter/Attack	150	130	12	40	19	11	112	41	27
Fighter/Interceptor	115	180	12	8	0	1	122	22	30
Recce/FGA Recce	8	0	0	0	12	0	10	8	0
AEW C4I/BM	0	1	0	0	0	0	5	0	0
MR/MPA**	6	0	0	0	7	0	0	0	0
OCU/COIN	0	18	0	11	13	0	36	15	0
Combat Trainers	92	200	0	11	22	0	66	35	12
Transport Aircraft**	68	34	3	4	14	5	49	20	19
Tanker Aircraft	4	2	0	0	0	0	16	0	0
Armed Helicopters**	100	120	10	16	0	20	12	42	8
Other Helicopters**	509	350	8	36	37	7	138	42	21
Major SAM Launchers	204	340	12	24	0	0	128	18	87
Light SAM Launchers	60	200	0	12	28	9	249	34	0
AA Guns	0	0	0	12	0	0	420	0	0
Navy Manpower	38,000	2,500	1,000	1,500	4,200	1,800	17,000	1,500	1,500
Major Surface Combatants									
Missile	5	0	3	0	0	0	8	0	0
Other	2	1	0	0	0	0	0	0	0
Patrol Craft									
Missile	10	1	4	2	4	3	9	10	7

(continues)

TABLE THIRTY-TWO (continued)

	Iran	Iraq	Bahrain	Kuwait	Oman	Qatar	Saudi Arabia*	UAE	Yemen
Other	26	7	5	12	8	6	20	18	3
Submarines	2	0	0	0	0	0	0	0	0
Mine Vessels	3	4	0	0	0	0	5	0	3
Amphibious Ships	8	0	0	0	2	0	0	0	2
Landing Craft	17	3	4	6	4	1	7	4	2

Notes: Does not include equipment in storage. Air Force totals include all helicopters, and all heavy surface to air missile launchers.

*60,000 reserves are National Guard Tribal Levies. The total for land forces includes active National Guard equipment. These additions total 262 AIFVs, 1,165 APCs, and 70 towed artillery weapons.

**Includes navy, army, national guard, and royal flights, but not paramilitary.

Source: Adapted by Anthony H. Cordesman from International Institute for Strategic Studies *Military Balance* (IISS, London), in this case, the 1995–1996 edition; *Military Technology, World Defense Almanac, 1994–1995*; and Jaffee Center for Strategic Studies, *The Military Balance in the Middle East, 1993–1994* (JCSS, Tel Aviv, 1994).

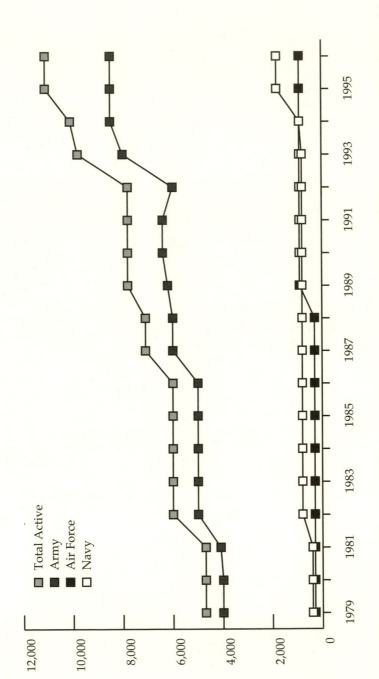

CHART FORTY Qatar: Military Manning—1979–1996. *Source:* Adapted by Anthony H. Cordesman from various editions of the IISS, *Military Balance,* the JCSS, *Military Balance in the Middle East,* and material provided by US experts.

Qatar's main problem in expanding its forces is a lack of total manpower. Even if one ignores the fact that 85% of the work force is foreign, the total male manpower pool is only about 219,400, counting the population from 15–49. The CIA estimates that only 115,000 males are fit for military service, and that only 3,915 reach military age each year. The IISS estimates that there are 21,200 native males between the ages of 13 and 17, 17,600 between the ages of 18 and 22, and 38,800 between the ages of 23 and 32.[427]

In the past, Qatar has depended heavily on nomadic tribes which crossed the Qatari-Saudi border for its native Arab recruits, but has recently been forced to increase its intake of urbanized Arabs. It now requires military service from male Qataris that do not complete secondary school. As a result, Qatar has created a growing pool of native personnel—who train in Britain, France, Jordan, Pakistan, and Saudi Arabia. Qatar also has an increasing number of competent young native officers, many from the ruling family and leading tribes.

Qatar is still dependent, however, on servicemen from more than 15 other nationalities, and seems to have British, Egyptian, French, Jordanian and Pakistani "advisors" who play an active military role. As much as 70% of Qatar's military manpower, however, is still foreign and largely Omani and Baluchi. Qatar still recruits military manpower directly in Oman.

The Qatari Army

The Qatari army has a nominal strength of 8,500 men, and its order of battle includes an armored battalion, three to four mechanized infantry battalions, a Royal Guard regiment, up to two armored car regiments, one artillery battery, a special forces battalion (company), a field artillery regiment, and one Rapier surface-to-air missile battery. The trends in Qatari army manpower have been shown in Chart Forty, and the trends in its major combat equipment are shown in Charts Forty-One and Forty-Two.

Qatar's regiments are small combat formations by Western standards, since the total manpower in the Qatari army is too small to fill out even one full Western brigade-sized formation plus support. The Emir guard and special forces units do, however, seem to be adequately trained as security and guard forces and the Emiri Guard has reserve native personnel it can use as "fillers" to supplement its regular manning.

The army is largely French equipped although many officers are British and Jordanian trained. Qatar shifted to reliance on French equipment both because of an active French effort to win Qatari defense contracts, and as a counterbalance to what it perceived as a British and US focus on Bahrain, Saudi Arabia, and the UAE.

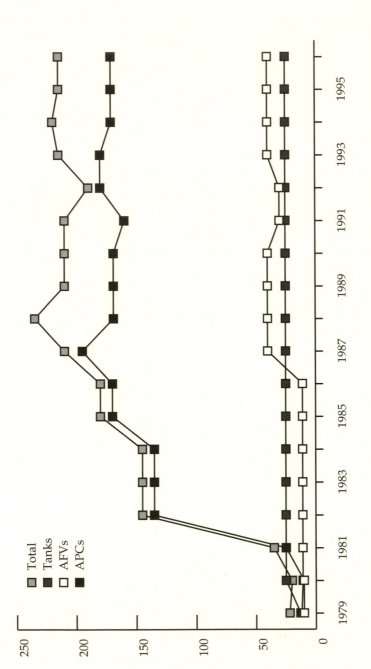

CHART FORTY-ONE Qatar: Armored Weapons Strength—1979–1996. *Source:* Adapted by Anthony H. Cordesman from various editions of the IISS, *Military Balance,* the JCSS, *Military Balance in the Middle East,* and material provided by US experts.

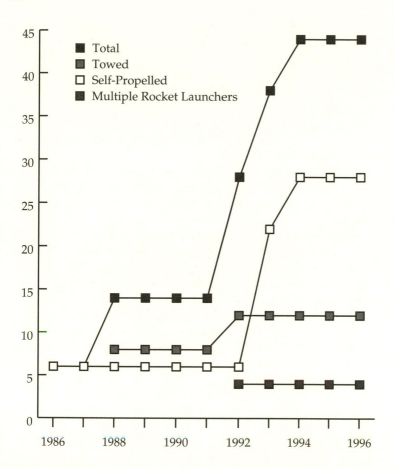

CHART FORTY-TWO   Qatar: Artillery Weapons Strength—1986–1996.
Source: Adapted by Anthony H. Cordesman from various editions of the IISS, *Military Balance,* the JCSS, *Military Balance in the Middle East,* and material provided by US experts.

Qatari Army Equipment

The Qatari Army played a creditable role in the battle of Khafji and other fighting during the war to liberate Kuwait. It is, however, lightly equipped. In 1996, it only had 24–28 obsolescent AMX-30 tanks. It had a diverse mix of other armored fighting vehicles. Its reconnaissance vehicles included 6 VBLs, 12 AMX-10RCs, and 8 V-150s. Its AIFVs included 40 AMX-10Ps, and its APCs included 160–180 VAB/VTTs, and 12 AMX-VCIs. It seems to have had 8 Saladins, 12 Ferrets and 22–25 Saracen armored cars in storage.

Qatar is currently in the process of seeking to modernize its armor. It is seeking 50 modern tanks to replace its AMX-30s and equip its armored battalion. The main candidates are the Leclerc, Challenger, and M-1A2. Qatar is also considering re-equipping its four motorized infantry battalions with other armored vehicles that can keep up with its tanks, but has not issued any formal tenders or requests for proposals. It is considering the purchase of AM General high-mobility multi-purpose wheeled vehicles with M-621 20 mm or M-781 30 mm automatic guns for reconnaissance and special operations missions.[428]

Qatar's anti-tank weapons defenses consisted of 25 HOT and 100 Milan anti-tank guided missile launchers, 40–50 106 mm recoilless rifles. Qatar also had an unknown number of Carl Gustav 84 mm light anti-tank rocket launchers.

Qatar's artillery strength has been modernized. It now has 28 AMX Mark F-3 155 mm self-propelled artillery weapons, and 12 G-5 155 mm towed howitzers. It also has 4–5 ASTROS II and 10 BM-21 122 mm multiple rocket launchers, 15–20 120 mm mortars, and 24 L-16 81 mm mortars, some self-propelled.[429]

The Qatari army has bought thermal imaging systems and inertial survey systems to support its artillery operations, and plans to buy artillery observation equipment and UAVs for target acquisition. It is considering buying 40–50 Giat 155TR 155 mm towed howitzers, Caesar 52 155 mm air transportable self-propelled howitzers, G6 155 mm self propelled howitzers, and/or VSEL Ultralight 155 mm field howitzers.[430]

The army has relied on Blowpipe and SA-7 man portable air defense missile systems. These systems give it only a very limited capability to cover one point target, or provide a loose defense screen over a wider area.[431] Qatar did, however, order 24 Mistral air defense system launchers and 500 missiles from Matra in 1989–1990 and these are now deployed. Qatar is also studying orders for the Stinger or Starburst missile.[432]

Qatari Army Readiness and Warfighting Capability

Qatar's land forces showed they could fight well in small actions during the Gulf War. They were able to deploy successfully to the Upper Gulf and maintained a good level of readiness. Qatar's forces have improved their exercise performance since the Gulf War, particularly since 1994. At the same time, these land forces are still limited in capability, strength, and equipment. They lack capability in combined arms and joint warfare. They are seriously undermanned and badly need a professional NCO corps.

Qatari army forces should be adequate for internal security purposes. Their main functions seem to be limited to border patrols, defense of the territory disputed with Bahrain, and defense of the capital, oil, and desalination facilities. They are also improving in proficiency. A French military assistance mission was established in Qatar in 1990, and a new Franco-Qatari defense cooperation agreement was signed on August 1, 1994. This has helped train the Qatari Army. but the logistic support of French-supplied systems remains poor. Two Franco-Qatari exercises—Pearl Gathering I and Pearl Gathering II—have helped with this training. Qatari forces are also beginning to receive training assistance from the US, although English language skills are a problem.[433]

Nevertheless, Qatari units have only a moderate overall ability to use their armor and artillery, and have limited maneuver, combined arms, and combined operations capability. Some Qatari mechanized infantry battalions are reasonably effective, but most army units can at best conduct limited defensive operations. The army has only limited overall maneuver training and has only token modern armored warfare capability against an enemy like Iran or Iraq. Qatar is only beginning to acquire the capability to use its artillery effectively in combined arms, counter-battery fire, or beyond visual range targeting.

The Qatari Navy

Qatar's navy is based in Doha and deploys to Halul Island. It has an authorized strength of over 1,800 men, including the marine police. Many of these men are expatriates.[434] The navy has French and Pakistani advisors. The trends in Qatari naval manpower have been shown in Chart Forty.

Qatari Navy Force Strength and Equipment

Qatar's main combat ships consist of three Combattante IIIM (Damsah-class) 395-ton fast missile patrol boats. These ships were commissioned during 1982–1983, and are each equipped with 8 Exocet MM-40 missiles, one 76 mm Oto Melara gun, two Breda 40 mm guns, and four twin 35 mm guns. Qatar plans to overhaul and modernize these ships, but no contracts have been issued.

Qatar also has six Vosper Thorneycroft (Barzan-class) 33.5 meter patrol boats. These are aging 120-ton ships which were commissioned in 1975–1976. Each is equipped with search radars and armed with four twin 35 mm guns.

Qatar ordered four Vita-class 350–400 ton fast attack boats to replace its six Barzan-class ships in June, 1992. These are 56 meter vessels from Vosper-Thorneycroft, and are being delivered in 1996–1997. They are equipped with a Thomson-CSF sensor and command suite, the NCS TACTICOS fully distributed combat management system, MM-40 Exocet ship-to-ship missiles, an Oto Melara 76 mm gun, and the Signal Goalkeeper 30 mm close-in defense system.[435]

Qatar's other ships consist of six, small, 18-ton, 14.5 meter Damen Polycat 1450- class coastal patrol boats delivered in 1980 (which may be operated by the Marine police). The Marine police also operate four Crestitalia MV-45 Class 17 ton coastal patrol boats, two Keith Nelson 13-ton 13.5 meter patrol boats, 25 4.3-ton Spear-class patrol boats, and five Watercraft P-1200 12.7 ton coastal patrol craft. Qatar has two tugs. It plans to acquire additional patrol boats for its coast guard.

Qatar has a small coastal defense force with a number of land based batteries, each of which has three MM-40 Exocet launchers with four missiles each. Its main base is near Doha, but it is building a naval base at Halul Island. Qatar is too small to play more than the most limited coastal defense role.

Qatari Navy Readiness and Warfighting Capability

The Qatari navy is still in the process of creating a force capable of more than short coastal operations. Readiness and proficiency are still low. Almost all maintenance and logistic support is done on a contract basis, and it only seems to be adequate for peacetime purposes. The logistic support of French-supplied equipment is poor and preventive maintenance schedules for most equipment are not being met.

The Qatari navy has no capability to defend Qatar's offshore gas resources like the North Dome, although it does patrol the area at regular intervals. Qatar does, however, have four Vita-class ships on order and is drawing up plans for procurement of two patrol craft with advanced air defense capabilities and a size of around 1,400 tons/34 meters.[436] If Qatar can provide the manpower, training, and sustainability necessary to operate these ships, it will significantly enhance its patrol capability. Qatar would still be unable to engage the Iranian Navy, but its forces would become adequate for local defense missions and could cooperate far more effectively with the US and British navies.

The Qatari Air Force

Qatar's air force is based at the military airfield at Doha. Many of its pilots and officers are from Qatar, but the air force is heavily dependent on French and other foreign support for training, maintenance, logistics, and many C[4]I functions. The Qatari air force currently has a strength of 800 men, only 12 combat aircraft, and 20 armed helicopters. The trends in Qatari air force manpower have been shown in Chart Forty, and the trends in its air strength are shown in Chart Forty-Three.

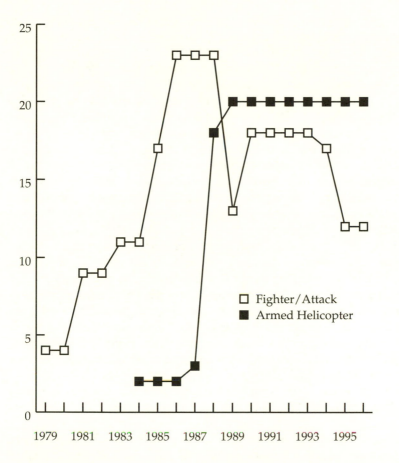

CHART FORTY-THREE   Qatar: Fixed Wing and Rotary Wing Combat Air Strength—1979–1996. *Source:* Adapted by Anthony H. Cordesman from various editions of the IISS, *Military Balance,* the JCSS, *Military Balance in the Middle East,* and material provided by US experts.

Qatari Air Units and Equipment

Qatar's combat aircraft include a fighter-ground attack squadron with 6 Alphajets, and an air defense squadron with 5 Mirage F-1E/Ds, plus one Mirage F-1E/D for training. The Mirages are armed with AM-39 air-to-ship missiles for its and R-530F Super and R-550 Magic air-to-air missiles. Qatar also has combat helicopter units equipped with 20 armed SA-342s (12 armed with HOT and 8 armed with Exocet).[437]

The Qatari Air Force has shelters for its Mirage fighters, and its facilities and stock levels are good. It trains with other GCC states and the US, and has had French and British advisors. It still has some maintenance and training problems in operating its combat aircraft, but its performance has improved since 1990.

Qatar has purchased 12–15 Mirage 2000-5 fighters from France, and has a large, modern air base under construction. This aircraft buy is part of a complex 3.5 billion franc deal. The Mirage 2000-5s will also have Thomson CSF RDY radars and Snecma M52 P2 engines. The deal also included Magic air-to-air and 50 MICA air-to-surface missiles. The MICA air-to-air missile has a range of up to 90 miles and will give Qatar a substantial beyond-visual-range (BVR) air combat capability.[438]

The deal allows Qatar to help pay for the Mirage 2000-5s by trading its Mirage F-1s back to France, who will recondition them and sell them to Spain. Qatar will also be able to defer any additional payments for several years.[439] This is an important first step towards creating a modern air force, but Qatar also needs to replace its Alphajets, upgrade them, or convert them to a training mission. It needs to build-up to a strength of around 36 modern combat aircraft if it is to be able to deal with any significant air raids or play a significant role in Gulf air defense.

At present, Qatar is considering the purchase of the British Aerospace Hawk 100 to supplement its Alphajets in the training and light attack role or converting them to a more modern mix of avionics and "glass cockpit" that improves the Alphajet's performance and makes it more interoperable with the Mirage 2000-5.[440] Qatar plans to upgrade its Westland Commando helicopters, and is considering equipping its Gazelle anti-tank helicopters with laser-range finder sights to improve their daylight attack capability.

Qatar's transport assets include 2 B-707 and 1–2 B-727 transport aircraft, 3 Whirlwind 3s, 1 Islander, and 4 Commando 2/3s. Its transport helicopter assets include 4 Westland Command s (1 VIP), 12 Gazelles, 6 Super Pumas, and 2 SA-341G liaison helicopters.[441]

Qatari Land-Based Air Defense Capability

The Qatari Air Force has nine Roland surface to air missile launchers, and 10–12 Rapiers.[442] Unless these Stinger systems have been serviced, they are no longer operational. Qatar seems likely to improve its land-based air defense assets, and is studying the improvement of its air defense system and may upgrade its Rolands with Glaive infra-red sights and Thomson-CSF VT-1 hypervelocity missiles. Qatar has considered an order for a Hawk MIM-23B surface-to-air missile battery, the Mistral, and two Shahine batteries, but it is unclear if it will make such a purchase.[443]

Qatar has Plessey land-based warning and surveillance radars, and an underground command center at Doha airfield. This command center is similar in some ways to the centers in Bahrain and Saudi Arabia, but it is unclear what kind of data links it has to other countries. Like Bahrain, Qatar would need assistance from a Saudi or US AWACS to provide adequate warning of an Iranian or Iraqi attack and suitable battle management. Like all the Southern Gulf states, it would benefit greatly from integration into a modern region-wide air defense system.

Qatari Air Force Readiness and Warfighting Capability

Qatar's air forces are still developing the first phases of modern war fighting capability. Its air units have minimal capabilities, and are more an assembly of individual pilots and aircraft than a cohesive force. Like a number of other Gulf Air forces, it consists of "knights of the air" rather than units organized for effective air defense, offensive air, and joint operations.

The air force's main problems are similar to those of most of the other small Southern Gulf states. They include a lack of sophisticated combat aircraft with advanced air defense and air attack mission capabilities, a lack of effective interoperability with other Southern Gulf aircraft in advanced air defense and strike-attack missions that would help compensate for Qatar's limited combat strength, and a lack of modern C^4I and battle management assets.

English language skills, logistic support, and preventive maintenance need improvement. The air force will need extensive advanced training and exercise experience to make use of its Mirage 2000s. It must reorganize to develop a capability to sustain higher sortie rates, conduct joint warfare, and fly interoperable air defense and offensive missions with US and Saudi air units. It will also be dependent on US and/or Saudi airborne C^4I/BM for effective force-wide operations, beyond-visual-range air combat operations, and targeting and damage assessment.

Qatar's land-based air defenses also have limited effectiveness. This is partly a matter of limited equipment, manpower quality, and readiness. It also, however, is a function of geography. Qatar's system requires close links to the system of Bahrain, Kuwait, and Saudi Arabia to be effective against Iran and Iraq. This is currently politically impossible because of political tensions between Qatar and its neighbors.

Qatari Paramilitary Forces and Internal Security Capabilities

Qatar did not experience major internal security problems until the problems within the royal family in 1996, and the recession caused by the decline in oil revenues has not created serious unrest among Qatari youth. While Qatar has some Islamic fundamentalist elements, its society is gradually becoming more modernized without becoming radicalized. The Al-Thani family has done a relatively good job of maintaining living standards and private sector opportunities in spite of declining oil revenues, and its recent cuts in government budgets and development activity have so far been well managed.

The Security Forces

The Qatari government operates an efficient internal security apparatus. The civilian security apparatus has been controlled by the Interior Ministry since 1990, and is comprised of two main sections: The regular police and the General Administration of Public Security. The General Administration of Public Security replaced Qatar's Criminal Investigation Department (CID) in 1991. It controls the Investigatory Police (Mubahathat), which is responsible for sedition and espionage cases.

The police force has a total of 5,000–6,500 men and some paramilitary elements. It is organized along British lines, with special internal security forces. This force is equipped with three Lynx, two SA-342, and two Gazelle helicopters. According to some sources, the police force includes a large number of expatriates, who seem to be carefully chosen to ensure their loyalty.[444]

The Mubahathat has special elements that deal with the control of foreign workers, immigration, intelligence, palace security, and surveillance operations. Like Bahrain, Qatar often uses cooption and informers rather than active repression. The police and security forces are believed to monitor the communications of suspected criminals, those considered to be security risks, and selected foreigners.[445]

There have been reports in the past that officers in the Mubahathat physically abused suspects. There have been no such reports since 1994, and there have been no reported instances of torture for several years. The Qatari government administers most corporal punishment prescribed by Islamic law but does not allow amputation. Qatar has no political prisoners. There have, however, been arbitrary detentions in security cases, and there were restrictions on worker rights and the freedoms of speech, press, assembly, and association when Sheik Khalid was Emir.

The armed forces have another enforcement organization under their jurisdiction, known as the Intelligence Service (Mukhabarat), which intercepts and arrests terrorists and monitors political dissidents. There are no permanent security courts. Security cases—which are rare—are tried by *ad hoc* military courts. There are no restrictions on internal travel, except around sensitive military and oil installations.[446]

Although suspects detained in security cases are generally not afforded access to counsel and may be detained indefinitely while under investigation—the US State Department reports there are no known recent cases of incommunicado detention. Involuntary exile is also rare, and there were no reported cases in 1994. The police rarely intrudes into private homes, and must normally obtain a warrant to search a residence or business, except in cases involving national security or emergencies. However, warrants are issued by police officials rather than by judicial authorities. The State Department reports there were no reports of unauthorized searches of homes in 1994.[447]

The Legal System

The legal system plays a major role in Qatar's internal security efforts. There are two types of civil courts: the civil courts which have jurisdiction in civil and commercial matters, and the Shari'a Court, which has jurisdiction in family and criminal cases. Neither type of court plays a formal role in internal security matters, although they may have jurisdiction over foreign workers. Defendants tried by all courts have the right to appeal. Suspects are usually charged within 48 hours. Defendants in the civil courts have the right to be represented by defense attorneys but are not always permitted to be represented by counsel in the Shari'a Court.

The judiciary is nominally independent, but most judges are foreign nationals who hold residence permits granted by the civil authorities and thus hold their positions at the government's pleasure. The legal system is biased in favor of Qataris and the government.

A Muslim litigant may request the Shari'a Court to assume jurisdiction in commercial or civil cases. Non-Muslims are not allowed to bring suits as plaintiffs in the Shari'a Court. This practice prevents non-Muslim residents from obtaining full legal recourse. Trials in the civil courts are public, but only the disputing parties, their relatives, associates, and witnesses are allowed in the courtroom in the Shari'a Court.

Lawyers do not play a formal role except to prepare litigants for their cases. Although non-Arabic speakers are provided with translators, foreigners are disadvantaged, especially in cases involving the performance of contracts. There is no provision for bail in criminal cases. However, foreigners charged with minor crimes may be released to a Qatari sponsor. They are prohibited from departing the country until the case is resolved.

Political Freedom and Freedom of the Press

There are still no political parties, human rights organizations, or unions, and there is no formal popular political activity in Qatar. Citizens may, however, express political opinions, and the Government tolerates generalized public criticism as long as it is not directed at specific senior officials or members of the ruling family. It discourages criticism of other Arab governments, but tolerates such criticism in the press.

Since Emir Hamad took power, Qatar has begun to relax its restrictions on the privately owned press and the state-owned electronic media. Censors used to review the content of local newspapers, books, and other locally published material for objectionable material, but journalists increasingly censor themselves and show steadily less restraint. Foreign journalists sometimes avoid challenging press restrictions because they fear the Government may cancel their residency permits, but international media like the BBC and CNN are freely available on the local cable system. There is no legal provision for academic freedom, but most instructors at the University of Qatar exercise self-censorship. Customs officials routinely screen imported video cassettes, audio tapes, books, and periodicals for pornographic content.[448]

Qatar seems to have only limited internal security problems with its Shi'ite minorities and foreign workers. Although the nation is about 15% Shi'ite, there have been few signs of support for Iran. The 12,000 Iranians working in Qatar are aware that they are under tight security supervision and have not presented problems

Foreign Workers and Labor Laws

The fact that 90% of Qatar's labor force is expatriate, and over 70% of its total population is expatriate, has not presented serious problems—except for foreign workers who stay or come without work permits. There are few reports of troubles between Qatar and its foreign workers. Relations with Indian workers have been particularly good. Pakistani workers have presented more problems, particularly with drugs. Qatar has recently strengthened its security surveillance of foreign workers—particularly of Iranians and Shi'ites.

Non-Qatari workers face discrimination, and foreigners are subject to immigration restrictions designed to control the size of the local labor pool. Foreign workers must be sponsored by a citizen or legally recognized organization to obtain an entry visa, and must have their sponsor's permission to depart the country. A foreign worker may seek legal relief from onerous work conditions, but domestic workers generally accept their situations in order to avoid repatriation. Those attempting to enter illegally, including persons seeking to defect from nearby countries, are refused entry.[449] In most cases involving foreigners, the police promptly notify the appropriate consular representative.

All workers, including foreigners, are prohibited from forming labor unions. The right to strike does not exist for government employees, domestic workers, or members of the employer's family. No worker in a public utility or health or security service may strike if such a strike would harm the public or lead to property damage. Other workers have the right to strike after their case has been presented to a Labor Conciliation Board and ruled upon.

Employers may, however, close a place of work or dismiss employees once the Conciliation Board has heard the case. Strikes are rare; there were none in 1994. Qatar's labor law also provides for the establishment of joint consultative committees composed of representatives of the employer and workers. The committees may consider issues including work organization and productivity, conditions of employment, training of workers, and safety measures and their implementation.[450]

Strategic Interests

Qatar plays an important strategic role in the Gulf, both because of its status as an oil and gas power and because of its strategic location in the Central Gulf. Qatar has supported the Arab-Israeli peace process and has taken steps to improve its relations with Israel. Qatar has also become an important partner in the US effort to improve USCENTCOM's power projection capabilities.

Qatar is not a major Gulf military power. Its forces are still small and relatively unsophisticated and cannot play a major role in regional defense efforts. However, Qatar's support of the UN Coalition in the Gulf War—particularly its support of Saudi forces in the battle of Khafji—has shown that its forces can fight. Qatar's plans to expand and improve its military capabilities should also steadily expand the role Qatar can play in defending its own territory and in collective security efforts.

Qatar will need continuing outside assistance in fully modernizing its combat equipment, and developing suitable training and support capabilities. Qatar does, however, need to place more emphasis on improving its collective defense capabilities and particularly on developing more advanced air defense and maritime surveillance capabilities.

Cooperation with the US and the West

Qatar has long cooperated with Britain and France and signed a defense agreement with Britain in 1987. It is playing a steadily greater role in US power projection capabilities. The US did not begin to develop security arrangements with Qatar until the tanker war of 1987–1988. Considerable tension existed over Qatar's purchase of smuggled Stinger missiles from Afghanistan during March, 1988 to November, 1990. Since that time, however, relations have improved.

The US and Qatar began to develop close security arrangements during the Gulf War. Qatar permitted US air units to stage out of Qatar during the Gulf War. Qatar provided a 1,600-man mechanized battalion with 25 tanks, 60 other armored vehicles, and 3–5 artillery weapons. This force fought well at the Battle of Khafji, and in Joint Forces Command (East). Qatar also committed 700 men, 21 fighters, and 12 armed helicopters from its small air force. Qatari Mirage F-1s flew 41 interdiction sorties, with a maximum of about 5 sorties per day. Qatari Alphajets flew two sorties. The Qatari Air Force was forced to cancel or abort 22 sorties, but 16 of these cancellations were due to weather.[451]

Unlike most Southern Gulf states, Qatar does not buy significant amounts of military equipment from the US and does not participate in the IMET program. It received only $30,000 in FMS delivers in 1990, $59,000 in 1991, $260,000 in 1992, $1.05 million, and $833,000 in 1995. Its commercial military imports from the US only totaled $2.2 million during 1990–1994.[452]

Qatar does, however, have close military relations with the US. On June 23, 1992, Qatar negotiated a bilateral security arrangement with the US that offers the US access to Qatari air and naval facilities, and a warehouse is now under construction in Doha which will preposition US equipment. In March, 1995, Qatar formally agreed to the prepositioning of the heavy equipment for one US Army mechanized brigade in Qatar—including up to 110 US M-1A2 tanks and Bradley armored infantry fighting vehicles—plus prepositioning of a division support base with up to 4,000 vehicles. The first elements of these forces were moved to two facilities near Doha in January 1996.[453] Qatar has also bought a substantial number of arms from France, and signed a defense agreement with France on August 1, 1994.

Further, Qatar allowed the US to deploy 30 F-15 and F-16 fighters to Qatar in May 1996, along with four KC-135 tankers, to support the enforcement of the "no-fly" zone over southern Iraq. This deployment was part of a process of similar rotations through Bahrain and Kuwait design to support both the enforcement of the "no fly" zone and demonstrate the ability of the USAF to rapidly reinforce Southern Gulf states.[454]

The Qatari military forces have begun to conduct joint air exercises with British, US, and French forces like the "Pearl Gathering" series of exercises.[455] While Qatar's force remain small, Qatar occupies a strategic position and has become critical to US prepositioning plans in the Gulf. This gives the West a strong strategic incentive to support the strengthening of Qatar's military forces and help improve its security.

Relations with Iran and Iraq

In spite of its close military relations with the US, Qatar must seek to strengthen its strategic position in other ways. Like the other Southern Gulf states, Qatar must try to find ways to "constructively engage" Iran and Iraq. Qatar has already taken useful steps in this direction. It has made it clear that it does not agree with the US strategy of "dual containment," and is seeking to maintain a dialog with Iran and Iraq even as it seeks to strengthen its defense.

The US must recognize Qatar's need to take these steps. Iran presents a special problem for Qatar because Iran has claimed a significant part of Qatar's North Field gas reserves in the past, and Qatar's future is dependent on the safe and stable development of these reserves. Iran also is an important potential source of water for Qatar, and may be able to provide supplies at considerably lower cost than further desalination plants.

Relations with Other Southern Gulf States

The tensions between Qatar and its neighbors are a different story. Qatar, Bahrain, Saudi Arabia, and the UAE urgently need to resolve their differences. Qatar largely ceased to play a role in Gulf Cooperation Council exercises in 1992 and did not take place in the Peninsula Shield exercises in 1995. The continuing tension between Bahrain, Qatar, and Saudi Arabia continues to limit any progress towards collective defense.

No one outside the region can hope to judge the merits of the conflicting claims of the three states, but it is clear that the strategic cost of these disputes is probably greater than the value of the land involved. It is clear that the Southern Gulf states are failing to make practical progress in virtually every major area of collective defense. While individual states and the Gulf Cooperation Council have sometimes shown that they are capable of formulating the right plans and rhetoric, they have either not made sufficient progress or have failed to make any progress in many priority areas. The Southern Gulf states need to develop collective or integrated defense capabilities. As a result, many aspects of Qatar's security will be determined by whether the Southern Gulf states can more forward in:

- Creating an effective planning system for collective defense, and truly standardized and/or interoperable forces.
- Integrating their C⁴I and sensor nets for air and naval combat, including beyond-visual-range and night warfare.
- Developing the capability to deploy forces to support the joint land defense of the Kuwaiti/Northwestern Saudi borders and reinforcing

other Gulf states like Oman in the event of any Iranian amphibious or air borne action.

- Creating joint air defense and air attack capabilities.
- Creating joint air and naval strike forces.
- Establishing effective cross reinforcement and tactical mobility capabilities.
- Preparing fully for outside or over-the-horizon reinforcement by the US and other Western powers.
- Setting up joint training, support, and infrastructure facilities.
- Creating common advanced training systems that develop a brigade and wing-level capability for combined arms and joint warfare, and which can support realistic field training exercises of the kind practiced by US and Israeli forces.
- Improving its capability to provide urban and urban area security and to fight unconventional warfare and low intensity combat.

Qatar is making little progress towards standardization with its upper Gulf neighbors in developing an effective deterrent and war fighting capability to deal with threats from Iran and Iraq. This is as much the fault of Bahrain, Kuwait, and Saudi Arabia as Qatar, but future military progress will depend heavily on the extent to which Qatar can move forward in procuring interoperable and/or standardized equipment to provide the capability to perform the following missions:

- Heavy armor, artillery, attack helicopters, and mobile air defense equipment for defense of upper Gulf.
- Interoperability and standardization with US power projection forces.
- Interoperable offensive air capability with stand-off, all-weather precision weapons and anti-armor/anti-ship capability.
- Interoperable air defense equipment, including heavy surface-to-air missiles, beyond-visual-range/all-weather fighters, AEW & surveillance capability, ARM & ECM capability. (Growth to ATBM and cruise missile defense capability)
- Maritime surveillance systems, and equipment for defense against maritime surveillance, and unconventional warfare.
- Mine detection and clearing systems.
- Improved urban, area, and border security equipment for unconventional warfare and low intensity conflict.
- Advanced training aids.
- Support and sustainment equipment.

At the same time, Qatar needs to develop more demanding procurement policies, and to focus on interoperability and standardization with

US power projection forces and the forces of its upper Gulf neighbors. Regardless of current political tensions in the Southern Gulf, Qatar must rationalize its military procurements and eliminate the waste of defense funds on:

- Non-interoperable weapons and systems.
- New types of equipment which increase the maintenance, sustainability, and training problem, or layer new types over old.

Internal Security Challenges

Finally, Qatar must continue to deal with its internal security challenges. Qatar is sufficiently small and wealthy so that it does not face the same near-term problems in continuing the distribution of oil and gas wealth to its citizens faced by many other Southern Gulf states. At the same time, Qatar's dependence on foreign labor does not offer a safe road to social change.

Qatar must deal with the problem of internal reform and find some effective way of systematically reducing its dependence on foreign labor. Qatar may have more time than states like Bahrain and Oman, but it still needs to increase popular participation in government, ensure that all state funds are included in its budget and state subsidies to the Al Thani family are reduced. It also needs to diversify its economy, privatize more operations, encourage native jobs and businesses, and reduce paternalism and welfare.

5

The United Arab Emirates

The United Arab Emirates (UAE) is composed of a group of tribally-based Emirates located along the southern coast of the Persian Gulf and the northwestern coast of the Gulf of Oman. It is a founding member of the Gulf Cooperation Council, and has supported most efforts to strengthen cooperation between the Southern Gulf states. It supported the US and Britain during the "tanker war" of 1987–1988, and strongly supported the UN Coalition during the Gulf War. It has steadily strengthened its strategic cooperation with the West since the Gulf War, and has offered to host a preposition US Army brigade on its soil.

The territory of the UAE dominates the Southern Gulf coast east of Bahrain and Qatar. It also divides the main territory of Oman from its enclave in the Musandam Peninsula, and reaches the Indian Ocean. The UAE's strategic importance lies in both this location and the fact that it possess around 5% of the world's oil reserves. The effective defense of the Gulf against Iran and of the flow of oil through the Gulf is heavily dependent on the UAE.

The UAE is a moderate-size state by Southern Gulf standards. It is roughly the size of Maine. It has a land area of about 83,600 square kilometers. Virtually all of its population of 2.4 million is concentrated along its 1,448 kilometer coastline on the Persian Gulf. Its borders with other states total 1,016 kilometers—20 kilometers with Qatar, 586 kilometers with Saudi Arabia, and 410 kilometers with Oman.

Like the other Gulf states, the UAE has tensions with its neighbors. Its border with Qatar is in dispute and the boundaries with Oman and Saudi Arabia are undefined. The UAE's claims over Gulf waters are defined by bilateral boundaries or an equidistant line with its neighbors. It claims a 200 nautical mile exclusive economic zone, and a territorial zone of three nautical miles, except for Ash Shariqah (Sharjah) with claims of 12 nautical miles. The UAE's most important territorial dispute with its neighbors are its claims to three islands strategically located in the lower Gulf, near the Straits of Hormuz. These islands include Jazirat Abu Musa (Jazireh-ye Abu Musa), Attunb al-Kubra (Jazireh-ye Tonb-e Bozorg or Greater Tunb), and Attunb al-Sughra (Jazireh-ye Tonb-e Kuchek or Lesser Tunb).

The Formation of the United Arab Emirates

The inhabitants of the area that makes up the UAE converted to Islam in the 7th century, and has been embroiled in dynastic disputes for most of its history. It had few resources to attract outside interference, but European and Arab navies increasingly patrolled local waters after the 17th century when raiders based in the Emirates harassed foreign shipping. Early British expeditions to protect the India trade route from raiders at Ras al-Khaimah led to campaigns against that Emirate and other harbors along the coast in 1819. A general peace treaty was signed in 1820 to which all the principal ruling Sheiks on the coast adhered, but pirate raids continued intermittently until 1835, when the Sheiks agreed not to engage in hostilities at sea.

In 1853, the ruling Sheiks signed a treaty with Great Britain, under which the Sheiks (the "Trucial Sheikdoms") agreed to a "perpetual maritime truce." This treaty was enforced by the United Kingdom, and disputes among the Sheiks were referred to the British for settlement. Primarily in reaction to the ambitions of other European countries, the United Kingdom and the Trucial Sheikdoms established a closer relationship in an 1892 treaty, which was similar to treaties entered into by Great Britain and other Gulf principalities. The Sheiks agreed not to dispose of any territory except to the United Kingdom and not to enter into relationships with any foreign government without the consent of Great Britain. In return, the British promised to protect the Trucial Coast from all aggression by sea and to help in the case of a land attack.

The treaties with Britain did little to affect the internal affairs of each Emirate, but gave Britain responsibility for their foreign relations and defense, prohibited them from conducting their own foreign relations, and placed British advisors at each court. Britain signed these treaties to secure the western approaches to India, and limit Turkish, Iranian, and other European expansion in the Gulf, and to halt piracy in the region. The treaties offered the sheiks of the Southern Gulf protection against their more powerful neighbors, a limited amount of security from each other, subsidies, and more stable trade.

Despite the treaties, the Emirates continued to be rivals. Each had a long history of border feuds and struggles for power between ruling royal families. Three of the states, however, emerged as more important than the others. Abu Dhabi became a major oil producer after 1959, Dubai became the region's commercial capital and found oil reserves of its own, and Sharjah was the center of British military operations in the Trucial States and had a small British trained military force called the Trucial Oman Scouts.[456]

The Emirates also continued to have problems with their neighbors. Abu Dhabi had a serious territorial dispute with Saudi Arabia in the early 1950s—a dispute that also affected Oman. Abu Dhabi's borders with Saudi Arabia had never been demarcated, and were tied as much to tribal and water rights as to geographic contiguity. The most important area in the undemarcated area was the Buraymi Oasis, which was an important agricultural area, source of water, and a potential oil field. In 1952, Saudi troops occupied the Buraymi Oasis with the aid of local Bedouin forces. Abu Dhabi responded by asking for aid from Oman, and Oman deployed troops near the area.

Saudi Arabia, Oman, and Abu Dhabi agreed to keep their forces in place on October 26, 1952. They subsequently agreed to formal arbitration in 1954. Saudi Arabia and Oman then withdrew their forces, leaving small police units in the area. Saudi Arabia, however, became actively involved in supporting a revolt in Oman, in which Imam Ghalib bin Ali attempted to seize power from the Sultan. The Saudis used the Buraymi Oasis to move arms and money to the Imam, and Britain was forced to become involved as the protector of Abu Dhabi and *de facto* protector of Oman. On October 26, 1956, the British trained and commanded Trucial Oman Scouts, and the personal guard of the Sultan of Oman occupied the Buraymi Oasis after a brief round of fighting.

A series of negotiations led to a 1974 agreement between Abu Dhabi and Saudi Arabia that would have settled the Abu Dhabi-Saudi border dispute. However, this agreement has yet to be ratified by the UAE Government and apparently is not formally recognized by the Saudi Government. The border with Oman also remains unsettled.

In 1968, the UK announced its decision to end its treaty relationships with the seven Trucial Sheikdoms that now make up the UAE, Bahrain, and Qatar in late 1971. This was part of a broad policy that ended British military commitments "East of Suez," and it meant that the Emirates would not be guaranteed British protection. Britain attempted to strengthen the Trucial States by persuading all nine Emirates to form a union, but they proved unable to agree on terms of the union. Bahrain and Qatar were strong rivals and chose independence in August 1971 and September 1971, respectively.

The Current Strategic Situation
of the United Arab Emirates

The UAE was formed on December 2, 1971, one day after the treaty between Britain and the Trucial Sheikdoms treaty expired. It initially included only six of the remaining Emirates—Abu Dhabi (Abu Zaby), Dubai, Sharjah (Ash Shariqah), Fujairah, Umm Al-Quwain, and Ajman. Ras al-Khaimah's ambitious Ruling Sheik—sometimes jokingly referred

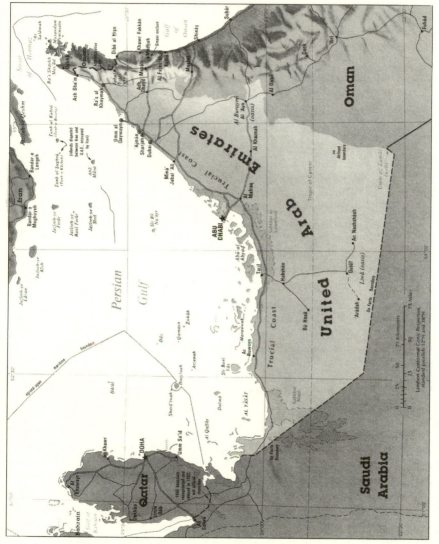

MAP FIVE The UAE

to as the "Napoleon of the Gulf"—initially tried to stand on his own, in part because of his long standing rivalry with a branch of the royal family in Sharjah and his jealousy of the oil wealth of Abu Dhabi and Dubai.

Ras al-Khaimah, however, soon came into conflict with Iran. Iran claimed the Greater and Lesser Tunb Islands and the island of Abu Musa in the Gulf. Ras al-Khaimah claimed the Tunbs, and Sharjah claimed Abu Musa. After some attempts to negotiate, Iran seized all three islands on November, 30, 1971—shortly after British forces left the Gulf.[457] Several Iranian soldiers and four of Ras al-Khaimah's policemen died in the fighting during Iran's seizure of Greater Tunb island.

These events made it clear that Ras al-Khaimah was too small, too weak, and too poor to stand on its own.[458] In addition, a realignment in the royal family in Sharjah produced leaders that were more acceptable to Ras al-Khaimah. As a result, Ras al-Khaimah joined the federation that became the United Arab Emirates in 1972. The Ruling Sheik, Saqr bin Muhammad al-Qasimi did not, however, give up his ambitions in the process, and these later led to considerable tension with Oman.

Since that time, Abu Dhabi has emerged as the dominant member of the UAE, in part because of its oil wealth and in part because of the leadership of its Ruling Sheik, Sheik Zayed bin Sultan Al Nahyyan. Dubai and Sharjah have also emerged as significant powers within the UAE because of their oil and gas resources. Under the federation charter, each Emirate is supposed to contribute 50% of its oil-related income to help finance the national budget. In practice, the situation has been different, and each Sheikdom still controls most of its own budget. The four Emirates with small or nonexistent petroleum resources are dependent on federal government subsidies for such essential services as health, electricity, water, and education.

The UAE's System of Government

Today, the UAE is a federation governed by a President, a Supreme Council of Rulers, a Prime Minister, and a Council of Ministers. The federation has specific powers delegated by the ruling Sheiks of each Emirate, which make up the Supreme Council of Rulers. All other powers are reserved to the Sheiks. The constitution established the positions of president (chief of state) and vice president, each serving 5-year terms; a Council of Ministers (cabinet), led by a prime minister (head of government); a Supreme Council of rulers; and a 40-member Federal National Council (Majlis Watani Itihad), a consultative body whose members are appointed by the Emirate rulers.

The Leadership of the UAE

The chief of state is Sheik Zayed bin Sultan Al Nahyyan, the ruler of Abu Dhabi. Sheik Zayed bin Sultan Al Nahyyan has been president of the

UAE, since the UAE was founded on December 2, 1971. His current 5-year term ends in December 2000. The Vice President is Sheik Maktum bin Rashid al-Maktum, the ruler of Dubai. He has served as Prime Minister since October 8, 1990, while Sheik Zayed has been deputy Prime Minister since November 20, 1990.

The UAE's principal government officials are members of the Supreme Council, which is composed of the seven ruling Sheiks. The Supreme Council is the highest constitutional authority in the UAE, and is the UAE's highest legislative and executive body. It selects a President and Vice President from its membership; the President in turn appoints the Prime Minister and Cabinet. The Council is supposed to meet four times a year, but it convenes more rarely at an official level, because the leaders meet frequently in more traditional settings.

The Supreme Council includes the President and ruler of Abu Dhabi—Sheik Zayed bin Sultan Al Nahyyan; the Vice President, Prime Minister, and ruler of Dubai—Sheik Maktum bin Rashid Al Maktum; the ruler of Sharjah—Sheik Sultan bin Muhammad al-Qasimi; the ruler of Ajman—Sheik Humaid bin Rashid al-Nuaimi; the ruler of Umm al-Qaiwain—Sheik Rashid bin Ahmad al-Mualla; the ruler of Ras al-Khaimah—Sheik Saqr bin Muhammad al-Qasimi; and the ruler of Fujairah—Sheik Hamad bin Muhammad al-Sharqi. The Supreme Council establishes general policies and sanctions federal legislation.

At least five members must agree on any important issue, and the rulers of Abu Dhabi and Dubai have veto power over its decisions. The Cabinet of the Supreme Council manages the Federation on a day-to-day basis. All decisions by the Supreme Council and at the federal level are generally made by consensus of the sheiks of all seven emirates and of leading families.

Military command is divided between Abu Dhabi and Dubai. President Zayed bin Sultan Al Nahyyan, the ruler of Abu Dhabi, is commander-in-chief of the armed forces. Mohamed bin Rashid al-Maktum—the crown prince of Dubai—is the Federal Minister of Defense. Lt. General Mohamed bin Zayed Al Nahyyan of Abu Dhabi is Chief of Staff. Sheik Khalifa bin Zayed Al Nahyyan—the crown prince of Abu Dhabi—is Deputy Commander.

The Role of Individual Emirates and the Role of the Consultative Council

Each Emirate retains control over its own oil and mineral wealth and some aspects of defense and internal security, although the Federal Government asserts primacy in most matters of law and government. Traditional rule has generally been patriarchal, with political allegiance defined in terms of loyalty to tribal leaders. Citizens may express their concerns directly to their leaders via traditional mechanisms, such as the open majlis, or council.

There are federal courts and a federal judicial system. There is a dual system of Shari'a (Islamic) and civil (secular) courts. The civil courts are generally part of the federal system and are answerable to the Federal Supreme Court, located in Abu Dhabi, which has the power of judicial review as well as original jurisdiction in disputes between emirates, or between the Federal Government and individual emirates.[459]

The Shari'a courts are administered by each emirate, but are also answerable to the Federal Supreme Court. In 1994 the President decreed that the Shari'a courts, and not the civil courts, would have the authority to try almost all types of criminal cases. The decree did not affect the emirates of Dubai, Umm Al-Qaiwain, and Ras Al-Khaimah, which have lower courts independent of the federal system.

Each court system has an appeals process, and death sentences may be appealed to the ruler of the emirate in which the offense was committed, or to the President of the Federation. Defendants are presumed innocent until proven guilty. Non-Muslims tried for criminal offenses in Shari'a courts may receive civil penalties at the discretion of the judge. Shari'a penalties imposed on non-Muslims may be overturned or modified by a higher court. The military has its own court system based on Western military judicial practice. Military tribunals try only military personnel. There is no separate national security court system.

There are no signs of a movement towards popular representation, but the government of Abu Dhabi has attempted to revitalize its Consultative Council. A new 52 man council was appointed in 1995, with members from all the major families and tribes. The previous Council had been appointed in 1990, and had not met since 1991. The powers of the new Council, however, will be sharply restricted. It will only be able to review laws after they are issued, although it can recommend changes to existing laws.

The Shifting Power Base Within the UAE

All real power rests with the individual ruling Sheiks of the UAE, and the unity of the United Arab Emirates depends heavily on the leadership and prestige of Sheik Zayed bin Sultan Al Nahyyan. Sheik Zayed has been able to use his personal prestige and Abu Dhabi's oil wealth to bridge the differences between the Emirates and reach compromises between Abu Dhabi, Dubai, and the smaller Emirates.

Sheik Zayed, however, is in his seventies, and time has not united the ruling families of the UAE. There is still tension between Abu Dhabi and Dubai, and senior members of the royal family of Dubai have raised questions about the leadership capabilities of Sheik Zayed's sons. Several members of the royal families of other Gulf states are uncertain whether the UAE will remain unified once Sheik Zayed dies or gives up power.

There are uncertainties regarding the future leadership within the Al-Nahyyan (Al-Nuhayyan) family. According to some reports, Sheik Zayed is already transferring power over domestic issues to the Crown Prince of Abu Dhabi, and plans to transfer authority over foreign relations to his son, the foreign minister. Such reports also indicate that Dubai and the Western Emirates will remain in the UAE because of the benefits of Abu Dhabi's immense oil wealth. According to other reports, Sheik Zayed's sons are quiet rivals for power, and there are divisions between them. Sheik Khalifa bin Zayed Al Nahyyan—the crown prince of Abu Dhabi and Deputy Commander of the Armed Forces—is reported to face a potential challenge from his younger brother, Lt. General Mohamed bin Zayed Al Nahyyan—the Chief of Staff of the armed forces.

Power may also be shifting in Dubai, because of the Emir's age. His brother—Mohamed bin Rashid al-Maktum—was appointed the crown prince of Dubai in January, 1995. He had already been serving as the Federal Minister of Defense, and has taken over much of the day-to-day running of the Emirate. Another brother, Hamdan, was appointed deputy ruler of Dubai.

These divisions between royal families have special importance, because they involve the next generation of princes, and not simply the current rulers. Further, the UAE has not developed strong unifying institutions that unite the Emirates at levels below the royal families. The military consists largely of officers loyal to a given Ruling Sheik commanding forces recruited from that Emirate with substantial numbers of foreign personnel that are largely Omani and Baluchi. The security services are divided by Emirate, and the UAE's technocrats are also divided by Emirate.

These problems are compounded by the fact that the native Arab population now makes up less than 20% of the total population of the UAE. More than 50% of the population is Asian, and more than 80% of the work force is foreign. This reliance on foreigners for virtually all productive economic activity, the divisions of the native population by Emirate, and the lack of unifying economic and political activity for native citizens provide few forces for nation-building. The elite of the UAE has become a "rentier" society living off oil wealth and the efforts of others.

External Security

The UAE has had troubled relations with its neighbors ever since it became an independent state. Sharjah and Ras al-Khaimah were immediately confronted with the Shah of Iran's takeover of Abu Musa and the Tunbs. Abu Dhabi was faced with border disputes with Qatar over territory at the base of the Qatari peninsula, and with Saudi Arabia over control of territory near the Buraymi Oasis. Abu Dhabi did not resolve its disputes with Saudi Arabia until late 1974, when the UAE traded territory to its southwest for Saudi agreement on a demarcation line with both the UAE and Oman.

Divisions Within the Emirates

These problems with neighboring states are compounded by divisions between the Emirates which must be kept in mind in any analysis of the UAE's external affairs. Abu Dhabi and Ajman tend to cooperate in foreign policy and security issues, while Dubai tends to cooperate with Sharjah and Umm Al-Quwain and has closer relations with Iran. The territory of Fujairah divides the main body of Oman from the Musandam Peninsula, and Fujairah has paid special attention to its relations with Oman.

The most striking division between the Emirates occurred in 1977, when the ruling Sheik of Ras al-Khaimah attempted to seize part of Oman's territory and offshore oil fields. His troops, more than half of whom were Omani, refused to attack Oman, and the Sheik was forced to back down. This confrontation also compelled the UAE to raise military pay by 50% in an attempt to ensure the loyalty of its foreign troops. Ras al-Khaimah still pursues a low level border dispute with Oman, although it does so against the opposition of the other ruling Sheiks in the UAE, and has exhibited some separatist ambitions towards creating a Qasimi state that would include Sharjah.

Since that time, the most important differences between the Emirates have been in their policies towards Iran and Iraq. Abu Dhabi strongly backed Iraq during the Iran-Iraq War, and strongly supported efforts to build-up the Gulf Cooperation Council. Dubai and Sharjah tilted more towards Iran during most of the Iran-Iraq War, and Dubai opposed efforts to strengthen the military forces of the GCC because this might have increased the influence of Abu Dhabi.

These differences ceased to be a matter of politics in November 1986, when Iran used its F-4s to attack the main pumping and loading facilities in the Al Bakush off-shore oil field in November, 1986. This Iranian attack seems to have been launched because Iraqi air strikes had damaged Iranian facilities that drew oil from the same reservoir Abu Dhabi used in producing from the Al Bakush field, and because Abu Dhabi had kept producing from this common reservoir in spite of Iranian protests.

Abu Dhabi responded by turning to the US and the West for aid in improving its air and naval defenses, and Iran then replied by using its Revolutionary Guards to plant mines in the waters near the UAE's offshore fields, and bombed one of Sharjah's offshore oil facilities in 1988.[460]

These Iranian attacks led to increasing cooperation between Abu Dhabi and the US during Operation Earnest Will in 1987 and 1988, and Dubai provided a recreational port and some support facilities to the US Navy. At the same time, Dubai continued to act as a major transshipping point to Iran and one of Iran's largest trading partners. Dubai effectively pursued a formal security policy opposing Iran, while it preserved its economic ties to the Khomeini regime.

In contrast, Iraq's invasion of Kuwait in August, 1990 galvanized considerably more unity. All of the Emirates denounced the Iraqi invasion and, provided support for the UN Coalition during Desert Storm. The UAE provided troops, extensive financial aid, basing rights, and aid in kind. It spent a total of roughly $10 billion on the war: $3.9 billion in 1990 and $5.7 billion in 1991.[461] This support for the UN reflected the fact that all the Emirates saw Iraq as a common threat, and the fact that Saddam Hussein had vigorously denounced the UAE's oil production policy in exactly the same way he had denounced Kuwait's oil production policy during the months before Iraq's August 1990 invasion.

The Problem of Iran and Iraq

Iran's seizure of full control over Abu Musa and the Tunbs in 1992 led to a more complex response. Once more, the Emirates took a unified formal stand in opposing Iran's actions, and once again Dubai and the individual Emirates kept up their economic relations with Iran.

The origins of this crisis over Abu Musa and the Tunbs predate the formation of the UAE and the revolution in Iran. Abu Musa and the Tunbs had long been claimed by both the Shahs of Iran and the ruling Qawasim family of Sharjah and Ras al-Khaimah. Title to the islands was disputed. Iranian control was intermittent before the British came to the Gulf, although the Qawasim paid occasional tribute to Iran. Further, the fact that the British had seized the islands after 1828, and had treated the claims of Sharjah and Ras al-Khaimah as legitimate for nearly a century, was treated more as a matter of British self-interest than a firm claim under international law.

The issue of sovereignty resurfaced in the 1930s when the Shah's father, Reza Shah, reasserted Iran's claims to the islands. The issue only became a serious source of contention, however, after Britain announced that it was leaving the Gulf, and the Shah of Iran sought to become the dominant military power in the region.

The Shah seized the islands of Abu Musa and the Greater and Lesser Tunbs from Sharjah and Ras al-Khaimah on November 30, 1971, in order to gain strategic positions in the lower Gulf. Furthermore, Abu Musa was in waters that many believed had offshore oil resources. The Shah also timed this seizure for maximum political effect and to demonstrate that Iran had become the power that would replace British influence in the Gulf. He seized the islands just as British forces were leaving and the day before Ras al-Khaimah and the United Arab Emirates gained their independence.[462]

Iran's Prime Minister Abbas Hoveida informed the Iranian Majlis that full Persian sovereignty "had been restored following long negotiations with the British government," and that Iran had "in no conceivable way relinquished or will relinquish its incontestable sovereignty and right of control over the whole of Abu Musa island."[463]

The Shah's seizure of the islands resulted in several casualties. At the same time, none of the islands had a large native population. The Greater Tunb (Tunb al-Kurba or Tonb-e Bozorg) is little more than a barren rock about 50 kilometers south of Bandr-e Lengeh, and was of interest only to a few visiting fishermen. The Lesser Tunb (Tunb al Soughra or Tonb-e Kuchek) was so small that its only previous strategic importance had been as a shipping hazard.

Abu Musa was the only island large enough to have a small port and a few square miles of territory, although it then had no surface flat enough to serve as a runway. Abu Musa then had a permanent population of well under 50, except for gangs of Arab laborers who mined the island's iron oxide deposits. Abu Musa was, however, of more strategic value than either Tunb. It is located about 50 kilometers east of Sirri, and in the middle of the lower Gulf, 50 kilometers further southeast of Bandr-e Lengeh. This made it a potential staging point for operations against Gulf shipping.

The Shah did, however, agree to share oil, to provide compensation to the ruling Sheik of Sharjah for the seizure of Abu Musa, to allow some Arabs from the UAE to remain on the island, and not to object to Sharjah's continued claim to sovereignty over the island.[464] As a result, the Shah did not pursue a claim to total sovereignty over the islands while he remained in power, and the new Khomeini government, when it assumed power, did little to change this situation because of its focus on the Iran-Iraq War.

In fact, a modus vivendi emerged between Iran and the UAE that permitted the UAE to play an economic and political role on the island and survive a significant Iranian military build-up on Abu Musa during the Iran-Iraq War. Iran surveyed several Silkworm and surface-to-air missile sites on the northern side of Abu Musa, built new ammunition bunkers, and constructed secure storage sites it could use to hold Silkworm and surface-to-air missiles. These sites were part of the network of facilities that Iran built to threaten Gulf tanker traffic during the "tanker war" of 1987–1988, and were similar to the Iranian facilities on islands like Sirri, and sites on the mainland near the Straits of Hormuz.

The Crisis Over Abu Musa and the Tunbs. This background helps explain why the UAE was surprised when Iran reasserted full control of Abu Musa in March, 1992. Iran suddenly expelled all workers that had UAE, rather than Iranian visas, and many of the Arab residents. These expulsions included the foreigners who ran the power station, the UAE-sponsored local school, and the island's only clinic.

Iran claimed it had taken this action, because it had not received a fair share of the offshore oil production from the island. The Iranian media soon, however, began to refer to the entire island as Iranian territory and as part of Hormuzgan province. Iran also supported its demonstrations with military action. During April 25–May 4, 1992, Iran staged its largest amphibious exercise since the end of the Iran-Iraq War. This exercise took place near the Straits of Hormuz while Iran was in the process of seizing control of Abu Musa. It lasted 11 days and practiced blocking the Strait to an outside invader (the US). The exercise covered an area of some 10,000 square miles of ocean, and involved 45 surface ships, 150 small craft, and an unknown number of Iranian Air Force aircraft. Iran continued such exercises in 1993, 1994, and 1995.

Iran and the UAE became involved in a major diplomatic clash. In September, 1992, the UAE obtained support from the Gulf Cooperation Council (GCC) and Arab League. Iran countered by charging that the GCC states and Arab League states had become US plotters. Iran broke off talks on the issue on September 28, 1992, after the UAE chose to make the issue the subject of GCC and Arab League diplomacy and renewed its claims to the two Tunbs. President Rafsanjani of Iran declared the issue a US "conspiracy . . . to justify its illegitimate presence in the Gulf."[465] Somewhat ironically, Iraq reacted by announcing that it was the only power that could protect the islands against Iran.[466]

While the UAE made efforts to refer the issue to the UN Security Council or the International Court of Justice in the Hague, Iran began deploying additional forces to Abu Musa. Iran sent additional Iranian Revolutionary Guard (IRGC) forces to the island beginning in late 1992, and Iranian President Rafsanjani declared that the Arabs would have to cross a "sea of blood" to get to the Islands. It was at this time, that several hard-line Iranian papers called for Iran to reassert its claim to Bahrain.[467]

During 1993 and 1994, Syria attempted to mediate the dispute, but had little success. Iran remained intransigent in discussing any peaceful resolution of the issue, and the UAE was forced to seek support from other Arab states. By late 1993, the UAE had obtained the support of the GCC, the Arab League and Syria in its effort to refer the dispute to either the UN Security Council or the International Court of Justice (ICJ) in the Hague. This Arab support, however, had little practical impact on Iran.

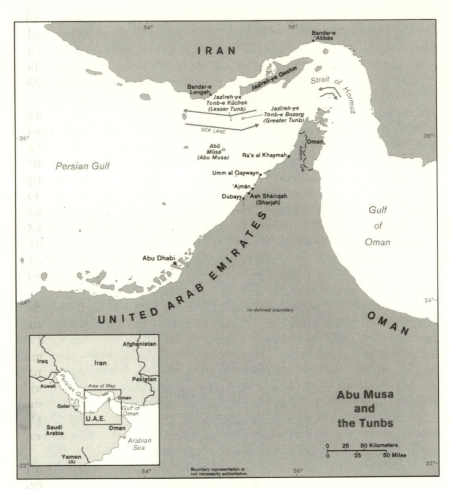

MAP SIX   Abu Musa, the Tunbs, and the Strait

Iran deployed new forces to the islands in the fall of 1994—at a time when the US was building up its forces in the Gulf to deal with an Iraqi threat to Kuwait. Iran deployed new IRGC forces, SA-6 air-to-surface missiles, 155 mm artillery, and CSSC-3 "Seersucker" anti-ship missiles. According to some reports, Iran increased the number of IRGC forces, marines and air defense personnel on Abu Musa from 700 to 4,000 by early 1995. Iran also rejected a new Saudi call for referring the dispute to the ICJ.[468]

By February, 1995, Iran had lengthened the runway on Abu Musa so that it could accept larger military cargo aircraft, built a new pier inside the breakwater, constructed a new command bunker, deployed IHawk missiles south of the runway, and established a new desalination plant. It also built its first CSSC-3 site on the south side of the island, near the UAE's ports. The CSSC-3 has a range of 150 kilometers and can reach the UAE's major ports. Some experts also felt Iran might be deploying a surface-to-surface modification of the SA-6 so it could pose at least a token threat to the UAE's cities.[469]

There is some dispute over the scale of the Iranian build-up. In the spring of 1995, Secretary of Defense William Perry referred to the Iranian deployment of chemical weapons on the island, including 155 mm shells and an Iranian force of up to 6,000. He called these deployments "very threatening." Some US experts feel, however, that Secretary Perry exaggerated the Iranian build-up and confused the deployment of poison gas with the deployment of non-lethal agents. They believe that the total Iranian presence on the islands and in the immediate vicinity is only about 3,700 men. What seems clear is that Iran now maintains a substantial garrison force, and has deployed added artillery and 10 older tanks in sheltered positions in the spring of 1995. Iran also seems to have deployed small stocks of CS gas, and to have created emplacements that might be used for anti-ship missiles.[470]

The aggressive nature of these Iranian actions should not be exaggerated, although some analysts have seen Abu Musa as a possible base for Iran's extended-range Scud missiles. Iran seems to have over-reacted to a fear of a US attack on the islands and a fear of either renewal of the tanker war of 1987–1988 or a broader US attack on Iran.

The strategic value of the islands must also be kept in perspective. The Tunbs have little value as bases, and even Abu Musa would be difficult to use as a survivable base for naval operations and siting missiles in the face of attacks by US airpower. While the three islands have a strategic position near the main shipping channels in the lower Gulf, Iran has long had anti-ship missiles deployed in other positions near the Straits. Iran possesses well developed bases at Sirri, Qeshem, Hengam, Forur, and Larak—islands which are capable of staging mining and Naval Guards operations against shipping in the lower Gulf or basing missiles for attacks on large vessels moving in and out of the Gulf.

Iran seems to have deployed Silkworm anti-ship missiles on Qeshem and Sirri with ranges of up to 90 kilometers, and CSSC-3 missiles. There are also reports that Iran has deployed advanced, long-range anti-ship missiles like the Sunburst on Sirri, although it seems more likely that it has deployed the CSSC-3. Iran also has SA-6 and/or IHawk units, or sites, on some of these islands, as well as runways, ammunition and missile storage facilities, POL storage, Revolutionary Guards units, and naval facilities.[471]

Current UAE Relations with Iran and Iraq.   The Emirates are formally united in resisting the Iranian takeover of the islands, but Dubai and Sharjah continue to be major trading and transshipment partners for Iran, and Iranian dhows and cargoes move in and out of UAE ports with little control and supervision. Even Abu Dhabi—the leader of the UAE's effort to claim the islands—has an Iranian dhow port and allows Iranians to trade extensively on its soil

The tensions between the UAE and Iran thus sometimes seem to be more show than substance. Abu Dhabi, as the leader of the UAE's military efforts, does structure its military buildup to deal with Iran. At the same time, these efforts show little regard for real-world contingency requirements and it is unclear that Abu Dhabi sees its efforts as more than a deterrent to further Iranian incursions against the UAE's offshore facilities in the Gulf. The other Emirates maintain relatively good informal relations with Iran, and even Abu Dhabi holds considerable informal dialogue with Iranian officials.

UAE officials do, however, express concern about two other aspects of the UAE's relations with Iran. The first is the potential "fifth column" created by the presence of nearly 100,000 Iranians in the UAE, and the constant flow of dhow traffic between Iran and the UAE. The second is the problems posed by Iran's potential claims over Gulf waters and the proximity of Dubai and the eastern Emirates to Abu Musa and Iran. Abu Dhabi is the only Emirate with any strategic depth relative to Iran. The shipping channels and coasts of the other Emirates are highly vulnerable and are within a few minutes flying time from Iran's air base at Bandar Abbas. Like Kuwait, and Oman's Musandam Peninsula, Dubai and the western emirates are highly vulnerable to attacks from the northern Gulf.

The UAE also takes a somewhat ambiguous attitude towards Iraq. The UAE firmly backed Kuwait in October, 1994, when Iraqi troops moved to the border area.[472] The Emirates do differ, however, over how long the current UN sanctions on Iraq should be enforced, and over how to deal with Iran. Abu Dhabi has tended to support a harder line approach towards Iraq than the other Emirates, although Sheik Zayed has made public statements indicating that the sanctions on Iraq may have to be lifted to ease the plight of the Iraqi people. In practice, Abu Dhabi would like to ease constraints on Iraq so that Iraq could act as a counterbalance to Iran, but has to act very cautiously because it needs support from Kuwait and Saudi Arabia in its dispute with Iran. This ambiguity illustrates yet another difference in strategic interests among the Southern Gulf states.

Relations with Qatar

The UAE has had a long-standing, though relatively minor, territorial dispute with Qatar. This dispute initially centered around the control of

Khaur al-Udaid, a long winding inlet at the base of the eastern side of the Qatari peninsula, and control over the territory behind it. The Al Thani family of Qatar and the Al Nahyyan family of Abu Dhabi had long disputed control over the Khaur al-Udaid. This dispute broadened in 1935, when Saudi Arabia asserted its own claims over the area, along with claims to much of Abu Dhabi.[473]

This issue seemed to be resolved by a complex series of negotiations over the Buraymi Oasis dispute and Sheik Zayed's mediation of some of the border disputes between Oman, Qatar, Saudi, and the UAE. The ruling Sheiks of the UAE have not, however, gotten along well with Qatar's new ruling Sheik, Hamad bin Khalifa al-Thani, and Qatar's foreign minister. Relations between the UAE and Qatar also deteriorated sharply in December, 1995, when Qatar walked out of the Gulf Cooperation Council meeting in protest over the nomination of a Saudi as Secretary General. The UAE felt that Qatar's new ruling Sheik had become a disruptive force in GCC relations and that Qatar's leaders had insulted Sheik Zayed when he attempted to mediate between Qatar and Saudi Arabia. As a result, Abu Dhabi retaliated by joining Saudi Arabia and Bahrain in receiving the Emir's deposed father Sheik Khalifa bin Hamad al-Thani on December 21, 1995, although Sheik Khalifa made it clear that he sought to regain power from Sheik Hamad.

The Sheik announced that he intended to return to power and would set up "temporary quarters" in Al-Ain until he returned to power in Doha. Sheik Khalifa bin Hamad pledged that he would improve relations between Qatar and its neighbors if he resumed power and would take a much harder line towards Iraq.[474] Sheik Khalifa bin Hamad then visited Cairo and Damascus. He referred to the Damascus Declaration and received at least some support from the Syrian press.

These tensions reached a near crisis point in early 1996 when Qatar charged that Bahrain, Saudi Arabia, and the UAE has at least tacitly supported a coup attempt by Sheik Khalifa bin Hamad while he was based in the UAE. This situation relaxed in March 1996, after mediation by Sultan Qabus and others and Qatar's agreement to accept the new Saudi Secretary-General of the GCC. Senior UAE officials made it clear, however, that they still regarded Qatar's rulers as provocative and unreliable, and that relations were anything but good.

Relations with Other Southern Gulf States

The UAE has not played a strong role in Gulf diplomacy. It has good relations with the rest of the Southern Gulf states, and has firmly supported Kuwait against Iraq, but the UAE as a whole has concentrated on domestic concerns while Sheik Zayed has played a mediating role in the southern Gulf as the "elder statesman" of the GCC.

Relations with Saudi Arabia are good, although the UAE is conscious of the fact that Saudi Arabia is the dominant power in the Southern Gulf and has acquired territory once claimed by Abu Dhabi. Relations with Bahrain are good, but not close. The UAE cooperates with Oman, and many of the UAE's military personnel are Omani. There is, however, a minor dispute between the UAE and Oman over the UAE's northeastern border, largely because a single tribe has historical claims to the border area.

The net result is that the UAE has rarely played much of a role in enhancing Gulf unity. Sheik Zayed is highly respected, and has helped resolve some past disputes between Southern Gulf states, but the divisions between the Emirates of the UAE, and the differences in strategic interest between the UAE and the upper Gulf states make the UAE a poor catalyst for major new efforts to improve collective security or economic cooperation.

Relations with the West, Russia, and Former Soviet Union

As is described later in this report, the UAE has cooperated closely with the West, and particularly the US, in strengthening bilateral military cooperation since the Gulf War. Abu Dhabi has offered the US the right to preposition a US Army brigade set on UAE soil, Dubai acts as a major port for the US 5th Fleet and forces in the Gulf, and the UAE conducts military exercises with a number of Western powers.

Perhaps the most striking shift in the UAE's cooperation with other states, however, is that Dubai has become a major trading partner and transshipment point for the former Soviet Union. It is often possible to see far more Russians in Dubai than natives, and trade with the nations of the former Soviet Union is now an important part of Dubai's economy.

Internal Security

The UAE has not been subject to major popular unrest, in part because its economy provides citizens with one of the world's highest per capita incomes, and in part because its citizens are so small a portion of the total population. There are few signs of ethnic differences within the indigenous population, and there are tight controls on foreign workers—who make up 80% of the population. The fact that the UAE is now more Asian than Arab does, however, present potential problems for the future, and the rivalries between the ruling families of the seven Emirates pose a risk of future clashes between them or even the break up of the UAE.

The Most Successful "Asian" Country in the Gulf

Oil income and an influx of foreign workers have increased the population of the UAE from 150,000 in 1972, 750,000 in 1982, 2.4 million in 1991, and finally up to 2.9 million in 1995. The total population of the UAE is now over 2.9 million, with a growth rate of 4.55%, and a birth rate of 27.02 births/1,000 population.[475] As might be expected, the UAE has a high net migration rate of 23.31 migrants/1,000 population.

There are a number of different estimates of the ethnic breakdown of this population. The IISS estimates a total population of around 1,830,000, of which 76% is expatriate. It estimates that 30% of the population is Indian, 16% is Pakistani, 12% is other Asian, 12% is other Arab, and 1% is European.[476] The CIA estimates that the UAE's population is only 19% Emirian. The rest of the population is 23% other Arab, 50% South Asian, and 8% other expatriates, including Westerners and East Asians. The CIA estimates the religious composition of the UAE to be about 96% Muslim (Shi'ite 16%), and 4% Christian, Hindu, and other.[477]

This degree of reliance on foreign workers presents potential security problems. There has been at least one major clash between Muslim and Hindu Asian workers. This clash took place in 1994 as a result of the destruction of the Ayoadha Mosque in India. It involved at least several hundred Asians, the security forces intervened, and there were well over 100 arrests and deportations.

The UAE is more careful in dealing with its foreign workers than some other Gulf states. Most foreign workers receive either employer-provided housing or housing allowances, medical care, and homeward passage from their employers. At the same time, most foreign workers do not earn the minimum salary of $1,090 per month required to obtain residency permits for their families (or $817 per month, if a housing allowance is provided in addition to the salary). Employers also have the option to petition for a 1 year ban from the work force against any foreign employee who leaves his job without fulfilling the terms of his contract. Employee appeals to the government because of mistreatment are rare because of fears of reprisals by native employers.

It seems unlikely that these problems will lead to any major clashes between Emiris and foreign workers in the near term, but riots are always a possibility and the UAE's dependence on foreigners has reached the point where it has become a joke in other parts of the Gulf. Omanis, for example, sometimes bet on how long it will be before they see a native Arab in Dubai. As is the case in Qatar and Kuwait, the rentier character of the UAE also raises existential questions about its future character. There is little work ethic in a society dominated by foreign non-Arab workers, and most UAE employers find it cheaper to hire foreign labor than natives from the poorer Emirates in the UAE or other Southern Gulf states.

The situation in Dubai is particularly uncertain, because the only outstanding evidence of a native society is a large annual horse race. Dubai now mixes Asian workers with Iranians involved in the re-export trade to Iran and an increasing number of citizens from the former Soviet Union engaged in re-export trade to their home countries. The end result is fascinating, but scarcely Arab. Dubai has effectively become the most successful Asian nation in the Gulf.

Rivalries Between Ruling Families

There are also important rivalries between and within the UAE's ruling elites. These rivalries began long before the formation of the UAE. In fact, the history of this part of the Gulf is largely the history of power struggles between the individual Emirates, or for power within the ruling family of a given Emirate. Much of this rivalry continues, although violent power struggles within a given ruling family may now be largely a thing of the past.

The only near coup within a ruling family in the UAE that has occurred since the country's formation took place on June 17, 1987, when the Sheik of Sharjah, Sultan bin Mohamed al-Qasimi, was deposed by his brother Abd al-Aziz Mohamed al-Qasimi. The coup occurred while the Sheik was in Britain, and immediately raised a potential challenge to the legitimacy of all rulers in the UAE. At the same time, the other Emirates divided over how to deal with the issue. Abu Dhabi backed Abd al-Aziz Mohamed al-Qasimi, and Dubai backed Sultan bin Mohamed al-Qasimi, and a real threat developed that Abu Dhabi and the troops of Sharjah might support Abd al-Aziz Mohamed al-Qasimi, while Dubai sent forces to aid Sultan bin Mohamed al-Qasimi.

The Supreme Council of Rulers eventually resolved this issue by persuading the two brothers to accept a compromise whereby Sultan bin Mohamed al-Qasimi returned to power, but Abd al-Aziz Mohamed al-Qasimi became crown prince and head of the Ruling Council. This compromise has proved unstable, however, and factions exist in Sharjah which compete for power and sometimes side with Abu Dhabi or Dubai.

Abu Dhabi has clearly emerged as the largest and most powerful member of the UAE, because of its much larger oil reserves, and Sheik Zayed has emerged as the UAE's *de facto* leader. The UAE has also steadily increased its federal institutions with the aid of an increasingly stronger group of technocrats. Nevertheless, the previous discussion has indicated that there are at least low level rivalries among Sheik Zayed's sons, and constant struggles for internal prestige between the Emirates.

These rivalries center around the differences between Abu Dhabi and Dubai, although Sharjah and Ras al-Khaimah have also taken independent stands on a number of issues. These rivalries have also affected the UAE's efforts to build up effective military forces. Despite an agreement to integrate their military forces in May, 1976, Abu Dhabi and Dubai have continued to build up military forces that they have never fully integrated. Sources in Dubai also claim that Sheik Zayed appointed his son as commander of the UAE armed forces in 1978 without consulting Sheik Rashid of Dubai. They state that Sheik Rashid reacted by creating his own Central Military Region Command; setting up his own armored forces, special forces, and air units; and buying his own air defense weapons.

Umm Al-Quwain, Fujairah, Ras al-Khaimah, and Sharjah all maintain their own national guard forces. The fact that Sharjah also has a limited amount of oil production, and Ras al-Khaimah has produced oil since 1977 has helped these sheikdoms to maintain police units, intelligence branches, security forces, and military forces of their own.

Some experts have argued that these rivalries could cause the UAE to gradually break up once Sheik Zayed dies or leaves power. This is a possibility, and much will depend on the strength of his eldest son and the level of support he receives from his brothers. It seems more likely, however, that the real issue is whether generational change in the UAE gives the ruling families leaders a willingness to make the UAE a true federation and address the issue of its future character and degree of dependence on foreign labor, or whether the UAE goes on divided into rentier Emirates.

Economy Stability and Security

The UAE is relatively wealthy as a federation, although much of its wealth is concentrated in Abu Dhabi. As is the case for all Gulf states, there are many conflicting statistics on its economy. Table Thirty-Three provides a summary of recent trends based on data developed by the Economist Intelligence Unit. These data show the critical role oil production still plays in the UAE's economy, and the short term impact of declining oil revenues and rising native and foreign population on the UAE's per capita income.

The CIA generates similar data, although its estimates of the UAE's GDP is based on purchasing power and gives the UAE a GDP equivalent to $62.7 billion in 1994. The CIA estimates that production, largely oil and gas, accounted for 50% of the GDP and had a growth rate of 1.9–2.3% per year. According to CIA estimates, the UAE's exports were worth $24 billion in 1994, and roughly 66% of these earnings came from exports of crude oil. The rest came from exports of natural gas, re-exports, and exports of dried fish and dates. The UAE had roughly $20 billion in imports, largely manufactured goods, machinery, and food. Agriculture accounted for only 2% of the UAE's GDP, and the UAE imported 75% of its food. The UAE's foreign debt totaled roughly $11.6 billion.[478]

TABLE THIRTY-THREE   Key Economic Indicators in the UAE

	1990	1991	1992	1993	1994
Production (1,000s of barrels per day)	2,123	2,420	2,290	2,170	2,200
Oil Exports (1,000s of barrels per day)	1,895	2,195	2,060	1,970	n/a
Oil Export Receipts ($ US current billions)	16.1	15.5	15.2	13.2	13.1
GDP ($ US current billions)	28.74	27.95	27.90	27.05	26.92
Annual Change in GDP (%)	14.0	–2.7	–0.2	–3.0	–0.6
Per Capita GDP ($ US current)	18,249	14,636	13,881	12,584	12,084
Annual Change in Per Capita GDP (%)	11.8	–6.1	–5.2	–9.3	–4.1
Total Government Revenue ($ US current billions)	4.08	3.98	4.80	4.23	4.46
Total Government Expenditures ($ US current billions)	3.93	3.88	4.24	4.20	4.27
Budget Balance ($ US current billions)	0.15	0.10	0.56	0.03	0.19

Source: Adapted by Wayne A. Larsen, NSSP, Georgetown University, from the EIU, Country Profile, *United Arab Emirates, 1995–1996,* pp. 41, 42, 43.

More recent data from the UAE indicate that the UAE had a GDP of $36.7 billion in 1994 (135 billion Dirhams) and $39.2 billion (143.9 billion Dirhams) in 1995—an increase of 6.5%.[479] The data in Chart Forty-Four also show that military expenditures and arms imports have been a relatively limited portion of the total GDP.[480]

Other estimates of the longer term trends in the UAE's economy, central government expenditures, total exports, military expenditures, and arms imports are shown in Chart Forty-Four. This chart is based on US State Department data and indicates that the UAE's total central government expenditures are relatively low as a percent of GDP for a Gulf state, and that exports have normally been substantially larger than central government expenditures.

The UAE's Evolving Oil Economy

The UAE has more wealth per capita than most Southern Gulf states, and a high per capita wealth for its native citizens. Like the other Southern Gulf states, however, the economic aspects of the UAE's security are determined largely by how it handles its oil wealth, and deals with the related impact of its population growth and foreign labor.

Chart Forty-Five supplements the trade data shown in Chart Forty-Four, and shows that oil and gas related revenues constitute the largest single component of GDP. The exact impact of these revenues on the UAE's economy is a matter of definition. The UAE's Ministry of Planning and Central Bank indicate that the oil sector accounted for 39 percent of its GDP in 1993, 51 percent of its export revenue, and 79 percent of its government revenues. US estimates of these percentages are about 15% higher because they include related goods and services.

According to US estimates, most of the UAE's workers work for the government or in service industries. Only 26.8% of the labor force is involved in industry, including the oil and gas sectors, and 7.8% of the UAE's labor force is currently involved in any form of agriculture (about 4 times the percent that agriculture contributes to the GDP).

Agriculture and Water. The UAE has little agricultural potential. It now allocates nearly 80% of its natural water to agriculture versus 13% for domestic needs and 7% for industry, but this figure disguises the fact that "agriculture" often consists of parks and urban areas. This helps explain why the ratio of workers to output is so high, although the Eastern Emirates do have some natives involved in traditional agriculture.

The UAE has only 50 square kilometers of irrigated land and very limited supplies of water. Even today, it only has about 0.42 cubic kilometers of internal, renewable water resources. This flow can only provide 189

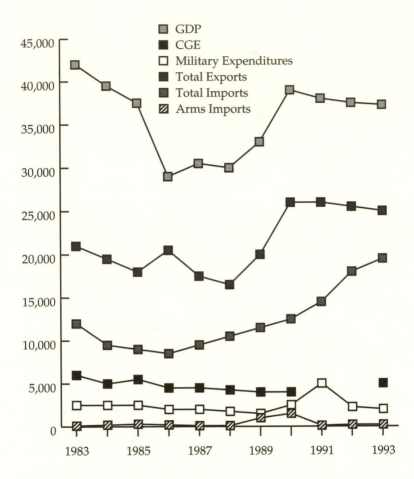

CHART FORTY-FOUR   UAE: GDP, Government Expenditures, Military
Expenditures, and Imports ($93 Constant Millions). *Source:* Adapted by Anthony
H. Cordesman from ACDA, *World Military Expenditures and Arms Transfers,
1993–1994*, ACDA/GPO, Washington, 1995.

cubic meters per person per year, less than one-sixth the total for a citizen
of the US. As a result, the UAE is forced to rely on desalination plants for
most of its water, although it recycles about 62 million cubic meters worth
of water a year.[481]

The UAE's rapid increase in population is exacerbating these water
problems. Desalination is too expensive to be a solution to meeting
anything other than civil and urgent industrial needs, and the World
Resources Institute and World Bank estimate that UAE natural per

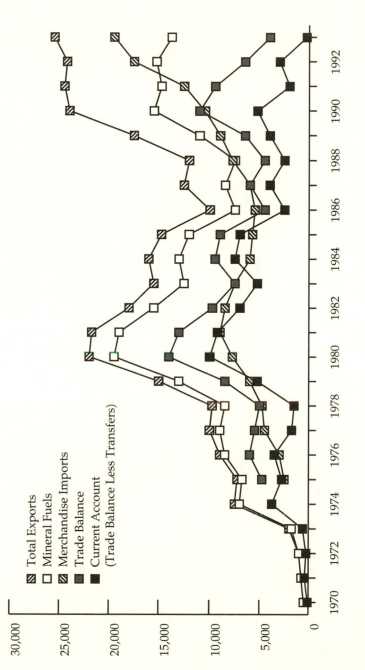
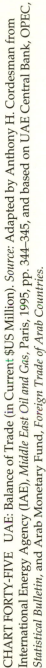

CHART FORTY-FIVE UAE: Balance of Trade (in Current $US Million). *Source:* Adapted by Anthony H. Cordesman from International Energy Agency (IAE), *Middle East Oil and Gas*, Paris, 1995, pp. 344–345, and based on UAE Central Bank, OPEC, *Statistical Bulletin*, and Arab Monetary Fund, *Foreign Trade of Arab Countries.*

capita water resources dropped from 3,000 cubic meters in 1960 to 189 cubic meters in 1990 and will drop to 113 cubic meters in 2025. Further, a recent US survey indicates that Abu Dhabi may deplete its ground water reserves in 20 to 50 years at even the current rate of use. The UAE may well have to reduce its use of water for urban decorative purposes. In general, water policy is problem that needs greater government attention.[482]

Trade and Diversification.   Chart Forty-Five shows that the UAE's trade balance has been considerably more favorable over time than the trade balance of most other Gulf states. More recent UAE data show that this favorable balance continues. The trade surplus was $329 million (1.21 billion Dirhams) in 1994 and $532 million (1.95 billion Dirhams) in 1995. It is estimated to be $250 million in 1996. These figures reflect the impact of a relatively low world oil price, and the UAE's trade surplus can rise sharply with increasing world oil prices. For example, it reached $3.51 billion (12.9 billion Dirhams) in 1992, after oil prices peaked following the Gulf War.

The UAE has sought to diversify its economy and has invested nearly $50 billion since the 1970s. As a result, the non-oil sector of the economy rose from 20% in the early 1970s to 67% in 1995. The UAE estimates that the non-oil sector grew in current dollars from $24.5 billion (89.9 billion Dirhams) in 1994, to $25.8 billion (94.7 billion Dirhams) in 1995, a growth rate of 5.3%. Light industries grew from $3.18 billion (11.7 billion Dirhams) in 1994, to $3.4 billion (12.5 billion Dirhams) in 1995. Construction grew from $3.48 billion (12.8 billion Dirhams) in 1994, to $3.62 billion (13.3 billion Dirhams) in 1995.[483]

Dubai has benefited from a major re-export trade with both Iran and the nations of the former Soviet Union. This re-export trade helped lead to a 6.6% increase in its GDP in 1995, which rose to 143.9 billion Dirhams. Fujirah is also benefiting from this trade, and the cargo shipped through its airport rose from 9,500 tons in 1994 to 33,000 tons in 1995.[484]

Much of this diversification, however, is the result of an increased dependence on imports and imported services, and a related construction boom—rather than diversification into productive economic activity. There are limits to the growth of such service activity, and there already are substantial numbers of empty homes and office units in Abu Dhabi and Dubai. Further, Dubai's economy has become increasingly dependent on re-exports to Iran and the former Soviet Union. This re-export market has already been hurt by Iranian measures to reduce imports, and both Iran and the FSU could shift their import markets with relatively little notice.

In short, the UAE is certain to remain dependent on oil and gas exports, and petroleum related products. This dependence is not likely to result in any significant near-term problems in supporting so small a native population, but it may lead to longer-term cuts in relative per capita wealth.

To put this risk in perspective, Charts Forty-Four, Forty-Five, and Fifty show the trends in the UAE's oil export earnings relative to its total exports, and reflect the sharp swings in the UAE's oil income. This fluctuation in the UAE's oil earnings is indicated by the fact that the UAE earned as much as $19 billion in current dollars per year in 1980, but steady cuts in oil prices reduced these earnings to $16 billion in 1981–1982, $12 billion in 1983–1984, and $7 billion in 1985–1988.[485] Oil revenues suddenly rose to $15 billion in 1989, but oil revenues then fell because of lower oil prices. In 1993, crude oil export revenues fell to $11.8 billion from $13.4 billion in 1992. This followed a 15 percent decline between 1990 and 1992, despite increased UAE oil production.[486] Oil revenues totaled about $12.3 billion in 1994 and just under $13 billion in 1995.[487]

As a result, the UAE's real GDP dropped by an average of 4.3% per year in constant dollars between 1980 and 1992, largely because of the drop in real oil prices. Combined with the impact of population growth, this made the annual per capita GDP drop from $31,600 in 1983 to $16,880 in 1986, and $13,910 in 1993. This trend is likely to continue in the future. Current estimates of future prices indicate that the UAE's per capita oil and gas earnings might drop by as much as another 25% per decade under a low oil price scenario unless the UAE makes major cuts in its birth rate and reliance on foreign labor.[488]

Oil Reserves and Resources

At the same time, the UAE does, have large oil and gas resources relative to its native population and can increase its oil and gas revenues by boosting production and expanding downstream and upstream operations. The UAE produced about 12.6 billion barrels of oil by the end of 1990, but still had a reserve to production ratio of 75/1.[489] As of 1994, the US Department of Energy estimated that the UAE had total proven oil reserves ranging up to 98.1 billion barrels—equivalent to 9.8% of the world's total reserves.[490]

Chart Forty-Six and Table Thirty-Four show EIA and IEA estimates of the UAE's reserves and of its present and future production capacity. Chart Forty-Seven shows the trends in the UAE's oil production. According to these figures, domestic demand has not risen in ways which significantly reduce export potential, and that there has been a significant increase in the export of refined products. It also indicates, however, that production levels have varied strikingly with world demand.

The UAE produced at a range of 2.2 to 2.4 MMBD of oil and oil equivalent during 1993–1995.[491] The UAE's biggest market for its crude was the

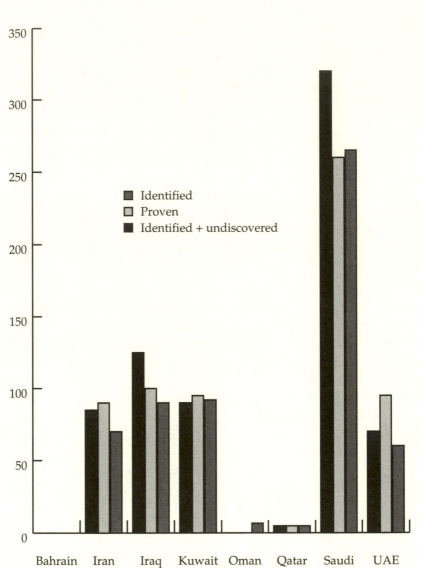

CHART FORTY-SIX Total Oil Reserves of the Gulf States (in Billions of Barrels).
Source: IEA, *Middle East Oil and Gas,* Paris, OECD, IEA, Annex 2, and data
provided by Bahrain and Oman. Bahrain's reserves are only 350 million barrels
and do not show up on the chart because of scale.

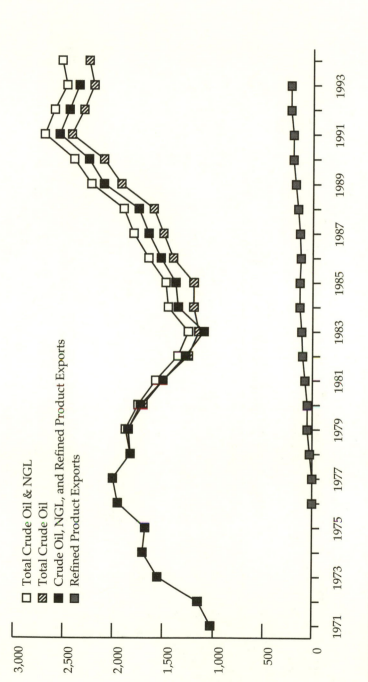

CHART FORTY-SEVEN   Trends in UAE Oil and NGL Production (Thousands of Barrels Per Day). *Source:* Adapted by Anthony H. Cordesman from IAE, *Middle East Oil and Gas*, Paris, OECD/IEA, 1995, pp. 334–344 and Cedigaz.

TABLE THIRTY-FOUR   Comparative Oil Reserves and Production Levels of the Gulf States

Comparative Oil Reserves in 1994 in Billions of Barrels

Country	Identified	Undiscovered	Identified and Undiscovered	Proven	% of World Total
Bahrain	—	—	—	.35	8.9
Iran	69.2	19.0	88.2	89.3	10.0
Iraq	90.8	35.0	125.8	100.0	9.7
Kuwait	92.6	3.0	95.6	96.5	NA
Oman	—	—	—	5.0	0.4
Qatar	3.9	0	3.9	3.7	26.1
Saudi Arabia	265.5	51.0	316.5	261.2	9.8
UAE	61.1	4.2	65.3	98.1	
Total	583.0	112.2	695.2	654.1	64.9
Rest of World	—	—	—	345.7	35.1
World	—	—	—	999.8	100.0

(continues)

TABLE THIRTY-FOUR (continued)

Comparative Oil Production in Millions of Barrels per Day

Country	1995		DOE/IEA Estimate of Actual Production					Maximum Sustainable		Announced Capacity in 2000
	Actual	OPEC Quota	1990	1992	2000	2005	2010	1995	2000	
Bahrain	—	—	—	—	—	—	—	—	—	—
Iran	3,608	3,600	3.2	3.6	4.3	5.0	5.4	3.2	4.5	4.5
Iraq	600	400	2.2	0.4	4.4	5.4	6.6	2.5	5.0	5.0
Kuwait	1,850	2,000	1.7	1.1	2.9	3.6	4.2	2.8	3.3	3.3
Oman	—	—	—	—	—	—	—	—	—	—
Qatar	449	378	0.5	0.4	0.6	0.6	0.6	0.5	0.6	0.6
Saudi Arabia	8,018	8,000	8.5	9.6	11.5	12.8	14.1	10.3	11.1	11.1
UAE	2,193	2,161	2.5	2.6	3.1	3.5	4.3	3.0	3.8	3.2
Total Gulf	—	—	18.6	17.7	26.8	30.9	35.0	23.5	28.2	28.2
World	—	—	69.6	67.4	78.6	84.2	88.8	—	28.2	—

Source: Adapted by Anthony H. Cordesman from estimates in IEA, *Middle East Oil and Gas*, Paris, OED/IEA, 1995, Annex 2 and DOE/EIA, *International Energy Outlook, 1995*, Washington, DOE/EIA, June, 1995, pp. 26–30, and *Middle East Economic Digest*, February 23, 1996, p. 3. IEA and DOE do not provide country breakouts for Bahrain and Oman. Reserve data estimated by author based on country data.

Far East, which accounted for over 80 percent of its crude oil exports. Japan alone imported about 1.2 million barrels per day of UAE crude, and approximately 27 percent of Japan's total oil imports came from the Emirates. Japan also imported large amounts of liquefied natural gas from the UAE.[492]

Production in the UAE is organized by Emirate. Under the federal constitution, each emirate has total responsibility and authority for its oil and gas development, production, and marketing. In practice, contracts and agreements have to be negotiated with the ruling Sheiks of Abu Dhabi, Dubai, Ras Al-Khaimah and Sharjah—the oil and gas producing Emirates. National oil companies account for about half of the oil output, and international companies took the rest. BP accounts for 14%, Total for 13%, Exxon for 2%, Mobil for 2%, Shell for 4% and others for 16%.

Some uncertainties exist as to how the UAE's reserves are divided by Emirate. According to some estimates, Abu Dhabi has estimated proven oil reserves of up to 92.2 billion barrels, and gas reserves of 182.8 trillion cubic feet. Dubai has estimated proven oil reserves of up to 4 billion barrels, and gas reserves of 4.6 trillion cubic feet. Ras al Khaimah has estimated proven oil reserves of up to 0.4 billion barrels, and gas reserves of 1.200 trillion cubic feet, and Sharjah had estimated proven oil reserves of up to 1.5 billion barrels, and gas reserves of 10.7 trillion cubic feet.[493] These figures would give Abu Dhabi about 94 percent of the UAE's total reserves.[494]

Table Thirty-Five shows a different estimate developed by the International Energy Agency. Their estimate indicates that Abu Dhabi has 94% of the UAE's oil reserves, Dubai has 4.1%, Sharjah has 1.5%, and the others have 0.4%. It indicates that Abu Dhabi has 92.1% of the UAE's gas reserves, Dubai has 2.2%, Sharjah has 5.1%, and the others have 0.6%.

Table Thirty-Five also shows that Abu Dhabi's share of crude oil production has risen from around 70% in 1983 to 85.8% in 1993, while Dubai's share has shrunk from about 30% to less than 15%. In contrast, Abu Dhabi's share of NGL production ranged from 33% to 70% during 1983-1993, while Dubai's share has shrunk from peaks of 47% to less than 12%, and Sharjah's share has shrunk from a little over 30% to less than 20%. These data clearly illustrate Abu Dhabi's dominant role as an oil and gas producer.

The UAE has a large internal pipeline network, but does not use this network for exporting. It has 14 oil and gas export terminals, the largest of which are in Abu Dhabi. Abu Dhabi has four terminals on the coast, three on islands, and two on off-shore terminals. Dubai has two on-shore and one off-shore; Sharjah has one on-shore and one off-shore.

TABLE THIRTY-FIVE   UAE: Comparable Oil Reserves and Production by Emirate

Relative Size and Oil Reserves in 1994

			Reserves	
	Area in Square Kilometers	*Population in 1,000s*	*Oil (Billion Bbls.)*	*Gas (BCF)*
Abu Dhabi	67,350	798	92.2	188.4
Dubai	3,900	501	4.0	4.5
Sharjah	2,600	314	1.5	10.5
Others	3,850	296	0.4	1.2
Total	77,700	1,909	98.1	204.6

Relative Crude Oil Production by Emirate (Thousands of Barrels Per Day)

	Abu Dhabi	*Dubai*	*Sharjah & Ras al-Khaimah*	*Total*
1983	802	338	3	1,143
1984	834	369	3	1,206
1985	831	363	3	1,197
1986	1,011	363	2	1,376
1987	1,098	393	3	1,494
1988	1,203	400	3	1,606
1989	1,496	408	3	1,907
1990	1,692	420	5	2,117
1991	2,022	390	4	2,416
1992	1,924	359	5	2,288
1993	1,840	320	5	2,166
1994	1,905	319	5	2,220

Relative Crude Oil and NGL Production by Emirate (Thousands of Barrels Per Day)

	Abu Dhabi	*Dubai*	*Sharjah & Ras al-Khaimah*	*Total*
1983	81	—	27	88
1984	110	72	55	237
1985	90	122	61	274
1986	110	110	56	276
1987	115	115	46	276
1988	125	110	49	284
1989	160	105	37	302
1990	187	55	32	274
1991	216	45	27	288

(continues)

TABLE THIRTY-FIVE   (continued)

	Abu Dhabi	Dubai	Sharjah & Ras al-Khaimah	Total
1992	210	34	52	296
1993	207	33	53	293
1994	204	35	56	294

Source: Adapted by Anthony H. Cordesman from *Oil and Gas Journal*, December 27, 1993; *The Middle East and North Africa, 1993*, Europa Publications, 1994; IEA, *Middle East Oil and Gas*, OECD/IEA, 1995, pp. 331, 336, 337.

Expanding Oil Resources. The UAE is investing heavily in expanding its oil production. Abu Dhabi has projects underway to increase sustainable production to 3.1 MMBD by 1997. The Abu Dhabi National Oil Company (ADNOC) is seeking to increase sustainable oil production by 50% by 2003. Dubai hopes to use enhanced recovery to boost sustainable production to 0.4 MMBD, which would raise the UAE's sustainable production capacity to 3.6 MMBD by 1997 and 3.8 MMBD by 2000.[495]

The Energy Information Agency of the US Department of Energy estimates that the UAE's daily production will increase from 2.5 MMBD in 1990 and 2.6 MMBD in 1992 to 3.1 MMBD by 2000, 3.5 MMBD by 2005, and 4.3 MMBD by 2010. This increase in output is similar to government plans which call for 2.6 MMBD by the late 1990s, and 3.0 MMBD by 2000. Such an expansion will steadily raise the UAE's oil revenues at currently projected oil prices and will be further supplemented by the UAE's plans to expand downstream and gas production.[496]

Most of the UAE's expansion activity with regards to oil production is occurring in the emirate of Abu Dhabi, which has the largest oil reserves and production capacity of the seven emirates. Abu Dhabi now has an OPEC export quota of 2.161 million barrels per day. Its oil production capacity is currently about 2.2–2.3 million barrels per day, of which 1.05 million barrels per day is located offshore and 1.15 million barrels per day onshore. Oil production and upstream capacity is planned to reach between 2.3 and 2.4 million barrels per day by the late 1990s, and reach 2.5 million barrels per day by 2000—although some estimates go as high as 2.9 million barrels per day.[497]

The Abu Dhabi National Oil Company (ADNOC) alone spent about $5.5 billion on new projects over the 13 year period ending in 1991, and has initiated projects with a total cost of $4.65 billion since 1991. Abu Dhabi plans to invest more than $3.28 billion more by the year 2000 to raise its oil production by more than 30 percent, and the Abu Dhabi National Oil Company indicated at a meeting in December, 1995 that it planned to spend a total of nearly $7 billion during 1996–2000 on its downstream oil capabilities and gas gathering network.[498] Dubai, with a much smaller oil and gas reserve base, is concentrating its efforts on diversifying its economy as oil production continues to decline. Sharjah, the third largest energy exporting emirate, has finally seen its finances boosted by recent natural gas finds, and has invested heavily in manufacturing industries.[499]

Abu Dhabi plans to raise output by a third to 1.2 million barrels per day by 1996/97. It has already completed the construction of three new oil storage tanks with the capacity of 1 million barrels each at the Jebel as Dhanah terminal in Abu Dhabi, raising storage capacity at the terminal to over 8.3 million barrels. Jebel as Dhanah opened in 1962 as a service center for oil from the Bab, Bu Hasa, Asab, Sahl and Shah fields.[500]

Plans call for a major increase in production capacity from the Bab field in central Abu Dhabi, from a current 100,000 barrels per day to 250,000 barrels per day. Overall, the project is expected to cost over $300 million and should be completed by the end of 1995. Another phase will eventually raise capacity at the field to 350,000 barrels per day. In addition, the capacity at the Bu Hasa field is being raised by 100,000 barrels per day to 550,000 barrels per day through gas injection. This upgrade is expected to be completed in 1994 at a cost of $90 million.[501]

A new field, Jarn Yaphour, came on line in Abu Dhabi in December 1993. The development of the field started in September 1991 and cost $70 million. The field is pumping 10,000 barrels per day of oil as feedstock for the nearby Umm Al-Nar refinery, plus 60 thousand cubic feet per day (Mcf/d) of natural gas. Zadco is developing production capacity at the offshore lower Zakum field. Capacity should reach 550,000 barrels per day, up from the present 350,000 barrels per day. The field is believed to have a production potential as high as 750,000 barrels per day.[502]

Dubai has not been as successful. Recent offshore exploration activity by the Dubai Petroleum Company (DPC) in its four fields (Fateh, Southwest Fateh, Rashid and Fallah) has not yielded any major finds.[503]

Downstream Operations and Petrochemicals. So far, the UAE has only made a limited investment in downstream operations. Abu Dhabi is the only emirate with refining capabilities. Both of the Emirates' two refineries (Ruwais and Umm al-Nar II) are operated by ADNOC. The $100 million first phase of expansion at the Ruwais refinery entails raising capacity to 250,000–300,000 barrels per day by 1995. The $1.2 billion second phase, which has not yet received approval from the Supreme Petroleum Council, would include the addition of visbreaking, catalytic reforming, kerosene processing, and vacuum topping units as well as an upgrade of the current hydrocracker unit.

The Umm-al Nar II refinery replaced the original Umm-al Nar refinery in July 1983. Umm al-Nar II processes crude from the Asab and Sahl structures, which are part of the Murban Basin. In Dubai, plans for a methyl tertiary butyl ether (MTBE) plant at Jebel Ali are progressing slowly, and work on the promised refinery there is presently stalled.[504]

The UAE is just beginning major petrochemical operations. It started fertilizer operations in the 1980s, but these proved to be an uncertain operation because of price and gas feedstock problems. A 500,000 ton a year MTBE plant began operation in 1995, however, and ADNOC is considering a 300,000 ton ethylene-based complex. Abu Dhabi is also considering a major expansion of its fertilizer plant at Ruwais.[505]

Growing Gas Resources. The US Department of Energy estimates that the UAE has gas reserves of 204.5 trillion cubic feet—giving it about 4.1% of the world's gas reserves and making it the world's fourth largest nation in terms of total gas reserves. Chart Forty-Eight and Table Thirty-Six show EIA and IEA estimates of the comparative size of the UAE's gas reserves relative to those of other Gulf states. Chart Forty-Nine shows the trend in total UAE gas production and that a steadily greater amount is reinjected, marketed, and exported.

The UAE produces about 901.1 billion cubic feet of gas per year, and estimates by the International Energy Agency indicate that Abu Dhabi alone has around 6,320 billion cubic meters (BCM) of gas and 7,280 BCM of ultimate resources—or more than 5% of the world's supply. Table Thirty-Seven shows the distribution of gas reserves and production by Emirate. As has been mentioned previously, Abu Dhabi has 92.1% of the UAE's gas reserves, Dubai has 2.2%, Sharjah has 5.1%, and the rest have 0.6%. Abu Dhabi's share of total UAE production has dropped from around 83% in 1975 to 60% in 1993, Dubai's share has ranged from 14% to 22%, Sharjah's share has risen from less than 3% to over 20%, and Ras al-Khaimah has shrunk from around 2% to 0.3%.

The UAE is seeking a major expansion of its gas production and marketing efforts. Abu Dhabi is seeking to double daily natural gas production between 1998 and 2003, and to export its ligquid natural gas (LNG) exports to Japan during 1996. The UAE has already allocated several billion dollars to expand its natural gas and refining sectors over the next few years.[506] New investments are also planned for UAE's natural gas liquids (NGL) industry. For example, NGL plants at the Bab and Bu Hasa fields are to be upgraded simultaneously to increase the percentage of liquid yielded.[507]

Exports of LNG to Japan began in 1977, and are currently about 2.5 million tons per year. They will probably double to 5 million tons per year by 2000, and the UAE has the potential to export 10 million tons per

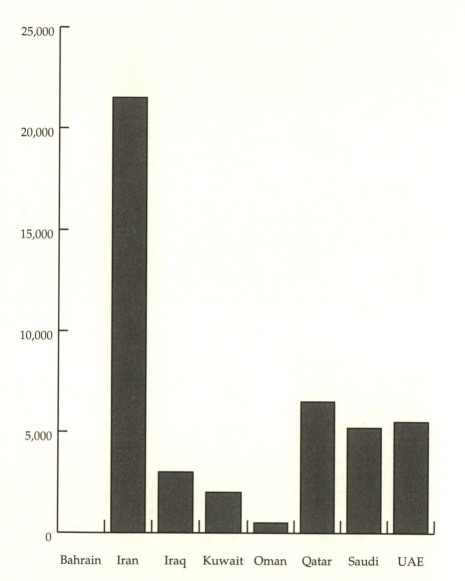

CHART FORTY-EIGHT   Total Oil Reserves of the Gulf States (in Billions of Cubic Meters). *Source:* Adapted by Anthony H. Cordesman from IEA, *Middle East Oil and Gas,* Paris, OECD, IEA, 1995, Annex 2, and data provided by Bahrain and Oman. Bahrain's reserves are too small to show on the chart because of scale.

TABLE THIRTY-SIX   Gulf and World Gas Reserves and Production

Nation	Reserves in 1995		Percent of Total World Supply	Production in 1993 (BCM)
	TCF	*BCM*		
Bahrain	—	—	—	—
Iran	741.6	21,000	14.9	60.0
Iraq	109.5	3,100	2.2	2.75
Kuwait	52.9	1,498	1.1	5.17
Oman	—	600–640	—	—
Qatar	250.0	7,070	5.0	18.4
Saudi Arabia	185.9	5,134	4.2	67.3
UAE	208.7	5,779*	4.2	31.63
Gulf	1,548.6	—	31.1	185.25
Rest of World	3,431.7	104,642	68.9	—
World Total	4,980.3	148,223	100.0	—

Note: *Other sources estimate 6,320–7,280 BCM for Abu Dhabi only.

Source: The reserve and production data are adapted by Anthony H. Cordesman from IEA, *Middle East Oil and Gas,* Paris, OECD, IEA, 1995, Annex 2.

year.[508] ADNOC has completed a major component of its natural gas expansion project at the offshore Abu al Bukhush field. The field will now produce 320 million cubic feet per day of gas and up to 10,000 barrels per day of condensates. The gas will be used as feedstock for the third LNG train on Das Island, which is currently under construction by ADGAS. This train, when completed by mid 1994, will raise Das Island's LNG capacity to 5 million tons per year, as compared to the current 2.5 million tons per year from the existing two trains. Additional feedstock will come from the Umm Shaif field.[509]

Japan's Tokyo Electric Power Co. (Tepco) has recently purchase 2.4 million metric tons per year of liquefied gas from Das Island, and signed an agreement in November of 1993 to double that amount to 5 mmt/y for 25 years starting in 1994.[510] The UAE's successful export partnership with Japan has prompted Thailand to consider similar long-term contracts for LNG purchases. As part of Adnoc's ongoing expansion program, a 25-mile (40-kilometer) pipeline from Zarkwa Island is being built to carry over 50 million cubic feet per day of associated gas to the Das Island treatment plant.[511]

ADNOC has been particularly aggressive in expanding its development of gas resources—partly to meet increases in domestic demand which are projected at 1,200 million cubic feet a day by 1999. It has spent $350 million to expand the Khuff reservoir and over $400 million on the

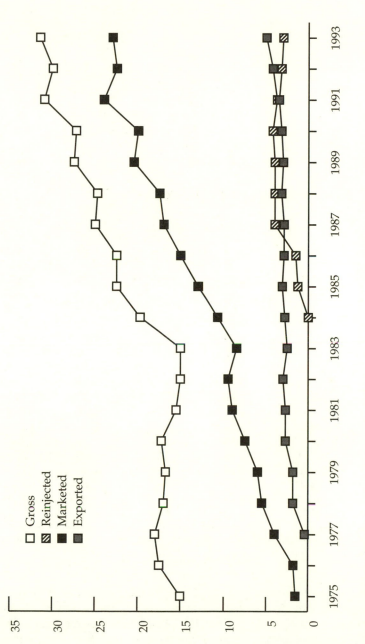

CHART FORTY-NINE Trends in UAE Natural Gas Production (Billions of Cubic Meters). *Source:* Adapted by Anthony H. Cordesman from IAE, *Middle East Oil and Gas,* Paris, OECD/IEA, 1995, pp. 340–341 and Cedigaz.

TABLE THIRTY-SEVEN   UAE: Comparable Gas Reserves and Production by
                      Emirate

Relative Size and Oil Reserves in 1994

| | | | Reserves | |
	Area in Square Kilometers	Population in 1,000s	Oil (Billion Bbls.)	Gas (BCF)
Abu Dhabi	67,350	798	92.2	188.4
Dubai	3,900	501	4.0	4.5
Sharjah	2,600	314	1.5	10.5
Others	3,850	296	0.4	1.2
Total	77,700	1,909	98.1	204.6

Relative Gross Gas Production by Emirate (Billions of Cubic Meters)

	Abu Dhabi	Dubai	Sharjah	Ras al-Khaimah	Total
1975	12.23	2.05	0.40	0.00	14.68
1976	14.31	2.50	0.40	0.00	17.21
1977	15.34	2.51	0.30	0.00	18.15
1978	13.55	2.80	0.25	0.00	16.60
1979	13.62	2.63	0.15	0.00	16.40
1980	14.40	2.60	0.10	0.00	17.10
1981	12.65	2.76	0.10	0.00	15.51
1982	10.72	3.32	0.84	0.00	14.88
1983	9.60	2.55	2.77	0.00	14.92
1984	10.92	3.13	5.29	0.31	19.65
1985	11.49	4.65	5.94	0.28	22.36
1986	12.15	4.65	5.19	0.48	22.47
1987	14.50	4.24	5.91	0.45	25.10
1988	14.98	4.34	5.01	0.40	24.73
1989	17.90	4.65	5.01	0.26	27.82
1990	17.83	4.96	4.86	0.10	27.75
1991	21.30	4.67	4.80	0.09	30.86
1992	18.67	4.65	6.72	0.09	30.13
1993	18.90	5.20	7.44	0.09	31.63

Source: Adapted by Anthony H. Cordesman from *CEDIGAS* and IEA, *Middle East Oil and Gas*, OECD/IEA, 1995, pp. 331, 341.

onshore gas development project. These investments are necessary to meet increased demand for reinjection gas and domestic feedstock that is projected to rise sharply through 2025. Demand for gas for purposes like reinjection is projected to rise from 1,730 million cubic feet per day in 1995 to around 3,000 million in 1999 and 3,700 million cfd in 2025.[512] This demand includes the increasing use of gas to produce water, which is projected to rise by 15% to 800 million cubic feet per day by 1999, and 1,200 million by 2025.

Industrial demand for gas is projected to rise by 30% by 1999, and reach 160 million cubic feet per day. It is estimated to be 500 million cubic feet per day. by 2025. Abu Dhabi is also planning to supply 500 million cubic feet per day to Dubai by 2000.[513] Part of this demand can be met by expanding the use of existing fields, but a substantial part will require new gas development projects. There is a possibility that Abu Dhabi's expansion of supply will fall short of projected demand during some of the period between 1996 and 2025.

In 1992, Amoco Sharjah announced the discovery of an additional 100 million cubic feet per day of natural gas and 15,000 barrels per day of condensates at its onshore concession areas (Sajaa and Moveyeid fields). Sharjah-based Crescent Petroleum is completing a $140 million gas and condensate investment program at the offshore Mubarak field, including the recent installation of a new $32 million production platform. Mubarak is within the territorial waters of Abu Musa, an island over which Iran also claims sovereignty. However, Crescent says it has not experienced any problems with Iran.[514]

Dubai is becoming a net importer of gas. It currently has a net demand of about 500 million cfd, and can meet 80% of that demand from domestic resources. The expansion of downstream facilities, however, will raise demand to around 800 million cfd by 2000. Dubai is considering purchases from Qatar, Oman, and Iran—as well as from Abu Dhabi.[515]

Wealth and Stability

If these oil and gas developments are successful, they should be adequate to maintain a high degree of per capita wealth in the UAE, in spite of its diversification problems. However, the UAE still needs to take steps to properly distribute its wealth, deal with the problems created by its dependence on foreign labor, and restructure its economy to create incentives for investment and creating productive jobs for its native population.

The UAE federal government currently uses fiscal policies that distribute its oil and gas wealth largely through patronage and welfare. The wealthier emirates of Abu Dhabi and Dubai provide support to the less wealthy emirates through the federal budget, which they largely fund, and by providing direct grants. Abu Dhabi alone pays up to 80% of the total federal budget. These efforts, however, leave serious differences in wealth between the Emirates. In 1993, the real per capita GDP in Abu Dhabi, the emirate with the most oil, was $20,664. The real per capita income of Ajman—the smallest and poorest of the seven emirate's—was $4,257.[516]

Furthermore, the UAE uses its oil and gas wealth to avoid taxation and provide subsidies to its population, while it adds other "welfare payments" through law and regulation. Foreigners are not permitted to own real estate in Abu Dhabi or Dubai. There still are no taxes on UAE nationals or income taxes on the large expatriate population. This reliance on the "welfare state" presents growing problems at a time when the UAE has been affected by the same cut in oil prices that has caused a recession or near recession in the other Gulf states. The UAE's real GDP (in 1995 prices) dropped from $29.5 billion in 1993 to $29.0 billion in 1994.[517] Real per capita GDP fell for the fifth consecutive year in every Emirate in 1995.

Budget Deficits and Reduced Welfare Payments. Chart Fifty shows that the UAE has a favorable balance of trade, and Chart Fifty-One shows that the federal government has not experienced a major structural budget crisis because of the growing cost of its subsidies relative to oil income. The UAE has, however, encountered growing budget deficit problems since the early 1980s, and has been in a state of deficit spending during virtually every year since 1981. Like Saudi Arabia and Kuwait, the UAE also encountered significant, near-term funding problems because of the Gulf War. It had a budget deficit of $311 million in 1991, which increased to $1.14 billion in 1992, as the UAE paid off the costs of its support for the UN Coalition.518

The UAE had to freeze its federal budget at its 1993 level through 1995. It announced in mid-1994 that its budget would be cut by 20 percent from planned levels and later that an additional 20 percent would be cut in 1995. As a result, the 1995 budget was kept at the 1994 level. This produced unexpected benefits when rises in oil prices during the first six months of 1995 changed the UAE's initial projections of a $288 million deficit for the period into an estimated $232 million surplus.[519] The UAE now calculates, however, that it had total expenditures of 17,950 million Dirhams ($65,953 million) in 1994 and revenues of 16,900 million Dirhams ($62,073 million)—a deficit of 1,050 million Dirhams ($3,857 million). Estimates for 1995 placed total expenditures of 18,250 million Dirhams ($67,032 million) and revenues of 17,400 million Dirhams ($63,910 million)—a deficit of 850 million Dirhams ($3,122 million). These changes illustrate both the difficulty of predicting oil revenues and the fact that the UAE is likely to experience at least moderate deficits during the immediate future.[520]

In the past, the authorities have attempted to deal with such budget problems by maintaining the distribution of wealth without generating inflation or drawing down on reserves accumulated in years of higher oil prices. The UAE's response to the decline in oil prices during 1985–86 was to draw down on foreign assets and decrease capital spending. The

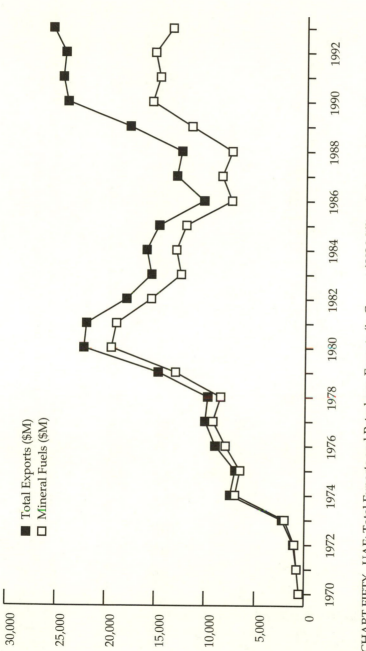

CHART FIFTY UAE: Total Exports and Petroleum Exports (in Current $US Millions). *Source:* Adapted by Anthony H. Cordesman from International Energy Agency (IEA), *Middle East Oil and Gas*, Paris, 1995, pp. 284, 294, and based on IMF, *International Financial Statistics, IMF, World Economic Outlook*, May, 1995, and OECD, *Main Economic Indicators*.

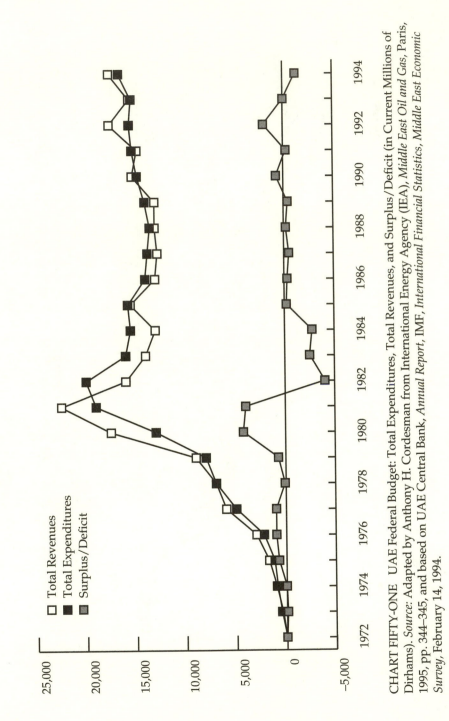

CHART FIFTY-ONE UAE Federal Budget: Total Expenditures, Total Revenues, and Surplus/Deficit (in Current Millions of Dirhams). *Source:* Adapted by Anthony H. Cordesman from International Energy Agency (IEA), *Middle East Oil and Gas*, Paris, 1995, pp. 344–345, and based on UAE Central Bank, *Annual Report*, IMF, *International Financial Statistics, Middle East Economic Survey*, February 14, 1994.

oil price decline of 1993–94 has been comparable to that of 1985–86, but now the UAE has had to both draw down on reserves, and adopt new and previously untried measures to raise revenue and cut expenditures.

These measures include cuts in social services and development. The governments of Abu Dhabi and Dubai have reduced spending on non-oil sector development projects.[521] They have also led the government to increase its income. Revenue raising measures have included raising water and electricity prices, and raising fees, primarily on expatriates, who make up about 70 percent of the population. Expatriates will pay more for visas, residence permits, water, electricity, and medical care. In 1995, expatriates paid an annual tax of $1,300 for each employed, household domestic.[522]

The government has taken other new measures to raise revenues. Effective August 1, 1994, the UAE instituted a new customs duty of four percent on the CIF value of imports which is now collected in full on items that are not exempt. This duty does not apply, however, to the higher tariffs on tobacco and alcohol. The list of exempt items is lengthy and includes items imported by the rulers or the government, items imported from Gulf Cooperation Council (GCC) states, religious materials imported by airlines and charitable institutions, medicines and pharmaceuticals, many different kinds of food, items to be re-exported, farm machinery, construction materials, and newspapers and periodicals.

Other changes include a ban on issuance of licenses authorizing the establishment of 42 different kinds of small business; a reduction in the number of expatriates permitted to bring family members with them to the UAE; and an increase in delay penalties applicable to contracts with the UAE federal government. While the government denies it, the UAE is also considering a sales tax.[523]

Retaining High Liquidity. The UAE has not faced anything like the economic and spending problems of Bahrain, Oman, and Saudi Arabia. It has not had to borrow extensively and economic pressures do not seem to be contributing to internal security problems at the current time.[524] Chart Fifty-Two shows that the UAE has been able to maintain a steady increase in liquidity in the face of the financial impact of shifts in oil prices, rising civil demand, the Iran-Iraq War, and the Gulf War.

The UAE federal government has no official foreign debt, though some individual Emirates are believed to have foreign commercial debts, and there is private external debt. While there are no reliable statistics on either, the amounts involved are not large. The foreign assets of the Abu Dhabi and Dubai governments and their official agencies are believed to be significantly larger than the reserves of the Central Bank.[525]

334

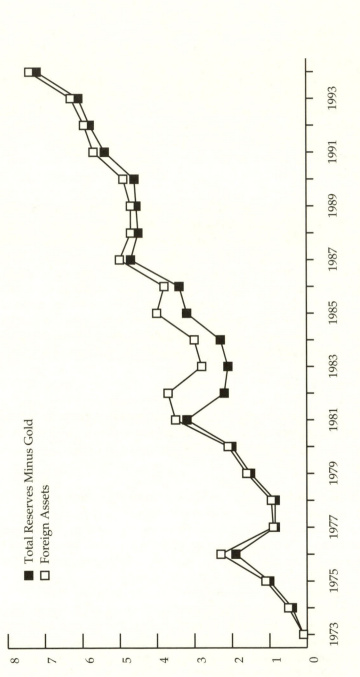

CHART FIFTY-TWO UAE: Liquidity in Billions of US Dollars: 1960–1993. *Source:* Adapted by Anthony H. Cordesman from International Energy Agency (IEA), *Middle East Oil and Gas*, Paris, 1995, pp. 298–299, and based on IMF, *International Financial Statistics*.

According to outside estimates, the UAE's short and long-term debt totaled $0.5 billion and $1.5 billion respectively in 1983. This was about the same as in 1983, even measured in current dollars. Debt as a share of GDP had fluctuated from 23% to 45% during 1982–1993, but only because of the oil-driven swings in GDP and not because of increases in total debt.[526] The UAE does, however, have a domestic debt total of around $19.5 billion with about $18.6 billion lent to business.[527] This debt is growing and does present a potential risk if oil prices should drop sharply in real terms at any point in the near future.

As a result, the UAE should be able to use its recent fiscal measures to achieve a near balance in its budget without further massive cuts in social services. This will minimize one source of economic unrest, but will still leave a serious structural problem in the UAE's economy. Like the other Southern Gulf states, the UAE has made no concerted effort to develop a native work ethic, reduce dependence on foreign labor, or reform its economy to reduce its dependence on the oil, gas, and service industries.

Demographics and the Problem of Foreign Labor

The most critical problem the UAE will face is dealing with the cumulative impact of its rapid population growth and dependence on foreign labor. Chart Fifty-Three shows that a conservative World Bank estimate projects that the UAE's population will grow from 1.6 million in 1990 and 1.8 million in 1995, to 2.0 million by the year 2000, 2.2 million by 2005, 2.3 million by 2010, and 2.6 million by 2020.[528] The CIA estimates that the UAE now has a total population of 2.92 million, including foreigners, a population growth rate of 4.55%, and a fertility rate of 4.53 children per mother. According to UN estimates, the population will double by 2018.[529]

About 35% of the UAE's population is under 14 years of age, and more than 50% is under 19. The total number of young men reaching job age (15–19 years) will rise from 61,000 in 1990 and 81,000 in 1995 to 86,000 in 2000, 93,000 in 2010, and 114,000 in 2020.[530] Chart Fifty-Four shows that the UAE's real per capita income has already dropped significantly in spite of a more favorable trend in its GDP, and this drop could become far more serious in the future.

As has been discussed earlier, over 80% of the total work force of roughly 580,000 is foreign, and 45% of it is Asian.[531] Given the current population growth rate of 4.55%—much of it driven by legal and illegal immigration—this raises serious questions about the UAE's future. Further, many private employers prefer Asian employees which they feel are cheaper, more productive, and easier to fire and hire. This is leading to

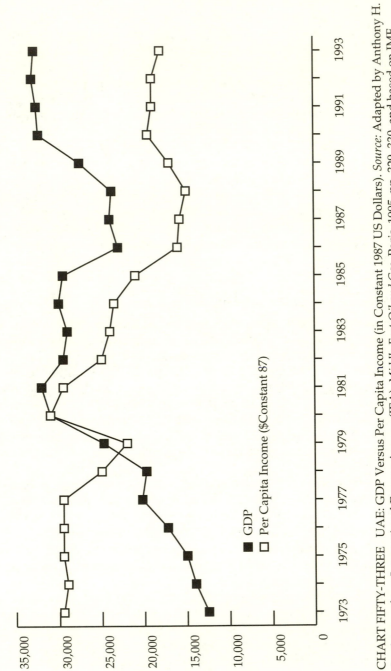

CHART FIFTY-THREE UAE: GDP Versus Per Capita Income (in Constant 1987 US Dollars). *Source:* Adapted by Anthony H. Cordesman from International Energy Agency (IEA), *Middle East Oil and Gas*, Paris, 1995, pp. 329–330, and based on IMF, *International Financial Statistics*, IMF, *World Economic Outlook*, May, 1995, and OECD, *Main Economic Indicators.*

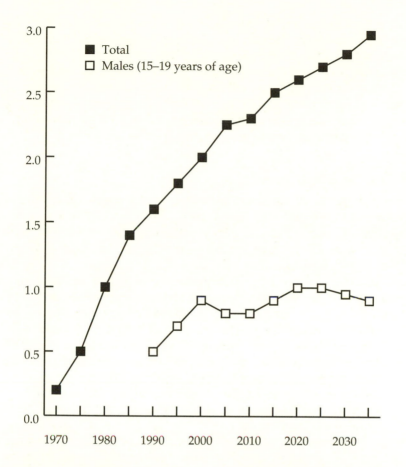

CHART FIFTY-FOUR Estimated Trends in the UAE Population During 1990–2035. *Source:* Adapted by Anthony H. Cordesman from World Bank, *World Population Projections, 1994–1995,* Washington, World.

thousands of illegal immigrants and direct unemployment among UAE nationals has reached 15%, or 15,600 people.[532]

It is extremely doubtful that the UAE can maintain a stable society, or suitable per capita earnings, without more drastic measures to cut its reliance on foreign labor. This, however, will require major shifts in the UAE's educational system and social structure to give native citizens the skills they need to replace foreign workers. Further, UAE laws and regulations now tend to penalize the hiring of UAE citizens because they require higher wages, far more benefits, and create barriers to firing unproductive employees.[533]

The UAE has talked about reforms to deal with this situation, but has done little to implement them. It also has experienced at least one major clash between its Asian foreign laborers and citizens and major riots took place in Dubai in 1994. Although the government quickly exiled troublesome foreign workers, and instituted tighter controls on foreign workers, it took no effective measures to deal with the longer term problem of growing dependence on foreign workers—and the cultural implications of the nation's growing dependence on non-Arab residents.[534]

The Need for Broader Reforms

In summary, the UAE must implement a broad range of economic reforms if it is to preserve the present level of real per capita wealth for its native citizens and avoid seeing its youth become little more than parasites living on an economy dominated by foreign labor, in a nation which has lost its Arab character.

The UAE needs to encourage much more rapid privatization—a step which should both improve development and create more efficient labor structures. To date, the government has made little progress in implementing privatization measures. The federal and individual Emirate governments own many enterprises outright and own shares in others. The government drafted a bill authorizing an official stock exchange in 1994, but the UAE's cabinet has taken no action on it.

The manner in which the government procures civil and military goods also creates problems for effective development. Foreign businesses, except those seeking to sell to the UAE Armed Forces, must have a UAE national sponsor. Agency and distributorship laws require that a business engaged in importing and distributing a foreign-made product must be 100 percent UAE national-owned. Other businesses must be at least 51 percent owned by nationals, and a 1994 law extended these requirements to service businesses for the first time. These policies again create disguised unemployment and profiteering, rather than development.

The end result is that the UAE has the same need for major economic and social reforms as the other Southern Gulf states. UAE officials recognize the need for most of these reforms and are taking some action, but the pace of their activity needs to be accelerated.[535] These action areas include the need to:

- Conduct a popular education program to limit population growth.
- Force radical reductions in the number of foreign workers, with priority for reductions in servants and in trades that allow the most rapid conversion to native labor. Eliminate economic disincentives

for employers hiring native labor, and creating disincentives for hiring foreign labor. The UAE's young and increasingly well-educated population needs to replace its foreign workers as quickly as possible, and it will only develop a work ethic and suitable skills once it is thrust into the labor market.

- Reduce those aspects of state subsidies and welfare that distort the economy and discourage the native population from seeking jobs. It must steadily reduce dependence on welfare, and replace subsidies with jobs.
- Price water, electricity, motor gasoline, basic foods, and other goods and services at market levels.
- Restructure the educational system to focus on job training and competitiveness. Create strong new incentives for faculty and students to focus on job-related education, sharply down-size other forms of educational funding and activity, and eliminate high overhead educational activities without economic benefits.
- Unify and reform the structure of the national budget to reduce the amount of money going directly to royal accounts, and ensure that most of the nation's revenues and foreign reserves are integrated into the national budget and into the planning process. Clearly separate royal and national income and investment holdings.
- Place limits on the transfer of state funds to princes and members of the royal family outside the actual ruling family, and transfers of unearned income to members of other leading families.
- Ensure that all income from enterprises with state financing is reflected in the national budget and is integrated into the national economic development and planning program.
- Freeze and then reduce the number of civil servants, and restructure and down-size the civil service to focus on productive areas of activity with a much smaller pool of manpower. Cut back sharply on state employees by the year 2000.
- Establish market criteria for all major state and state-supported investments. Require detailed and independent risk assessment and projections of comparative return on investment, with a substantial "penalty" for state versus privately funded projects and ventures. Down-size the scale of programs to reduce investment and cash flow costs and the risk of cost-escalation.
- Carry out much more rapid and extensive privatization to increase the efficiency of UAE investments in downstream and upstream operations, to create real jobs and career opportunities for native workers, and to open investment opportunities to a much wider range of investors. Privatization must be managed in ways ensuring an opportunity for all native citizens to share in the privatization

process. Privatization must not be conducted in a manner that benefits a small, elite group of investors and discourages popular confidence and willingness to invest in the UAE.

- Stop subsidizing firms and businesses in ways which prevent realistic economic growth and development, and which deprive the government of revenue. Present policies strongly favor UAE citizens and UAE-owned companies, but in ways which encourage unproductive investments in real estate, construction, and import-driven service industries.
- Avoid offset requirements that simply create disguised unemployment or non-competitive ventures that act as a further state-sponsored distortion of the economy.
- Eliminate economic disincentives for employers hiring native labor, and create disincentives for hiring foreign labor.
- Create new incentives to invest in local industries and business and disincentives for the expatriation of capital. Encourage outside investment.
- Create market driven incentives for foreign investment in major oil and gas projects, refineries, and petrochemical operations. Avoid offset requirements that simply create disguised unemployment or non-competitive ventures that act as a further state-sponsored distortion of the economy.
- Tax earnings and sales with progressive taxes that reduce or eliminate budget deficits, encourage local investment, and create strong disincentives for the expatriation of capital, including all foreign holdings of capital and property by members of elite and ruling families.
- Establish a firm rule of law for all property, contract, permitting, and business activity and reduce state bureaucratic and permitting barriers to private investment.
- Place national security spending on the same basis as other state spending, and fully implement the law the National Assembly passed in 1993 to insure that all direct and indirect defense costs—including arms—are reflected in the national budget. Integrate it fully into the national budget, including investment and equipment purchases.
- Replace the present emphasis on judging arms purchases on the basis of initial procurement costs and technical features with a full assessment of life cycle cost—including training, maintenance, and facilities.
- Cease buying arms in an effort to win outside political support and establish specific procedures and regulations for evaluating the value of standardization and interoperability with existing national

equipment and facilities, those of other Gulf states, and those of the US and other power projection forces.

- Subject all offset proposals relating to government military and non-military expenditures to the same risk and cost-benefit analyses used by the private sector, and create independent auditing procedures to ensure that offsets do not become a concealed government subsidy or a way of benefiting influential government officials.
- Create a long-term planning effort focusing on periods five, ten, and twenty years into the future to set goals for Kuwait's social, economic, and military development, with special attention to the problems of population growth, reducing dependence on foreign labor, diversifying the economy, and linking development to a clear set of social goals. Use contingency and risk analysis, not simply growth-oriented models.

The UAE's Military Forces

The federal armed forces of the UAE were created on May 5, 1976—some five years after independence—when the Trucial Oman Scouts were merged with the Abu Dhabi Defense Forces. The current size of the UAE's forces relative to Iran, Iraq, Saudi Arabia and the total forces of the GCC is shown in Table Thirty-Eight. It is clear from these figures that the UAE can only defend against Iranian intimidation or military action with the help of its neighbors and the West.

The forces of Abu Dhabi, Dubai, Ras Al Khaimah, and Sharjah were formally merged in 1976, but much of the UAE's defense and arms efforts are still wasted on internal rivalry.[536] Elements of the UAE's military forces remain under the *de facto* command of individual ruling Sheiks, and Dubai maintains two independent brigades while the other smaller Emirates maintain independent control over other elements of their forces.

The command of the UAE's forces is divided so that the Ministry of Defense is in Dubai and the General Headquarters is in Abu Dubai, and each of the Emirates retains control over its own forces. The command of the armed forces reflects a similar split between Abu Dhabi and Dubai. The armed forces are under the command of President Zayed bin Sultan Al Nahyyan, the ruler of Abu Dhabi. Mohamed bin Rashid al-Maktum—the crown prince of Dubai—is the Federal Minister of Defense. Lt. General Mohamed bin Zayed Al Nahyyan of Abu Dhabi is Chief of Staff. Sheik Khalifa bin Zayed Al Nahyyan—the crown prince of Abu Dhabi—is Deputy Commander.[537]

While the UAE's arms purchases were supposed to be centralized after 1976, this simply did not occur. Dubai, for example, has bought Italian-made tanks to have a supply of arms that Abu Dhabi could not influence.

TABLE THIRTY-EIGHT Gulf Military Forces in 1996

	Iran	Iraq	Bahrain	Kuwait	Oman	Qatar	Saudi Arabia*	UAE	Yemen
Manpower									
Total Active	320,000	382,500	10,700	16,600	43,500	11,100	161,500	70,000	39,500
Regular	220,000	382,500	10,700	16,600	37,000	11,100	105,500	70,000	39,500
National Guard & Other	100,000	0	0	0	6,500	0	57,000	0	0
Reserve	350,000	650,000	0	23,700	0	0	0	0	40,000
Paramilitary	135,000	24,800	9,250	5,200	4,400	0	15,500	2,700	30,000
Army and Guard									
Manpower	260,000	350,000	8,500	10,000	31,500	8,500	127,000	65,000	37,000
Regular Army Manpower	180,000	350,000	8,500	10,000	25,000	8,500	70,000	65,000	37,000
Reserve	350,000	450,000	0	0	0	0	20,000	0	40,000
Tanks	1,350	2,700	81	220	85	24	910	133	1,125
AIFV/Recce, Lt. Tanks	515	1,600	46	130	136	50	1,467	515	580
APCs	550	2,200	235	199	7	172	3,670	380	560
Self Propelled Artillery	294	150	13	38	6	28	200	90	30
Towed Artillery	2,000	1,500	36	0	96	12	270	82	483
MRLs	890	120	9	0	0	4	60	48	220
Mortars	3,500	2,000+	18	24	74	39	400	101	800
SSM Launchers	46	12	0	0	0	0	10	6	30
Light SAM Launchers	700	3,000	65	48	62	58	650	36	700
AA Guns	1,700	5,500	0	0	18	12	10	62	372
Air Force Manpower	20,000	15,000	1,500	2,500	4,100	800	18,000	3,500	1,000
Air Defense Manpower	15,000	15,000	0	0	0	0	4,000	0	0

(continues)

TABLE THIRTY-EIGHT (continued)

	Iran	Iraq	Bahrain	Kuwait	Oman	Qatar	Saudi Arabia*	UAE	Yemen
Total Combat Aircraft	295	353	24	76	46	12	295	97	69
Bombers	0	6	0	0	0	0	0	0	0
Fighter/Attack	150	130	12	40	19	11	112	41	27
Fighter/Interceptor	115	180	12	8	0	1	122	22	30
Recce/FGA Recce	8	0	0	0	12	0	10	8	0
AEW C4I/BM	0	1	0	0	0	0	5	0	0
MR/MPA**	6	0	0	0	7	0	0	0	0
OCU/COIN	0	18	0	11	13	0	36	15	0
Combat Trainers	92	200	0	11	22	0	66	35	12
Transport Aircraft**	68	34	3	4	14	5	49	20	19
Tanker Aircraft	4	2	0	0	0	0	16	0	0
Armed Helicopters**	100	120	10	16	0	20	12	42	8
Other Helicopters**	509	350	8	36	37	7	138	42	21
Major SAM Launchers	204	340	12	24	0	0	128	18	87
Light SAM Launchers	60	200	0	12	28	9	249	34	0
AA Guns	0	0	0	12	0	0	420	0	0
Navy Manpower	38,000	2,500	1,000	1,500	4,200	1,800	17,000	1,500	1,500
Major Surface Combatants									
Missile	5	0	3	0	0	0	8	0	0
Other	2	1	0	0	0	0	0	0	0
Patrol Craft									
Missile	10	1	4	2	4	3	9	10	7

(continues)

TABLE THIRTY-EIGHT (continued)

	Iran	Iraq	Bahrain	Kuwait	Oman	Qatar	Saudi Arabia*	UAE	Yemen
Other	26	7	5	12	8	6	20	18	3
Submarines	2	0	0	0	0	0	0	0	0
Mine Vessels	3	4	0	0	0	0	5	0	3
Amphibious Ships	8	0	0	0	2	0	0	0	2
Landing Craft	17	3	4	6	4	1	7	4	2

Notes: Does not include equipment in storage. Air Force totals include all helicopters, and all heavy surface to air missile launchers.

*60,000 reserves are National Guard Tribal Levies. The total for land forces includes active National Guard equipment. These additions total 262 AIFVs, 1,165 APCs, and 70 towed artillery weapons.

**Includes navy, army, national guard, and royal flights, but not paramilitary.

Source: Adapted by Anthony H. Cordesman from International Institute for Strategic Studies *Military Balance* (IISS, London), in this case, the 1995–1996 edition; *Military Technology, World Defense Almanac, 1994–1995*; and Jaffee Center for Strategic Studies, *The Military Balance in the Middle East, 1993–1994* (JCSS, Tel Aviv, 1994).

Even the command structure is uncertain. As a result of the power struggles between Abu Dhabi and Dubai, the responsibility for command, personnel, logistics, support matters, and procurement seems to vary according to the nature of internal politics and external crises. Abu Dhabi's forces are the only elements of the UAE armed forces that regularly participate in GCC exercises, although Dubai has sometimes contributed to such exercises.

UAE Military Spending and Arms Imports

Recent trends in UAE military expenditures and arms imports, measured in constant dollars, are shown in Chart Fifty-Five. This chart shows that the Emirates have collectively spent a great deal of their total central government budget on military forces. Other reporting indicates that expenditures reached a peak of 66.9% of all central government expenditures during the Gulf War.

The broad trends in UAE military expenditures reflect its response to the threat Iran posed during the Iran-Iraq War and then the threat Iraq posed during the Gulf War. The UAE increased its annual military expenditures from around $822 million in 1978, to $1,900 to $2,100 million during 1981 through 1985. Defense spending dropped to around $1.6 billion during 1986–1990, but climbed in 1991 in reaction to Iraq's invasion of Kuwait, peaking at $4.9 billion. Military spending has since dropped to a little under $2 billion a year, although the UAE has faced far fewer cash flow problems than many of its neighbors.[538]

The US Arms Control and Disarmament Agency (ACDA) estimates that the UAE's annual military expenditures in current dollars totaled $1,197 million in 1979, $1,724 million in 1980, $1,980 million in 1982, $1,973 million in 1983, $1,919 million in 1984, $1,888 million in 1985, $1,569 million in 1986, $1,577 million in 1987, $1,577 million in 1988, $1,577 million in 1989, $2,572 million in 1990, $4,867 million in 191, $2,083 million in 1992, $2,100 million in 1993, and $1,907 million in 1994.[539] The IISS estimates that the UAE spent $2,110 million on military forces in 1993, $1,910 million in 1995, and $1,880 billion in 1995.[540]

ACDA estimates that UAE has spent from 6 to 14 percent of its GDP on military forces during the last decade, and 37% to 67% of its central government expenditures.[541] These expenditures represent a steadily more significant level of effort for a small country. Much of this effort has been wasted, however, because of divisions between the Emirates and because the UAE has emphasized the "glitter factor" of acquiring unique mixes of military technology over military effectiveness.

Chart Fifty-Five shows that the UAE's arms imports were relatively moderate through 1989, ranging from $60 million to $294 million annu-

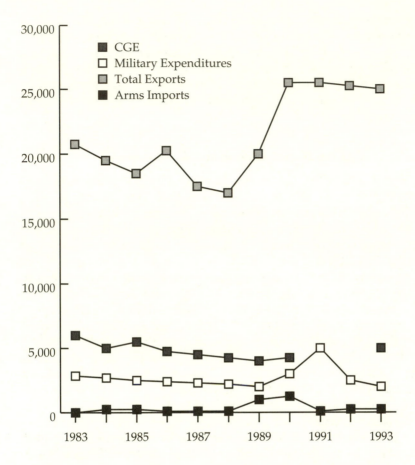

CHART FIFTY-FIVE   UAE Central Government Expenditures, Military
Expenditures, Total Exports, and Arms Import Deliveries: 1983–1993 (Constant
$93 Millions). *Source:* Adapted by Anthony H. Cordesman from ACDA, *World
Military Expenditures and Arms Transfers, 1993–1994,* ACDA/GPO, Washington,
1995.

ally in constant dollars. ACDA estimates of deliveries in current dollars
indicate that the UAE imported $150 million worth of arms in 1979, $170
million in 1980, $240 million in 1981, $50 million in 1982, $40 million in
1983, $190 million in 1984, $220 million in 1985, $170 million in 1986, $150
million in 1987, $120 million in 1988, $875 million in 1989, $1,400 million
in 1990, $370 million in 1991, $360 million in 1992, and $430 million in
1993, and $200 million in 1994.[542]

These annual arms import expenditures reflect reasonable levels of
effort for a state the size of the UAE, but the Emirates have made little

effort to make use of a standard set of arms suppliers, or to emphasize the necessary degree of interoperability and standardization within their own forces. The UAE has fluctuated between political arms purchases designed to reinforce its relations with a given Western country, and an effort to produce the most advanced weapon possible with some unique features that the UAE feels gives the weapon special status or prestige. As a result, the UAE has often insisted on mixes of weapons that force the supplier to attempt new forms of weapons system integration, and features that may have individual value but are difficult to integrate into effective war fighting capability.

While the arms buys of other Gulf countries also emphasize supplier politics and technological "glitter" over military effectiveness, the UAE has the worst track record in managing its military procurements of any Gulf state. These procurement problems are reflected in the UAE's shift in its choices of supplier country. The UAE's total arms imports during 1979–1983 totaled $620 million. Roughly $20 million came from the US, $350 million came from France, $90 million from the UK, $110 million from Germany, $30 million from Italy, and $20 million from other states.[543] Its total arms imports during 1984–1988 totaled $620 million, and showed a shift towards imports from the US. Some $20 million came from the USSR, $350 million came from the US, $180 million from the UK, $70 million from the Germany, and $30 million from other states.[544]

The UAE shifted back to dependence on European suppliers before the Gulf War. ACDA estimates that the UAE signed a total of $2,175 million worth of new arms agreements during 1987–1991, with $20 million coming from Russia, $450 million from the US, $1,400 million from France, $5 million from the UK, $20 million from China, $90 million from West Germany, $60 million from other European countries, $90 million from East Asian countries, $20 million from Middle Eastern countries, and $20 million from other countries.[545]

The UAE then shifted suppliers again after the Gulf War. ACDA estimates that the UAE took delivery on a total of $995 million worth of new arms agreements during 1992–1994, with $260 million coming from Russia, $360 million from the US, $110 million from France, $10 million from other European countries, $5 million from Middle Eastern countries, $30 million from East Asian countries, and $190 million from other countries.[546]

Chart Fifty-Six shows the broad trends reflected in more recent US government data on UAE arms imports. It is based on data taken from work by Richard F. Grimmett of the Congressional Research Service and indicates that the UAE signed a total of $1 billion worth of major new arms agreements in current dollars during 1987–1990. A total of $300 million came from the US, $300 million from major West European countries, and $400 million from all other countries.

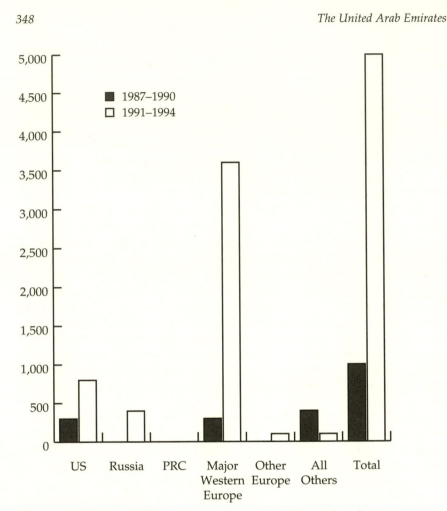

CHART FIFTY-SIX   UAE Arms Sales Agreements by Supplier Country:
1987–1994 ($Current Millions). *Source:* Adapted by Anthony H. Cordesman from
work by Richard F. Grimmett in *Conventional Arms Transfers to Developing
Nations, 1987–1994,* Congressional Research Service 95-862F, August 4, 1995,
pp. 56–57.

Chart Fifty-Six also indicates that the UAE made major increases in
its orders as a result of both the Gulf War and growing concern with the
Iranian threat following its seizure of Abu Musa and the Tunbs. The
UAE signed $5.0 billion worth of new agreements during 1991–1994,
with $800 million coming from the US, $400 million coming from Russia, $3.6 billion from major West European countries, $100 million com-

ing from other European countries, and $100 million from all other countries.[547]

This same source reports a total of $2.5 billion worth of major new arms deliveries during 1987–1990, with $300 million coming from the US, $2.1 billion from major Western European countries, and $100 million from all other countries. The delay between new orders and deliveries has meant that the UAE only received $1.3 billion worth of major deliveries during 1991–1994, with $600 million coming from the US, $300 million coming from Russia, $200 million coming from major West European states, and $200 million from all other states.[548]

Table Thirty-Nine shows how the UAE's major investments in military modernization and arms since the Gulf War break down by major weapons system. As the following discussion indicates, most of these purchases involve some aspect of the UAE's search for unique mixes of weapons technology and for high performance "glitter."

The recent trends in UAE orders from the US are shown in more detail in Table Forty. Reporting by the US Defense Security Assistance Agency shows that the delivery of past UAE arms orders was accelerated during the Gulf War, and that the UAE signed significant new FMS sales agreements as a result of the Gulf War. It ordered $492 million worth of arms in fiscal year 1992, $69 million worth in 1993, and $227 million worth in 1994. This was only a limited portion of the UAE's total orders, however, and the UAE has placed comparatively few orders for commercial sales from the US.

All US sales to the UAE are cash transactions. The UAE does not make use of US military construction services, the International Military Education and Training (IMET) program, or Military Assistance Program (MAP) aid.[549]

The UAE does impose some of the stiffest offset requirements of any nation in the developing world. Contractors are often required to finance joint ventures over a seven to ten year period that are equal to 60% of the value of the contract. These requirements are often eased, however, if the offset provides the UAE with added technology and/or training. This requirement sometimes imposes problems, because the UAE's economy is relatively small and lacks trained native labor. A number of "offset" ventures have notable amounts of disguised unemployment and their long-term profitability is uncertain.

UAE Military Manpower

The CIA estimates that there are now about 1,072,000 males in the age group between 15 and 49, and 584,000 are estimated to be fit for military

TABLE THIRTY-NINE   Key UAE Equipment Developments

- Examining the option of joining Saudi Arabia in accepting a West German proposal to up-engine the AMX-30, and install a new fire control system, and make other improvements.
- On February 21, 1993, announced it would purchase 390 "tropicalized" Leclerc tanks—and 46 recovery vehicles and logistic support. Leclercs will have advanced thermal sights. Training for conversion to the Leclerc began in January 1995, and deliveries of tanks and ammunition will continue through 1999. Package will include Giat squadron-level command systems with regimental, command systems under development, and digitally sorted mapping systems within the tank.[550]
- Dubai considering the purchase of 72–100 additional tanks for its forces to replace its 36 aging OF-40s, and expand its forces from one armored battalion to three—creating an armored brigade. It is also considering the purchase of up to 100 Leclercs, T-72s, or T-80Us.
- In May 1992, Abu Dhabi ordered 240–250 Russian BMP-3 mechanized infantry combat vehicles, with an option for 400 more.
- Dubai is considering additional purchases of 130–150 BMP-3s and/or BTR-80s.
- Abu Dhabi has ordered 78 155 mm self-propelled G-6 gun systems from Denel of South Africa in 1990.
- The UAE has acquired 18 LAU-97 70 mm and 24–40 FIROS-25 122 mm multiple rocket launchers, and has purchased 85–87 surplus M-109A3 self-propelled 155 mm howitzers from the Netherlands, which will be upgraded with NBC protection and to use extended range Swiss round with ranges of 25 kilometers (32 kilometers with an assisted range round).
- Examining possible purchases of 120 mm towed rifle mortars from France, French self-propelled or towed 155 mm howitzers, and Russian BM-9A52 Smerch 300 mm multiple rocket launch systems.
- Abu Dhabi has ordered the advanced twin launcher version of the French Mistral air defense systems mounted on "Humvees." Dubai is also interested in the British short-range Starburst system. The UAE recognizes that it also needs longer range systems, and is currently studying possible purchases of systems like the Crotale.
- Considering the purchase of up to 70–80 F-16Us, F-15Us, Mirage-2000Cs, Mirage 2000-5s, Rafales, MiG-29s, Su-25TKs, Su-27Bs, Su-30MK5s, or Su-35s—although an initial purchase of 32–40 aircraft seems more likely. Seeks aircraft tailored to improve BVR combat capability, as well as attack capability.
- Considering buying as many as 10 more Mirage 2000 fighters.
- Seeking to procure a new long range stand off attack missile.
- Considering the purchase of up to 40 more Hawk 100 trainers, including 40 for Dubai.
- Has actively investigated ordering C-130s equipped for electronic warfare, ordering E-2C Hawkeyes for the AWACS and maritime surveillance role, and ordering two BN-Defender AEW aircraft.

(continues)

TABLE THIRTY-NINE   (continued)

- Has 20 AH-63 Apache attack helicopters, which it purchased with 4,000 Hydra rockets and 360 Hellfire missiles.
- Some reports indicate that the UAE has 30 A-129 Mangustas and Lynx helicopters on order. Other reports indicate that the UAE is considering plans to acquire up to 40 Agusta AB-412HP Griffons, 10 IAR 330-L Pumas, and/or a significant number of AS-532 Cougar or Westland WS-70 Black Hawk helicopters. The UAE also seems to be considering purchase of more C-130s, or CASA/IPTN CN-235 aircraft.
- Evaluating the purchase of 10 Patriot missile launchers, or three batteries of Russian SV-300 (SA-10/12) missiles.
- Purchased a far more sophisticated C⁴I/BM system from Westinghouse. It purchased this system in February 1993, and it will include radars, computers, communications systems, and software—including radars mounted on tethered ballons to provide some of the range and look-down capabilities of an AWACS. The UAE is also examining the possible purchase of Lockheed Martin FPS-117(E)1, Marconi Martello 743-D, Westinghouse W-2100, Thomson-CSF TRS 22-XX, and Alenia RAT-31SL long range surveillance radars.
- Issued a statement of requirements in mid-1993 for four to eight frigates of about 2,500 tons, equipped with a helicopter with dipping sonar, surface-to-surface missile, surface-to-air missile, and ASW capability.
- The UAE is also examining the purchase of ASW systems to refit its existing ships.
- Considering the purchase of mine warfare vessels like the Eridan and Sandown class vessels. Also considering purchase of rapid interception craft.
- Bought seven new AS-565SA Panthers and will retrofit five AS-552 Cougar helicopters to upgrade its naval air forces with ASW and improved anti-surface capability. (Panthers will be delivered in mid-1998, and will have AS15TT antiship.) The Cougars will have AM39 Exocet missiles.

---

service.[551] The IISS estimates that there are 82,600 males between the ages of 13 and 17, 72,000 between the ages of 18 and 22, and 140,400 between the ages of 23 and 32. This population, however, is only about 19% native Emirian and only about 19,300 male citizens reach the age of 16 each year.

There are an increasing number of native Emirians in the armed forces, but the UAE is forced to recruit extensively from other foreign countries.[552] The UAE has talked about conscription, but has not implemented it, and lacks the population and political consensus to do so. As a result, the UAE has been able to increase the number of Emirians in its armed forces but remains dependent on foreign manpower from Jordan, Oman, the Sudan and Pakistan. There are also Pakistani contract pilots, and some contract British officers.

TABLE FORTY   US Foreign Military Sales (FMS), Commercial Arms Export Agreements, Military Assistance Programs (MAP), and International Military Education and Training (IMET) Programs with the UAE: FY1985–1994 (Current Millions)

	1985	1986	1987	1988	1989	1990	1991	1992	1993	1994
Foreign Military Financing Program Payment Waived	—	—	—	—	—	—	—	—	—	—
DoD Direct	—	—	—	—	—	—	—	—	—	—
DoD Guarantee	—	—	—	—	—	—	—	—	—	—
FMS Agreements	60.8	1.9	99.5	156.4	51.8	8.8	24.1	491.8	69.3	226.7
Commercial Sales	17.0	22.4	4.7	8.8	19.8	33.6	17.8	-6.7	5.1	4.1
FMS Construction Agreements	5.1	—	—	—	—	—	—	—	—	—
FMS Deliveries	—	10.7	83.9	37.3	86.3	66.7	282.3	205.3	97.7	41.0
MAP Program	—	—	—	—	—	—	—	—	—	—
MAP Deliveries	—	—	—	—	—	—	—	—	—	—
MAP Excess Defense Articles Program	—	—	—	—	—	—	—	—	—	—
MAP Excess Defense Articles Deliveries	—	—	—	—	—	—	—	—	—	—
IMET Program/ Deliveries	—	—	—	—	—	—	—	—	—	—

Source: Adapted from US Defense Security Assistance Agency (DSAA), "Foreign Military Sales, Foreign Military Construction Sales and Military Assistance Facts as of September 30, 1994," Department of Defense, Washington, 1995.

The UAE's forces have suffered in recent years from friction between native UAE and Omani personnel. Some 6,000–7,000 Omanis have been forced to leave the UAE's armed forces—largely because of concerns over the loyalty of the Omanis and possible Omani ambitions regarding the eastern Emirates. The UAE also seems to have dismissed some of its Jordanian and Sudanese personnel as a result of the Gulf War, although the number of Jordanians was reduced even before Jordan aligned itself with Iraq in 1990.

Despite these manpower problems, Chart Fifty-Seven shows that the UAE has expanded its total military forces from 25,000 men in the early 1980s to 44,000 in 1985, and 70,000 in mid-1996. This latter figure may be exaggerated, given the loss of Omani personnel and reports that the UAE is reducing its manning in some areas to free up funds for modernization.

Manpower quality, however, remains a problem. Although the UAE has been able to train an increasing number of native personnel, its current military forces still seem to be 30–50% expatriate. They include many Asian and still include some Omanis. The UAE does not have a strong NCO corps, and provides inadequate technical training. Although a number of UAE military personnel train overseas—up to 1,000 in the US—it still needs to make major improvements in its military training and military schools. The UAE is the only Southern Gulf army to have trained women for combat. During the build-up following Iraq's invasion of Kuwait, Sheik Zayed sent 74 women to the US for training by US Army female personnel. This training, however, was largely a political gesture.[553]

The UAE Army

The UAE Army has a nominal strength of 65,000 men, including significant numbers of Omanis. Its order of battle is largely under the control of Abu Dhabi, and these forces include six brigades, with one armored brigade, one mechanized infantry brigade, two infantry brigades, a royal guard brigade, and artillery brigade. Dubai controls two additional brigades, and the other Emirates have small units.[554]

Abu Dhabi has the Western Command with most of the UAE's military manpower, one armored brigade, one mechanized brigade and the royal guard brigade. Dubai has the Central Military Region with 5,000 men and one brigade. Ras al-Khaimah has the Northern Military District with 1,700 men, and one brigade. Sharjah has its own regimental or brigade sized unit. Each military district is under the command of a son of the ruling sheik of the individual sheikdom involved, and the smaller Sheikdoms have their independent guard forces and commands. Abu Dhabi contributes elements of its mechanized brigade to the Peninsular Defense Force at King Khalid Military City in Saudi Arabia.

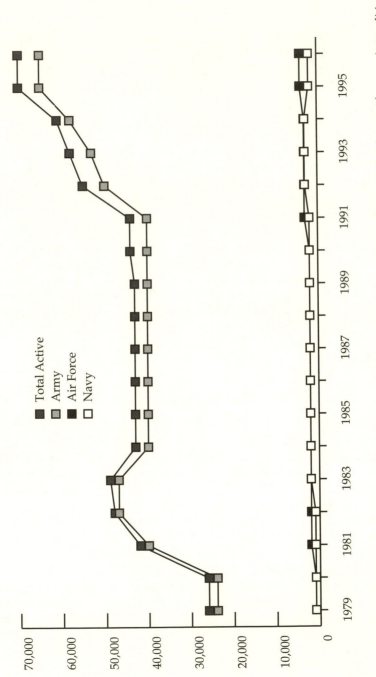

CHART FIFTY-SEVEN UAE: Military Manning—1979–1996. *Source:* Adapted by Anthony H. Cordesman from various editions of the IISS, *Military Balance,* the JCSS, *Military Balance in the Middle East,* and material provided by US experts.

Major Equipment

Chart Fifty-Seven has shown the trend in army manpower, and Charts Fifty-Eight and Fifty-Nine show the build-up in UAE military manpower. Army equipment is a problem for a number of reasons, primarily standardization, interoperability, and obsolescence.

The UAE's heavy armor now consists of 133 main battle tanks, divided into 95 AMX-30s, 30–36 OF-40 Lions, and 2 Leclercs.[555] The AMX-30s are in two battalions in Abu Dhabi, and sources disagree as to whether there are 64 AMX-30s plus four recovery vehicles, or all 95 AMX-30s plus six recovery vehicles, in active service. In any case, the AMX-30s are lightly armored, lack modern firepower systems, and are obsolete. For several years, Abu Dhabi has been examining the option of joining Saudi Arabia in accepting a German proposal to up-engine the AMX-30, install a new fire control system, and make other improvements.

The OF-40s are Italian versions of the German Leopard, and are virtually part of a different force. Dubai took delivery on the first 18 OTO Melara OF-40s in 1981, and then 18 more plus three armored recovery vehicles. It has converted all of its OF-40s to the improved Mark 2 version, but its tank force has never had more than minimal effectiveness.[556]

The UAE recognizes that it needs new tanks if it is to develop the kind of strength that can help its neighbors deal with a threat from either Iraq or Iran. It began to examine possible replacements for its tanks in combination with Saudi Arabia in the late 1980s. Candidates included the Leclerc, the EE-T1 with either a 105 mm or 120 mm gun, the Challenger, the M-1A1/2, and the T-80.

According to some reports, the UAE came close to signing an order for 337 M-1A1 tanks, and 160–164 Bradley M-2 fighting vehicles, and 800–900 high mobility multi-purpose wheeled vehicles in 1991, but delayed the order pending further trials of the M-1, Challenger, and Leclerc in Kuwait. The UAE delayed ordering US tanks in part because of financing problems, and in part because it was told it could not get Congressional approval of the sale of a version of the M-1A2 with both advanced armor and shells with depleted uranium.

The UAE ultimately decided on the Leclerc—which it had been examining for several years—because France promised to provide both capabilities equivalent to the M-1A2 and depleted uranium rounds.[557] On February 21, 1993, the UAE announced that it would purchase 390 "tropicalized" Leclerc tanks, 46 recovery vehicles, crew training, and logistic support—at a cost of roughly $4.3 billion. The Leclercs will have advanced thermal sights—the value of such sights is one of the key lessons of the Gulf War—and a 1,500 horsepower MTU-833 power pack and Renk transmission. Training for conversion to the Leclerc began in

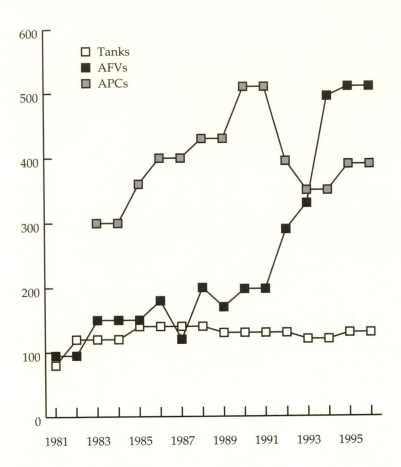

CHART FIFTY-EIGHT   UAE: Armored Weapons Strength—1981–1996.
Source: Adapted by Anthony H. Cordesman from various editions of the IISS,
Military Balance, the JCSS, *Military Balance in the Middle East,* and material
provided by US experts.

January, 1995, and deliveries of tanks and ammunition will continue
through 1999. France has agreed to a generous offset package, which will
include Giat squadron-level command systems with regimental, command systems under development, and digitally sorted mapping systems within the tank.[558]

   These purchases present potential problems for a number of reason.
Although it has very good specifications, the Leclerc is unproven in com-
bat and extensive field operations and past experience with tanks like the
M-1A1 and Challenger has shown that Western tanks rarely are truly oper-

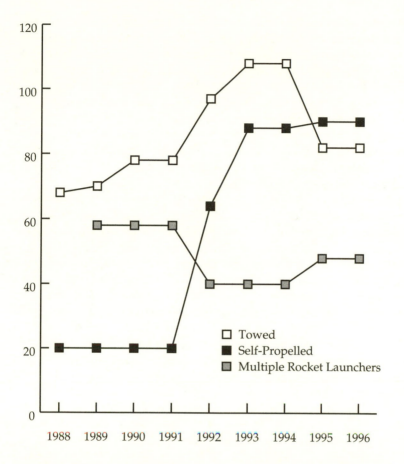

CHART FIFTY-NINE   UAE: Artillery Weapons Strength—1988–1996.
Source: Adapted by Anthony H. Cordesman from various editions of the IISS,
Military Balance, the JCSS, *Military Balance in the Middle East,* and material
provided by US experts.

ational at the point they enter combat units. In spite of field trials, modern
test and evaluation techniques virtually always fail to bring complex combat systems to the point where they are combat ready until they have had
several years of use by actual combat units. Virtually all Western-made
modern weapons systems require major modification to perform well in
sustained combat. Further, the Leclerc is not standardized with other tanks
in the Gulf, and is not interoperable in terms of supply and sustainment.

The Giat deal has also become something of a nightmare for the UAE
because the firm failed to properly cost the contract, and members of the

corporate staff concealed the true cost of production of the tank and speculated in foreign currency exchange rates with loses in excess of $524 million. As a result, Giat stands to lose $2.38 billion on the Leclerc, and $1.17 billion of this loss will come from the $3.6 billion Leclerc contract with Abu Dhabi. Further, Giat has $645.2 million in offset liabilities to the UAE, with up to $201.6 million in penalties if it does meet these requirements. It also must bring all of the tanks up to the latest French standard by the time the contract is complete and evidently did not fully include this cost in the contract—which might reach $443.6 million. Giat is effectively bankrupt and this confronts the UAE with having to down-size the contract, force the company into collapse, or rebid the contract. There is a strong possibility that Abu Dhabi may have to cut back its tank purchases to around 300 tanks if it does go forward with the present contract.[559]

Dubai is considering the purchase of 72–100 additional tanks for its forces to replace its 36 aging OF-40s, and expand its forces from one armored battalion to three—creating an armored brigade. It is also considering the purchase of up to 100 Leclercs, T-72s or T-80Us.[560] Dubai's plans to buy 72–100 tanks could make the UAE's standardization problems worse, if it does not standardize on the Leclerc but any such standardization is now cast into doubt by Giat's problems.

The UAE's other armor includes about 894 operational other fighting vehicles. These systems include 76 Scorpion light tanks, 90 AML-90s and VBC-40s in the armored reconnaissance role, and 18 AMX-10P and 330 BMP-3 infantry fighting vehicles. The UAE has a wide range of APCs, including 60–96 Engessa EE-11 Urutus (some with TOW), 200–240 Panhard M-3 AML/VTTs, 80 VCRs, and 20 VAB/ VBCs. The UAE has 60 armored recovery vehicles, including EE-9s and AMX-30s. It has over 100 armored cars—including AML-60s, 20 Ferrets, 50 Saladins, some Saracens, and some Shoreland Mark 2s.

These figures show the UAE now has far too wide a range of types of armored weapons from far too many seller countries to allow effective support and sustainability and to provide the proper standardization of maintenance and training. Further, many of the UAE's other armored fighting vehicles are obsolete.

Abu Dhabi has been aware of these problems for several years. It examined a wide range of possible new armored vehicle purchases during 1990–1992—including the possible purchase of the Russian BMP, Bradley M-2, M-113A2, Egyptian Fahd, Vickers Valkyr, and M-998 "Humvee" light reconnaissance vehicle. In May 1992, Abu Dhabi decided to order 240–250 Russian BMP-3 mechanized infantry combat vehicles, with an option for 400 more. The UAE felt the Russian offer gave the UAE both the ability to standardize on a new combat vehicle, and an excellent bargain.[561] According to some reports, the UAE paid under $1 million per BMP-3 which compares with over $2 million for the Bradley.[562]

The BMP and other Soviet armored vehicles did perform relatively poorly in the Iran-Iraq War, the Gulf War, and the fighting in Afghanistan. However, Russian armored vehicles have been extensively modified as a result of these conflicts, and the BMP-3 seems to have corrected many of the crippling ergonomic problems that limited the effectiveness of the BMP-1 and BMP-2. The BMP-3 also has a much more effective 100 mm gun and its use of a gun-launched variant of the AT-10 "Bastion" (9M117) missile may give it the first effective anti-tank guided missile capability ever deployed on a BMP. Nevertheless, the BMP requires different tooling, support and sustainment, and repair capabilities than any of the Western armored vehicles now in Gulf service, and is both heavy for its power train and has serious initial reliability problems.[563] Once again, Abu Dhabi's insistence on mixing systems from different countries and buying new systems is likely to present war fighting problems.

Dubai is considering additional purchases of 130–150 BMP-3s and/or BTR-80s.[564] This would improve its standardization with the rest of the UAE. Conversely, if Dubai bought armored vehicles different from the BMP-3 and BTR-80, this would further complicate the UAE's interoperability and sustainment problems.[565]

The UAE has significantly improved its artillery strength in recent years. The UAE army has 18–20 155 mm AMX Mark F-3 self-propelled howitzers, 72 G-6 155 mm self-propelled guns, 20 Type 59-1 130 mm towed guns, 62 light ROD 105 mm towed howitzers, 18–36 M-56 105 mm pack howitzers, 20–24 120 mm mortars and 80 81 mm mortars. The UAE has also acquired 18 LAU-97 70 mm and 48 FIROS-25 122 mm multiple rocket launchers.

These holdings reflect the delivery of the UAE's new G-6 self-propelled guns, and the UAE has additional weapons on order. Abu Dhabi ordered 78 G-6 155 mm self-propelled gun systems from Denel of South Africa in 1990. The G-6 has a maximum range of 39 kilometers, and developmental rounds exist with ranges of over 40 kilometers.[566] The UAE has also purchased 87 surplus M-109A3 self-propelled 155 mm howitzers from the Netherlands, which will be upgraded with NBC protection and will be able to use extended range Swiss round with ranges of 25 kilometers (32 kilometers with an assisted range round).[567] It is examining possible purchases of 120 mm towed rifled mortars from France, French self-propelled or towed 155 mm howitzers, and Russian BM-9A52 Smerch 300 mm multiple rocket launch systems.[568]

This mix of artillery weapons will give the UAE considerable firepower. The UAE will, however, have problems in target acquisition and maneuver warfare and needs improved artillery radars and fire control systems. It also needs to improve its artillery training to support armored and combined arms operations.

The UAE has an adequate number of anti-tank guided weapons launchers, including 25 BGM-71A Improved TOW launchers (Some on EE-11s), 25–35 HOT launchers (some on armored vehicles), 65–70 Milans on EE-11s and 120–230 man portable Milan launchers, and an unknown number of obsolete Vigilant launchers. Its other anti-tank weapons include 30 106 mm recoilless rifles, and 84 mm Carl Gustav M-2 recoilless rifles. Anti-tank capabilities are improving, but the UAE has too many different types of anti-tank weapons, too few of any given system, and poor overall training.

Army short range air defenses include some SA-14s, 10 SA-16s, and 18–24 man portable Blowpipe and Mistral surface-to-air missile fire units. They include 48 M-3 VDA self-propelled twin 30 mm guns, 20 GCF-BM2 self-propelled twin 20 mm guns, and a mix of roughly 100 14.5 mm, 20 mm, 30 mm., and 35 mm towed guns. Abu Dhabi has ordered the advanced twin launcher version of the French Mistral air defense systems mounted on "Humvees". Dubai is also interested in the British short-range Starburst system. The UAE recognizes that it also needs longer range systems to protect its armored forces, and is currently studying possible purchases of systems like the Crotale.[569]

Readiness and Warfighting Capabilities

The UAE Army has steadily improved over time. Its divided force structure limits the standardization of equipment and training, however, as well as the ability to conduct combined arms training, and the ability to develop effective career structures and manpower management.

The UAE has some good units at the battalion level, but cannot operate defensively or offensively as a coherent force—particularly at any distance from its normal peacetime bases and casernes. Armored operations, air defense operations, maneuver warfare, combined arms, and combined operations are all critical weaknesses, and the UAE cannot operate effectively at the brigade level.

The situation is gradually improving—largely as the result of a slow decline in the rivalry between the Emirates and an understanding that more professionalism is vital if the army is to have any real value as either a deterrent or operational force. The UAE conducts joint exercises with France and the US, French instructors are improving the UAE's armored warfare training, and the UAE Army now conducts joint exercises units of the French rapid action force.

The UAE Army is, however, still under-trained. There is no effective combat training above the brigade level, and the quality of logistics, maintenance, service support, and combat support capabilities vary by unit and Emirate. The UAE's forces are heavily dependent on operating near their peacetime casernes and facilities—a major weakness if the army has to deal with threats to other Southern Gulf states.

The Army lacks effective combined arms training and all of the UAE's forces lack effective organization and training for combined warfare. The UAE has some of the poorest maintence and sustainment capabilities in the Gulf.

The UAE also lacks a clear doctrine as to how it will fight in wartime. It has conducted exercises in the upper Gulf, but it is not tailored to rapidly reinforce Kuwait and defend the upper Gulf against Iran and Iraq. Its weaknesses in interoperability, sustainability, and combined arms training preclude it from having anything like the effectiveness its weapons strength might indicate, and UAE field training and exercises are far too undemanding to prepare the UAE's army for extensive combat against a well organized Iraqi armored threat.

The UAE Army has only minimal amphibious capabilities to deal with a threat in the Gulf. As a result, it is in many ways a large and expensive garrison force without a real war fighting mission. This reality may be cloaked by the rhetoric of cooperation used by the Gulf Cooperation Council, but it is scarcely a mystery to Iraq and Iran. As a result, the UAE Army has limited deterrent, as well as war fighting, capability.

The UAE Air Force

The UAE's air force is its most prestigious service. It now has 3,500 men, including the air defense forces and police air wing. It has 97 combat aircraft, 22 transport aircraft, and 42 armed helicopters. The air force's main air bases at Abu Dhabi and Jebel Ali (Dubai) are sheltered and have light anti-aircraft defenses. It has military fields at Batin in Abu Dhabi, Dubai, Fujairah, Ras al-Khaimah, and Sharjah. Abu Dhabi is creating a major modern air base at Suwaihan. The trends in its air force manpower have been shown in Chart Fifty-Seven and the trends in its air strength are shown in Chart Sixty.

It is important to note, however, that Dubai has a separate force element, which includes about 700 men out of a total of 3,500. This is a low overall manning level for an air force with the UAE's number of combat air force, and the UAE is heavily dependent on foreign contractor support for any kind of air operation.

Major Units, Equipment, and Modernization

The UAE now has 9 Mirage 2000s and 18 Hawk 102s in fighter-ground attack roles, and 14 Hawk Mark-63s in attack/training missions. It has one air defense squadron of 22 Mirage 2000EADs, and one reconnais-

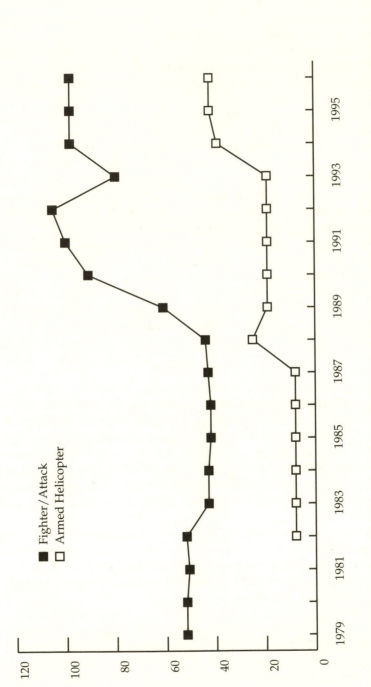

CHART SIXTY UAE: Fixed Wing and Rotary Wing Combat Air Strength—1979–1996. *Source:* Adapted by Anthony H. Cordesman from various editions of the IISS, *Military Balance,* the JCSS, *Military Balance in the Middle East,* and material provided by US experts.

sance squadron of 8 Mirage 2000RADs. It also maintains a mixed training/combat squadron with 7 Hawk M-61s, 2 MB-339As, and 6 Mirage-2000DADs, and the UAE has 5 SF-260 and 30 PC-7 trainers. Some reports indicate there are also 6–8 MB-326K and 5 MB-339A light attack aircraft operating in the COIN and training role.

The UAE's advanced air ordnance includes R-550 Magic air-to-air missiles, and AGM-A, AGM-B, AS-11, AS-12, and AM-39 Exocet air-to-ground missiles. It has Hydra 70s, HOT, and Hellfire for its attack helicopters. The UAE is currently conducting acceptance tests of the Hakim family of 500 lb. and 2,000 lb. laser and TV-guided rocket-assisted bombs. It is seeking to procure a new long range stand off attack missile.[570] The UAE air force also has some Beech MQM-107A RPVs, which it uses as target drones.

Proficiency varies by type of aircraft. The Hawk is a relatively simple aircraft to operate and maintain, and British experts indicate that the UAE is able to keep it at reasonable levels of effectiveness. The UAE is considering the purchase of up to 40 more Hawk 100 trainers, including 40 for Dubai.

The UAE Air Force has had trouble absorbing its Mirage 2000s. Although these aircraft are equipped with Marconi PGM A/B air-to-ground missiles, they have only moderate performance in the attack role. They also have not performed up to the UAE's hopes in the air defense role.[571] Pilot proficiency is relatively high, but the UAE is just beginning to acquire the capability to sustain moderate sortie rates, and its C4I/BM capabilities do not allow it to fully exploit the capabilities of its aircraft.

Part of the UAE's problems in absorbing the Mirage 2000 was caused by differences between the UAE and France. Abu Dhabi refused to take delivery on the first 18 of the 36 Mirage 2000s for its air defense forces in early 1987 because they were not equipped to a special standard as specified. The UAE's dispute with France over the aircraft began in March, 1986. In spite of an agreement by Dassault-Breuget to modify the Mirage 2000s, the aircraft that Dassault proposed to deliver did not have the quality of avionics that the UAE expected, could not fire special laser-guided ordnance being developed by ISC-Ferranti, could not fire the same US ordnance as other Gulf aircraft, and did not have fully compatible communications, IFF, and data links. Dassault stated that the problems were the fault of ISC-Ferranti, and sought to deliver the aircraft first, and then modify them later.[572]

The UAE finally agreed to accept the aircraft in November, 1987, but the agreement was only reached after the UAE foreign minister visited Paris and threatened the French prime minister and minister of foreign affairs with the exclusion of Dassault from the UAE market, and Dassault agreed to complete the necessary changes later and pay penalties.[573] The agreement has been successful enough, however, for the UAE to consider buying as many as 10 more Mirage 2000 fighters. The UAE is also seeking to improve its performance with the Mirage 2000 by having Ferranti (USA) make major improvements to its training ranges, and by having France's Airco improve the training of its flight engineers.[574]

Although it is still fully integrating the Mirage 2000 into its forces, the UAE still needs to improve the capability of its combat aircraft—particularly its low altitude and stand-off attack capabilities. Small air forces like that of the UAE need to maximize force capability. At the same time, basing, maintenance, training, and support costs are so high that such air forces suffer from severe diseconomies of scale, and the incremental life cycle cost of high performance fighters is relatively limited—particularly when the lower maintenance costs of newer types of high performance fighters are taken into consideration.

As a result, the UAE has considered the purchase of F-16Us, F-15Us, Mirage-2000Cs, Mirage 2000-5s, Eurofighter 2000s, Rafales, MiG-29s, Su-25TKs, Su-27Bs, Su-30MK5s, or Su-35s. The UAE has discussed the purchase of up to 70–80 new aircraft, although an initial purchase of 32–40 aircraft seems more likely. The UAE has been conducting trials of such aircraft since 1993.[575]

The UAE is seeking an advanced aircraft with features that will be different from those of other aircraft in the region and which will give the UAE "status" relative to its neighbors. It wants a long-range high-endurance air superiority aircraft with advanced beyond-visual-range (BVR) combat capabilities similar to those of the F-15Is purchased by Israel and the F-15Ss purchased by Saudi Arabia. The UAE would like an aircraft with the capability to use the AMRAAM or a similar very long range radar-guided missile. As a result, virtually all of the aircraft manufacturers are proposing for sale are being tailored to improve BVR combat capability, as well as attack capability.

For example, Lockheed-Martin has proposed an F-16U which would have added fuel and a larger delta wing to provide up to 40% more range-payload capability needed, an a advanced, forward looking, infrared sensor system. McDonnell Douglas has proposed an F-15U with some added avionics features. The US has also taken the unusual step of offering the UAE the source code to be used in the avionics of the F-15 or F-16, and a possible thrust vectoring option for either aircraft, although it has not approved sale of the AIM-120 AMRAAM to the UAE.

Russia and France are countering by proposing the sale of advanced air-to-air missiles, as well as aircraft. Russia is proposing sale of the AA-12 Adder fire and forget missile, and France is proposing sale of the Matra MICA. The UK is offering the UAE lease of a Tornado IDS force until the Eurofighter 2000 is ready.[576]

France has evidently offered the Rafale to Abu Dhabi and Dubai at a cost of $6.8 billion for a force of 80 aircraft. It displayed the Rafale at the Dubai air show in November, 1988. The Rafale, however, has run into severe cost-escalation problems and a report by the French National Assembly's finance committee indicated that the cost of the aircraft could escalate to 618 million francs per plane. The report also indicated that French plans to buy 234 fighters for its air force and 86 fighters for its navy could cost in excess of $40 billion.[577]

The UAE has a clear mission requirement for a more advanced aircraft with BVR capability, but discussions with aircraft manufacturers indicate the UAE may also be seeking a unique configuration simply for the sake of prestige. If so, such "gold plating" is likely to be an extremely wasteful proposition. Even minor system integration and support problems can greatly complicate support and training, and raise total life cycle costs by 20% or more. Standardization and interoperability almost invariably provide more real-world, military effectiveness than technological "glitter." Further, Abu Dhabi has the problem that it has only one major military air base. As a result, some experts believe it will buy additional upgraded Mirage 2005s in the near term, and look at more advanced US or French fighters in the future.[578]

The UAE employs CASA C-212s in an electronic warfare role, but these aircraft are of uncertain effectiveness. The UAE has actively investigated ordering C-130s equipped for electronic warfare, ordering E-2C Hawkeyes for the AWACS and maritime surveillance role, and ordering two BN-Defender AEW aircraft.

The UAE has 20 AH-64 Apache attack helicopters, which it purchased with 4,000 Hydra rockets and 360 Hellfire missiles.[579] It has done a good job of absorbing the AH-64s, and these aircraft furnish the kind of long range strike system that provides the UAE with the ability to defend both its coast line, territory, and off-shore platforms, and to conduct all-weather and night armed reconnaissance to deal with any amphibious landing. They also can be used to reinforce Saudi Arabia, Bahrain, or Kuwait.[580]

The UAE is also reported to be studying purchases of additional attack helicopters, including 10 more AH-64s, the Lynx, fast attack, helicopter armed with Sea Skua missiles.[581]

The UAE has 10 SA-342K Gazelle attack helicopters with HOT anti-tank guided missiles, 5 AS-332-Fs (3 with Exocet AM-39 anti-ship missiles), 7 SA-316/319 Alouette III with AS-11 and AS-12 air-to-surface missiles. These assets make the UAE air force the most advanced attack helicopter force in the Southern Gulf, and the UAE is considering the purchase of 10 more Pumas.

Reports differ as to the UAE Air Force's transport force. It may include 2 L-100-30, 4 C-130Hs, 1 BN-2 Islander, 4 C-212s. 7 CN-235M-100s, and 4

IL-76s. Its transport helicopter holdings seem to include 8 AB-205/Bell 205s, 9 Bell 206As, 5 206Ls, 4 Bell 214s, 8 AS-332s (2 VIP), and 1 AS-350. There are 3 Bo-105 helicopters and 1 SA-76 in the SAR role.

Some reports indicate that the UAE has 30 A-129 Mangustas and Lynx helicopters on order. Other reports indicate that the UAE is considering plans to acquire up to 40 Agusta AB-412HP Griffons, 10 IAR 330-L Pumas, and/or a significant number of AS-532 Cougar or Westland WS-70 Black Hawk helicopters. The UAE also seems to be considering purchase of more C-130s, or CASA/IPTN CN-235 aircraft.[582]

Readiness and Warfighting Capabilities

The UAE's air force is steadily improving in capability, and some elements should now perform well in air defense intercept missions. Overall proficiency levels, however, are low—particularly in conducting realistic air strike and close air support missions. The UAE is heavily dependent on foreign technical support for all operations.

Individual pilot training is good, but the UAE is only slowly evolving from an air force with limited training in day combat, and with little central direction and overall organization, to a modern air force. It is dependent on foreign technical personnel for the operation of virtually all its aircraft, and Saudi and British pilots indicate that the UAE does very little realistic air-to-air combat training, would have serious problems in low altitude air defense and attack missions, has no real experience in combined operations, and needs to improve its munitions and ground-based intercept training.

Equally important, the UAE remains a force of individual combat aircraft, rather than an integrated air force. It has some good individual pilots who can perform well in technical training exercises, but its efforts at integrating its air power into joint operations are more cosmetic than real. The air force has failed to give adequate weight to advanced training, airborne C⁴I/BM needs, its ability to manage beyond-visual-range combat, targeting and management of offensive air operations, joint warfare doctrine and training, achieving high sortie rates. sustainment, and maintenance.

UAE air force has no real capability to manage an effective unified air defense battle and cannot really develop such a capability without integrated Southern Gulf AWACS and C⁴I systems. It is unable to organize its air force for a cohesive offensive operation and is only beginning to acquire the capability to operate effectively with US or Saudi C⁴I, battle management, and targeting support. Like most Gulf air forces, it is organized more to produce individual "knights of the air" than develop a modern war fighting capability.

Land-Based Air Defenses

The UAE Air Force merged with the UAE Air Defense Force in January, 1988. This merger occurred because of growing coordination problems between the fighter force and land based air defenses.[583] The decision placed both commands under the former chief of the Air Force, Colonel Sheik Mohamed bin Zayed Al Nahyyan, while the head of the air defense force became the deputy commander. He described the merger as leading to, "faster decision making and closer cooperation, ... better performance in the use of weapons, and also flexibility in relaying orders from headquarters and carrying them out."[584]

The UAE is making progress along these lines. The UAE has five MIM-23B Improved Hawk batteries with 42 launchers (342 missiles) and has done a good job of absorbing this weapons system.[585] It has also deployed an air defense brigade with three battalions. These are armed with 12 Rapier, 9 Crotale fire units, 13 RBS-70 light surface-to-air missiles, and 100 Mistral light surface-to-air missile fire units. The UAE's total land-based air defenses also include some SA-14s, 10 SA-16s, and 20–24 Blowpipe manportable surface-to-air missile weapons, a number of light unguided anti-aircraft guns, and Skyguard radar guided twin Oerlikon 35 mm anti-aircraft guns. The UAE is considering the purchase of Crotale NG systems with VT-1 hypersonic missiles, the Norwegian NFT-NASAMS, and British Aerospace Jernas to improve its short range defense capabilities. Dubai is considering purchasing the Shorts Starburst for its very short range air defenses, while Abu Dhabi has evidently purchased the Matra Atlas for this requirement.[586]

The UAE's most serious land-based air defense requirement is for a long range system with upgrade potential for cruise missile and ATBM defense. The UAE is evaluating the purchase of 10 Patriot missile launchers or three batteries of Russian SV-300 (SA-10/12) missiles. If the UAE should decide to buy the Patriot, this could be an important step forward in standardizing the air defense of the Gulf. More than 25 Patriot launchers have already been sold to Kuwait and Saudi Arabia, and the Patriot radar and C4I/BM system could be integrated into a common Patriot defense net as well as improve the warning and cueing data provided to the IHawk missile units that are already widely deployed in the region.[587]

At the same time, Russia is offering the SA-10/12 at a very low cost. The SA-10/SA-12 is an effective system and Russia already owes the UAE $500 million for past debts. The UAE also wants the PAC-3 version of Patriot, which is still in development. The sale of such a US system to another country could present transfer and disclosure problems.[588]

The UAE Air Force currently relies on a mix of Marconi, AN/TSQ-73, and AN-TPS-70 warning radars and a relatively limited C⁴I/BM system. This is largely the fault of Western defense contractors. The UAE was supposed to have acquired a modern automated air defense command and control system along with its improved Hawks, but its overall command and control, and air control and warning capabilities are questionable. Some of the systems integration was evidently supposed to be carried out by ISC and Ferranti as part of a project called GMX or Al-Hakim. Ferranti's performance has evidently been questionable, and part of the contract may have been fraudulent.[589]

The UAE has, however, purchased a far more sophisticated C⁴I/BM system from Westinghouse in February, 1993. The new system will include radars, computers, communications systems, and software—including radars mounted on tethered balloons to provide some of the range and look-down capabilities of an AWACS. The UAE is also examining the possible purchase of Lockheed Martin FPS-117(E)1, Marconi Martello 743-D, Westinghouse W-2100, Thomson-CSF TRS 22-XX, and Alenia RAT-31SL long range surveillance radars. These radars have ranges of 320–400 kilometers and would improve coverage against aircraft, cruise missiles, and UAVs, with an option to provide anti-tactical ballistic missile coverage in the future. The Lockheed Martin FPS-117(E)1 is an improved version of the radar being installed in Saudi Arabia as part of the Peace Shield air defense system, with its range extending from 320 to 400 kilometers.[590] Once these new systems are installed, the UAE should acquire an effective battle management and warning capability, effective secure voice and data links to the Saudi Air Force, and a compatible IFF system. Like the other small Gulf states, it would also benefit greatly from full integration into the Saudi air defense system.

The UAE Navy

The UAE's small 1,500 man navy is now expanding from a coastal defense force operated by Abu Dhabi to a navy designed to help the UAE defend its islands and offshore oil facilities from an Iranian and Iraqi threat. It also plans to acquire an anti-submarine warfare (ASW) capability against Iran's Kilo-class submarines.

The trends in UAE Navy manning have been shown in Chart Fifty-Seven. The relative strength of the UAE and other Gulf navies is shown in Chart Sixty-One. Such strength data are only a rough indication of capability, however, because they do not reflect ship quality, tonnage, training, or operational activity. The Navy's main base is at Abu Dhabi, with others at Dalma and Mina Zayed in Abu Dhabi; at Mina Rashid and

Mina Jebal (Jebel Ali) in Dubai; at Mina Khalid and Khor Fakkan (west coast) in Sharjah; and Mina Sakr in Ras al Khaimah. A naval facility is under construction at al-Qaffay Island.

Major Naval Equipment

The UAE's larger ships are modern, highly capable vessels within their class. The UAE's major combat ships currently include two 630-ton German Type 62 Lurssen (Muray Jip-class) corvettes delivered in 1990 and 1991. Each is armed with 2 quad MM-40 Exocet anti-ship missile launchers. The Exocet is a sea-skimming missile with a maximum range of 70 kilometers, a speed of Mach 0.9, and a 165 kilogram warhead. Each corvette is also equipped with Crotale anti-air missiles, 1 76 mm gun, and can support 1 Alouette helicopter. The corvettes do not have anti-submarine warfare capability but are equipped with modern radars, countermeasures, and fire control systems. There are unconfirmed reports that Abu Dhabi has ordered two more Lurssen 62 meter patrol boats with Exocet, 76 mm guns, and Goalkeeper close-in defense systems.

The UAE has two 250-ton Lurrsen 45 meter fast attack (Murbarraz-class) craft commissioned in 1990. Each is armed with two twin Exocet launchers, one six cell Mistral (Sadral) anti-air missile launcher, and one 76 mm gun. These ships have modern radars and countermeasures systems, but no ASW capability.

Other major combat ships include six 260-ton Lurssen TNC-45 (Ban Yas-class) guided missile patrol boats, each equipped with two twin MM-40 Exocet launchers, one 76 mm gun, and two twin Breda 40 mm guns. These ships were commissioned in the early 1980s and now have dated electronics. The UAE is, however, overhauling these ships in its own yards in Abu Dhabi at a cost of $15 million each, and is considering proposals for a major upgrading of their capabilities.[591]

The UAE issued a statement of requirements in mid-1993 for four to eight frigates of about 2,500 tons, equipped with a helicopter with dipping sonar, surface-to-surface missile, surface-to-air missile, and ASW capability. A total of 14 contractors made proposals and the UAE pre-selected five in the first half of 1994. It then conducted its own evaluation of Blohm and Voss, Lurssen, Vosper Thorneycroft, Royal Schelde, Newport News and used US Navy ships. The ships involved included the French Souverainte type, British 83 and 105 meter frigates, a derivative of the Karl Doorman-class, the Lurssen FPB-62, the Newport News FF-21 and the leasing of the Oliver Hazard Perry-class from the US. The UK may also have proposed lease of Royal Navy F-23 ships.[592]

The UAE's evaluation focused on the need for both better air defense capability, and ASW capability against Iran's new Kilo-class submarines,

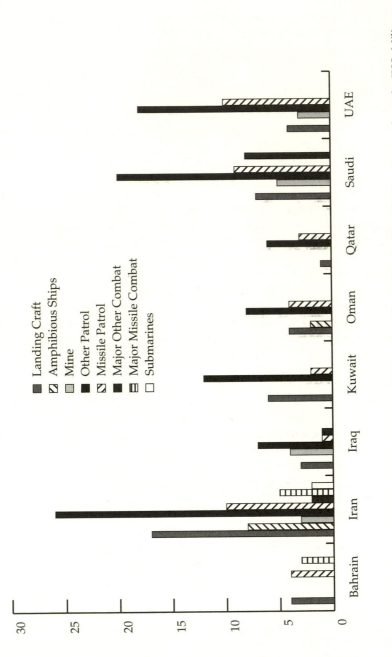

CHART SIXTY-ONE Gulf Naval Ships by Category in 1996. *Source:* Adapted by Anthony H. Cordesman from the IISS, *Military Balance, 1995–1996,* and material provided by US experts.

CHART SIXTY-ONE (continued)

	Bahrain	Iran	Iraq	Kuwait	Oman	Qatar	Saudi	UAE
Submarines	—	2	—	—	—	—	—	—
Major Surface Combat								
Missile	3	5	—	—	—	—	8	—
Other	—	2	1	—	—	—	—	—
Patrol Craft								
Missile	4	10	1	2	4	3	9	10
Other	—	26	7	12	8	6	20	18
Mine Vessels	0	3	4	—	—	—	5	3
Amphibious Ships	0	8	0	0	2	0	0	0
Landing Craft	4	17	3	6	4	1	7	4

and the UAE initially seemed likely to issue an award to procure a total of four ships equipped with a mix of sensors, fire control, and weapons systems from different countries. Such a purchase would have reflected the UAE's interest in advanced technology and unique equipment, but would also have presented major problems in systems integration and substantially degrade both the capability of its new ships and their inter-operability with other naval forces.

The UAE announced on April 2, 1996, that it would lease two used Dutch S-class frigates—the HMS Piet Heijn and HMS Abraham—to pro-vide an interim capability and had agreed on an a option to buy up to six Royal Schelde-built LCF-type 6,044 ton air defense frigates. The $362 million contract called for Netherlands Maritime Consortium to over-haul the two ships with new radars and other equipment before they were delivered, including the UAE's usual emphasis on special features and high technology systems. It called for the addition of the Goalkeeper systems for short-range missile defense, and new Scout short-range radar systems. It also called for fitting Scout radars on eight other UAE ships, the construction of a Goalkeeper maintenance facility and NBCD training school in Abu Dhabi, the construction of two tugs to move the frigates in and out of port, and training the 140 men required to crew the new ships.[593]

It was not clear from the contract, however, that the UAE would pur-chase the LCF-type missile frigates or how many it would buy. At least one source in the UAE claimed that the contract for new frigates was still "wide open."[594]

The UAE has six 110-ton Vosper Thorneycroft (Ardhana-class) 33.5 meter patrol boats with twin 30 mm guns. These ships date back to the mid 1970s, and have limited search radar capability, but the UAE is con-sidering British and French proposals to modernize them. The UAE has purchased eight Arctic 28 meter small patrol boats, each capable of car-rying 10 combat-equipped men, for use by its special forces. The UAE is also examining the purchase of ASW systems to refit its existing ships.[595]

The rest of the UAE's naval forces consist of three 38-ton Keith Nelson (Kawkab-class) 17 meter patrol boats, one diving tender, two Cheverton tenders, four LCU landing craft, one LCM, one support craft, and one 795-ton tug. The UAE is considering the purchase of mine warfare vessels like the Eridan and Sandown class vessels. It is also considering purchase of rapid interception crafts.

The UAE has seven Aerospatiale SA-316/319S Alouette helicopters which are capable of shipboard deployment, but which lack modern sen-sors and are largely inoperable. It has eight AS-535/552 Cougar land-based helicopters with radars, which are widely used in the transport role. It also has two long-range Britten-Norman Maritime Defender aircraft for coastal patrol and surveillance missions. These aircraft have nose mounted search radars, search lights, and rocket and gun pods. They are slow flying aircraft and have a maximum range of 1,500 nautical miles (2,775 kilometers), but are seldom used in the coastal patrol and surveillance roles.

The UAE has bought seven new AS-565 Panthers and will retrofit five of its AS-552 Cougar helicopters to upgrade its naval air forces with ASW and improved anti-surface capability. The Panthers will be delivered in mid-1998, and will have AS15TT anti-ship missiles (a radar-guided system with a range of 15 kilometers). The Cougars will have AM39 Exocet missiles. Both aircraft can be fitted with dipping sonars and light weight torpedoes for the ASW mission. The UAE is also examining the purchase of four new maritime patrol aircraft (MPA), up to 10 more AS-532 Cougars, and 8 AS-565F Panther ASW helicopters. The candidates for the MPA roles include the P-3C, Fokker Maritime Enforcer, Atlantique 2, and CN-235MPA. The Panthers might be used aboard the UAE's new frigates.[596]

The UAE has a small coast guard, which is part of the Ministry of Interior, operates 31 small coastal patrol boats, 10 watercraft, 38 harbor patrol boats, and two Crestitalia 30-meter diver support vessels. Abu Dhabi is considering providing its shoreline, islands, and off-shore facilities with anti-ship missiles. Possible candidates include the MM-40 Exocet, Matra Otobreda Otomat, and Rockwell/Bofors Hellfire.[597]

There have been reports that Dubai has already purchased 30 Chinese HY-2 (CSSC-3 Seersucker) missiles, but US experts do not believe that this is the case.[598] The UAE has reached an agreement with Newport News Shipbuilding to build a $30 million ship construction and repair facility in Abu Dhabi next to the Abu Dhabi shipyard, although construction has not begun. Newport News will be a 40% investor in the new yard and manage it for the UAE. The consortium that operates the new yard is the one refitting the UAE's six TNC-45s.[599]

Readiness and Warfighting Capabilities

The UAE navy conducts relatively limited realistic exercise training, but its proficiency has improved since the late 1980s. It is training with the British, Indian, and US navies. Some of its individual ships are beginning to acquire significant capability, although the UAE Navy is scarcely capable of challenging Iran without massive US or British assistance.

Overall readiness is uncertain, and UAE crews do a poor job of routine maintenance and maintenance at sea. The UAE Navy is, however, acquiring an improved capability to support its combat ships. It has recently signed a contract with Newport News Shipbuilding Corp. in the US to build a new yard called the Abu Dhabi Ship Building Company, which will be located in the Mussafah Industrial Areas near the Mussafah Channel.

Paramilitary and Security Forces

Like the other Southern Gulf States, the UAE has large paramilitary police forces, and security and intelligence units organized along British lines. Each Emirate maintains its own police force, but only the Federal Government (Abu Dhabi) and the Emirate of Dubai have internal security and intelligence organizations.[600]

In Abu Dhabi's case, these security forces are controlled by the Ministry of Interior. The security forces also include a small coast guard and border security force. None of these forces seem to be particularly repressive, although the UAE obviously exerts careful control over foreign laborers, maintains surveillance on its armed forces, particularly foreign soldiers, and must be concerned with Iranian and Iraqi infiltration.

The UAE's internal security forces are subject to more legal constraints than those of many other Southern Gulf states. The UAE's constitution prohibits arrest, search, detention, or imprisonment except in accordance with the law, and the laws of each Emirate prohibit arrest or search without probable cause. The police must report arrests within 48 hours to the Attorney General who then must determine within the next 24 hours whether to charge, release, or order further detention pending an investigation. The Attorney General may order detainees held for up to 21 days without charge. After that time, the authorities must obtain a court order for further detention without charge. Troublesome foreigners, however, can be expelled on the next available flight.[601]

With the exception of a few security cases, these reporting requirements are complied with, and detainees are brought to trial reasonably expeditiously. There is no formal system of bail, but the authorities may temporarily release detainees who deposit money or an important document such as a passport. The law permits incommunicado detention, but prohibits exile. The exiling of political opponents and critics of the government of the Emirates is not practiced. There are no known political prisoners, and there is no known surveillance of private correspondence.[602]

The Role of the Legal System

The UAE has a complex dual system of Shari'a (Islamic) and civil (secular) courts which affect the internal security structure of each Emirate. The Constitution designates the Shari'a as the basis of all legislation. Judicial procedures reflect a mixture of Western and Islamic models. In February, 1994, the President decreed that the Shari'a courts, and not the civil courts, would have the authority to try virtually all criminal cases. The decree did not affect the Emirates of Dubai, Umm Al-Quwain, and Ras al-Khaimah which have lower courts independent of the federal system. Nevertheless, despite the decree, judges in criminal cases involving non-Muslims may decide to impose civil court penalties, and appeals courts may overturn or modify Shari'a penalties imposed on non-Muslims by lower courts.

The nature of the case determines the venue. The civil courts are generally part of the federal system and are answerable to the Federal Supreme Court in Abu Dhabi. The Shari'a courts are administered by each Emirate and are also answerable to the Federal Supreme Court. The court systems in the Emirates of Dubai and Ras al-Khaimah are independent of the federal system, although they apply the Civil Procedure Code. Each court system has an appeals process, and death sentences may be appealed to the President. Legal procedures are uniform in both Shari'a and civil courts. In practice, there has been so little internal political unrest that this mix of conflicting jurisdictions has had little impact on internal security operations.

The UAE does not hold jury trials. A single judge normally renders the verdict in each case, whether in the Shari'a or civil court system. All trials are public, except national security cases and those deemed by the judge likely to harm public morality. Most judges are foreign nationals, primarily from other Arab countries; however, the Ministry of Justice has begun to train UAE citizens as judges and prosecutors. The military has its own court system based on Western military judicial practice. Military tribunals try only military personnel. There is no separate national security court system.[603]

The legal system has two other potential roles in internal security. It has the authority to resolve disputes between the Emirates, and the power of judicial review and original jurisdiction over all disputes between Emirates and between the Federal Government and Emirates.

Freedom of Speech and Dissent

While the UAE generally respects the rule of law, its internal security systems do place tight limits on political activity and freedom of speech, and on the activity of domestic and foreign labor. Political organizations are prohibited, and all organized public gatherings require a government permit. Each Emirate determines its own practice on public gatherings. Abu Dhabi and Dubai are more tolerant of seminars and conferences on sensitive subjects, but citizens normally confine political discussions to the numerous assemblies or "majlises," held in private homes, which are not subject to any restrictions.[604]

Although the Constitution provides for freedom of speech, most people, especially foreign nationals, refrain from criticizing the Government in public. The Ministry of Information and Culture performs internal security functions, and controls the domestic press through a mix of subsidies and the threat of suspending publication. Many of the local English and Arabic-language newspapers are privately owned, but receive government subsidies. Journalists censor their own reporting on government policy, the ruling families, national security, religion, and relations with neighboring states. In May 1995, the Government banned distribution of the Arabic-language, daily *Al-Sharq Al-Awsat* for one week after the newspaper commented on a memorandum from the Minister of Economy and Commerce on the UAE's possible inclusion on the United States Trade Representative's "priority-watch" list.[605]

Foreign publications are routinely censored before distribution. Censors at the Ministry of Information and Culture review imported newspapers, periodicals, books, films, and videos and ban any material considered pornographic, violent, derogatory to Islam, favorable to Israel, unduly critical of friendly countries, or critical of the Government or the ruling family. All television and radio stations are government owned and conform to government reporting guidelines. However, satellite receiving dishes are widespread and provide access to international broadcasts without apparent censorship.[606]

Control of Foreign Labor

Control of the labor force plays an important role in internal security, because 80% of the total work force of roughly 580,000 is foreign.[607] The law does not grant workers the right to engage in collective bargaining, and there is no legislated or administrative minimum wage. Laborers in the industrial and service sectors are employed under contracts that are subject to review by the Ministry of Labor and Social Affairs. The Ministry resolves work-related disputes through conciliation committees or special labor courts. Complaints may be appealed to the Ministry and ultimately to the courts. However, the Ministry of Labor and Social Affairs is understaffed and under-budgeted, so that complaints and compensation claims are backlogged. Further, many workers do not protest for fear of reprisals or deportation.[608]

Foreign labor is regarded as the main potential source of internal unrest, and the legal and internal security system favors both the employer and deportation of foreign workers who cause problems. Foreign workers are often denied the right to work in the UAE or are deported if they engage in labor disputes. The government also has repeatedly cracked down on illegal immigrants, and police and coast guard units have arrested and expelled a total of 25,000 illegal foreign workers over the last two decades. The UAE also extends careful surveillance over Iranian workers, which it sees as a potential "fifth column."[609]

Labor laws do not cover domestic servants and agricultural workers (which total about 10% of the labor force). Other foreign workers do have legal protection as to the number of hours they can be asked to work, and the maximum temperature in the work place. They normally receive either employer-provided housing or a housing allowance, medical care, and homeward passage from their employers. Most do not, however, earn the minimum salary of approximately $1,370 a month required to obtain a residency visa for their families. This makes it easy to deport foreign workers rapidly, and employers can also exercise control over foreign workers by petitioning for a one-year ban from the work force against any foreign employee who leaves his job without fulfilling the terms of his contract.[610]

Strategic Interests

The UAE is a moderate state which is friendly to the West. It played an important role in supporting US and British forces during the "tanker war" of 1987–1988 and Gulf War. The UAE helped found the Gulf Cooperation Council, and has strengthened its ties to the West since the Gulf War. Its strategic location makes it critical to collective defense efforts in the Southern Gulf and ensures that it will play an important future role in defending against the threat of Iranian intimidation or military action.

The UAE also deployed forces as part of the UN Coalition during the Gulf conflict. It committed a motorized infantry battalion to the Joint Forces Command (East) and created a joint aviation battalion with Kuwait. It used its 7,000-man air force to fly 109 sorties, including 58 Mirage 2000 interdiction sorties, 45 C-212 and C-130 airlift sorties, and six Mirage 2000 reconnaissance sorties. The UAE Air Force had reasonable readiness. It canceled or aborted 18 sorties, but only two for maintenance reasons. Its Mirage 2000 fighters attacked targets like Iraqi infantry and mechanized forces, artillery positions, and supply areas.[611]

Military Cooperation with the West

The UAE is of considerable military importance to the US. The US and UAE cooperated closely during both the tanker war and Gulf War. The UAE provided port call facilities and support during Operation Earnest Will. The US Navy and US Marine Corps have conducted joint exercises with the UAE since July, 1990, when Saddam Hussein first began to threaten the UAE. The UAE provided the US with $6.572 billion in direct aid during the Gulf War, and $218 million in goods and services, for a total of $6.455 billion.[612]

The UAE negotiated a security arrangement with the US in 1992 that offered the US access to UAE air and naval facilities. It signed a more comprehensive defense agreement with the US on July 23, 1994. As a result, the US Navy now makes nearly 300 ship visits a year to the UAE. The UAE signed a similar agreement with France on January 18, 1995, and is negotiating an agreement for joint exercises and training with the Netherlands and the United Kingdom.

The US Navy maintains a small prepositioning facility at Jebel Ali, uses Dubai as its main "R&R" port in the Gulf, and has a small naval support facility at Fujayrah. Fujayrah has ports on the Gulf of Oman, and allows the US to provide logistic support to reach destinations in the Gulf without going through the Straits of Hormuz by moving from ports in Fujayrah along a modern highway to locations in the Southern Gulf.[613]

The UAE lets US tanker aircraft operate out of the country in support of the "no fly" zone in southern Iraq, and cooperates with the US in contingency planning. The US maintains a Military Liaison Office with a staff of six military, one civilian, and two local personnel to manage the US side of military programs in the country, and the UAE agreed in 1995 to preposition one US Army armored brigade in the country. The force would include 120 tanks and 70 AIFVs. The UAE is negotiating a status of forces agreement with the US and the details of a prepositioning agreement and suitable cost sharing.[614]

The UAE and the US have, note, however, reached full agreement on a status of forces agreement and jurisdiction over the US military personnel who visit the UAE. The UAE has been reluctant to sign a draft agreement that would give the US jurisdiction in most cases, and has made its terms for a status of forces agreement a bargaining chip in evaluating the purchase of US fighters. There has already been at least one incident where the UAE arrested a US sailor for a traffic fatality and refused to turn him over to the US. This could be a source of growing problems, given the frequency of US visits and the differences between the two countries over jurisdiction and legal proceedings.

The Need for Better Military Cohesion and Priorities

There are significant problems in the UAE's military forces, however, that affect its strategic position. The UAE forces are not standardized, and some of the UAE's new arms acquisitions may limit the interoperability of the UAE's forces with those of other GCC states and with Western power projection forces.

The UAE needs to look beyond its current fascination with buying unique and high status technologies, and individual subsystems with the best available technology. It has to make hard decisions about its next fighter aircraft, frigates, and whether to buy the Patriot, but it should then put a halt to its major equipment buys and focus on systems integration, sustainability, and collective defense. It also needs to focus on interoperability, coalition warfare, and exercise performance. At present, it is buying fighter and armored warfare capabilities it cannot support with adequate manpower, training, C^4I/BM, sustainment, and maintenance and spares.

The divisions within the UAE also raise a continuing question as to whether the UAE will work to create an effective deterrent, suitable defensive capabilities, and improved capacity to accept friendly power projection forces, or will become bogged down in the rivalry between individual Emirates.

More broadly, the UAE cannot develop effective forces on its own. For the foreseeable future, it will need the support of US and British power projection forces in any major confrontation with Iran. It also needs to be part of a collective defense effort that is far more effective than the present faltering efforts of the Gulf Cooperation Council—an organization whose good intentions have not been transformed into substantive action.

The UAE is in a unique position in that it faces only a limited threat of direct invasion, but depends on other Southern Gulf states and the US for its security. More than any other Southern Gulf state, it needs to focus on developing effective collective and integrated defense capabilities by:

- Creating an effective planning system for collective defense, and truly standardized and/or interoperable forces.
- Integrating its C^4I and sensor nets for air and naval combat, including BVR and night warfare.
- Focusing on deploying its forces to support the joint land defense of the Kuwaiti/Northwestern Saudi borders and reinforcing other Gulf states like Oman in the event of any Iranian amphibious or air borne action.
- Creating joint air defense and air attack capabilities.
- Creating joint air and naval strike forces.
- Establishing effective cross reinforcement and tactical mobility capabilities.
- Preparing fully for outside or over-the-horizon reinforcement by the US and other Western powers.
- Setting up joint training, support, and infrastructure facilities.

- Creating common advanced training systems that develop a brigade and wing-level capability for combined arms and joint warfare, and which can support realistic field training exercises of the kind practiced by US and Israeli forces.
- Improving its capability to provide urban and urban area security and to fight unconventional warfare and low intensity combat.

UAE forces also need to cease their present emphasis on political purchases and "glitter factor" procurements. The UAE needs to reduce its number of different suppliers and major weapons types and to focus on procuring interoperable and/or standardized equipment to provide the capability to perform the following missions:

- Heavy armor, artillery, attack helicopters, and mobile air defense equipment for defense of the upper Gulf.
- Interoperability and standardization with US power projection forces.
- Interoperable offensive air capability with stand-off, all-weather precision weapons and anti-armor/anti-ship capability.
- Interoperable air defense equipment, including heavy surface-to-air missiles, BVR/AWX fighters, AEW & surveillance capability, ARM & ECM capability. (Growth to ATBM and cruise missile defense capability)
- Maritime surveillance systems, and equipment for defense against maritime surveillance, and unconventional warfare.
- Mine detection and clearing systems.
- Improved urban, area, and border security equipment for unconventional warfare and low intensity conflict.
- Advanced training aids.
- Support and sustainment equipment.

In the process, the UAE needs to recognize the mistakes it has made in the past. More than any other Southern Gulf state, it needs to rationalize its military procurements and to eliminate the waste of funds on:

- Unique equipment types and one-of-a-kind modifications.
- "Glitter factor" weapons; developmental equipment and technology.
- Non-interoperable weapons and systems.
- Submarines and ASW systems.
- Major surface warfare ships.
- Major equipment for divided or "dual" forces.
- New types of equipment which increase maintenance, sustainability, and training problems, or layer new types over old.

The Long-Term Need to Emphasize
Economic Development and Native Labor

The UAE also must deal with the need for internal change. Its oil and gas wealth does not exempt it from the need to emphasize the private sector and reliance on native labor that affects all of the Southern Gulf states. The UAE's military build-up, and its alliance with the US and the other Southern Gulf states, should provide a high degree of external security—although it cannot guarantee the return of Abu Musa and the Tunbs. In the long run, however, the UAE's security will be determined by how well it meets the needs of its people, and this means creating expanded private economic opportunities and steadily reducing its dependence on low cost foreign labor.

Like Qatar, the UAE has the wealth to avoid this problem for at least half a decade—although at the expense of the poorer emirates. The end result of delaying reform, however, will be to institutionalize added reliance on the UAE's welfare system, widen the gap between rich and poor, and deny new, economically valid, job opportunities for the UAE's youth and labor from the poorer Southern Gulf states. This, in turn, will tend to alienate the UAE's young population and make the process of evolutionary political reform more difficult. As a result, the most important single security challenge the UAE faces is to decide whether it will use the time it has available to implement economic and labor reform, or wait until it inevitably faces the same problems as its less wealthy neighbors.

As a result, the UAE's highest security priority is not more arms or to strengthen collective defense, but rather to implement the following list of internal reforms:

- Conduct a popular education program to limit population growth.
- Force radical reductions in the number of foreign workers, with priority for reductions in servants and in trades that allow the most rapid conversion to native labor. Eliminate economic disincentives for employers hiring native labor, and creating disincentives for hiring foreign labor. The UAE's young and increasingly well-educated population needs to replace its foreign workers as quickly as possible, and it will only develop a work ethic and suitable skills once it is thrust into the labor market.
- Reduce those aspects of state subsidies and welfare that distort the economy and discourage the native population from seeking jobs. It must steadily reduce dependence on welfare, and replace subsidies with jobs.
- Price water, electricity, motor gasoline, basic foods, and many services at market levels.

- Restructure the educational system to focus on job training and competitiveness. Create strong new incentives for faculty and students to focus on job-related education, sharply down-size other forms of educational funding and activity, and eliminate high overhead educational activities without economic benefits.
- Unify and reform the structure of the national budget to reduce the amount of money going directly to royal accounts, and ensure that most of the nation's revenues and foreign reserves are integrated into the national budget and into the planning process. Clearly separate royal and national income and investment holdings.
- Place limits on the transfer of state funds to princes and members of the royal family outside the actual ruling family, and transfers of unearned income to members of other leading families.
- Ensure that all income from enterprises with state financing is reflected in the national budget and is integrated into the national economic development and planning program.
- Freeze and then reduce the number of civil servants, and restructure and down-size the civil service to focus on productive areas of activity with a much smaller pool of manpower. Cut back sharply on state employees by the year 2000.
- Establish market criteria for all major state and state-supported investments. Require detailed and independent risk assessment and projections of comparative return on investment, with a substantial penalty for state versus privately funded projects and ventures. Down-size the scale of programs to reduce investment and cash flow costs and the risk of cost-escalation.
- Carry out much more rapid and extensive privatization to increase the efficiency of UAE investments in downstream and upstream operations to create real jobs and career opportunities for native workers, and to open investment opportunities to a much wider range of investors. Privatization must be managed in ways ensuring an opportunity for all native citizens to share in the privatization process. Privatization must not be conducted in a manner that benefits a small, elite group of investors and discourages popular confidence and willingness to invest in the UAE.
- Stop subsidizing firms and businesses in ways which prevent realistic economic growth and development, and which deprive the government of revenue. Present policies strongly favor UAE citizens and UAE-owned companies in ways which encourage unproductive investments in real estate, construction, and import-driven service industries.
- Avoid offset requirements that simply create disguised unemployment or non-competitive ventures that act as a further state-sponsored distortion of the economy.

- Eliminate economic disincentives for employers hiring native labor, and create disincentives for hiring foreign labor.
- Create new incentives to invest in local industries and business and disincentives for the expatriation of capital. Encourage outside investment.
- Create market driven incentives for foreign investment in major oil and gas projects, refineries, and petrochemical operations. Avoid off-set requirements that simply create disguised unemployment or non-competitive ventures that act as a further state-sponsored distortion of the economy.
- Tax earnings and sales with progressive taxes that reduce or eliminate budget deficits, which encourage local investment, and which create strong disincentives for the expatriation of capital, including all foreign holdings of capital and property by members of elite and ruling families.
- Establish a firm rule of law for all property, contract, permitting, and business activity and reduce state bureaucratic and permitting barriers to private investment.
- Place national security spending on the same basis as other state spending. Integrate it fully into the national budget, including investment and equipment purchases. Replace the present emphasis on judging purchases on the basis of initial procurement costs and technical features with a full assessment of life cycle cost—including training, maintenance, and facilities—and with specific procedures for evaluating the value of standardization and interoperability with existing national equipment and facilities, those of other Gulf states, and those of the US and other power projection forces.

Sources and Methods

This volume is part of a series of volumes on each of the Gulf states which has been developed by the Center for Strategic and International Studies as part of a dynamic net assessment of the Middle East. This project has had the sponsorship of each of the Southern Gulf states as well as US sponsors of the CSIS, and each text has been widely distributed for comment to experts and officials in each Southern Gulf country, to US experts and officials, and to several international agencies and institutions, and various private experts.

Sources

The author has drawn heavily on the inputs of outside reviewers throughout the text. It was agreed with each reviewer, however, that no individual or agency should be attributed at any point in the text except by specific request, and that all data used be attributed to sources that are openly available to the public. The reader should be aware of this in reviewing the footnotes. Only open sources are normally referred to in the text, although the data contained in the analysis has often been extensively modified to reflect expert comment.

There are other aspects of the sources used of which the reader should be aware. It was possible to visit each Southern Gulf state at various times during the preparation of this book and to talk to local officials and experts. Some provided detailed comments on the text. Interviews also took place with experts in the United States, United Kingdom, France, Switzerland and Germany. Portions of the manuscript were circulated for informal review by European officials and diplomats in some cases. Once again, no details regarding such visits or comments are referenced in the text.

Data from open sources are deliberately drawn from a wide range of sources. Virtually all of these sources are at least in partial conflict. There is no consensus over demographic data, budget data, military expenditures and arms transfers, force numbers, unit designations, or weapons types.

While the use of computer data bases allowed some cross-correlation and checking of such source, the reporting on factors like force strengths, unit types and identities, tactics often could not be reconciled and citing multiple sources for each case was not possible because it involved many detailed judgments by the author in reconciling different reports and data.

The Internet and several on-line services were also used extensively. Since such the data bases are dynamic, and change or are deleted over time, there is no clear way to footnote much of this material. Recent press sources are generally cited, but are often only part of the material consulted.

Methods

A broad effort has been made to standardize the analysis of each country, but it became clear early in the project that adopting a standard format did not suit the differences that emerged between countries. The emphasis throughout this phase of the CSIS net assessment has been on analyzing the detailed trends within individual states and this aspects of the analysis has been given priority over country-to-country consistency.

In many cases, the author adjusted the figures and data use in the analysis on a "best guess" basis, drawing on some thirty years of experience in the field. In some other cases, the original data provided by a given source were used without adjustment to ensure comparability, even though this leads to some conflicts in dates, place names, force strengths, etc. within the material presented—particularly between summary tables surveying a number of countries and the best estimates for a specific country in the text. In such cases, it seemed best to provide contradictory estimates to give the reader some idea of the range of uncertainty involved.

Extensive use is made of graphics to allow the reader to easily interpret complex statistical tables and see long-term trends. The graphic program used was deliberately standardized, and kept relatively simple, to allow the material portrayed to be as comparable as possible. Such graphics have the drawback, however, that they often disguise differences in scale and exaggerate or minimize key trends. The reader should carefully examine the scale used in the left-hand axis of each graphs.

Most of the value judgments regarding military effectiveness are made on the basis of American military experience and standards. Although the author has lived in the Middle East, and worked as a US advisor to several Middle Eastern governments, he believes that any attempt to create some Middle Eastern standard of reference is likely to be far more arbitrary than basing such judgments on his own military background.

Mapping and location names presented a major problem. The author used US Army and US Air Force detailed maps, commercial maps, and in some cases commercial satellite photos. In many cases, however, the place names and terrain descriptions used in the combat reporting by both sides, and by independent observers, presented major contradictions that could not be resolved from available maps. No standardization emerged as to the spelling of place names. Sharp differences emerged in the geographic data published by various governments, and in the conflicting methods of transliterating Arabic and Farsi place names into English.

The same problem applied in reconciling the names of organizations and individuals—particularly those being transliterated from Arabic and Farsi. It again became painfully obvious that no progress is being made in reconciling the conflicting methods of transliterating such names into English. A limited effort has been made to standardize the spellings used in this text, but many different spellings are tied to the relational data bases used in preparing the analysis and the preservation of the original spelling is necessary to identify the source and tie it to the transcript of related interviews.

Notes

Chapter 1

1. Data for 1992–1994 are taken from US Arms Control and Disarmament Agency print out for the author, dated May 14, 1996, 11:37.

Chapter 2

2. The military manpower, force strength, and equipment estimates in this section are made by the author using a wide range of sources, including computerized data bases, interviews, and press clipping services. Most are impossible to reference in ways of use to the reader. The force strength statistics are generally taken from interviews, and from the sources reference for each paragraph. They also draw heavily on his *The Gulf and the Search for Strategic Stability* (Boulder, Westview, 1984) *The Gulf and the West* (Boulder, Westview, 1988), *and After the Storm, The Changing Military Balance in the Middle East* (Boulder, Westview, 1993).

Extensive use has also been made of the annual editions of the International Institute for Strategic Studies *Military Balance* (IISS, London); *Military Technology, World Defense Almanac*; and the Jaffee Center for Strategic Studies, *The Military Balance in the Middle East* (JCSS, Tel Aviv). Material has also been drawn from computer print outs from NEXIS, the United States Naval Institute data base, and from the DMS/FI Market Intelligence Reports data base.

Weapons data are taken from many sources, including computerized material available in NEXIS, and various editions of *Jane's Fighting Ships* (Jane's Publishing); *Jane's Naval Weapons Systems* (Jane's Publishing); *Jane's Armor and Artillery* (Jane's Publishing); *Jane's Infantry Weapons* (Jane's Publishing); *Jane's Military Vehicles and Logistics* (Jane's Publishing); *Jane's Land-Base Air Defense* (Jane's Publishing); *Jane's All the World's Aircraft* (Jane's Publishing); *Jane's Battlefield Surveillance Systems*, (Jane's Publishing); *Jane's Radar and Electronic Warfare Systems* (Jane's Publishing), *Jane's C³I Systems* (Jane's Publishing); *Jane's Air-Launched Weapons Systems* (Jane's Publishing); *Jane's Defense Appointments & Procurement Handbook (Middle East Edition)* (Jane's Publishing); *Tanks of the World* (Bernard and Grafe); *Weyer's Warships* (Bernard and Grafe); and *Warplanes of the World* (Bernard and Grafe).

Other military background, effectiveness, strength, organizational, and history data are taken from Anthony H. Cordesman, *Weapons of Mass Destruction in the Middle East, London*, Brassey's/RUSI, 1991; Anthony H. Cordesman and Abraham Wagner, *The Lessons of Modern War, Volume II*, Boulder, Westview, 1989; the relevant country or war sections of Herbert K. Tillema, *International Conflict Since 1945*, Boulder, Westview, 1991; Department of Defense, *Conduct of the Persian Gulf War; Final Report to Congress*, Washington, Department of Defense, April, 1992; Department of Defense and Department of State, *Congressional Presentation for Security Assistance Programs, Fiscal Year 1995*, Washington, Department of State, 1992; various annual editions of John Laffin's *The World in Conflict* or *War Annual*, London, Brassey's, and John Keegan, *World Armies*, London, Macmillan, 1983.

3. For the details of the battles for control of Bahrain from the early 1500s on, see Dr. Peter Vine, *The Bahrain National Museum*, London, Immel Publishing, 1993, pp. 75–110.

4. J. B. Kelley, *Arabia, the Gulf and the West*, New York, Basic Books, pp. 54–56, 87, 179–180.

5. *Defense News*, April 10, 1995, p. 4, October 23, 1995, p. 6; *Jane's Defense Weekly*, July 8, 1995, p. 15, September 30, 1995, p. 32; US Department of State, *Congressional Presentation: Foreign Operations Fiscal Year 1996*, Washington, State Department, pp. 493–499; *Periscope Daily Defense News*, July 6, 1995.

6. Reuters, December 4, 1995, 0933.

7. J. B. Kelley, *Arabia, the Gulf and the West*, New York, Basic Books, pp. 54–56, 87, 179–180.

8. This description is excerpted in part from Anthony H. Cordesman, *The Gulf and the West*, Boulder, Westview, 1984, pp. 587–589.

9. The author was briefed on these incidents several times during visits to Bahrain in the 1980s. Also see Emil Nakleh, "Democracy in the Gulf," *Middle East*, August, 1980, pp. 32–35; *Washington Post*, November 25, 1982, *8 Days*, May 23, 1981.

10. *Wall Street Journal*, June 12, 1995, p. 1; *Los Angeles Times*, May 3, 1995, p. A-2, June 26, 1995, p. A-2.

11. *Washington Times*, February 2, 1996, p. A-16.

12. *Defense News*, April 10, 1995, p. 4; *Wall Street Journal*, June 12, 1995, p. 1; *Los Angeles Times*, May 3, 1995, p. A-2, June 26, 1995, p. A-2; *Jane's Defense Weekly*, February 28, 1996, p. 18.

13. *Washington Times*, June 4, 1996, p. A-11; Reuters, June 6, 1996; *Daily Telegraph*, Internet, June 4, 1996; *Washington Post*, June 4, 1996, p. A-13, June 6, 1996, p. A-25.

14. Fax from Embassy of Bahrain, June 6, 1996, 11:50

15. *Gulf Times*, June 3, 1996, p. 2; *Khaleej Times*, June 3, 1996, p. 1.

16. *Washington Times*, June 4, 1996, p. A-11; Reuters, June 6, 1996; *Daily Telegraph*, Internet, June 4, 1996; *Washington Post*, June 4, 1996, p. A-13, June 6, 1996, p. A-25.

17. Reuters, June 6, 1996; *Daily Telegraph*, Internet, June 4, 1996; *Washington Post*, June 6, 1996, p. A-25.

18. J. B. Kelly, *Arabia, the Gulf, and the West*, New York, Basic Books, 1980, pp. 56–57; Helen Chapin Metz, *Persian Gulf States*, Washington, Department of the Army, DA Pam 550-185, January 1993, pp. 157–160.

19. *Defense and Foreign Affairs Weekly*, May 26–June 1, 1986, p. 4.

20. *Jane's Defense Weekly*, 14 June, 1986, p. 1087, and *Defense and Foreign Affairs Weekly*, May 26, 1986, p. 4.

21. Herbert K. Tillema, *International Conflict Since 1945*, Boulder, Westview, 1991, p. 156.

22. Helen Chapin Metz, *Persian Gulf States*, Washington, Department of the Army, DA Pam 550-185, January 1993, pp. 191–194.

23. *Washington Times*, December 27, 1995, p. A-10, January 17, 1996, p. A-10; *Middle East Economic Digest*, January 12, 1996, p. 6; January 26, 1996, p. 5; *The Estimate*, January 19, 1996, p. 1.

24. *Middle East Economic Digest*, January 26, 1996, p. 5.

25. J. B. Kelly, *Arabia, the Gulf, and the West*, New York, Basic Books, 1980, pp. 56–57; Helen Chapin Metz, *Persian Gulf States*, Washington, Department of the Army, DA Pam 550-185, January 1993, pp. 191–194.

26. Helen Chapin Metz, *Persian Gulf States*, Washington, Department of the Army PAM 550-185. pp. 137–140; US State Department, *Country Reports on Human Rights Practices for 1994*, Report Submitted to the Committee on Foreign Relations, Washington, GPO, February, 1995, pp. 1055–1063; US State Department, *Country Reports on Human Rights Practices for 1995*, country chapter on Bahrain, accessed from the Internet on March 14, 1996; Amnesty International, *Report 1994*, New York. Amnesty International, 1994, pp. 66–67.

27. US State Department, *Country Reports on Human Rights Practices for 1994*, Report Submitted to the Committee on Foreign Relations, Washington, GPO, February, 1995, pp. 1055–1063; US State Department, *Country Reports on Human Rights Practices for 1995*, country chapter on Bahrain, accessed from the Internet on March 14, 1996; Amnesty International, *Report 1994*, New York. Amnesty International, 1994, pp. 66–67; *Wall Street Journal*, June 12, 1995, p. 1; *Los Angeles Times*, May 3, 1995, p. A-2, June 26, 1995, p. A-2.

28. US State Department, *Country Reports on Human Rights Practices for 1995*, country chapter on Bahrain, accessed from the Internet on March 14, 1996.

29. *Khaleej Times*, June 2, 1996.

30. Data from the *Middle East Economic Digest*, the CIA, *World Factbook, 1995*, "Bahrain," and World Bank, *The World Bank Atlas, 1996*, Washington, World Bank, 1996, p. 8.

31. World Bank, "Forging a Partnership for Environmental Action," Washington, The World Bank, December, 1994, p. 24; World Bank, *The World Bank Atlas, 1996*, Washington, World Bank, 1996, p. 8.

32. World Bank, *The Middle East and North Africa: Issues in Development*, Washington, World Bank, Fall, 1995, p. 47.

33. Forecast International/DMS Market Intelligence Report, *Middle East and Africa—Bahrain*, April 1994, p. 3.

34. *Middle East Economic Digest*, November 24, 1995, p. 26.

35. *Middle East Economic Digest*, November 24, 1995, p. 26; Wall Street Journal, June 4, 1996, p. A-14.

36. CIA, *World Factbook, 1995*, "Bahrain"; World Bank, *World Population Projections, 1994–1995*, Washington, World Bank, 1995, p. 132.

37. See World Bank, *The Middle East and North Africa: Issues in Development*, Washington, World Bank, Fall, 1995, p. 47

38. Energy Information Agency (EIA), *International Energy Outlook, 1994*, DOE/EIA 0484(94), July, 1994, pp. 14–26; EIA, *International Petroleum Status*

Report, DOE/EIA 0520(94)1), November, 1994, pp. 6–7, BAPCO, working estimate, April, 1994 and July 1995; *OJJ Special, Oil and Gas Journal,* December 30, 1991, pp. 43–49; and *International Petroleum Encyclopedia, 1993,* Tulsa, PennWell Publishing Co., 1993, pp. 96, 284–285. Other estimates indicate 260 billion barrels of proven reserves and 42 billion barrels of probable reserves. See Joseph P. Riva, Jr. of the Congressional Research Service, writing in the *Oil and Gas Journal,* September 23, 1991, p. 62. These estimates have gotten increasingly more political in recent years as each major producer in the Gulf has tried to exaggerates its reserves and relative importance.

39. BAPCO, working estimate, April, 1994 and July 1995; *Middle East Economic Review,* November 22, 1991, pp. 13–16; and *International Petroleum Encyclopedia,* Tulsa, PennWell Publishing Co., 1993, pp. 96, 284–285.

40. BAPCO, working estimate, April, 1994 and July 1995; *Middle East Economic Review,* November 22, 1991, pp. 13–16; and *International Petroleum Encyclopedia,* Tulsa, PennWell Publishing Co., 1993, pp. 96, 284–285.

41. BAPCO, working estimate, April, 1994 and July 1995; Alan Richards, "Economic Roots of Instability in the Middle East," USCENTCOM, Tampa, Florida, 17–18 May, 1994; and D. F. Hepburn, "Observations from Oil Vantage Point," USCENTCOM, Tampa, Florida, 17–18 May, 1994; CIA, *World Factbook, 1994,* Washington, GPO, 1994, p. 33.

42. BAPCO, working estimate, April, 1994 and July 1995; *Middle East Economic Review,* November 22, 1991, pp. 13–16; and *International Petroleum Encyclopedia,* Tulsa, PennWell Publishing Co., 1993, pp. 96, 284–285.

43. CIA, *World Factbook, 1995,* "Bahrain"; Helen Chapin Metz, *Persian Gulf States,* Washington, Department of the Army, DA Pam 550-185, January 1993, pp. 122–124.

44. *Middle East Economic Digest, Special Report Bahrain ,* November 24, 1995, pp. 29–32.

45. *Middle East Economic Digest,* January 26, 1996, p. 7; World Bank, *The Middle East and North Africa: Issues in Development,* Washington, World Bank, Fall, 1995, p. 55.

46. CIA, *World Factbook, 1995,* "Bahrain"; Helen Chapin Metz, *Persian Gulf States,* Washington, Department of the Army, DA Pam 550-185, January 1993, pp. 122–124.

47. World Bank, *The Middle East and North Africa: Issues in Development,* Washington, World Bank, Fall, 1995, p. 54. Also see CIA, *World Factbook, 1995,* "Bahrain"; Helen Chapin Metz, *Persian Gulf States,* Washington, Department of the Army, DA Pam 550-185, January 1993, pp. 122–124.

48. CIA, *World Factbook, 1995,* "Bahrain."

49. *Middle East Economic Digest, Money,* November 11, 1995, p. 3; *EIU Country Report,* 2nd Quarter, 1995, pp. 10–11.

50. *Middle East Economic Digest,* November 24, 1995, p. 39; *EIU Country Report,* 2nd Quarter, 1995, pp. 10–11.

51. *Middle East Economic Digest,* November 24, 1995, p. 40; *EIU Country Report,* 2nd Quarter, 1995, pp. 10–11.

52. *EIU Country Report,* 2nd Quarter, 1995, pp. 10–11.

53. BAPCO, working estimate, April, 1994 and July 1995.

54. *Middle East Economic Digest, Special Report Bahrain*, November 24, 1995, pp. 29–32.

55. *Defense News*, March 16, 1992, p. 16; CIA, World Factbook, 1995, "Bahrain"; ACDA, *World Military Expenditures and Arms Transfers, 1993–1994*, GPO, Washington, 1995, p. 53; World Bank, *The World Bank Atlas*, 1996, Washington, World Bank, 1996, p. 18.

56. *Middle East Economic Digest, Money*, November 10, 1995, pp. 2–3.

57. *Defense News*, March 16, 1992, p. 16; CIA, World Factbook, 1995, "Bahrain"; ACDA, *World Military Expenditures and Arms Transfers, 1993–1994*, GPO, Washington, 1995, p. 53.

58. Population data are derived from the CIA data base; growth rate is estimated by the World Bank.

59. World Bank, *World Population Projections, 1994–1995*, Washington, World Bank, 1994; *Middle East Economic Digest*, July 28, 1995, p. 11; *CIA World Factbook*, 1995, "Iran."

60. Interviews, CIA, *World Factbook, 1995*, "Bahrain;" *Washington Post*, April 4, 1996, p. A-21.

61. This definition residency was the criteria for being able to vote for Bahrain's parliament before it was dissolved in 1976. Only 3% of the male population qualified.

62. Financial Affairs, Budget Directorate, *The Budget for Fiscal Year, 1995*, Ministry of Finance and National Economy, 1995; CIA, *World Factbook, 1995*, "Bahrain"; BAPCO, working estimate, April, 1994; Alan Richards, "Economic Roots of Instability in the Middle East," USCENTCOM, Tampa, Florida, 17–18 May, 1994; and D. F. Hepburn, "Observations from Oil Vantage Point," USCENTCOM, Tampa, Florida, 17–18 May, 1994; *Middle East Economic Digest, Special Report Bahrain*, November 24, 1995, pp. 29–32.

63. CIA, *World Factbook, 1995*, "Bahrain." US State Department, "Bahrain—Country Report," US Embassy Bahrain, 1994. The IISS estimates a total population of around 560,000, of which 32% is expatriate. It estimates that 10% of the population is other Arab, 13% is Asian, 8% is Iranian, and 1% is European. IISS, *Military Balance, 1995–1996*, p. 129.

64. These conclusions are based on World Bank and CIA demographic data.

65. CIA, *World Factbook, 1995*, "Bahrain"; Helen Chapin Metz, *Persian Gulf States*, Washington, Department of the Army, DA Pam 550-185, January 1993, pp. 118–119.

66. Based on interviews in Bahrain and comments by US and British experts.

67. Based on interviews in Bahrain and comments by US and British experts.

68. The coup involved arms shipped from Iran to Bahrain, the use of the Iranian embassy to support the coup attempt, and the training of Bahraini citizens in Iran. While some expatriate were arrested, the core force in the coup was some 73 Bahraini youths, all Shi'ite.

69. The coup involved arms shipped from Iran to Bahrain, the use of the Iranian embassy to support the coup attempt, and the training of Bahraini citizens in Iran. While some expatriate were arrested, the core force in the coup was some 73 Bahraini youths, all Shi'ite.

70. CIA, *World Factbook, 1994,* Washington, GPO, 1991, p. 32; CIA, *World Factbook, 1995,* "Bahrain"; Helen Chapin Metz, *Persian Gulf States,* Washington, Department of the Army, DA Pam 550-185, January 1993, pp. 118–119.

71. BAPCO, working estimate, April, 1994; Alan Richards, "Economic Roots of Instability in the Middle East," USCENTCOM, Tampa, Florida, 17–18 May, 1994; and D. F. Hepburn, "Observations from Oil Vantage Point," USCENTCOM, Tampa, Florida, 17–18 May, 1994.

72. *Wall Street Journal,* June 12, 1995, p. 1.

73. World Bank, "Will Arab Workers Prosper?," Washington, The World Bank, August, 1995.

74. CIA, *World Factbook, 1995,* "Bahrain"; BAPCO, working estimate, April, 1994; Alan Richards, "Economic Roots of Instability in the Middle East," USCENTCOM, Tampa, Florida, 17–18 May, 1994; and D. F. Hepburn, "Observations from Oil Vantage Point," USCENTCOM, Tampa, Florida, 17–18 May, 1994.

75. World Bank, "Forging a Partnership for Environmental Action," Washington, The World Bank, December, 1994, p. 24.

76. International Labor Office, "State of Bahrain: Labor Market Requirements and the Outputs of the Educational System," Geneva, ILO, May, 1995, draft.

77. The following details are based on interviews in Bahrain and a wide variety of press reports. For typical reporting, see Dr. Andrew Rathmell, "The Troubled State of Bahrain," *Jane's Intelligence Review,* Volume 7, Number 6, pp. 267–269,

78. *Washington Times,* April 19, 1995, p. A-12; *Los Angeles Times,* May 3, 1995, p. A-2; *Washington Post,* June 13, 1995, p. A-15.

79. *Washington Times,* April 19, 1995, p. A-12; *Los Angeles Times,* May 3, 1995, p. A-2; *Washington Post,* June 13, 1995, p. A-15.

80. Reports that troops were used are false. Some of these reports may stem from the deployment of Bahraini armed forces on routine exercises.

81. *Los Angeles Times,* June 26, 1995, p. A-2; *Washington Post,* June 13, 1995, p. A-15.

82. *Daily Times* (Bahrain), June 27, 1995, p. 1; *Wall Street Journal,* June 12, 1995, p. 1; *Los Angeles Times,* May 3, 1995, p. A-2, June 26, 1995, p. A-2; *Baltimore Sun,* December 18, 1995, p. 28; *Washington Times,* April 19, 1995, p. A-12; *Washington Post,* June 13, 1995, p. A-15; *Middle East Economic Digest,* July 7, 1995, p. 21.

83. *Middle East Economic Digest,* September 15, 1995, p. 4.

84. *TIR/EW,* August 4, 1995, p. 12.

85. *Middle East Economic Digest,* September 22, 1995, November 17, 1995, p. 18.

86. *Washington Post,* February 11, 1996, p. A-20.

87. Reuters, January 19, 1996, 23:08 BC Cycle.

88. Reuters and Associated Press, February 19, 20, 21, 22, 23, 24, 1996; *Washington Post,* February 15, 1996, p. A-20.

89. *The Estimate,* March 29, 1996, p. 1; Reuters, March 26, 1996, 1416; *Washington Post,* March 27, 1996, p. A-25; *Washington Times,* April 3, 1996, p. A-12.

90. *Orlando Sentinel Tribune,* May 5, 1996, p. A22; *Guardian,* May 6, 1996, p. 9; *Dallas Morning News,* April 25, 1996; *New York Times,* April 24, 1996, p. A-8; *The Independent,* April 16, 1996, p. 10.

91. Washington Times, June 4, 1996, p. A-11; Reuters, June 6, 1996; Daily Telegraph, Internet, June 4, 1996; Washington Post, June 4, 1996, p. A-13, June 6, 1996, p. A-25.

92. Reuters, June 6, 1996; Daily Telegraph, Internet, June 4, 1996; Washington Post, June 6, 1996, p. A-25.

93. See for example the interview with Foreign Minister , Sheik Mohammed bin Mubarak al-Khalifa in the Financial Times, April 12, 1996, p. 19.

94. Financial Times, April 12, 1996, p. 19; Washington Post, April 4, 1996, p. A-21.

95. Interviews, Washington Post, April 4, 1996, p. A-21.

96. Financial Times, April 12, 1996, p. 19; Washington Post, April 4, 1996, p. A-21.

97. Bahraini defense expenditure was officially set at 50.7 million dinars ($135 million) in 1986, and 53.9 billion dinars ($143 million) in 1987, and 62 billion dinars in 1988 ($165 million). It seems to have risen to an average of around $200 million annually in 1987 if one includes Saudi aid. Estimate based on Bahraini data and reporting in Jane's Defense Weekly, March 15, 1986, p. 452.

98. Arms Control and Disarmament Agency (ACDA), World Military Expenditures and Arms Transfers, 1990, Washington, GPO, 1992, Table I; and Arms Control and Disarmament Agency (ACDA), World Military Expenditures and Arms Transfers, 1993–1994, Washington, GPO, 1995, Table I; ACDA print out, May 14, 1996.

99. IISS, Military Balance, various editions.

100. Middle East Economic Digest, November 22, 1991, pp. 13–16.

101. Arms Control and Disarmament Agency (ACDA), World Military Expenditures and Arms Transfers, 1990, Washington, GPO, 1992, Table II; Arms Control and Disarmament Agency (ACDA), World Military Expenditures and Arms Transfers, 1993–1994, Washington, GPO, 1995, Table II; ACDA print out, May 14, 1996.

102. Arms Control and Disarmament Agency (ACDA), World Military Expenditures and Arms Transfers, 1985, Washington, GPO, 1985, pp. 133–134; and Arms Control and Disarmament Agency (ACDA), World Military Expenditures and Arms Transfers, 1993–1994, Washington, GPO, 1995, Table II; ACDA print out, May 14, 1996.

103. Arms Control and Disarmament Agency (ACDA), World Military Expenditures and Arms Transfers, 1989, Washington, GPO, 1990, pp. 117–118; ACDA print out, May 14, 1996.

104. Richard F. Grimmett in Conventional Arms Transfers to Developing Nations, 1987–1994, Congressional Research Service 95-862F, August 4, 1995, pp. 56–57 and 68.

105. US Defense Security Assistance Agency (DSAA), "Foreign Military Sales, Foreign Military Construction Sales and Military Assistance Facts as of September 30, 1994," Department of Defense, Washington, 1995.

106. Some estimates are as low as 7,150–7,400 men.

107. CIA, World Factbook, 1995, "Bahrain."

108. IISS, Military Balance, 1994–1995, and Military Technology, World Defense Almanac, 1994–1995, Vol. XIX, Issue 1, 1995, ISSN 0722-3226, pp. 207–208. While Iran occasionally shows women in military roles for propaganda purposes, it does not employ them in any meaningful military roles.

109. Estimate derived from interviews and *Defense News*, May 9, 1994, IISS; *Military Balance, 1995–1996, "Bahrain,"* and Military Technology, *World Defense Almanac, 1994–1995,* Vol. XIX, Issue 1, 1995, ISSN 0722-3226, pp. 207–208.

110. *Defense News,* April 17, 1995, p. 1; *Jane's Defense Weekly,* September 30, 1995, p. 32.

111. *Defense News,* June 26, 1995, p. 18; *Jane's Defense Weekly,* September 30, 1995, p. 32.

112. *Defense News,* March 16, 1992, p. 6; *Jane's Defense Weekly,* September 30, 1995, p. 32.

113. *Defense News,* March 16, 1992, p. 6; *Jane's Defense Weekly,* September 30, 1995, p. 32.

114. *Defense News,* February 2, 1987, p. 15, March 30, 1992, p. 22; April 17, 1995, p. 1; *Jane's Defense Weekly,* September 30, 1995, pp. 32–33.

115. One Bahraini source claims 40 Crotale launchers. This estimate seems to be too high. IISS, *Military Balance, 1995–1996, "Bahrain,"* and Military Technology, *World Defense Almanac, 1994–1995,* Vol. XIX, Issue 1, 1995, ISSN 0722-3226, pp. 207–208; *Jane's Defense Weekly,* September 30, 1995, pp. 32–33.

116. *Defense News,* April 17, 1995, p. 1.

117. *Jane's Defense Weekly,* March 28, 1992, p. 530.

118. There were unconfirmed reports in 1989 that Bahrain was also recruiting Sudanese. If so, some of these may also have left Bahrain's armed forces.

119. *Jane's Defense Weekly,* February 13, 1988, p. 247, September 30, 1995, pp. 32–33; IISS *Military Balance, 1995–1996, "Bahrain,"* and Military Technology, *World Defense Almanac, 1994–1995,* Vol. XIX, Issue 1, 1995, ISSN 0722-3226, pp. 207–208; *Jane's Fighting Ships, 1994,* pp. 38–49.

120. *Defense News,* April 17, 1995, p. 1; June 26, 1995, p. 18.

121. *Jane's Defense Weekly,* February 13, 1988, p. 247, September 30, 1995, pp. 32–33; IISS *Military Balance, 1995–1996, "Bahrain,"* and Military Technology, *World Defense Almanac, 1994–1995,* Vol. XIX, Issue 1, 1995, ISSN 0722-3226, pp. 207–208; *Jane's Fighting Ships, 1994,* pp. 38–49.

122. *Jane's Defense Weekly,* February 13, 1988, p. 247, September 30, 1995, pp. 32–33; *Defense News,* December 6, 1993, December 13, 1993; IISS *Military Balance, 1995–1996, "Bahrain,"* and Military Technology, *World Defense Almanac, 1994–1995,* Vol. XIX, Issue 1, 1995, ISSN 0722-3226, pp. 207–208; ; *Jane's Fighting Ships, 1994,* pp. 38–49.

123. *Jane's Defense Weekly,* February 13, 1988, p. 247; *Defense News,* December 6, 1993, December 13, 1993; IISS *Military Balance, 1995–1996, "Bahrain,"* and Military Technology, *World Defense Almanac, 1994–1995,* Vol. XIX, Issue 1, 1995, ISSN 0722-3226, pp. 207–208; *Jane's Fighting Ships, 1994,* pp. 38–49.

124. Other estimates indicate the Coast Guard is equipped with 6 coastal patrol craft, 10 motorized dhows, 3 landing craft, and one Hovercraft. *Defense News,* March 16, 1992, p. 16247; IISS *Military Balance, 1995–1996, "Bahrain,"* and Military Technology, *World Defense Almanac, 1994–1995,* Vol. XIX, Issue 1, 1995, ISSN 0722-3226, pp. 207–208; *Jane's All the World's Navies, 1994,* pp. 38–49.

125. At a cost of $114 million, and as part of a package including 60 AIM-9-P3 missiles. DMS Intelligence data base.

126. *Jane's Defense Weekly*, September 30, 1995, pp. 32–33; US DSSA, June, 1996.

127. *Defense News*, May 6, 1996, p. 3.

128. *Defense News*, June 26, 1995, p. 18; *Jane's Defense Weekly*, September 30, 1995, pp. 32–33.

129. US State Department, *Country Reports on Human Rights Practices for 1994*, Report Submitted to the Committee on Foreign Relations, Washington, GPO, February, 1995, pp. 1055–1063; ; US State Department, *Country Reports on Human Rights Practices for 1995*, country chapter on Bahrain, accessed from the Internet on March 14, 1996; Amnesty International, *Report 1994*, New York. Amnesty International, 1994, pp. 66–67.

130. IISS, Based on interviews, wire service reports, faxes from the Bahrain Freedom Movement, and; Helen Chapin Metz, *Persian Gulf States*, Washington, Department of the Army PAM 550–185. pp. 140–143; *Wall Street Journal*, June 12, 1995; *Financial Times*, April 12, 1996, p. 19; *Christian Science Monitor*, April 23, 1996, p. 19; *Defense News*, May 6, 1996, p. 16.

131. Based on interviews, wire service reports, faxes from the Bahrain Freedom Movement, and US State Department, *Country Reports on Human Rights Practices for 1994*, Report Submitted to the Committee on Foreign Relations, Washington, GPO, February, 1995, pp. 1055–1063; US State Department, *Country Reports on Human Rights Practices for 1995*, country chapter on Bahrain, accessed from the Internet on March 14, 1996; Amnesty International, *Report 1994*, New York. Amnesty International, 1994, pp. 66–67.

132. Based on interviews, wire service reports, faxes from the Bahrain Freedom Movement, and US State Department, *Country Reports on Human Rights Practices for 1994*, Report Submitted to the Committee on Foreign Relations, Washington, GPO, February, 1995, pp. 1055–1063; US State Department, *Country Reports on Human Rights Practices for 1995*, country chapter on Bahrain, accessed from the Internet on March 14, 1996; Amnesty International, *Report 1994*, New York. Amnesty International, 1994, pp. 66–67; Helen Chapin Metz, *Persian Gulf States*, Washington, Department of the Army PAM 550-185. pp. 142–143.

133. Interviews, US State Department, *Country Reports on Human Rights Practices for 1995*, country chapter on Bahrain, accessed from the Internet on March 14, 1996.

134. Interviews, US State Department, *Country Reports on Human Rights Practices for 1995*, country chapter on Bahrain, accessed from the Internet on March 14, 1996.

135. US State Department, *Country Reports on Human Rights Practices for 1995*, country chapter on Bahrain, accessed from the Internet on March 14, 1996.

136. Interviews, US State Department, *Country Reports on Human Rights Practices for 1995*, country chapter on Bahrain, accessed from the Internet on March 14, 1996.

137. Interviews, US State Department, *Country Reports on Human Rights Practices for 1995*, country chapter on Bahrain, accessed from the Internet on March 14, 1996.

138. US State Department, *Country Reports on Human Rights Practices for 1995*, country chapter on Bahrain, accessed from the Internet on March 14, 1996.

139. US State Department, *Country Reports on Human Rights Practices for 1995*, country chapter on Bahrain, accessed from the Internet on March 14, 1996.

140. *Dallas Morning News*, April 25, 1996.

141. US State Department, *Country Reports on Human Rights Practices for 1995*, country chapter on Bahrain, accessed from the Internet on March 14, 1996.

142. Based on interviews, wire service reports, faxes from the Bahrain Freedom Movement; US State Department, *Country Reports on Human Rights Practices for 1994*, Report Submitted to the Committee on Foreign Relations, Washington, GPO, February, 1995, pp. 1055–1063; US State Department, *Country Reports on Human Rights Practices for 1995*, country chapter on Bahrain, accessed from the Internet on March 14, 1996; Report Submitted to the Committee on Foreign Relations, Washington, GPO, February, 1995, pp. 1055–1063; Amnesty International, *Report 1994*, New York. Amnesty International, 1994, pp. 66–67.

143. Interviews in Bahrain in March, 1991. Saudi MODA briefing aid, March, 1991. Cohen, Dr. Eliot A, Director, *Gulf War Air Power Survey, Volume V*, Washington, US Air Force/Government Printing Office, 1993, pp. 232–233, 319, 338, 340.

144. Deutsche Press-Agentur, October 19, 1994.

145. *Defense News*, May 6, 1996, p. 16.

146. *Washington Times*, August 29, 1995; *Jane's Defense Weekly*, August 26, 1995, p. 3.

147. Executive News Service, October 17, 1995, 1225 and October 23, 1995, 1610; *Washington Post*, October 17, 1995, p. A-16.

148. *New York Times*, January 30, 1996, p. A-6.

149. Defense Security Assistance Agency (DSAA), Foreign Military Sales, *Foreign Military Construction Sales, and Military Assistance Facts As of September 30, 1993*, Washington, DC; FMS Control and Reports Division, Comptroller, DSAA, 1994, pp. 2–3, 16–17.

150. Defense Security Assistance Agency (DSAA), Foreign Military Sales, *Foreign Military Construction Sales, and Military Assistance Facts As of September 30, 1993*, Washington, DC; FMS Control and Reports Division, Comptroller, DSAA, 1994, pp. 2–3, 16–17. Covers FY1991–FY1993.

151. Defense Security Assistance Agency (DSAA), Foreign Military Sales, *Foreign Military Construction Sales, and Military Assistance Facts As of September 30, 1993*, Washington, DC; FMS Control and Reports Division, Comptroller, DSAA, 1994, pp. 94–95, 102–103.

Chapter 3

152. There are many good Western histories of Oman. For a good Omani summary on the nation's history see Malallah bin Ali Habib Allawati, *Outline of the History of Oman*, Muscat, Mazoon Printing Press, 1993. Also see Dr. Peter Vine, *Oman in History*, Immel Publishing, London, 1995; Miriam Joyce, *The Sultanate of Oman, A Twentieth Century History*, Praeger, Westport, 1995; and Joseph A. Kechichian, *Oman and the World*, Santa Monica, Rand, 1995.

153. The Ibadhis have become relatively liberal and tolerant, although they long resisted secular change during the time the Imam's rivaled the Sultans. They

make up about 75% of Oman's native population. CIA, *World Factbook, 1995,* Washington, GPO, 1994, "Oman."

154. The military manpower, force strength, and equipment estimates in this section are made by the author using a wide range of sources, including computerized data bases, interviews, and press clipping services and Ronald D. McLaurin, "Strategic Evolution in Oman," *Times of Oman,* December 16, 1992. Many are impossible to reference in ways of use to the reader. Extensive use has also been made of the annual editions of the International Institute for Strategic Studies *Military Balance* (IISS, London), in this case, the 1995–1996 edition, and of the Jaffee Center for Strategic Studies, *The Military Balance in the Middle East* (JCSS, Tel Aviv), especially the 1993–1994 edition; and Military Technology, *World Defense Almanac, 1994–1995,* Vol. XIX, Issue 1, 1995, ISSN 0722-3226, pp. 207–240. Material has also been drawn from computer print outs from NEXIS, the United States Naval Institute data base, and from the DMS/FI Market Intelligence Reports data base. Weapons data are taken from many sources, including computerized material available in NEXIS, and various editions of *Jane's Fighting Ships* (Jane's Publishing); *Jane's Naval Weapons Systems* (Jane's Publishing); *Jane's Armor and Artillery* (Jane's Publishing); *Jane's Infantry Weapons* (Jane's Publishing); *Jane's Military Vehicles and Logistics* (Jane's Publishing); *Jane's Land-Base Air Defense* (Jane's Publishing); *Jane's All the World's Aircraft* (Jane's Publishing); *Jane's Battlefield Surveillance Systems,* (Jane's Publishing); *Jane's Radar and Electronic Warfare Systems* (Jane's Publishing), *Jane's C³I Systems* (Jane's Publishing); *Jane's Air-Launched Weapons Systems* (Jane's Publishing); *Jane's Defense Appointments & Procurement Handbook (Middle East Edition)* (Jane's Publishing); *Tanks of the World* (Bernard and Grafe); *Weyer's Warships* (Bernard and Grafe); and *Warplanes of the World* (Bernard and Grafe).

Other military background, effectiveness, strength, organizational, and history data are taken from Anthony H. Cordesman, *After The Storm: The Changing Military Balance in the Middle East,* Boulder, Westview, 1993; *The Gulf and the Search for Strategic Stability,* Boulder, Westview, 1984, *The Gulf and the West,* Boulder, Westview, 1988, and *Weapons of Mass Destruction in the Middle East,* London, Brassey's/RUSI, 1991; Anthony H. Cordesman and Abraham Wagner, *The Lessons of Modern War, Volume II,* Boulder, Westview, 1989; the relevant country or war sections of Herbert K. Tillema, *International Conflict Since 1945,* Boulder, Westview, 1991; Department of Defense and Department of State, *Congressional Presentation for Security Assistance Programs, Fiscal Year 1996,* Washington, Department of State, 1992; various annual editions of John Laffin's *The World in Conflict* or *War Annual,* London, Brassey's, and John Keegan, *World Armies,* London, Macmillan, 1983.

155. Iran's naval forces are largely based at Bandar Abbas inside the Gulf and to the northwest of the Strait of Hormuz. Iran has discussed Jask as a possible submarine base, and began the construction of a major naval base at Bandar Abbas at the time of the Shah. Work on Bandar Abbas stopped in 1979, when the Shah fell, but seems to have been renewed. See *Jane's Defense Weekly,* May 8, 1996, p. 4.

156. *Washington Times,* October 25, 1995.

157. Reuters, June 3, 1995.

158. Reuters, July 10, 1995, 0552.

159. Sheik Saqr made several attempts to take territory from his neighbors, and was anything but a popular ruler.

160. *Middle East Economic Digest,* October 13, 1995, p. 20; *Philadelphia Inquirer,* October 2, 1995, p. B-5; *Washington Times,* January 28, 1996, p. A-19.

161. US Embassy, Sultanate of Oman, "Country Commercial Guide: Sultanate of Oman," July, 1994, pp. 9–10, A-1 to A-2; Anne Joyce, "Interview with Sultan Qabus Bin Said Al Said," *Middle East Policy,* Spring, 1995, pp. 1–6.

162. Ministry of Information, *Oman, 1993,* Muscat, Ministry of Information, 1994; Oman, *Statistical Yearbook, Twenty Second Issue,* Information and Documentation Center, Muscat, October, 1994.

163. *Oman: A Financial Times Survey,* November 20, 1991, pp. I-IV; US Embassy, Sultanate of Oman, "Country Commercial Guide: Sultanate of Oman," July, 1994; Peter Kemp, "MEED Special Report: Oman," *Middle East Economic Digest,* May 5, 1995, pp. 8–15; Ministry of Information, *Oman, 1993,* Muscat, Ministry of Information, 1994; Oman, *Statistical Yearbook, Twenty Second Issue,* Information and Documentation Center, Muscat, October, 1994.

164. Speeches by His Majesty Sultan Qabus Bin Said al Said, November 18, 1994, and December 26, 1994; Sultanate of Oman, *Majles A'Shurea; Documents of Establishment, the First Term;* Muscat, Government of Oman, 1992; Ministry of Information, *Oman, 1993,* Muscat, Ministry of Information, 1994; *Middle East Economic Digest,* November 17, 1995, p. 8.

165. Speech by His Majesty Sultan Qabus Bin Said al Said, December 26, 1994; Sultanate of Oman, *Majles A'Shurea; Documents of Establishment, the First Term;* Muscat, Government of Oman, 1992.

166. *Oman: A Financial Times Survey,* November 20, 1991, pp. I-IV; US Embassy, Sultanate of Oman, "Country Commercial Guide: Sultanate of Oman," July, 1994; Peter Kemp, "MEED Special Report: Oman," *Middle East Economic Digest,* May 5, 1995, pp. 8–15.

167. US Embassy, Sultanate of Oman, "Country Commercial Guide: Sultanate of Oman," July, 1994, pp. 9–10, A-1 to A-2.

168. *The Estimate,* March 29, 1996.

169. Ministry of Development, *Localities, Housing Units, Household, and Population in the Sultanate, 1993,* Muscat, Ministry of Development, January, 1995; Oman, *Statistical Yearbook, Twenty Second Issue,* Information and Documentation Center, Muscat, October, 1994; CIA, *World Factbook,* 1995, "Oman."

170. CIA, *World Factbook,* 1995, "Oman"; US Embassy, Sultanate of Oman, "Country Commercial Guide: Sultanate of Oman," July, 1994, pp. A-1 to A-2. The IISS estimates a total population of around 2,018,000, of which 27% is expatriate. IISS, *Military Balance, 1995–1996,* "Oman."

171. Interviews, *The Estimate,* August 19, 1994, p. 1, October 77, 1995, p. 3, March 29, 1996, pp. 1–9.

172. Speech by His Majesty Sultan Qabus Bin Said al Said, November 18, 1994; US State Department, Country Report on Human Rights Practices in 1994, Washington, GPO, 1994, Internet on-line edition, May, 1995; reporting by Amnesty International and Middle East Watch; *The Estimate,* March 29, 1996.

173. Ministry of Development, *Localities, Housing Units, Household, and Population in the Sultanate, 1993*, Muscat, Ministry of Development, January, 1995; Oman, *Statistical Yearbook, Twenty Second Issue*, Information and Documentation Center, Muscat, October, 1994.

174. World Bank, *World Population Projections, 1994–1995*, Washington, World Bank, 1994; *Middle East Economic Digest*, July 28, 1995, p. 11; *CIA World Factbook*, 1995, "Oman."

175. World Bank, *World Population Projections, 1994–1995*, Washington, World Bank, 1994; *Middle East Economic Digest*, July 28, 1995, p. 11; *CIA World Factbook*, 1995, "Oman."

176. Oman, *Statistical Yearbook, Twenty Second Issue*, Information and Documentation Center, Muscat, October, 1994.

177. Ministry of Information, *Oman, 1993*, Muscat, Ministry of Information, 1994; Oman, *Statistical Yearbook, Twenty Second Issue*, Information and Documentation Center, Muscat, October, 1994.

178. CIA, *World Factbook, 1995*, Washington, GPO, 1994, "Oman."

179. Sultanate of Oman, Ministry of Development, *Basic Components and Main Indicators of the Fifth Five Year Plan (1996–2000)*, Muscat, Government of Oman, January, 1996, pp. 57–64.

180. Sultanate of Oman, Ministry of Development, *Basic Components and Main Indicators of the Fifth Five Year Plan (1996–2000)*, Muscat, Government of Oman, January, 1996, p. 63.

181. The CIA estimates that Oman had a GDP with a purchasing power of around $17 billion in 1994. It had total exports of approximately $4.8 billion, and imports worth $4.1 billion. Oman's external debt totaled a relatively low $3 billion. CIA, *World Factbook, 1995*, "Oman."

182. US Embassy, Sultanate of Oman, "Country Commercial Guide: Sultanate of Oman," July, 1994; Ministry of Information, Oman, 1993, Muscat, Ministry of Information, 1994; Oman, Statistical Yearbook, Twenty Second Issue, Information and Documentation Center, Muscat, October, 1994.

183. CIA, *World Factbook, 1995*, Washington, GPO, 1995; *Middle East Economic Digest*, May 3, 1996, p. 10.

184. CIA, *World Factbook, 1995*, Washington, GPO, 1995, "Oman"; Ministry of Information, *Oman, 1993*, Muscat, Ministry of Information, 1994; Oman, *Statistical Yearbook, Twenty Second Issue*, Information and Documentation Center, Muscat, October, 1994.

185. MEED estimates a per capita income of $6,480 in 1995. *MEED*, May 5, 1995, p. 8; Anne Joyce, "Interview with Sultan Qabus Bin Said Al Said," *Middle East Policy*, Spring, 1995, pp. 1–6; World Bank, "Forging a Partnership for Environmental Action," Washington, World Bank, December, 1994, p. 24.

186. Peter Kemp, "MEED Special Report: Oman," *Middle East Economic Digest*, May 5, 1995, pp. 8–15; US Embassy, Sultanate of Oman, "Country Commercial Guide: Sultanate of Oman," July, 1994; Ministry of Information, *Oman, 1993*, Muscat, Ministry of Information, 1994; Oman, *Statistical Yearbook, Twenty Second Issue*, Information and Documentation Center, Muscat, October, 1994.

187. *Washington Times*, November 18, 1995, p. C-1; Peter Kemp, "MEED Special Report: Oman," *Middle East Economic Digest*, May 5, 1995, pp. 8–15, December 15,

1995, p. 17; US Embassy, Sultanate of Oman, "Country Commercial Guide: Sultanate of Oman," July, 1994; Ministry of Information, *Oman, 1993*, Muscat, Ministry of Information, 1994; Oman, *Statistical Yearbook, Twenty Second Issue*, Information and Documentation Center, Muscat, October, 1994.

188. Oman, *Statistical Yearbook, Twenty Second Issue*, Information and Documentation Center, Muscat, October, 1994.

189. Sultanate of Oman, *Basic Components and Main Indicators of the Fifth Five Year Plan (1996–2000)*, Muscat, Ministry of Development, January 1996, pp. 7, 13–15, 24–25, and 50.

190. *Middle East Economic Digest*, July 21, 1995, p. 25.

191. EIA Internet on-line data base, analysis section, country chapters, July 16, 1995.

192. *Oil and Gas Journal*, September 23, 1991, p. 62.

193. Mark Nicholson, "A Tough Hurdle," *Oman: A Financial Times Survey*, November 20, 1991, pp. I-IV; *International Petroleum Encyclopedia, 1993*, Tulsa, PennWell Press, 1993, pp. 101–102, 280, 284–285; DOE/EIA, *International Energy Outlook, 1994*, Washington, DOE/EIA, 1994, p. 26; Peter Kemp, "MEED Special Report: Oman," *Middle East Economic Digest*, May 5, 1995, pp. 8–15; Ministry of Information, *Oman, 1993*, Muscat, Ministry of Information, 1994; Oman, *Statistical Yearbook, Twenty Second Issue*, Information and Documentation Center, Muscat, October, 1994.

194. EIA Internet on-line data base, analysis section, country chapters, July 16, 1995.

195. Oman, *Statistical Yearbook, Twenty Second Issue*, Information and Documentation Center, Muscat, October, 1994.

196. EIA, *Middle East Economic Digest*, May 3, 1996, pp. 10–16.

197. EIA Internet on-line data base, analysis section, country chapters, July 16, 1995; *Middle East Economic Digest*, July 21, 1995, pp. 25–26, May 3, 1996, pp. 10–16.

198. Mark Nicholson, "A Tough Hurdle," *Oman: A Financial Times Survey*, November 20, 1991, pp. I-IV; *International Petroleum Encyclopedia, 1993*, Tulsa, PennWell Press, 1993, pp. 101–102, 280, 284–285; DOE/EIA, *International Energy Outlook, 1994*, Washington, DOE/EIA, 1994, p. 26; Peter Kemp, "MEED Special Report: Oman," *Middle East Economic Digest*, May 5, 1995, pp. 8–15; Ministry of Information, *Oman, 1993*, Muscat, Ministry of Information, 1994; Oman, *Statistical Yearbook, Twenty Second Issue*, Information and Documentation Center, Muscat, October, 1994.

199. These estimates do not include up to 30 billion barrels of heavy crude, which may eventually be producable. *Oil and Gas Journal Special, Oil and Gas Journal*, December 30, 1991, pp. 43–49; Peter Kemp, "MEED Special Report: Oman," *Middle East Economic Digest*, May 5, 1995, pp. 8–15. Other estimates indicate 4.3 billion barrels of proven reserves and 2 billion barrels of probable reserves. See Joseph P. Riva, Jr. of the Congressional Research Service, writing in the *Oil and Gas Journal*, September 23, 1991, p. 62. These estimates have gotten increasingly more political in recent years as each major producer in the Gulf has tried to exaggerates its reserves and relative importance.

200. Sultanate of Oman, *Basic Components and Main Indicators of the Fifth Five Year Plan (1996–2000)*, Muscat, Ministry of Development, January 1996, pp. 33–35.

201. EIA Internet on-line data base, analysis section, country chapters, July 16, 1995; *Middle East Economic Digest,* July 21, 1995, pp. 25–26.

202. Sultanate of Oman, *Basic Components and Main Indicators of the Fifth Five Year Plan (1996–2000),* Muscat, Ministry of Development, January 1996, pp. 33–35.

203. EIA Internet on-line data base, analysis section, country chapters, July 16, 1995; *Middle East Economic Digest,* July 21, 1995, pp. 25–26.

204. EIA Internet on-line data base, analysis section, country chapters, July 16, 1995; *Middle East Economic Digest,* July 21, 1995, pp. 25–26.

205. EIA Internet on-line data base, analysis section, country chapters, July 16, 1995; *Middle East Economic Digest,* July 21, 1995, pp. 25–26.

206. EIA Internet on-line data base, analysis section, country chapters, July 16, 1995; *Middle East Economic Digest,* July 21, 1995, pp. 25–26.

207. EIA Internet on-line data base, analysis section, country chapters, July 16, 1995; *Middle East Economic Digest,* July 21, 1995, pp. 25–26.

208. EIA Internet on-line data base, analysis section, country chapters, July 16, 1995; *Middle East Economic Digest,* July 21, 1995, pp. 25–26.

209. EIA Internet on-line data base, analysis section, country chapters, July 16, 1995; *Middle East Economic Digest,* July 21, 1995, pp. 25–26.

210. EIA Internet on-line data base, analysis section, country chapters, July 16, 1995; *Middle East Economic Digest,* July 21, 1995, pp. 25–26.

211. IEA, *Oil, Gas, and Coal Supply Outlook,* Paris, OECD/IEA, 1995, p. 144.

212. World Bank working report, 1993; Peter Kemp, "MEED Special Report: Oman," *Middle East Economic Digest,* May 5, 1995, pp. 8–15, May 3, 1996, p. 10. Key reserve areas include the Ghaba salt basin, and fields at Saih Rawl, Barik, and Saih Nihayda.

213. Sultanate of Oman, *Basic Components and Main Indicators of the Fifth Five Year Plan (1996–2000),* Muscat, Ministry of Development, January 1996, pp. 33–35.

214. Sultanate of Oman, *Basic Components and Main Indicators of the Fifth Five Year Plan (1996–2000),* Muscat, Ministry of Development, January 1996, pp. 33–35.

215. Sultanate of Oman, *Basic Components and Main Indicators of the Fifth Five Year Plan (1996–2000),* Muscat, Ministry of Development, January 1996, pp. 33–35.

216. Sultanate of Oman, *Basic Components and Main Indicators of the Fifth Five Year Plan (1996–2000),* Muscat, Ministry of Development, January 1996, pp. 33–35.

217. EIA Internet on-line data base, analysis section, country chapters, July 16, 1995; *Middle East Economic Digest,* July 21, 1995, pp. 25–26.

218. EIA Internet on-line data base, analysis section, country chapters, July 16, 1995; *Middle East Economic Digest,* July 21, 1995, pp. 25–26, December 15, 1995, p. 17, May 3, 1996, pp. 13–15; IEA, *Oil, Gas, and Coal Supply Outlook,* Paris, OECD/IEA, 1995, pp. 143–144.

219. EIA Internet on-line data base, analysis section, country chapters, July 16, 1995; *Middle East Economic Digest,* July 21, 1995, pp. 25–266, December 15, 1995, p. 17, May 3, 1996, pp. 13–15; IEA, *Oil, Gas, and Coal Supply Outlook,* Paris, OECD/IEA, 1995, pp. 143–144.

220. *Middle East Economic Digest,* May 3, 1996, pp. 13–15.

221. EIA Internet on-line data base, analysis section, country chapters, July 16, 1995; *Middle East Economic Digest,* July 21, 1995, pp. 25–266; IEA, *Oil, Gas, and Coal Supply Outlook,* Paris, OECD/IEA, 1995, pp. 143–144.

222. *Middle East Economic Digest*, August 18, 1995, p. 23, May 3, 1996, pp. 13–15.
223. Ministry of Information, *Oman, 1993*, Muscat, Ministry of Information, 1994; Oman, *Statistical Yearbook, Twenty Second Issue*, Information and Documentation Center, Muscat, October, 1994.
224. US Embassy, Sultanate of Oman, "Country Commercial Guide: Sultanate of Oman," July, 1994, pp. 9–10, A-1 to A-2; Peter Kemp, "MEED Special Report: Oman," *Middle East Economic Digest*, May 5, 1995, pp. 8–15, December 15, 1995, p. 17.
225. Omani government data; *Jane's Defense Weekly*, February 7, 1996, p. 15; Peter Kemp, "MEED Special Report: Oman," *Middle East Economic Digest*, May 5, 1995, pp. 8–15, December 15, 1995, p. 17.
226. Sultanate of Oman, *Basic Components and Main Indicators of the Fifth Five Year Plan (1996–2000)*, Muscat, Ministry of Development, January 1996, pp. 28–29, 33–35.
227. Omani government data; *Jane's Defense Weekly*, February 7, 1996, p. 15; Peter Kemp, "MEED Special Report: Oman," *Middle East Economic Digest*, May 5, 1995, pp. 8–15, December 15, 1995, p. 17.
228. *Washington Times*, November 18, 1995, p. C-1; Reuters, September 17, 1995, 1146; *Middle East Economic Digest*, December 15, 1995, p. 17.
229. US Embassy, Sultanate of Oman, "Country Commercial Guide: Sultanate of Oman," July, 1994, pp. 9–10, A-1 to A-2; Peter Kemp, "MEED Special Report: Oman," *Middle East Economic Digest*, May 5, 1995, pp. 8–15.
230. Sultanate of Oman, *Basic Components and Main Indicators of the Fifth Five Year Plan (1996–2000)*, Muscat, Ministry of Development, January 1996, pp. 28–29.
231. World Bank, "Will Arab Workers Prosper?" Washington, World Bank, August, 1995, p. 8.
232. World Bank, "Forging a Partnership for Environmental Action," Washington, World Bank, December, 1994, pp. 22–23.
233. *Los Angeles Times*, January 28, 1992, p. C-1; working papers from the Royal Institute of International Affairs (RIIA) conference on Saudi society, economy, and security, October 4–5, 1993.
234. *Middle East Economic Digest*, March 1, 1996, p. 3.
235. Ministry of Information, *Oman, 1993*, Muscat, Ministry of Information, 1994; *Los Angeles Times*, January 28, 1992, p. C-1; *Oman: A Financial Times Survey*, November 20, 1991, pp. I-IV; World Bank, "Forging a Partnership for Environmental Action," Washington, World Bank, December, 1994, pp. 19, 22–23.
236. Sultanate of Oman, *Basic Components and Main Indicators of the Fifth Five Year Plan (1996–2000)*, Muscat, Ministry of Development, January 1996, pp. 47–49, 50.
237. Sultanate of Oman, *Basic Components and Main Indicators of the Fifth Five Year Plan (1996–2000)*, Muscat, Ministry of Development, January 1996, pp. 47–49.
238. *Middle East Economic Digest*, March 1, 1996, p. 3; Sultanate of Oman, *Basic Components and Main Indicators of the Fifth Five Year Plan (1996–2000)*, Muscat, Ministry of Development, January 1996, pp. 14–19.
239. Sultanate of Oman, *Basic Components and Main Indicators of the Fifth Five Year Plan (1996–2000)*, Muscat, Ministry of Development, January 1996, p. 27.
240. Sultanate of Oman, *Basic Components and Main Indicators of the Fifth Five Year Plan (1996–2000)*, Muscat, Ministry of Development, January 1996, p. 19.

241. For a summary of Oman's effort, see the speech by H. E. Mohammed Bin Musa Al Yousef, Minister of State for Development Affairs, at the closing session of the Conference on Vision for Oman's Economy, "Oman: 2020," June 3–4, 1995.

242. US Embassy, Sultanate of Oman, "Country Commercial Guide: Sultanate of Oman," July, 1994, pp. 9–10, A-1 to A-2; *Washington Post* January 30, 1995.

243. US Embassy, Sultanate of Oman, "Country Commercial Guide: Sultanate of Oman," July, 1994, pp. 9–10, A-1 to A-2; *Washington Post* January 30, 1995.

244. *Defense News*, June 26, 1995, p. 10; *Jane's Defense Weekly*, July 30, 1994, p. 35.

245. Arms Control and Disarmament Agency (ACDA), *World Military Expenditures and Arms Transfers, 1990*, Washington, GPO, 1992, Table I, and Arms Control and Disarmament Agency (ACDA), *World Military Expenditures and Arms Transfers, 1994–1995*, Washington, GPO, 1995, Table I.

246. Arms Control and Disarmament Agency (ACDA), *World Military Expenditures and Arms Transfers, 1994–1995*, Washington, GPO, 1995, Table I; ACDA print out, May 14, 1996.

247. Arms Control and Disarmament Agency (ACDA), *World Military Expenditures and Arms Transfers, 1994–1995*, Washington, GPO, 1995, Table I; ACDA print out, May 14, 1996.

248. IISS, *Military Balance*, 1995–1996, "Oman."

249. Arms Control and Disarmament Agency (ACDA), *World Military Expenditures and Arms Transfers, 1994–1995*, Washington, GPO, 1995, Table I; ACDA print out, May 14, 1996.

250. *Jane's Defense Weekly*, February 7, 1996, p. 15; May 1, 1996, p. 14; *Wall Street Journal*, June 4, 1996, p. A-14.

251. Arms Control and Disarmament Agency (ACDA), *World Military Expenditures and Arms Transfers, 1990*, Washington, GPO, 1992, Table II.

252. Arms Control and Disarmament Agency (ACDA), *World Military Expenditures and Arms Transfers, 1989*, Washington, GPO, 1990, pp. 102; CIA, World Factbook, 1991, pp. 341–342; CIA, *World Factbook, 1995*, Washington, GPO, 1994, "Oman."

253. Arms Control and Disarmament Agency (ACDA), *World Military Expenditures and Arms Transfers, 1985*, Washington, GPO, 1985, pp. 134.

254. Arms Control and Disarmament Agency (ACDA), *World Military Expenditures and Arms Transfers, 1989*, Washington, GPO, 1990, pp. 134; and Arms Control and Disarmament Agency (ACDA), *World Military Expenditures and Arms Transfers, 1993–1994*, Washington, GPO, 1995, Table II.

255. Arms Control and Disarmament Agency (ACDA), *World Military Expenditures and Arms Transfers, 1990*, Washington, GPO, 1991, Table III.

256. Arms Control and Disarmament Agency (ACDA), *World Military Expenditures and Arms Transfers, 1993–1994*, Washington, GPO, 1995, Table III.

257. Richard F. Grimmett in *Conventional Arms Transfers to Developing Nations, 1987–1994*, Congressional Research Service 95-862F, August 4, 1994, pp. 56–57. Major European countries include France, the UK, Germany and Italy. East Asia excludes the PRC.

258. US Defense Security Assistance Agency (DSAA), "Foreign Military Sales, Foreign Military Construction Sales and Military Assistance Facts as of September 30, 1994," Department of Defense, Washington, 1995.

259. CIA, *World Factbook, 1995*, Washington, GPO, 1994, "Oman." The IISS estimates a total population of around 2,125,089, of which 27% is expatriate. IISS, *Military Balance, 1995–1996*, "Oman."

260. IISS, *Military Balance, 1995–1996*, "Oman"; Ministry of Information, *Oman, 1993*, Muscat, Ministry of Information, 1994, pp. 58–62.

261. *Moneyclips*, January 30, 1993, June 23, 1993; Agence France Presse, January 29, 1993; *Jane's Defense Weekly*, July 3, 1993, p. 8, November 25, 1995, p. 23; September 11, 1993, p. 16; *Defense News*, June 26, 1995, p. 10; *Jane's Defense Weekly*, July 30, 1994, p. 35, November 25, 1995, p. 23.

262. *Jane's Defense Weekly*, September 30, 1995, pp. 34–38, November 25, 1995, p. 23.

263. *Jane's Defense Weekly*, August 9, 1992, May 28, 1994, p. 11; *Moneyclips*, June 23, 1993; *Defense News*, June 13, 1994, p. 19; *Defense News*, June 26, 1995, p. 10; *Jane's Defense Weekly*, July 30, 1994, p. 35, September 30, 1995, pp. 34–38.

264. *Jane's Defense Weekly*, August 9, 1992, May 28, 1994, p. 11; *Moneyclips*, June 23, 1993; *Defense News*, June 13, 1994, p. 19; *Defense News*, June 26, 1995, p. 10; *Jane's Defense Weekly*, July 30, 1994, p. 35, September 30, 1995, pp. 34–38, November 25, 1995, p. 23.

265. *Jane's Defense Weekly*, April 23, 1994, May 28, 1994, p. 11, November 25, 1995, p. 23; *Defense News*, June 26, 1995, p. 10.

266. *Jane's Defense Weekly*, September 30, 1995, pp. 34–38.

267. *Jane's Defense Weekly*, September 30, 1995, pp. 34–38, November 25, 1995, p. 23.

268. *Jane's Defense Weekly*, September 30, 1995, pp. 34–38; *Jane's Military Exercise & Training Monitor*, January–March 1996, p. 10.

269. Strength estimates adapted from the IISS, *Military Balance*, various years.

270. Ministry of Information, *Oman, 1993*, Muscat, Ministry of Information, 1994; Oman, *Statistical Yearbook, Twenty Second Issue*, Information and Documentation Center, Muscat, October, 1994.

271. Strength estimates adapted primarily from *Jane's Fighting Ships, 1994*, pp. 468–474, the IISS, *Military Balance, 1995–1996*, "Oman," and *Jane's Defense Weekly*, September 30, 1995, pp. 34–38.

272. *Defense News*, June 26, 1995, p. 10; *Jane's Defense Weekly*, July 30, 1994, p. 35, September 30, 1995, pp. 34–38.

273. *Jane's Defense Weekly*, September 7, 1991, p. 387, February 22, 1992, p. 273, May 23, 1992, p. 881, November 11, 1995, p. 26; *Jane's Fighting Ships, 1994*, pp. 468–474; *Sea Power*, December, 1994, p. 31.

274. *Sea Power*, December, 1994, p. 31; *Jane's Fighting Ships, 1994*, pp. 468–474; *Jane's Defense Weekly*, October 1, 1994, p. 15; September 18, 1993, p. 18, October 10, 1992, p. 22, May 23, 1992, p. 881, September 7, 1991, p. 387, August 3, 1991, p. 189, November 11, 1995, p. 26; *International Defense Review*, No. 6, 1992, p. 617, 1/1996, p. 11.

275. *Jane's Fighting Ships, 1994*, pp. 468–474; IISS, *Military Balance, 1995–1996*, "Oman."

276. *Jane's Defense Weekly*, October 29, 1994, p. 11; *Jane's Fighting Ships, 1994*, pp. 468–474; *Jane's Defense Weekly*, September 11, 1993, p. 6, July 17, 1993, p. 5; *Defense News*, June 26, 1995, p. 10; *Jane's Defense Weekly*, July 30, 1994, p. 35, September 30, 1995, pp. 32–37.

277. *Jane's Fighting Ships, 1994*, pp. 468–474 , IISS, *Military Balance, 1995–1996*, "Oman," and *Jane's Defense Weekly*, July 30, 1994, p. 35, September 30, 1995, pp. 32–37.

278. Estimates of Oman's support ships differ significantly by source. *Jane's Fighting Ships, 1994*, pp. 468–474, *Military Balance, 1995–1996*, "Oman," and *Jane's Defense Weekly*, July 30, 1994, p. 35, September 30, 1995, pp. 32–37.

279. *Jane's Military Exercise & Training Monitor*, January–March 1996, p. 10.

280. *Jane's Military Exercise & Training Monitor*, January–March 1996, p. 10. For a discussion of the role of the Air Force in development, see Ministry of Information, *Oman, 1993*, Muscat, Ministry of Information, 1994, pp. 62–66.

281. For a discussion of the role of the Air Force in development, see Ministry of Information, *Oman, 1993*, Muscat, Ministry of Information, 1994, pp. 62–66.

282. Oman bought some 300 AIM-9P4s in late October, 1985. *Baltimore Sun*, October 11, 1985, p. 9A; *Oman: A Financial Times Survey*, November 20, 1991, pp. I–IV.

283. Economist Intelligence Unit, *EIU Regional Review: The Middle East and North Africa, 1986*, Economist Publications, New York, 1986, p. 193.

284. *Oman: A Financial Times Survey*, November 20, 1991, pp. I–IV; *Defense News*, June 26, 1995, p. 10; *Jane's Defense Weekly*, July 30, 1994, p. 35, September 30, 1995, pp. 32–37.

285. *Jane's Defense Weekly*, July 30, 1994, pp. 35, September 30, 1995, pp. 32–37.

286. *Defense News*, June 26, 1995, p. 10; *Jane's Defense Weekly*, July 30, 1994, p. 35, September 30, 1995, pp. 32—37, April 24, 1996, pp. 23.

287. *Jane's Defense Weekly*, July 30, 1994, pp. 35, September 30, 1995, pp. 32–37.

288. *Jane's Defense Weekly*, July 30, 1994, p. 35, September 30, 1995, pp. 32–37.

289. *Washington Times*, May 9, 1985, p. 7; *Jane's World Air Defense Systems, 1994*, "Oman."

290. *Washington Times*, May 9, 1985, p. 7; *Jane's World Air Defense Systems, 1994*, "Oman."

291. *Jane's Defense Weekly*, May 1, 1996, p. 14.

292. *Jane's Defense Weekly*, May 1, 1996, p. 14.

293. IISS, *Military Balance, 1995–1996*, "Oman"; Ministry of Information, *Oman, 1993*, Muscat, Ministry of Information, 1994, pp. 69–72.

294. The text in this section is adapted from reporting in the US State Department, Country Report on Human Rights Practices in 1994, Washington, GPO, 1994, Internet on-line edition, May, 1995, reporting by Amnesty International and Middle East Watch, and Ministry of Information, *Oman, 1993*, Muscat, Ministry of Information, 1994.

295. The text in this section is adapted from reporting in the US State Department, Country Report on Human Rights Practices in 1994, Washington, GPO, 1994, Internet on-line edition, May, 1995, reporting by Amnesty International and Middle East Watch, and Ministry of Information, *Oman, 1993*, Muscat, Ministry of Information, 1994.

296. The text in this section is adapted from reporting in the US State Department, Country Report on Human Rights Practices in 1994, Washington, GPO, 1994, Internet on-line edition, May, 1995, and reporting by Amnesty International and Middle East Watch.

297. The text in this section is adapted from reporting in the US State Department, Country Report on Human Rights Practices in 1994, Washington, GPO, 1994, Internet on-line edition, May, 1995, and reporting by Amnesty International and Middle East Watch.

298. The text in this section is adapted from reporting in the US State Department, Country Report on Human Rights Practices in 1994, Washington, GPO, 1994, Internet on-line edition, May, 1995, and reporting by Amnesty International and Middle East Watch.

299. The text in this section is adapted from reporting in the US State Department, Country Report on Human Rights Practices in 1994, Washington, GPO, 1994, Internet on-line edition, May, 1995, and reporting by Amnesty International and Middle East Watch.

300. The text in this section is adapted from reporting in the US State Department, Country Report on Human Rights Practices in 1994, Washington, GPO, 1994, Internet on-line edition, May, 1995, and reporting by Amnesty International and Middle East Watch.

301. The text in this section is adapted from reporting in the US State Department, Country Report on Human Rights Practices in 1994, Washington, GPO, 1994, Internet on-line edition, May, 1995, and reporting by Amnesty International and Middle East Watch.

302. Sultanate of Oman, *Basic Components and Main Indicators of the Fifth Five Year Plan (1996–2000)*, Muscat, Ministry of Development, January 1996, pp. 61–65.

303. The text in this section is adapted from reporting in the US State Department, Country Report on Human Rights Practices in 1994, Washington, GPO, 1994, Internet on-line edition, May, 1995, Ministry of Information, *Oman, 1993*, Muscat, Ministry of Information, 1994; Oman, *Statistical Yearbook, Twenty Second Issue*, Information and Documentation Center, Muscat, October, 1994; and reporting by Amnesty International and Middle East Watch.

304. Speeches by His Majesty Sultan Qabus Bin Said al Said, November 18, 1994, and December 26, 1994.

305. The text in this section is adapted from reporting in the US State Department, Country Report on Human Rights Practices in 1994, Washington, GPO, 1994, Internet on-line edition, May, 1995, and reporting by Amnesty International and Middle East Watch.

306. The text in this section is adapted from reporting in the US State Department, Country Report on Human Rights Practices in 1994, Washington, GPO, 1994, Internet on-line edition, May, 1995, and reporting by Amnesty International and Middle East Watch.

307. The US spent over $300 million on upgrading these facilities. *Washington Post*, July 19, 1985, p. A-29.

308. Dale Bruner, "US Military and Security Relations with the Southern Gulf States," Washington, NSSP, Georgetown University, May 8, 1995; Michel A. Palmer, *Guardians of the Gulf: A History of America's Expending Role in the Persian Gulf, 1833–1992*, New York, The Free Press, 1992, p. 93.

309. There are two major radars at Goat Island. It is garrisoned by 250 Omani soldiers and marines and 10 Britons. *New York Times*, December 22, 1986, p. A18;

Defense News, December 1, 1986, p. 6; *Washington Post*, March 24, 1986, p. A-13; *Christian Science Monitor*, October 30, 1979; *Time*, December 2, 1985, p. 58.

310. Deutsche Press-Agentur, October 19, 1994.

311. *Jane's Defense Weekly*, September 30, 1995, p. 35.

312. *Jane's Defense Weekly*, September 30, 1995, p. 35.

313. Defense Security Assistance Agency (DSAA), Foreign Military Sales, *Foreign Military Construction Sales, and Military Assistance Facts As of September 30, 1993*, Washington, DC; FMS Control and Reports Division, Comptroller, DSAA, 1994, pp. 2–3, 16–17.

314. Defense Security Assistance Agency (DSAA), Foreign Military Sales, *Foreign Military Construction Sales, and Military Assistance Facts As of September 30, 1993*, Washington, DC; FMS Control and Reports Division, Comptroller, DSAA, 1994, pp. 2–3, 16–17. Covers FY1991–FY1993.

315. Defense Security Assistance Agency (DSAA), Foreign Military Sales, *Foreign Military Construction Sales, and Military Assistance Facts As of September 30, 1993*, Washington, DC; FMS Control and Reports Division, Comptroller, DSAA, 1994, pp. 94–95, 102–103.

316. Richard Green, Editor, *Middle East Review, 1986*, London, Middle East Review Company, 1986, pp. 168–167; *New York Times*, December 22, 1986, p. A18; *Defense News*, December 1, 1986, p. 6; *Jane's Defense Weekly*, November 22, 1986 and December 6, 1986; *Chicago Tribune*, November 18, 1985, p. I-12.

317. *Defense News*, May 22, 1995, p. 46; June 26, 1995, p. 10.

318. *Defense News*, December 9, 1991, p. 42.

319. Gulf Cooperation Council, *Preliminary Evaluation of Pipeline Transportation of Crude Oil from Gulf Cooperation Council Countries, Volumes I, II, and III*, Secretariat General of the Cooperation Council of the Arab Gulf States,/Research Institute University of Petroleum & Minerals, Dhahran, Saudi Arabia, April, 1985.

320. Sultanate of Oman, *Basic Components and Main Indicators of the Fifth Five Year Plan (1996–2000)*, Muscat, Ministry of Development, January 1996, p. 19.

Chapter 4

321. DOE/EIA Internet data base, analysis section, country chapters, accessed July 17, 1995.

322. J. B. Kelly, *Arabia, the Gulf, and the West*, New York, Basic Books, 1980, pp. 56–57; Helen Chapin Metz, *Persian Gulf States*, Washington, Department of the Army, DA Pam 550-185, January 1993, pp. 157–160.

323. The company also has some Dutch, French, and US participation.

324. *Defense and Foreign Affairs Weekly*, May 26–June 1, 1986, p. 4.

325. *Jane's Defense Weekly*, 14 June, 1986, p. 1087, and *Defense and Foreign Affairs Weekly*, May 26, 1986, p. 4.

326. Herbert K. Tillema, *International Conflict Since 1945*, Boulder, Westview, 1991, p. 156.

327. Helen Chapin Metz, *Persian Gulf States*, Washington, Department of the Army, DA Pam 550-185, January 1993, pp. 191–194.

328. *Washington Times*, December 27, 1995, p. A-10, January 17, 1996, p. A-10; *Middle East Economic Digest*, January 12, 1996, p. 6; January 26, 1996, p. 5; *The Estimate*, January 19, 1996, p. 1.

329. *Middle East Economic Digest*, January 26, 1996, p. 5.

330. J. B. Kelly, *Arabia, the Gulf, and the West*, New York, Basic Books, 1980, pp. 56–57; Helen Chapin Metz, *Persian Gulf States*, Washington, Department of the Army, DA Pam 550-185, January 1993, pp. 191–194.

331. For maps of the disputed claims, and a controversial but detailed history of the dispute, see J. B. Kelly, *Arabia, the Gulf, and the West*, New York, Basic Books, 1980, pp. 56–57, and pp. 65–76.

332. J. B. Kelly, *Arabia, the Gulf, and the West*, New York, Basic Books, 1980, pp. 187–188; Helen Chapin Metz, *Persian Gulf States*, Washington, Department of the Army, DA Pam 550-185, January 1993, pp. 191–194.

333. J. B. Kelly, *Arabia, the Gulf, and the West*, New York, Basic Books, 1980, pp. 56–57; Helen Chapin Metz, *Persian Gulf States*, Washington, Department of the Army, DA Pam 550-185, January 1993, pp. 191–194.

334. *Middle East Economic Digest*, January 26, 1996, March 1, 1996, p. 13, 21; *Wall Street Journal*, March 21, 1996, p, A-1.

335. *Middle East Economic Digest*, January 26, 1996, March 1, 1996, p. 13, 21; *Wall Street Journal*, March 21, 1996, p, A-1.

336. *Wall Street Journal*, March 21, 1996, p. A-1; *Jane's Defense Weekly*, March 13, 1996, p. 14; *The Estimate*, January 19, 1996, March 1, 1996, p. 1.

337. *Middle East Economic Digest*, March 1, 1996, p. 13, 21, March 8, 1996, p. 33; *Jane's Defense Weekly*, March 13, 1996, p. 14.

338. *Middle East Economic Digest*, March 1, 1996, p. 13, 21; *Jane's Defense Weekly*, March 13, 1996, p. 14.

339. *Wall Street Journal*, March 21, 1996, p. A-1; *The Estimate*, January 19, 1996, February 16, 1996, March 1, 1996; *Jane's Defense Weekly*, March 13, 1996, p. 14, March 27, 1996, p. 16.

340. *Middle East Economic Digest*, March 1, 1996, p. 13.

341. *Middle East Economic Digest*, April 5, 1996, p. 19; *Khaleej Times*, March 26, 1996, p. 7; Kuwaiti New Service, March 25, 1996.

342. Saudi MODA briefing aid, March, 1991. Dr. Eliot A. Cohen, Director, *Gulf War Air Power Survey, Volume V*, Washington, US Air Force/Government Printing Office, 1993, pp. 232–233, 304–305, 317, 319, 329, 401.

343. US Central Command (USCENTCOM), *Posture Statement, 1995*, pp. 11, 57.

344. Deutsche Press-Agentur, October 19, 1994; USCENTCOM, *Posture Statement, 1995*, pp. 11, 57; *Moneyclips*, June 10, 1993; *Washington Post*, June 5, 1992; *New Arabia*, June 11, 1992, p. 1.

345. *Washington Times*, March 24, 1995, p. 15; David C. Morrison, "Gathering Storm," *National Journal*, August 20, 1994, p. 1963; US Central Command (USCENTCOM), *Posture Statement, 1995*, pp. 11, 57; *Jane's Defense Weekly*, April 1, 1995. p. 20; *Defense News*, November 28, 1993, p. 1; *Jane's Defense Weekly*, March 27, 1996, p. 16.

346. *The Estimate*, May 10, 1996, p. 4.

347. *Le Monde*, January 29, 1992, p. 16; Middle East News Network, January 6, 1992; *Washington Post*, October 1, 1992, p. A-19; *Washington Times*, October 1, 1992, p. A-7.

348. *Washington Times*, April 3, 1996; *Arab Times*, March 31, 1996.

349. Helen Chapin Metz, *Persian Gulf States*, Washington, Department of the Army, DA Pam 550-185, January 1993, pp. 188–191.

350. Reuters, June 27, 1995, 0331, June 28, 1995, 1358; UPI, June 27, 1995, 1607; AFX, June 27, 1995, strip feed; *Washington Times,* June 28, 1995, p. A-17; *New York Times,* June 27, 1995, p. A-3, June 29, 1995, p. A-13; *International Herald Tribune,* June 28, 1995, p. 1; Executive News Service, July 5, 1995, 1312, 1305; *Chicago Tribune,* June 29, 1995, p. I-6; *Washington Post,* June 28, 1995, p. A-23; Helen Chapin Metz, *Persian Gulf States,* Washington, Department of the Army, DA Pam 550-185, January 1993, pp. 183.

351. There is some evidence that Sheik Hamad consulted with the other Gulf states and the US before he acted, and that the US had consulted with Saudi Arabia before it acted to recognize Hamad as Emir. This has led to some rumors of foreign support for the coup, but there seems to be no evidence of outside action as distinguished from non-interference in sheik Hamad's actions.

352. *Washington Times,* June 28, 1995, p. A-17.

353. *Middle East Economic Survey,* July 3, 1995, pp. 1–3; Reuters, June 27, 1995, 0331, June 28, 1995, 1358; UPI, June 27, 1995, 1607; AFX, June 27, 1995, strip feed; *Washington Times,* June 28, 1995, p. A-17; *New York Times,* June 27, 1995, p. A-3, June 29, 1995, p. A-13; *International Herald Tribune,* June 28, 1995, p. 1; Executive News Service, July 5, 1995, 1312, 1305; *Chicago Tribune,* June 29, 1995, p. I-6; *Washington Post,* June 28, 1995, p. A-23; *Jane's Intelligence Review Pointer,* August, 1995, p. 8.

354. *Jane's Defense Weekly,* September 30, 1995, pp. 29–30; Reuters, June 27, 1995, 0331, June 28, 1995, 1358; UPI, June 27, 1995, 1607; AFX, June 27, 1995, strip feed; *Washington Times,* June 28, 1995, p. A-17; *New York Times,* June 27, 1995, p. A-3, June 29, 1995, p. A-13; *International Herald Tribune,* June 28, 1995, p. 1; Executive News Service, July 5, 1995, 1312, 1305; *Chicago Tribune,* June 29, 1995, p. I-6; *Washington Post,* June 28, 1995, p. A-23.

355. Reuters, June 27, 1995, 0331, June 28, 1995, 1358; UPI, June 27, 1995, 1607; AFX, June 27, 1995, strip feed; *Washington Times,* June 28, 1995, p. A-17; *New York Times,* June 27, 1995, p. A-3, June 29, 1995, p. A-13; *International Herald Tribune,* June 28, 1995, p. 1; Executive News Service, July 5, 1995, 1312, 1305; *Chicago Tribune,* June 29, 1995, p. I-6; *Washington Post,* June 28, 1995, p. A-23.

356. Reuters, July 11, 1995, 0547.

357. *Jane's Defense Weekly,* September 30, 1995, pp. 29–30

358. *Washington Times,* December 27, 1995, p. A-10, January 17, 1996, p. A-10; *Middle East Economic Digest,* January 12, 1996, p. 6; January 26, 1996, p. 5; *The Estimate,* January 19, 1996, p. 1.

Interviews, and on-line Internet version of the US State Department Human Rights reports for 1994 and 1995. Accessed June 6, 1995.

359. *Middle East Economic Digest,* January 26, 1996, p. 5.

360. *Middle East Economic Digest,* January 26, 1996, p. 5.

361. *Washington Post,* February 21, 1996.

362. Interviews, and on-line Internet version of the US State Department Human Rights reports for 1994 and 1995. Accessed June 6, 1995.

363. Interviews, and on-line Internet version of the US State Department Human Rights reports for 1994 and 1995. Accessed June 6, 1995.

364. Interviews, and on-line Internet version of the US State Department Human Rights reports for 1994 and 1995. Accessed June 6, 1995.

365. World Bank, "Forging a Partnership for Environmental Action," December, 1994, p. 23.

366. This estimate of total foreign workers would only equal 88,400 workers. The CIA estimate of the total work force, however, only seems to include regular salaried employees and not domestic or unsalaried workers. Other estimates indicate that Qatar's expatriate work force increased from 57,000 in 1975 to 230,000 in 1985, and that 78% of Qatar's population is foreign. Harry Brown, "Population Issues in the Middle East and North Africa," *RUSI Journal*, February, 1995, pp. 32–43. More recent work by Professor Alan Richards at the University of California at Santa Cruz indicates that the current total labor force in Qatar exceeds 179,000 and will expand to 213,000 by 2000.

367. These data are based upon the CIA, *World Factbook, 1994*, pp. 324–325, and Harry Brown, "Population Issues in the Middle East and North Africa," *RUSI Journal*, February, 1995, pp. 32–43. The IISS estimates that the total population is 590,000, of which 75% is expatriate. The major expatriate groups are estimated to be Pakistani's (18%), Indians (18%), and Iranians (10%). IISS, *Military Balance, 1994–1995*; Arms Control and Disarmament Agency (ACDA), *World Military Expenditures and Arms Transfers, 1989*, Washington, GPO, 1990, pp. 62, 104 and 117.

368. CIA, *World Factbook, 1995*, "*UAE*"; Los Angeles Times, January 28, 1992, p. C-1.

369. World Bank, *World Population Projections, 1994–1995*, Washington, World Bank, 1994; *Middle East Economic Digest*, July 28, 1995, p. 11; *CIA World Factbook, 1995*, "Iran".

370. CIA, *World Factbook, 1995*, "Qatar."

371. Dresdener Bank, and *Financial Times*, April 21, 1995, p. 6.

372. Dresdener Bank, and *Financial Times*, April 21, 1995, p. 6.

373. D. F. Hepburn, "Observations from the Oil Vantage Point," Working Paper at the USCENTCOM Symposium, Tampa Florida, May 17, 1994, p. 13.

374. Estimates based upon the data in ACDA, World Military Expenditures and Arms Transfers, 1993–1994, Table I, and CIA, *World Factbook, 1995*. Further statistical and analytic background is taken from material provided by the World Bank, including "Will Arab Workers Prosper or Be Left Out in the Twenty-First Century?," August, 1995; "Forging a Partnership for Environmental Action," December, 1994; and "A Population Perspective on Development: The Middle East and North Africa," August, 1994.

375. D. F. Hepburn, "Observations from the Oil Vantage Point," Working Paper at the USCENTCOM Symposium, Tampa Florida, May 17, 1994, p. 13.

376. *International Financial Statistics*, December, 1995; *Middle East Economic Digest*, January 26, 1996, p. 5, February 2, 1996, p. 24.

377. *Middle East Economic Digest*, April 19, 1996, p. 19, May 10, 1996, pp. 2–3.

378. Qatar produced about 4.4 billion barrels of oil by the end of 1990, and had a moderate reserve to production ratio of 19/1.

379. *Middle East Economic Digest*, September 29, 1995, p. 17; CIA, *World Fact Book, 1995*; Energy Information Agency (EIA), *International Energy Outlook, 1994*, DOE/EIA 0484(94), July, 1994, pp. 14–26; EIA, *International Petroleum Status Report*, DOE/EIA 0520(94)1), November, 1994, pp. 6–7, and *International Petroleum*

Encyclopedia, 1993, Tulsa, PennWell Press, 1993, p. 280. Estimates of reserve have gotten increasingly more political in recent years as each major producer in the Gulf has tried to exaggerates its reserves and relative importance. The CIA estimates reserves at the lower end of the range, the EIA estimates them at the higher end of the range.

380. DOE/EIA Internet data base, analysis section, country chapters, accessed July 17, 1995.

381. *Middle East Economic Digest,* September 29, 1995, p. 17; CIA, *World Fact Book, 1995;* Energy Information Agency (EIA), *International Energy Outlook, 1994,* DOE/EIA 0484(94), July, 1994, pp. 14–26; EIA, *International Petroleum Status Report,* DOE/EIA 0520(94)1), November, 1994, pp. 6–7, and *International Petroleum Encyclopedia, 1993,* Tulsa, PennWell Press, 1993, p. 280. Estimates of reserve have gotten increasingly more political in recent years as each major producer in the Gulf has tried to exaggerates its reserves and relative importance. The CIA estimates reserves at the lower end of the range, the EIA estimates them at the higher end of the range.

382. DOE/EIA Internet data base, analysis section, country chapters, accessed July 17, 1995; *Middle East Economic Digest,* September 1, 1995, pp. 25–39, September 29, 1995, pp. 17–18, May 10, 1996, pp. 2–3.

383. DOE/EIA Internet data base, analysis section, country chapters, accessed July 17, 1995; *Middle East Economic Digest,* September 1, 1995, pp. 25–39, September 29, 1995, pp. 17–18.

384. DOE/EIA Internet data base, analysis section, country chapters, accessed July 17, 1995.

385. DOE/EIA Internet data base, analysis section, country chapters, accessed July 17, 1995.

386. *Middle East Economic Digest,* September 1, 1995, pp. 25–39, September 29, 1995, pp. 17–18.

387. DOE/EIA Internet data base, analysis section, country chapters, accessed July 17, 1995; *Middle East Economic Digest,* September 1, 1995, pp. 25–39, September 29, 1995, pp. 17–18.

388. DOE/EIA Internet data base, analysis section, country chapters, accessed July 17, 1995.

389. DOE/EIA Internet data base, analysis section, country chapters, accessed July 17, 1995.

390. IEA, *Middle East Oil and Gas,* Paris, OECD/IEA, 1995. p. 390; *Middle East Economic Digest,* May 10, 1996, p. 2.

391. *Oil and Gas Journal,* February 20, 1995, p. 41.

392. Internet version, US State Department Note on Qatar, accessed from State Department Data base, June 6, 1995.

393. IEA, *Middle East Oil and Gas,* Paris, OECD/IEA, 1995. pp. 370–371.

394. DOE/EIA Internet data base, analysis section, country chapters, accessed July 17, 1995; *Middle East Economic Digest,* September 1, 1995, pp. 25–39, September 29, 1995, pp. 17–18.

395. IEA, *Middle East Oil and Gas,* Paris, OECD/IEA, 1995. p. 183.

396. DOE/EIA Internet data base, analysis section, country chapters, accessed July 17, 1995.

397. IEA, *Middle East Oil and Gas*, Paris, OECD/IEA, 1995. pp. 174–175.

398. IEA, *Middle East Oil and Gas*, Paris, OECD/IEA, 1995. p. 183.

399. *Financial Times*, May 23, 1995.

400. Energy Information Agency (EIA), *International Energy Outlook, 1994*, DOE/EIA 0484(94), July, 1994, pp. 14–26; EIA, *International Petroleum Status Report*, DOE/EIA 0520(94)1), November, 1994, pp. 6–7, and *International Petroleum Encyclopedia, 1993*, Tulsa, PennWell Press, 1993, p. 280. These estimates have gotten increasingly more political in recent years as each major producer in the Gulf has tried to exaggerates its reserves and relative importance.

401. International Energy Agency, *Oil, Gas & Coal Supply Outlook*, Paris, IEA, 1995, pp. 142–143; *Financial Times*, April 20, 1995, May 1, 1995, May 23, 1995; *Oil and Gas Journal*, April 24 ,1995, p. 24.

402. DOE/EIA Internet data base, analysis section, country chapters, accessed July 17, 1995; *Middle East Economic Digest*, September 1, 1995, pp. 25–39, September 29, 1995, pp. 17–18; IEA, *Middle East Oil and Gas*, Paris, OECD/IEA, 1995. Annex 1, Qatar.

403. IEA, *Oil, Gas, and Coal Supply Outlook*, Paris, OECD/IEA, 1995. pp. 142–143.

404. DOE/EIA Internet data base, analysis section, country chapters, accessed July 17, 1995; *Middle East Economic Digest*, September 1, 1995, pp. 25–39, September 29, 1995, pp. 17–18; IEA, *Middle East Oil and Gas*, Paris, OECD/IEA, 1995. Annex 1, Qatar.

405. DOE/EIA Internet data base, analysis section, country chapters, accessed July 17, 1995; *Middle East Economic Digest*, September 1, 1995, pp. 25–39, September 29, 1995, pp. 17–18; IEA, *Middle East Oil and Gas*, Paris, OECD/IEA, 1995. Annex 1, Qatar.

406. DOE/EIA Internet data base, analysis section, country chapters, accessed July 17, 1995.

407. DOE/EIA Internet data base, analysis section, country chapters, accessed July 17, 1995; *Middle East Economic Digest*, September 1, 1995, pp. 25–39, September 29, 1995, pp. 17–18; IEA, *Middle East Oil and Gas*, Paris, OECD/IEA, 1995. Annex 1, Qatar.

408. DOE/EIA Internet data base, analysis section, country chapters, accessed July 17, 1995; *Middle East Economic Digest*, September 1, 1995, pp. 25–39, September 29, 1995, pp. 17–18; IEA, *Middle East Oil and Gas*, Paris, OECD/IEA, 1995. Annex 1, Qatar.

409. DOE/EIA Internet data base, analysis section, country chapters, accessed July 17, 1995; *Middle East Economic Digest*, September 1, 1995, pp. 25–39, September 29, 1995, pp. 17–18; IEA, *Middle East Oil and Gas*, Paris, OECD/IEA, 1995. Annex 1, Qatar.

410. DOE/EIA Internet data base, analysis section, country chapters, accessed July 17, 1995; *Middle East Economic Digest*, September 1, 1995, pp. 25–39, September 29, 1995, pp. 17–18.

411. DOE/EIA Internet data base, analysis section, country chapters, accessed July 17, 1995; *Middle East Economic Digest*, September 1, 1995, pp. 25–39, September 29, 1995, pp. 17–18; IEA, *Middle East Oil and Gas*, Paris, OECD/IEA, 1995. Annex 1, Qatar.

412. DOE/EIA Internet data base, analysis section, country chapters, accessed July 17, 1995; *Middle East Economic Digest*, September 1, 1995, pp. 25–39, September 29, 1995, pp. 17–18; IEA, *Middle East Oil and Gas*, Paris, OECD/IEA, 1995. Annex 1, Qatar.

413. OECD, *Financing and External Debt of Developing Countries*, IEA, *Middle East Oil and Gas*, Paris, OECD, IEA, 1995, Annex 2.

414. *Wall Street Journal*, June 4, 1996, p. A-14.

415. Arms Control and Disarmament Agency (ACDA), *World Military Expenditures and Arms Transfers, 1994–1995*, Washington, GPO, 1996, Table I.

416. IISS, *Military Balance*, 1990–1991 and 1994–1995 editions.

417. Based on working data provided by the Arms Control and Disarmament Agency (ACDA.

418. Arms Control and Disarmament Agency (ACDA), *World Military Expenditures and Arms Transfers, 1990*, Washington, GPO, 1992, Table III, and *World Military Expenditures and Arms Transfers, 1994–1995*, Washington, GPO, 1996, Table III.

419. Arms Control and Disarmament Agency (ACDA), *World Military Expenditures and Arms Transfers, 1985*, Washington, GPO, 1985, pp. 134.

420. Arms Control and Disarmament Agency (ACDA), *World Military Expenditures and Arms Transfers, 1989*, Washington, GPO, 1990, pp. 134; and Arms Control and Disarmament Agency (ACDA), *World Military Expenditures and Arms Transfers, 1993–1994*, Washington, GPO, 1995, Table II.

421. Richard F. Grimmett, *Conventional Arms Transfers to the Third World, 1986–1993*, Washington, Congressional Research Service 94-612F, July 29, 1994, pp. 57 and 68.

422. Arms Control and Disarmament Agency (ACDA), *World Military Expenditures and Arms Transfers, 1990*, Washington, GPO, 1991, Table III.

423. Arms Control and Disarmament Agency (ACDA), *World Military Expenditures and Arms Transfers, 1993–1994*, Washington, GPO, 1995, Table III.

424. Arms Control and Disarmament Agency (ACDA), *World Military Expenditures and Arms Transfers, 1995–1995*, Washington, GPO, 1996, Table III.

425. US Defense Security Assistance Agency (DSAA), "Foreign Military Sales, Foreign Military Construction Sales and Military Assistance Facts as of September 30, 1994," Department of Defense, Washington, 1995.

426. The military manpower, force strength, and equipment estimates in this report are made by the author using a wide range of sources, including computerized data bases, interviews, and press clipping services. Many are impossible to reference in ways of use to the reader. Extensive use has also been made of the annual editions of the International Institute for Strategic Studies *Military Balance* (IISS, London), in this case, the 1994–1995 edition, and of the Jaffee Center for Strategic Studies, *The Military Balance in the Middle East* (JCSS, Tel Aviv), especially the 1993–1994 edition; and Military Technology, *World Defense Almanac, 1994–1995*, Vol. XIX, Issue 1, 1995, ISSN 0722-3226, pp. 207–240. Material has also been drawn from computer print outs from NEXIS, the United States Naval Institute data base, and from the DMS/FI Market Intelligence Reports data base. Weapons data are taken from many sources, including computerized material available in NEXIS, and various editions of *Jane's Fighting Ships* (Jane's Publish-

ing); *Jane's Naval Weapons Systems* (Jane's Publishing); *Jane's Armor and Artillery* (Jane's Publishing); *Jane's Infantry Weapons* (Jane's Publishing); *Jane's Military Vehicles and Logistics* (Jane's Publishing); *Jane's Land-Base Air Defense* (Jane's Publishing); *Jane's All the World's Aircraft* (Jane's Publishing); *Jane's Battlefield Surveillance Systems,* (Jane's Publishing); *Jane's Radar and Electronic Warfare Systems* (Jane's Publishing), *Jane's C³I Systems* (Jane's Publishing); *Jane's Air-Launched Weapons Systems* (Jane's Publishing); *Jane's Defense Appointments & Procurement Handbook (Middle East Edition)* (Jane's Publishing); *Tanks of the World* (Bernard and Grafe); *Weyer's Warships* (Bernard and Grafe); and *Warplanes of the World* (Bernard and Grafe).

Other military background, effectiveness, strength, organizational, and history data are taken from Anthony H. Cordesman, *After The Storm: The Changing Military Balance in the Middle East*, Boulder, Westview, 1993; *The Gulf and the Search for Strategic Stability*, Boulder, Westview, 1984, *The Gulf and the West*, Boulder, Westview, 1988, and *Weapons of Mass Destruction in the Middle East*, London, Brassey's/RUSI, 1991; Anthony H. Cordesman and Abraham Wagner, *The Lessons of Modern War, Volume II*, Boulder, Westview, 1989; the relevant country or war sections of Herbert K. Tillema, *International Conflict Since 1945*, Boulder, Westview, 1991; Department of Defense and Department of State, *Congressional Presentation for Security Assistance Programs, Fiscal Year 1996*, Washington, Department of State, 1992; various annual editions of John Laffin's *The World in Conflict* or *War Annual*, London, Brassey's, and John Keegan, *World Armies*, London, Macmillan, 1983.

427. IISS, *Military Balance, 1995–1996*; CIA *World Factbook, 1995*, "Qatar."

428. *Jane's Defense Weekly*, September 30, 1995, p. 36; *Defense News*, November 6, 1995, p. 6.

429. These numbers are very uncertain. They are based on interviews and have been round to the nearest 5.

430. *Jane's Defense Weekly*, September 30, 1995, p. 36.

431. Qatar bought at least 12 Stinger units stolen from the Afghan rebels. The US refused to support these systems, however, and demanded their return, and Qatar seems to lack the powerpacks to keep its Stingers operational. *Los Angeles Times*, April 1, 1988, p. B-4.

432. *Jane's Defense Weekly*, September 30, 1995, p. 36.

433. *Jane's Defense Weekly*, September 30, 1995, p. 36.

434. Some estimates put actual manning as low as 700.

435. *Jane's Defense Weekly*, June 13, 1992, October 31, 1992, p. 17, September 30, 1995, p. 36.

436. *Jane's Defense Weekly*, November 4, 1995, p. 4.

437. Three Hunter FGA-78/T-79 and 1 T-79 seem to be in storage.

438. *Jane's Defense Weekly*, September 30, 1995, p. 36.

439. *Financial Times*, August 2, 1994, p. 5, *April 5, 1995*, p. 32; *Aviation Week*, August 8, 1994, p. 26; *Defense News*, May 9, 1994, p. 8, August 8, 1994, p. 34; *Jane's Defense Weekly*, August 13, 1994, p. 8.

440. *Jane's Defense Weekly*, April 24, 1996, p. 20.

441. This estimate of transport assets is based upon *Military Technology*, 1/1995, p. 229.

442. The US demanded their return and was refused.

443. This estimate is based upon the IISS, *Military Balance, 1994–1995. Military Technology*, 1/1995, p. 229, indicates Qatar already has one IHawk battery, 18 Rapiers, and 6 Rolands. Also see *Jane's Defense Weekly*, September 30, 1995, p. 36.

444. Interviews; on-line Internet versions of the US State Department Human Rights reports for 1994 and 1995. Accessed June 6, 1995 and March 15, 1996. Also Helen Chapin Metz, Persian Gulf States, Washington, Department of the Army, DA Pam 550-185, January 1993, pp. 359–360.

445. Interviews; on-line Internet versions of the US State Department Human Rights reports for 1994 and 1995. Accessed June 6, 1995 and March 15, 1996. Also Helen Chapin Metz, Persian Gulf States, Washington, Department of the Army, DA Pam 550-185, January 1993, pp. 359–360.

446. Interviews; on-line Internet versions of the US State Department Human Rights reports for 1994 and 1995. Accessed June 6, 1995 and March 15, 1996. Also Helen Chapin Metz, Persian Gulf States, Washington, Department of the Army, DA Pam 550-185, January 1993, pp. 359–360.

447. Interviews; on-line Internet versions of the US State Department Human Rights reports for 1994 and 1995. Accessed June 6, 1995 and March 15, 1996. Also Helen Chapin Metz, Persian Gulf States, Washington, Department of the Army, DA Pam 550-185, January 1993, pp. 359–360.

448. Interviews; on-line Internet versions of the US State Department Human Rights reports for 1994 and 1995. Accessed June 6, 1995 and March 15, 1996. Also Helen Chapin Metz, Persian Gulf States, Washington, Department of the Army, DA Pam 550-185, January 1993, pp. 359–360.

449. Interviews; on-line Internet versions of the US State Department Human Rights reports for 1994 and 1995. Accessed June 6, 1995 and March 15, 1996. Also Helen Chapin Metz, Persian Gulf States, Washington, Department of the Army, DA Pam 550-185, January 1993, pp. 359–360.

450. Interviews; on-line Internet versions of the US State Department Human Rights reports for 1994 and 1995. Accessed June 6, 1995 and March 15, 1996. Also Helen Chapin Metz, Persian Gulf States, Washington, Department of the Army, DA Pam 550-185, January 1993, pp. 359–360.

451. Saudi MODA briefing aid, March, 1991. Cohen, Dr. Eliot A, Director, *Gulf War Air Power Survey, Volume V*, Washington, US Air Force/Government Printing Office, 1993, pp. 232–233, 304–305, 317, 319, 329, 401.

452. Defense Security Assistance Agency, *Foreign Military Sales, Foreign Military Construction Sales, and Military Assistance Facts*, Washington, DC September 30, 1994.

453. *Jane's Defense Weekly*, January 17, 1996, p. 14.

454. *Washington Post*, May 15, 1996, p. A-7; *Washington Times*, May 15, 1996, p. A-15.

455. *Washington Times*, March 24, 1995, p. 15; David C. Morrison, "Gathering Storm," *National Journal*, August 20, 1994, p. 1963.

Chapter 5

456. Formed in 1966, when Britain began its withdrawal from Aden. The main British military base was at Bahrain.

457. See J. B. Kelly, *Arabia, the Gulf, and the West*, New York, Basic Books, 1980, pp. 87–97.

458. Herbert K. Tillema in *International Conflict Since 1945*, Boulder, Westview, 1991, p. 149.

459. Based on the computerized version of the US State Department annual reports on human rights for 1994, 1995, and 1996; US State Department data net, Internet access, June 4, 1995, and April 9, 1996.

460. For more details, see the author's *After the Storm* and *Lessons of Modern War, Volume II*.

461. *Baltimore Sun*, January 18, 1993, p. 5A.

462. The Shah had, however, discussed his actions with the British government, and had made a massive 100 million pound purchase of Chieftains in May, 1971.

463. See J. B. Kelly, *Arabia, the Gulf, and the West*, New York, Basic Books, 1980, pp. 96, and Dan Caldwell, "Flashpoints in the Gulf: Abu Musa and the Tunb Islands," *Middle East Policy*, March 1996, pp. 50–57.

464. A development that did Sheik Khalid of Sharjah little good. The British had deposed his predecessor, Saqr ibn Sultan of the Bani Sultan branch of the royal family, six years earlier for hostile political activity. In January, 1972, Saqr ibn Sultan returned covertly by dhow and led a coup financed with Iraqi money. He attacked Khalid for giving up Abu Musa, stormed the palace with his supporters, and killed Khalid and several others. Saqr ibn Sultan, in turn, was arrested by the Trucial Oman Scouts and Abu Dhabi Defense Forces and was imprisoned in Abu Dhabi. Another member of the royal family, Sultan ibn Muhammed then became the ruling Sheik.

465. *Washington Post*, April 17, 1992, p. A-18, September 25, 1992, p. 31, September 29, 1992, p. A-15; *New York Times*, April 16, 1992, September 17, 1992, p. A-12; *Armed Forces Journal*, July, 1992, p. 23.

466. Reuters, September 19, 1992.

467. Dan Caldwell, "Flashpoints in the Gulf: Abu Musa and the Tunb Islands," *Middle East Policy*, March 1996, p. 54, Reuters, December 25, 1992.

468. *Middle East Economic Digest*, December 23, 1994, p. 10.

469. Such reports about the SA-6 are very uncertain. Its warhead only weighs 80 kilograms and its maximum range is under 100 miles. *Jane's Intelligence Review*, October, 1995, pp. 454–455.

470. EIU Country Report, *United Arab Emirates*, 1st Quarter, 1995, p. 5; *Armed Forces Journal*, May, 1995, p. 30; *Jane's Defense Weekly*, March 11, 1995, p. 2, April 1, 1995, p. 3; *Washington Times*, March 27, 1995, p. A-1.

471. *Jane's Defense Weekly*, March 11, 1995, p. 2, and March 18, 1995, p. 5; *Defense News*, February 6, 1995, p. 1; *Jane's Intelligence Review*, October, 1995, pp. 454–455; EIU Country Report, *United Arab Emirates*, 1st Quarter, 1995, p. 5; *Armed Forces Journal*, May, 1995, p. 30.

472. Agence France Presse, October 13, 1994, 05:19.

473. For maps of the disputed claims, and a controversial but detailed history of the dispute, see J. B. Kelly, *Arabia, the Gulf, and the West*, New York, Basic Books, 1980, pp. 56–57, and pp. 65–76.

474. J. B. Kelly, *Arabia, the Gulf, and the West*, New York, Basic Books, 1980, pp. 56–57; Helen Chapin Metz, *Persian Gulf States*, Washington, Department of the Army, DA Pam 550-185, January 1993, pp. 191–194.

475. CIA, *World Factbook, 1995*, "UAE."

476. CIA, *World Factbook, 1995,* "UAE"; IISS, *Military Balance, 1995–1996,* "UAE."

477. CIA, *World Factbook, 1995,* "UAE."

478. CIA, *World Factbook, 1995,* "UAE."

479. UAE Planning Ministry, March, 1996.

480. UAE Planning Ministry, March, 1996.

481. CIA, *World Factbook, 1995, "UAE"*; Los Angeles Times, January 28, 1992, p. C-1.

482. *Middle East Economic Digest,* March 1, 1996, p. 3; *Jane's Intelligence Review, Pointer,* June, 1996, p. 5.

483. UAE Planning Ministry, March, 1996.

484. *Jane's Intelligence Review, Pointer,* Juine, 1996, p. 5.

485. D. F. Hepburn, "Observations from Oil Vantage Point," USCENTCOM Symposium, Tampa, Florida, May 17, 1994; US State Department, on-line data base, *Annual Economic Report for the UAE,* June 5, 1995; CIA, *World Factbook, 1995,* "UAE."

486. DOE/EIA Internet Data base, analysis section, country chapter. As accessed on July 14, 1995.

487. *Middle East Economic Digest,* December 1, 1995, p. 34.

488. Estimates based upon the data in ACDA, World Military Expenditures and Arms Transfers, 1993–1994, Table I, and CIA, *World Factbook, 1995.* Further statistical and analytic background is taken from material provided by the World Bank, including "Will Arab Workers Prosper or Be Left Out in the Twenty-First Century?," August, 1995; "Forging a Partnership for Environmental Action," December, 1994; and "A Population Perspective on Development: The Middle East and North Africa," August, 1994.

489. *Oil and Gas Journal,* September 23, 1991, p. 62.

490. Energy Information Agency (EIA), *International Energy Outlook, 1994,* DOE/EIA 0484(94), July, 1994, pp. 14–26; EIA, *International Petroleum Status Report,* DOA/EIA 0520(94)1), November, 1994, pp. 6–7.

491. Energy Information Agency (EIA), *International Energy Outlook, 1994,* DOE/EIA 0484(94), July, 1994, pp. 14–26; EIA, *International Petroleum Status Report,* DOE/EIA 0520(94)1), November, 1994, pp. 6–7, and *International Petroleum Encyclopedia, 1993,* Tulsa, PennWell Press, 1993, p. 280. Other estimates indicate that the UAE as a whole has 56.2 billion barrels of proven reserves and 49 billion barrels of probable reserves. See Joseph P. Riva, Jr. of the Congressional Research Service, writing in the *Oil and Gas Journal,* September 23, 1991, p. 62. These estimates have gotten increasingly more political in recent years as each major producer in the Gulf has tried to exaggerates its reserves and relative importance. *Washington Post,* September 25, 1992, p. A-31, September 29, 1992, p. A-15; *Christian Science Monitor,* September 18, 1992, p. 6; *New York Times,* September 13, 1992, p. A-22, September 17, 1992, p. A-19. These estimates have gotten increasingly more political in recent years as each major producer in the Gulf has tried to exaggerates its reserves and relative importance.

492. DOE/EIA Internet Data base, analysis section, country chapter. As accessed on July 14, 1995; *IEA, Middle East Oil and Gas,* Paris, OECD/IEA, 1995, Annexes 1F and 2L; *Middle East Economic Digest,* December 1, 1995, p. 32.

493. *OJJ Special, Oil and Gas Journal,* December 30, 1991, pp. 43–49; and *International Petroleum Encyclopedia, 1993,* Tulsa, PennWell Press, 1993, pp. 284–285. Also see Joseph P. Riva, Jr. of the Congressional Research Service, writing in the *Oil and Gas Journal,* September 23, 1991, p. 62; and *Washington Post,* September 25, 1992, p. A-31, September 29, 1992, p. A-15; *Christian Science Monitor,* September 18, 1992, p. 6; *New York Times,* September 13, 1992, p. A-22, September 17, 1992, p. A-19.

494. DOE/EIA Internet Data base, analysis section, country chapter. As accessed on July 14, 1995.

495. *IEA, Middle East Oil and Gas,* Paris, OECD/IEA, 1995, Annex 1F.

496. Energy Information Agency (EIA), *International Energy Outlook, 1995,* DOE/EIA 0484(95), June, 1995, pp. 14–26; EIA, *International Petroleum Status Report,* DOE/EIA 0520(94)1), November, 1994, pp. 6–7, *International Petroleum Encyclopedia, 1993,* Tulsa, PennWell Press, 1993, p. 280; and EIU Country Report, *United Arab Emirates, 1st Quarter 1995,* pp. 1–6. Other estimates indicate that the UAE as a whole has 56.2 billion barrels of proven reserves and 49 billion barrels of probable reserves. See Joseph P. Riva, Jr. of the Congressional Research Service, writing in the *Oil and Gas Journal,* September 23, 1991, p. 62. These estimates have gotten increasingly more political in recent years as each major producer in the Gulf has tried to exaggerates its reserves and relative importance. *Washington Post,* September 25, 1992, p. A-31, September 29, 1992, p. A-15; *Christian Science Monitor,* September 18, 1992, p. 6; *New York Times,* September 13, 1992, p. A-22, September 17, 1992, p. A-19. These estimates have gotten increasingly more political in recent years as each major producer in the Gulf has tried to exaggerates its reserves and relative importance.

497. Executive News Service, September 5, 1995, 0918; DOE/EIA Internet Data base, analysis section, country chapter. As accessed on July 14, 1995.

498. *Middle East Economic Digest,* December 1, 1995, p. 32.

499. Executive News Service, September 5, 1995, 0918; DOE/EIA Internet Data base, analysis section, country chapter. As accessed on July 14, 1995; *Middle East Economic Digest,* December 1, 1995, p. 32.

500. DOE/EIA Internet Data base, analysis section, country chapter. As accessed on July 14, 1995; IEA, *Middle East Oil and Gas,* Paris, OECD/IEA, 1995, Annexes 1F and 2L; *Middle East Economic Digest,* December 1, 1995, p. 32.

501. DOE/EIA Internet Data base, analysis section, country chapter. As accessed on July 14, 1995; IEA, *Middle East Oil and Gas,* Paris, OECD/IEA, 1995, Annexes 1F and 2L; *Middle East Economic Digest,* December 1, 1995, p. 32.

502. DOE/EIA Internet Data base, analysis section, country chapter. As accessed on July 14, 1995; IEA, *Middle East Oil and Gas,* Paris, OECD/IEA, 1995, Annexes 1F and 2L; *Middle East Economic Digest,* December 1, 1995, p. 32.

503. DOE/EIA Internet Data base, analysis section, country chapter. As accessed on July 14, 1995; IEA, *Middle East Oil and Gas,* Paris, OECD/IEA, 1995, Annexes 1F and 2L; *Middle East Economic Digest,* December 1, 1995, p. 32.

504. DOE/EIA Internet Data base, analysis section, country chapter. As accessed on July 14, 1995; *IEA, Middle East Oil and Gas,* Paris, OECD/IEA, 1995, Annexes 1F and 2L; *Middle East Economic Digest,* December 1, 1995, p. 32.

505. IEA, *Middle East Oil and Gas*, Paris, OECD/IEA, 1995, Annexes 1F and 2L; *Middle East Economic Digest*, December 1, 1995, p. 32.

506. DOE/EIA Internet Data base, analysis section, country chapter. As accessed on July 14, 1995; IEA, *Middle East Oil and Gas*, Paris, OECD/IEA, 1995, Annexes 1F and 2L; *Middle East Economic Digest*, December 1, 1995, p. 32.

507. DOE/EIA Internet Data base, analysis section, country chapter. As accessed on July 14, 1995; IEA, *Middle East Oil and Gas*, Paris, OECD/IEA, 1995, Annexes 1F and 2L; *Middle East Economic Digest*, December 1, 1995, p. 32.

508. International Energy Agency, *Oil, Gas and Coal Supply Outlook, 1995*, Paris, IEA, 1995, pp. 140–142; Energy Information Agency (EIA), *International Energy Outlook, 1994*, DOE/EIA 0484(94), July, 1994, pp. 14–26; EIA, *International Petroleum Status Report*, DOE/EIA 0520(94)1), November, 1994, pp. 6–7, *International Petroleum Encyclopedia, 1993*, Tulsa, PennWell Press, 1993, p. 280; and EIU Country Report, *United Arab Emirates, 1st Quarter 1995*, pp. 1–6. Other estimates indicate that the UAE as a whole has 56.2 billion barrels of proven reserves and 49 billion barrels of probable reserves. See Joseph P. Riva, Jr. of the Congressional Research Service, writing in the *Oil and Gas Journal*, September 23, 1991, p. 62. These estimates have gotten increasingly more political in recent years as each major producer in the Gulf has tried to exaggerates its reserves and relative importance. *Washington Post*, September 25, 1992, p. A-31, September 29, 1992, p. A-15; *Christian Science Monitor*, September 18, 1992, p. 6; *New York Times*, September 13, 1992, p. A-22, September 17, 1992, p. A-19. These estimates have gotten increasingly more political in recent years as each major producer in the Gulf has tried to exaggerates its reserves and relative importance.

509. DOE/EIA Internet Data base, analysis section, country chapter. As accessed on July 14, 1995; IEA, *Middle East Oil and Gas*, Paris, OECD/IEA, 1995, Annexes 1F and 2L; *Middle East Economic Digest*, December 1, 1995, p. 32.

510. DOE/EIA Internet Data base, analysis section, country chapter. As accessed on July 14, 1995; IEA, *Middle East Oil and Gas*, Paris, OECD/IEA, 1995, Annexes 1F and 2L; *Middle East Economic Digest*, December 1, 1995, p. 32.

511. DOE/EIA Internet Data base, analysis section, country chapter. As accessed on July 14, 1995; IEA, *Middle East Oil and Gas*, Paris, OECD/IEA, 1995, Annexes 1F and 2L; *Middle East Economic Digest*, December 1, 1995, p. 32.

512. *Middle East Economic Digest*, February 16, 1996, p. 2.

513. *Middle East Economic Digest*, February 16, 1996, p. 2.

514. DOE/EIA Internet Data base, analysis section, country chapter. As accessed on July 14, 1995; IEA, *Middle East Oil and Gas*, Paris, OECD/IEA, 1995, Annexes 1F and 2L; *Middle East Economic Digest*, December 1, 1995, p. 32.

515. *Middle East Economic Digest*, December 1, 1995, pp. 40–42.

516. US State Department, on-line data base, *Annual Economic Report for the UAE*, June 5, 1995.

517. It rose from $35.5 billion to $35.9 billion in current prices.

518. *The Middle East*, February, 1992, pp. 19–20, and *World Military Expenditures, 1993–1994*, Washington, GPO, 19952, Table I.

519. *Middle East Economic Digest*, December 1, 1995, p. 34; EIU Country Report, *United Arab Emirates, 1st Quarter 1995*, pp. 1–6; US State Department, on-line data base, *Annual Economic Report for the UAE*, June 5, 1995.

520. *Middle East Economic Digest,* April 19, 1996, p. 23.

521. EIU Country Report, *United Arab Emirates, 1st Quarter 1995,* pp. 1–6; US State Department, on-line data base, *Annual Economic Report for the UAE,* June 5, 1995.

522. EIU Country Report, *United Arab Emirates, 1st Quarter 1995,* pp. 1–6; US State Department, on-line data base, *Annual Economic Report for the UAE,* June 5, 1995.

523. EIU Country Report, *United Arab Emirates, 1st Quarter 1995,* pp. 1–6; US State Department, on-line data base, *Annual Economic Report for the UAE,* June 5, 1995.

524. US State Department, on-line data base, *Annual Economic Report for the UAE,* June 5, 1995.

525. US State Department, on-line data base, *Annual Economic Report for the UAE,* June 5, 1995.

526. Based on OECD, *Financing and External Debt of Developing Countries,* and IEA, *Middle East Oil and Gas,* Paris, OECD/IEA, 1995, p. 351.

527. *Middle East Economic Digest,* December 1, 1995, p. 34.

528. World Bank, *World Population Projections, 1994–1995,* Washington, World Bank, 1994; *Middle East Economic Digest,* July 28, 1995, p. 11; *CIA World Factbook, 1995,* "Iran."

529. CIA, *World Factbook, 1995,* "UAE;" Economist Intelligence Unit, *Country Profile: UAE 1995–1996,* pp. 16–17.

530. World Bank, *World Population Projections, 1994–1995,* Washington, World Bank, 1994; *Middle East Economic Digest,* July 28, 1995, p. 11; *CIA World Factbook, 1995,* "Iran."

531. CIA, *World Factbook, 1995,* "UAE."

532. *Jane's Inrelligence Review,* Pointer, June 1996, p. 5.

533. CIA, *World Factbook, 1995,* "UAE"; Further statistical and analytic background is taken from material provided by the World Bank, including "Will Arab Workers Prosper or Be Left Out in the Twenty-First Century?," August, 1995; "Forging a Partnership for Environmental Action," December, 1994; and "A Population Perspective on Development: The Middle East and North Africa," August, 1994.

534. CIA, *World Factbook, 1995,* "UAE."

535. *Middle East Economic Digest,* December 1, 1995, p. 32.

536. The force strength data in this section are adapted from interviews, and various editions of the IISS, *Military Balance,* and the JCSS, *Middle East Military Balance.*

537. *Jane's Defense Weekly,* March 18, 1995, p. 46.

538. Estimates for 1978–1988 are based on ACDA data. Estimates for 1989–1991 are based on IISS and CIA data.

539. Arms Control and Disarmament Agency, *World Military Expenditures, 1990,* Washington, GPO, 1992, Table I, and *World Military Expenditures, 1993–1994,* Washington, GPO, 19952, Table I.

540. IISS, *Military Balance, 1995–1996,* "UAE."

541. Arms Control and Disarmament Agency, *World Military Expenditures, 1990,* Washington, GPO, 1992, Table I; ACDA computer printout, May 14, 1996.

542. Arms Control and Disarmament Agency (ACDA), *World Military Expenditures and Arms Transfers, 1990,* Washington, GPO, 1992, Table II; Arms Control and Disarmament Agency (ACDA), *World Military Expenditures and Arms Transfers, 1993–1994,* Washington, GPO, 1995, Table II; ACDA computer printout, May 14, 1996.

543. Arms Control and Disarmament Agency, *World Military Expenditures, 1986,* Washington, GPO, 1987.

544. Arms Control and Disarmament Agency (ACDA), *World Military Expenditures and Arms Transfers, 1989,* Washington, GPO, 1990, pp. 134; Arms Control and Disarmament Agency (ACDA), *World Military Expenditures and Arms Transfers, 1993–1994,* Washington, GPO, 1995, Table II; ACDA computer printout, May 14, 1996.

545. Arms Control and Disarmament Agency (ACDA), *World Military Expenditures and Arms Transfers, 1990,* Washington, GPO, 1991, Table III.

546. Arms Control and Disarmament Agency (ACDA), *World Military Expenditures and Arms Transfers, 1993–1994,* Washington, GPO, 1995, Table III; ACDA computer printout, May 14, 1996.

547. Richard F. Grimmett, *Conventional Arms Transfers to the Third World, 1987–1994,* Washington, Congressional Research Service 95-862F, August 4, 1995, pp. 57 and 68. Major European countries include France, the UK, Germany and Italy. East Asia excludes the PRC.

548. Richard F. Grimmett, *Conventional Arms Transfers to the Third World, 1987–1994,* Washington, Congressional Research Service 95-862F, August 4, 1995, pp. 57 and 68. Major European countries include France, the UK, Germany and Italy. East Asia excludes the PRC.

549. US Defense Security Assistance Agency (DSAA), "Foreign Military Sales, Foreign Military Construction Sales and Military Assistance Facts as of September 30, 1994," Department of Defense, Washington, 1995.

550. *Defense News,* April 22, 1991, p. 1; September 16, 1991, p. 1; December 9, 1991, p. 1, November 16, 1992, p. 36, April 12, 1993, July 4, 1994; *Jane's Defense Weekly,* August 7, 1993, p. 28, March 18, 1995, p. 49; *Washington Times,* February 15, 1993, p. A-9; *Armed Forces Journal,* June, 1993, p. 50; *Washington Post,* February 15, 1993, p. A-3; Reuters, February 14, 1993; *Financial Times,* February 15, 1993.

551. CIA, *World Factbook, 1995,* "UAE"; IISS, *Military Balance, 1995–1996,* "UAE."

552. CIA, *World Factbook, 1995,* "UAE"; IISS, *Military Balance, 1995–1996,* "UAE"; Further statistical and analytic background is taken from material provided by the World Bank, including "Will Arab Workers Prosper or Be Left Out in the Twenty-First Century?," August, 1995; "Forging a Partnership for Environmental Action," December, 1994; and "A Population Perspective on Development: The Middle East and North Africa," August, 1994.

553. *Wall Street Journal,* August 8, 1991, p. A-1.

554. *Military Technology,* 4/93, pp. 28–31.

555. The Italian-made OF-40s are the only tanks operational in the world in this configuration.

556. France demonstrated the AMX-40 in trials in both Qatar and the UAE. *Jane's Defense Weekly*, June 6, 1987, p. 1092.

557. *Military Technology*, 4/93, p. 28.

558. *Defense News*, April 22, 1991, p. 1; September 16, 1991, p. 1; December 9, 1991, p. 1, November 16, 1992, p. 36, April 12, 1993, July 4, 1994; *Jane's Defense Weekly*, August 7, 1993, p. 28, March 18, 1995, p. 49; *Washington Times*, February 15, 1993, p. A-9; *Armed Forces Journal*, June, 1993, p. 50; *Washington Post*, February 15, 1993, p. A-3; Reuters, February 14, 1993; *Financial Times*, February 15, 1993.

559. *Defense News*, January 22, 1996, p. 1; *Financial Times*, January 18, 1996.

560. *Jane's Defense Weekly*, August 7, 1993, p. 5, March 18, 1995, p. 42; *Armed Forces Journal*, April, 1933, p. 13, July, 1994, pp. 33–34.

561. *Military Technology*, 4/93, p. 28; *Armed Forces Journal*, July, 1994, pp. 33–34.

562. These reports are dubious. Brazilian firms often leak false orders while trying to win new business. The EDT-FILA is a three radar system with a scanning area of 2—25 kilometers. *Defense News*, April 22, 1991, p. 1; December 9, 1991, p. A-1, May 25, 1991, p. 1.

563. *Jane's Intelligence Monthly*, Volume 7, Number 6, pp. 261–264, and Volume 7, Number 7, pp. 299–304.

564. *Jane's Defense Weekly*, August 7, 1993, p. 5, March 18, 1995, p. 42.

565. *Jane's Defense Weekly*, March 18, 1995, p. 42, April 15, 1995, p. 20.

566. *Jane's Defense Weekly*, April 23, 1994, May 28, 1994, p. 11

567. *Jane's Defense Weekly*, September 9, 1995, p. 23.

568. *Jane's Defense Weekly*, March 18, 1995, p. 42, April 15, 1995, p. 20.

569. *Military Technology*, 4/93, pp. 28–31.

570. *Jane's Defense Weekly*, April 8, 1995, p. 13, December 5, 1995, p. 13.

571. *Armed Forces Journal*, September, 1995, p. 22; *TIR/EW*, August 4, 1995, p. 12; *Defense Week*, July 17, 1995, p. 8.

572. *Financial Times*, December 21, 1991, p. 1; *Washington Times*, December 25, 1989, p. A-2.

573. *Defense News*, January 5, 1987, p. 19; *Jane's Defense Weekly*, October 17, 1987, December 5, 1987, p. 1302; February 20, 1988, p. 301, March 18, 1995, p. 42.

574. *Defense News*, January 5, 1987, p. 19; *Jane's Defense Weekly*, October 17, 1987, December 5, 1987, p. 1302; February 20, 1988, p. 301, March 18, 1995, p. 42.

575. Reuters, January 4, 1996, 0555; *Defense News*, August 22, 1994, *Jane's Defense Weekly*, March 18, 1995, p. 38, November 25, 1995, p. 19, April 24, 1996, pp. 22–23; *Armed Forces Journal*, September, 1995, p. 22; *TIR/EW*, August 4, 1995, p. 12; *Defense Week*, July 17, 1995, p. 8.

576. Reuters, March 18, 1996, 1017; *Jane's Defense Weekly*, March 18, 1995, p. 38, April 24, 1996, pp. 22–23.

577. *Jane's Defense Weekly*, November 18, 1995, p. 11, April 24, 1996, pp. 22–23.

578. *Jane's Defense Weekly*, November 25, 1995, p. 19.

579. *Defense News*, March 7, 1994.

580. *Jane's Defense Weekly*, June 15, 1991, p. 1001.

581. Reuters, February 18, 1995; *Defense News*, March 7, 1994; *Jane's Defense Weekly*, February 20, 1988, p. 301, March 18, 1995, p. 42.

582. *Defense News*, August 22, 1994, *Jane's Defense Weekly*, March 18, 1995, p. 38; *Armed Forces Journal*, September, 1995, p. 22; *TIR/EW*, August 4, 1995, p. 12; *Defense Week*, July 17, 1995, p. 8.

583. *Jane's Defense Weekly*, February 20, 1988, p. 301, March 18, 1995, p. 42.

584. The deputy commander was not named due to UAE security policies. *Jane's Defense Weekly*, February 20, 1988, p. 301.

585. The US temporarily delayed the sale of a $170 million upgrade package for the IHawks in June, 1987, because of the coup attempt in Sharjah.

586. *Defense News*, August 22, 1994, July 17, 1995, p. 8; *Jane's Defense Weekly*, March 18, 1995, p. 38; *Armed Forces Journal*, September, 1995, p. 22; *TIR/EW*, August 4, 1995, p. 12.

587. *Jane's Defense Weekly*, April 1, 1995, p. 10, March 18, 1995, p. 38; *Defense News*, August 22, 1994, July 17, 1995, p. 8; *Armed Forces Journal*, September, 1995, p. 22; *TIR/EW*, August 4, 1995, p. 12; *Defense Week*, July 17, 1995, p. 8.

588. *Defense News*, February 19, 1995, p. 29.

589. *Financial Times*, December 21, 1991, p. 1.

590. *Financial Times*, February 15, 1993, p. 1; Agence Presse, February 15, 1993, UPI, February 15, 1993; *Jane's Defense Weekly*, April 1, 1995, p. 6; *Washington Post*, February 16, 1993, p. C-1; *Defense and Aerospace Electronics*, February 22, 1993, Vol. 3, No. 7, p. 5; *Armed Forces Journal*, May, 1995, p. 30.

591. *Jane's Defense Weekly*, April 1, 1995, p. 8, April 17, 1996, p. 5.

592. *Jane's Defense Weekly*, March 18, 1995, p. 14.

593. *International Defense Review*, 1/1994, p. 14; *Flight International*, November 23, 1994; *Jane's Defense Weekly*, April 17, 1993, p. 9, April 16, 1994, p. 25, April 17, 1996, p. 5; *Defense News*, December 13, 1993, p. 32, April 8, 1996, p. 6; *Armed Forces Journal*, May, 1995, p. 30; *Sea Power*, October, 1993, p. 42.

594. *International Defense Review*, 1/1994, p. 14; *Flight International*, November 23, 1994; *Jane's Defense Weekly*, April 17, 1993, p. 9, April 16, 1994, p. 25, April 17, 1996, p. 5; *Defense News*, December 13, 1993, p. 32, April 8, 1996, p. 6; *Armed Forces Journal*, May, 1995, p. 30; *Sea Power*, October, 1993, p. 42.

595. *Jane's Defense Weekly*, February 27, 1993, April 17, 1993, p. 9.

596. *Jane's Defense Weekly*, March 18, 1995, p. 14; April 1, 1995, p. 5; *Defense News*, March 27, 1995, p. 32.

597. *Jane's Defense Weekly*, March 18, 1995, p. 14; April 1, 1995, p. 5; *Defense News*, March 27, 1995, p. 32.

598. *Jane's Defense Weekly*, March 18, 1995, p. 14; April 1, 1995, p. 5; *Defense News*, March 27, 1995, p. 32.

599. *Jane's Defense Weekly*, April 17, 1996, p. 5.

600. Based on interviews and the computerized version of the US State Department annual reports on human rights for 1994 and 1995, US State Department data net, Internet access, June 4, 1995; and for 1996, Internet access April 11, 1996. For additional background, see DR. Andrew Rathnell, Threats to the Gulf—Part 2," Jane's Intelligence Review, Volume 7, Number 4, pp. 180–183.

601. Based on interviews and the computerized version of the US State Department annual reports on human rights for 1994 and 1995, US State Department data net, Internet access, June 4, 1995; and for 1996, Internet access April 11, 1996.

602. Based on interviews and the computerized version of the US State Department annual reports on human rights for 1994 and 1995, US State Department data net, Internet access, June 4, 1995; and for 1996, Internet access April 11, 1996.

603. Based on interviews and the computerized version of the US State Department annual reports on human rights for 1994 and 1995, US State Department data net, Internet access, June 4, 1995; and for 1996, Internet access April 11, 1996.

604. Based on interviews and the computerized version of the US State Department annual reports on human rights for 1994 and 1995, US State Department data net, Internet access, June 4, 1995; and for 1996, Internet access April 11, 1996.

605. Based on interviews and the computerized version of the US State Department annual reports on human rights for 1994 and 1995, US State Department data net, Internet access, June 4, 1995; and for 1996, Internet access April 11, 1996.

606. Based on interviews and the computerized version of the US State Department annual reports on human rights for 1994 and 1995, US State Department data net, Internet access, June 4, 1995; and for 1996, Internet access April 11, 1996.

607. CIA *World Factbook, 1994*, computerized on-line edition, June 4, 1995.

608. Based on interviews and the computerized version of the US State Department annual reports on human rights for 1994 and 1995, US State Department data net, Internet access, June 4, 1995; and for 1996, Internet access April 11, 1996.

609. CIA *World Factbook, 1994*, computerized on-line edition, June 4, 1995; EIU Country Report, *United Arab Emirates*, 1st Quarter, 1995, p. 8.

610. Based on interviews and the computerized version of the US State Department annual reports on human rights for 1994 and 1995, US State Department data net, Internet access, June 4, 1995; and for 1996, Internet access April 11, 1996.

611. Saudi MODA briefing aid, March, 1991. Cohen, Dr. Eliot A, Director, *Gulf War Air Power Survey, Volume V*, Washington, US Air Force/Government Printing Office, 1993, pp. 232–233, 304–305, 317, 401.

612. Stephen Dagget and Gary J. Pagliano, "Persian Gulf War: US Costs and Allied Financial Contributions," Congressional Research Service IB91019, September, 21, 1992, pp. 11–13.

613. Reuters, November 28, 1995, 0838; Deutsche Press-Agentur, October 19, 1994; Alfred B. Prados and Ross Kaplan, "United Arab Emirates: Background and US Relations," Congressional Research Service 95-730F, June 19, 1995; *Jane's Defense Weekly*, March 18, 1995, pp. 38–45.

614. *Defense and Security Electronics*, November 13, 1995, p. 1; US Department of State, *Congressional Presentation: Foreign Operations in Fiscal Year 1996*, p. 510; *Defense News*, November 19, 1995.

About the Book and Author

This volume examines the changing economic and internal security challenges faced by the Gulf countries and the problems they face with Iran, Iraq, and other Gulf states. The special military and security needs of Bahrain, Oman, Qatar, and the United Arab Emirates are analyzed here in detail, as are their growing demographic problems and export plans.

Anthony H. Cordesman has served in senior positions in the office for the secretary of defense, NATO, and the U.S. Senate. He is currently a senior fellow at the Center for Strategic and International Studies and a special consultant on military affair for ABC News. He lives in Washington, D.C.